● *1986 California Edition* ●

THE COMPLETE GUIDE TO

WHITEWATER RAFTING TOURS

/

• 1986 California Edition •

THE COMPLETE GUIDE TO

WHITEWATER RAFTING TOURS

• Rena K. Margulis •

AQUATIC ADVENTURE PUBLICATIONS • PALO ALTO • 1986

The following are registered trademarks: Bullfrog, Oceanside Laboratories, Inc.; Neutrogena Norwegian Formula, Neutrogena Corp.; Riverguide, Rivers and Mountains; Ziploc, Dow Consumer Products, Inc.

ISBN 0-9616150-0-1
Printed in the United States of America

Aquatic Adventure Publications
P.O. Box 60494
Palo Alto, CA 94306

Important Note: The publisher or anyone connected with it cannot be held responsible for loss or damages suffered through reliance on any information provided by this guide. Readers should understand that trips, schedules, and prices may be changed by the outfitters, lodgings, and stores listed in this publication. No one can accept the information in this book without the acceptance of this disclaimer.

To George M. Fleck
who predicted this book

Acknowledgments

This book required the assistance of whitewater professionals and enthusiasts from throughout the state. The extensive compilation of data would not have been possible without the cooperation of whitewater rafting companies in submitting information about their tours. Additional background on some rivers was provided by Julie Buer of Great Out of Doors, Jim Foust of Sunshine River Adventures, Noah Hague of Noah's World of Water, Bill Mashek of Rubicon Whitewater Adventures, John Munger of Spirit Whitewater, Dean Munroe of Wilderness Adventures, and Andrew Price of Trinity Wilderness Travel. My special appreciation goes to Mark Helmus of Wild Water West and to Bill McGinnis of Whitewater Voyages, both of whom reviewed and suggested improvements for the safety appendix.

The book's usefulness was enhanced by information from persons in the Bureau of Land Management, the Forest Service, the Department of Parks and Recreation, the Department of Water Resources, and the El Dorado County Planning Department. I must particularly note the assistance of Linda Armentrout, Kevin Clark, Jack Darnell, Mark Dymkoski, David Harris, Charlie Hellens, Bill Helms, Fran Herbst, Carol Herman, Bill Lane, Arlan Nickel, Ron Otrin, Jim Sandner, Shelley Spindler, Fred Tomlins, and Paul Wheaton from those agencies.

Friends of the River supplied the latest information on the status and potential threats to the rivers described in this book; Betty Andrews and Bea Cooley contributed extensively to this effort.

Also, the book benefits from the considerable advice and market research provided by my associates. I must especially note the ideas provided by Larry Ingram and by Beth Charlesworth.

Jim Cassady, co-author of *California White Water*, and Kevin Wolf, River Program Director for Friends of the River, reviewed the entire text under the most restrictive of deadlines. My editors, Holly Stafford and Dan Margulis, salvaged the text from a jumble of meaningless verbosity.

Finally, Claire Palmatier compiled the information on hotels, motels, bed and breakfast inns, campgrounds, and where to buy or rent equipment. She also performed all database entry.

Preface

All the information in this book is correct to the best of my knowledge, and no person or organization paid to be listed or discussed in the book. Each trip description was double-checked by the outfitter after formatting and typing to ensure that the information presented here is accurate. In addition, a complete listing of all tours and guide schools offered on a particular river was provided to the appropriate river authority to ensure that all trips described were legal and within an existing permit (as of December, 1985).

It has not been possible, however, for me to go on each of the 600 tours listed here. If, in the course of your touring, you find that any of the information here is inaccurate, please write to me care of the publisher and let me know, and I will see that it is corrected in next year's edition.

A brief note on the various listings: A serious effort was made to contact every outfitter operating in the state that held river permits as of May 1985. Some could not be reached despite repeated attempts, and a few others chose not to be included or failed to meet required deadlines. No judgments were made on the inclusion of outfitters in the listings, provided that they held permits where required.

In contrast, only selected sources were used to identify lodgings, campgrounds, outdoor equipment shops, etc. If you know other motels, companies, stores, etc., that should be included in future editions of this book, please let me know.

Table of Contents

Appendices

Introduction

You are perched on a 21-inch tube, feet inside a 16-foot grey whitewater raft, paddle at the ready. With you in the raft are five other novice rafters, similarly attired in bathing suits and life jackets. At the stern moves your guide, twisting his well-muscled torso while steering the raft toward some small ripples in the middle of a clear shallow stream. More like a creek than the Mississippi, the river winds through a golden high-walled canyon, dotted with chaparral, Ponderosa pine, and California oak.

From around the bend you hear the sound of swiftly falling water. The woman behind you starts humming the theme from Jaws. You grin, but your mind comes to attention. Your heart, too. Now you see four huge granite boulders redirecting the current, churning thousands of cubic feet of water to a noisy white before the river disappears below the horizon. You wonder just how steep the rapid can be. You subtly shift your weight toward the interior of the raft.

The guide turns the raft bow downstream. He calls out "Hard Forward!", and six rafters drive six paddles into the water, thrusting the raft towards the roaring rapid. One stroke, two, three, four, and the spray reaches your face. Now the bow falls and your raft crashes through a three-foot standing wave, leaving you drenched. Yet you hang onto your paddle, trying to maintain the pace of your fellow rafters. You rise over another wave, and yet another, concentrating as much on the shouts of your guide as on the water's movement. Suddenly you're through, and you join your paddle crew in a cry of triumph. You're wet, you're wild, and you made it!

This book will tell you how to put yourself in that picture, how to select a trip that is right for your level of experience and activity, a trip that will excite your senses without offending your anatomy or deflating your pocketbook. Here you will find descriptions of the 29 California river sections that will be commercially rafted in 1986, and extensive information on over 600 different tours offered by 67 companies on those rivers.

Good luck, and good rafting.

Chapter 1

General Information About Whitewater Trips

Rafting companies offer hundreds of different river trips in California every year. With so many choices, you can practically design the trip that is just right for you.

This chapter identifies many factors that differ from river to river and sometimes from trip to trip. You will have to judge which aspects of a trip are most important to you, and therefore which rivers and outfitters can provide the kind of whitewater adventure you seek.

Type of experience

The first decisions you need to make in selecting a river trip involve the type of experience you wish to have. Do you want roaring whitewater or placid streams? Do you want access to lodges and services, or do you want to immerse yourself in the wilderness? Finally, do you want to power your craft through rapids by paddling the boat, or do you want the guide to row while you enjoy the ride?

How much whitewater? Rafting trips are divided into two major types: float trips and whitewater adventures. Float trips have relatively little whitewater; they offer a placid experience that permits you to relax and enjoy the river environment. You can lean back and unwind, or you can calmly paddle through the wilderness, as time and the wild birds fly by.

Or, you can use rafts to their fullest extent and have a whitewater adventure. Shoot four-foot falls. Ride a succession of standing waves. Get wet.

Whitewater comes in a broad spectrum of difficulty, from that suitable for the novice to that reserved for the expert. River and rapid difficulties are discussed in detail later in this chapter.

Easy access or wilderness? Whitewater trips by their very nature require mountainous country, which somewhat reduces access. However, given that requirement, you can select the extent of your wilderness involvement.

Some whitewater trips take you where neither roads nor fishermen roam. Your only companions are birds, wild animals, snakes, and other rafters. You camp out by the river, with the most primitive facilities and total quiet.

At the other end of the spectrum, some rivers offer lodges for indoor overnights, easy access (lowering costs and permitting more time on the river), and even improved campgrounds.

Paddle boat, oar boat, inflatable kayak or you-oar? On most river trips, you will have the option of deciding how the raft will be powered.

A **"paddle boat"** generally holds six clients and one guide. The six clients receive paddles (similar to canoe paddles), and they are taught to stroke together as a team. The guide steers. In most rapids, it is necessary for paddlers to keep both hands on their paddles. Therefore they cannot hold on to the raft while it jolts about. The challenge and teamwork in a paddle boat create a special atmosphere of victory and togetherness. The paddle boat is the craft of choice for the overwhelming majority of rafters.

In an **"oar boat"**, an oar frame is strapped to the raft. The raft holds two to four clients and one guide. The guide uses two 10-foot oars (similar to those used in rowboats), and he or she powers the raft through shallows and steers the raft through rapids. An oar boat has superior control and stability relative to a paddle boat. Also, because the guide does all the work, you have the opportunity to hang, white-knuckled, onto the boat as it goes through wild rapids and over waterfalls. Despite the security of being able to hold onto the raft, I find that an oar boat provides a wilder ride. In a paddle boat your paddle, when thrust in the water, acts as a sort of crutch, a third point of stability. Further, in an oar boat you can let loose at any time the exuberant Rebel yell that you perfected at Great America or some other source of amusement. In a paddle boat, cries of victory wait for the bottom of the rapid, because otherwise you could miss paddle commands.

Since many people find rafting in an oar boat too passive, several outfitters now offer an **oar boat with paddle assist**. In such a raft, the clients receive paddles and work along with the guide. This provides the team feeling of a paddle boat with the controlled steering of an oar boat. In rapids where tight maneuvering is required, the paddle assist can be extremely valuable. In some wide rapids, the paddle assist can seem extraneous.

Also, on some relatively easy rivers, many rafting companies offer an **inflatable kayak**, which is basically a raft shaped like a canoe. An inflatable kayak seats one or two, and you are responsible for both power and steering. The small size of an inflatable kayak makes it much more responsive to minor rapids. What I'm saying here is that you get a lot of action in a little rapid with an inflatable. One advantage of the inflatable option is that if your group includes those that want a float trip and those who want adventure, then a good trip choice is an easy river where the venturesome can kayak while the floaters raft. On the other hand, powering an inflatable kayak can be a lot of work, especially on flat water after the wind rises in the afternoon. You won't be able to slack off and let others paddle for you. Also, inflatable kayaks turn over easily; all kayakers should be able to swim.

Finally, the **"you-oar"** oar boat provides an individual the responsibility and challenge of an inflatable kayak with the size and stability of a raft. In a you-oar oar boat, clients are taught to row themselves through rapids, with a guide-powered boat in the lead (first boat) and sweep (last boat) positions.

Level of difficulty

No factor is more important in determining your suitability for a trip than the difficulty of the river. Too difficult, and you will finish a day physically and emotionally exhausted. Too easy, and you will find yourself disappointed with a sport that can thrill better than Hitchcock.

Whitewater rapids are divided into six classes. Rivers receive the same class as their most difficult rapids, but a single difficult rapid will not usually increase a river's rating. Rafters usually choose Class III rivers the first time, and the more venturesome advance to Class IV or ultimately Class V.

The following discussion of rapid difficulty uses the International Whitewater scale, the standard for California rivers. Descriptions come from the American Whitewater Affiliation (AWA) and my observations.

In evaluating your suitability for the different classes of whitewater, remember that you must wear a life jacket whenever you are on or near the river.

Class I. "Moving water with a few riffles and small waves. Few or no obstructions".

A Class I rapid may be caused by shallows or a small narrowing or a river channel. The rapid will have waves of about one foot. As you raft over a Class I rapid, you will notice little or no vertical movement, just the sound of the small waves slapping against the bottom of the raft.

Raft, schmaft you say. You grumble that your eight-year-old could run these in an inflatable kayak, and you'd be right.

Class II. "Easy rapids with waves up to 3 feet, and wide, clear channels that are obvious without scouting [going to shore and looking at the rapid]. Some maneuvering is required."

A Class II rapid may result from a small (two-foot) fall, a couple of large boulders, or an abrupt narrowing of the river. In a Class II rapid, a raft will glide rather slowly down falls, and vertical movement in waves will be limited to perhaps one or two feet. Depending on the height of the raft's tubes and your position in the raft, you may be sprayed with a small amount of water.

In a Class II rapid you appreciate the raft. It's the guide you could do without (provided you don't mind doing all the steering or rowing). Class II rivers provide opportunities for float trips.

If you choose an inflatable kayak, however, understand that a Class II rapid provides a challenge unsuitable for small children. Boats may rise over waves at angles of 30 or 40 degrees. Good balance and the ability to change direction quickly become important. Inflatable kayaks can flip in Class II water.

Class III. "Rapids with high irregular waves often capable of swamping an open canoe. Narrow passages that often require complex maneuvering. May require scouting from shore."

A Class III rapid may be caused by a combination of a narrowing river bed, many standing waves, small falls, and large boulders around which the raft must steer. Also, a high volume of water may cause waves over three feet. Even in the absence of boulders or falls, such waves rate a Class III. As the raft passes through a Class III rapid, it may knock sharply against rocks and rise or fall three or more feet. Everyone gets wet in a Class III rapid; the people in the bow get quite wet.

You want that guide. Teenagers may fall out of the raft; adults may fall into the raft, especially if they have not braced themselves. A Class III river is usually suitable for children, senior citizens, or the handicapped, and indeed, will provide an adrenalin lift at any age. On occasion, an entire raft may flip in Class III water, especially if it is a paddle boat manned by novices. The overwhelming majority of people taking rafting tours choose Class III rivers.

In an inflatable kayak, a Class III rapid daunts some adults. Each rapid requires scouting and special instructions. To carry out those instructions, a paddler must be reasonably strong, coordinated, and able to direct the craft without looking at the paddle.

Class IV. "Long, difficult rapids with constricted passages that often require precise maneuvering in very turbulent waters. Scouting from shore is often necessary [rare on commercial trips] and conditions make rescue difficult."

Class IV rapids occur in narrow channels, often at bends in the river. In California, the current is usually obstructed by clusters of large boulders. The rapid may include a fall of four or five feet. Standing waves of four to six feet may follow or obstruct the main rapid. Somewhere in the rapid there may be one or two places where a portion of the river current turns upstream (called a hole). While holes occur to some extent in all classes of rapids, at the Class IV level holes start to be referred to as "boat-eating", which means that the hole can stop a raft dead in the water or even flip it. As you travel through a Class IV rapid, the raft will pitch and lunge at angles up to 50 degrees. Persons in the raft's bow will receive a wave of substantial force right in the chops. Everyone in the boat will get soaked.

If you get a little queasy on a roller coaster, this is not your rapid. If you're not big on swimming, be sure to request an oar boat. I have observed that on a two-day trip some 35% of novice paddlers will inauspiciously exit their rafts (80% of teenagers, 25% of adults). Others report that this figure is high, that only about 20% fall out, but you get the idea. Children, if permitted, must travel in oar boats. A Class IV river is usually considered intermediate for commercial raft trips, but if you love water and roller coasters, then go ahead, make your day.

Class IV rapids are unsuitable for all but those who have had considerable experience with inflatable kayaks. Even experts will frequently flip their boats.

Class V. "Extremely difficult, long, and very violent rapids with highly congested routes which nearly always must be scouted from shore. Rescue conditions are difficult and there is a significant [risk of injury and] hazard to life in the event of a mishap."

I have problems providing a precise description of a Class V rapid, because every time I have been in one, I have been either (a) under water or (b) paddling like hell. Imagine, if you will, rock walls or boulders with only narrow chutes between them, where a miss is as good as a swim. After navigating the first chute, you must row or paddle across the current to the next, and the next, and the next, after which you reposition for a seven-foot drop into a huge hole. Boat angles can go up to 80 degrees (yes, you will be nearly perpendicular to the ground, wherever it is). You should plan for a flipped raft. Only about one percent of all California raft trips are on Class V rivers, mainly because a lot of people are into survival.

Class V rapids are hazardous. In the absence of other information, you can identify a Class V rapid because the guide will say "You absolutely do not want to fall out in this rapid." Swimming a Class V rapid is a religious experience. I have seen it drive a teetotaler to the bottle. Your disability insurance should be up to date. You should not consider rafting a Class V rapid or river if you have not previously rafted a Class IV river.

Class VI. "Difficulties of Class V carried to the extreme of navigability. Nearly impossible and very dangerous. For teams of experts only, after close study and with all precautions taken."

Class VI rapids are usually sets of falls that present special technical problems. For example, they are twelve feet high. Or, the hole at the bottom of the fall is large enough to eat three rafts. Or, there is an undercut ledge at the end of the rapid, which could cause swimmers to drown. It is extremely rare for a commercial operation to raft a Class VI rapid.

At a Class VI rapid a fellow paddler told me: "I don't care what [the guide] says. I'm going to hang on [to the raft]." We did. Your life insurance should definitely be up to date.

Unrunnable. To the best of my information no one has run this rapid in a raft and survived. Your life insurance may be canceled under the suicide clause.

Portages. Sometimes discretion is the better part of avoiding total humiliation. At these times, your guide will steer your raft to shore, and you will carry the boat around the rapid (or falls). This is called a portage (pronounced **port•ij** or sometimes por•**tahsh**). Portages range in difficulty from a short walk on a concrete and rock road (the Lower Kern) to a difficult clamber over dozens of granite boulders. If a rapid is especially difficult to portage, lines or cables may be used to direct the raft downstream.

Commercially rafted rivers usually include few—if any—portages. Those that do are identified with a "p" after the difficulty classification, for example, Class IVp. In most cases, portages require that that rafters be rather agile and rugged. Rivers that include portages may be less well-suited for senior citizens and the handicapped. Also, portages usually require a minimum of half an hour of concerted effort by guides and a good deal of waiting by those who choose not to help. The fastidiously helpless and the easily frustrated may wish to avoid trips with portages.

Whether a particular rapid is portaged may depend on the water level. Thus, where this book may indicate only one portage, the water level during your trip may force two or more. If you have concerns about portages on your trip, call and ask your outfitter.

When to raft

Frequently people wonder what is the best time of year to go rafting. They read guidebooks or brochures that imply that any time is a good time to go rafting. While many of us will in fact raft any river at any time in any weather, all rafting seasons (and days) are not created equal.

Spring. Rivers rise to their highest heights in the spring time (mid-April to mid-June). This season offers the widest variety of runnable rivers, abundant wildflowers on green hills, the company of enthusiastic rafting fanatics, and of course, high water. High water multiplies the excitement of river rafting: it makes currents faster and the waves higher. However, that fast and cold water requires wetsuits, and many summer rafters are unwilling to squeeze into them. Also, spring high water is more difficult to run than summer low water. An outfitter may be forced to convert your spring paddle trip to an oar trip without notice or, if the river rises still higher, to cancel your long-planned tour altogether because the river cannot be run safely. Finally, you will need to prepare for inclement weather (tents and rain gear).

Should one of your objectives be to find raft during a river's period of highest water, you face the difficult task of trying to predict when high water will occur. Or, you may simply wish to know how long the rafting season will last. Free-flowing rivers run while the snow is melting or the rain is falling, with no respect for the calendar. A river's rafting season may be either much shorter or much longer than this book indicates. In 1985, for example, the Sierra snow pack was only about 70% of normal, and the season ended early.

To get the best information on expected water levels, write to the California Department of Water Resources and request a free pamphlet called Water Supply Outlook for Boaters. This pamphlet, available after April 1, provides an estimate of water levels over the coming month as well as a whole season outlook.

The address is: P.O. Box 388
Room 1615
Sacramento, CA 95802

If you live in Northern California, you may wish to pick up the *San Francisco Chronicle* on Mondays. The Outdoors section of the Sporting Green includes a weekly column on river water levels written by Jim Cassady and Fryar Calhoun, authors of *California White Water.*

If you are considering rafting in the near future, say over the next week or so, you can call the "flow phone", a recorded message listing California river levels at various locations. The number is long distance for most Californians, (916) 322-3327, and it is frequently busy on Tuesdays, Thursdays, and Fridays, when the message is updated. Try calling after 11 p.m. to save money and aggravation. Check the river descriptions to determine how to convert the flow phone river levels to rafting conditions on individual rivers.

Summer. After the Sierra snows have melted and the free-flowing wild rivers of spring have dried to mere creeks, California rafting continues on rivers with upstream dams. With lower river levels, navigating "rock gardens" replaces the challenge of climbing surfer-sized waves. This does not mean that the excitement is gone. Indeed, some rivers that offer too much excitement in the spring only become runnable in the summer. Also, damming usually permits a constant daily level of water flow (not always provided, however), and this allows rafting guides to become quite knowledgeable about the behavior of a river at a particular level. And in the summer the hills, valleys, and canyons of the river country turn golden. By night you camp under the stars; by day you work on your tan.

On the other hand, summer is traditionally a time for vacation and travel. The number of people who want to take rafting tours increases as the number of rivers available decreases. So, crowding on those rivers also increases. Strategies on how to bypass the teeming masses are discussed below.

Fall. Dam-controlled rivers don't dry up after Labor Day the way crowds do. Try it; you'll like the privacy. Bring warmer clothes, however, and be prepared for rain.

Day of the week. Four major factors may affect your choice of the day of the week to raft: cost, crowding, dam type, and permit system.

(1) Cost. Rafting companies frequently offer discounts to attract you to weekday rafting. This is caused by the cost structure of the industry (a substantial investment is required to buy rafts and other equipment, but the cost of assembling an individual trip is rather low), and the

concentration of demand on the weekends. It benefits an outfitter to shift demand from the weekends to weekdays. From this discussion you can perceive that your odds of negotiating a good price on a large tour improve when you request a weekday.

(2) Crowding. On many a river, the number of people who raft is so small that the day of the week has no discernible effect on the river's population. However, on most rivers, you will find more people rafting on the weekends than on weekdays. The least crowded days are Tuesday, Wednesday, and Thursday. If one of your rafting objectives is to experience the wilderness, then avoid the weekends, particularly summer weekends on easy access and low difficulty rivers. On a river clogged with many boats, your rafting party will have to stop and regroup frequently. Also, you may find delays at the put-in (trip start point) and lines everywhere.

(3) Dam type. Once the spring run-offs have ended, rafters run at the mercy of dam releases. The quantity and timing of water releases from a dam depend on the purpose of the dam. A dam that provides irrigation water will release approximately the same amount of water week in and week out, as crops know no weekends. The dam above the Lower Kern is a good example. On the other hand, a dam that serves chiefly to produce power will frequently release much less water on the weekends, when the demand for power drops. The dam above the two Tuolumne runs is an example of this type. For each summer river described in Chapter 3, this book provides a description of the type of dam and its usual release pattern.

(4) Permit system. Most of the rivers described in this book are regulated by the Forest Service or the Bureau of Land Management. Simple regulation usually involves a limit to the number of people a company can bring down a river in one day, but no limit to the number of companies that can run the river on that day. The effect of this type of regulation is to allow a concentration of river activity on the weekends, which becomes self-perpetuating, as rafting companies then book individuals only on weekend trips. One sees examples such as the Middle Fork of the American, where on a summer weekend 28 boats may start, while on a weekday the river may be empty. Complex regulation involves the assignment of start dates among outfitters, mainly to avoid adverse environmental impact in the river area but also to reduce crowding. Assigned start dates also spread demand through the week. Because more people need to start on weekdays when weekends are full, small groups will find it easier to book into a weekday trip. While passenger volume on a river with assigned start dates will still be somewhat higher on the weekends than on the weekdays, the demand variation will have no resemblance to what occurs on the forks of the American river over a given week. In Chapter 3, this book discusses the regulatory system used on each river and how that system may affect your choice of where and when to raft.

Who can come?

Well, to paraphrase the cereal commercial, rafting is right for just about everyone, but you may not be right for just about every river.

Non-swimmers. People differ on whether or not you need to know how to swim to raft. The rafting companies generally say that on a Class II, III, or IV river it doesn't matter, because a life jacket will keep you afloat. And it's hard to break Olympic swimming records in a life jacket.

It may be more important to consider how you feel about the water. If your past experiences in water have been unpleasant, you may be so discomfited by the possibility of falling out of the boat that you will not enjoy the trip.

If you are a non-swimmer, or a swimmer lacking confidence, you may wish to consider requesting an oar boat, because your likelihood of falling out is substantially reduced. You will feel better if you can hang on.

Finally, a personal opinion: I don't believe that someone who cannot swim should go through a Class V *rapid*, let alone raft a Class V *river*. *Paddle* rafters on Class V rivers usually have to take a swimming proficiency test, which eliminates weak swimmers. However, some mainly Class IV rivers (such as the Middle Fork of the American and the Main Tuolumne) include one or more Class V rapids. In a Class V rapid, your ability to swim quickly and calmly away from trouble will reduce (but not eliminate) the risk of injury. There is no shame in walking around a Class V rapid. There may be a considerable amount of wisdom.

Rivers that include Class V rapids are identified in the river descriptions in Chapter 3. If you wish to walk around a Class V rapid, simply tell your guide.

And in an oar boat? Well, if you have strong hands, you may consider that you will probably not fall out. However, oar boats have been known to go vertical and even turn upside down in a Class V rapid. Although the risk is much less, non-swimmers should be leery of Class V rapids even in an oar boat.

Seniors. Yes, seniors raft too. I am awed and impressed by stories of septuagenarians paddling their way through the Grand Canyon. My father, age 60, survived to his surprise an oar boat trip down the South Fork of the American last year. Yet, while rafting trips can make the wilderness accessible to almost everyone (see below), seniors are rarely seen on the river. Try it; think of the stories you'll have for your grandchildren. Better yet, bring your grandchildren with you.

Seniors interested in rafting should be in good health and should consult with their doctors about the advisability of such a trip. Tell your outfitter your age if you are over 55. Also tell the outfitter if you have had surgery recently. Persons who suffer from osteoporosis should approach rafting with extreme caution; I do not recommend it.

Children. In selecting a river for your children, keep in mind both their swimming abilities and their attitudes toward water thrills. If you have to say no the twelfth time your daughter wants to shoot the mile-high water slide, you have a rafter on your hands.

In my opinion, children should be at least six years old and water-safe (able to float without a life jacket) to run a Class II river, eight years old to run Class III, ten years old to run Class III +, twelve to run Class IV, and sixteen to run Class V. During high water periods, add four years. Outfitters have their own minimum age rules for each river: check the river trip descriptions.

Much more important than chronological age is attitude (relative fearlessness), weight (affects the likelihood of falling out of the raft), river experience (better skills), and swimming ability (reduces fear and increases safety). Therefore, if your 15-year-old has paddled six rivers, weighs in at 150 pounds, and is captain of the high school swim team, some accommodation on a Class V river may just be possible. Call the outfitter and ask.

Age requirements for an oar boat may be less stringent than for a paddle boat, especially if the parent will be in the oar boat with the child. Again, ask your outfitter.

All children should be drilled on safety procedures, especially the importance of (a) not tying themselves to the boat (bad news if the boat flips), and (b) not leaving the boat without the permission of the guides. Review the appendix on safety with your child before you reach the put-in.

Handicapped. Rafts enable the handicapped to venture into the wilderness. Paraplegics, many of whom have considerable upper body strength, often make better paddlers (and swimmers) than those without handicaps. Wheelchairs can sometimes be strapped to the raft, or the handicapped rafter can sit on the tube. At no time is any rafter ever strapped to a boat.

Both commercial companies and non-profit organizations offer special trips for the handicapped, often at large discounts. These are discussed in Chapter 2. One commercial guide told me that she didn't know who had more fun on a tour for the handicapped, the clients or the guides. If you are, or if you know, someone who is "handicapable", I urge you to explore these opportunities.

River comparison charts

The following chart defines some of the key variables differentiating river trips. For each river, the chart provides:

Class (difficulty) of the river. Recall that Class I is very easy and Class V is extremely difficult. P means that a portage is required. This book utilizes with permission the same class judgments for river sections as provided by *California White Water*. However, sections rafted by commercial outfitters do not always conform with sections as defined by that excellent river guide, and river classes have been adjusted accordingly.

Season. The rafting season (a) as started and ended by outfitters on dam-controlled rivers, (b) as started by outfitters and as ended according to *California White Water* on free-flowing rivers, or (c) as limited by the Forest Service. Note that for free-flowing streams the season may be longer during a high water year such as 1983 and shorter during a low water year such as 1985. In many instances outfitters were rather optimistic about their seasons in reporting their start dates, so use these seasons as a planning guide.

Minimum age. Youngest child any outfitter will permit on this river.

Distance. In miles from LA (Los Angeles Downtown) and SF (San Francisco Downtown)

Wild. A subjective judgment as to whether or not this is a wilderness run. The major factor in this judgment was the availability of road access. This does not include the effect of overcrowding. "Part" means that the river (a) has substantial wilderness character, or (b) that a portion of the run occurs in a wilderness area.

Crowds. An even more subjective estimate of the extent of crowding, both by rafters and by other users of the river, on *in-season weekends*. River populations will always be lower during the week and in the off-season.

1 = Yours will probably the only party you will see on the river.

50 = River will be a zoo; you will be able to walk from boat to boat.

Days. Range of number of days a trip may last.

Cost. Range of individual costs for a trip starting on a weekend.

The Complete Guide to

River comparison chart

River	Class	Season	Min. Age	Distance from LA	SF	Wild	Crowds	Days	Cost
Forks-Kern	V	Apr-Jun	13	154	318	yes	2	2-4	$315-470
U Kern	II-Vp	Apr-Jun	6	133	308	no	6	.25-2	15-214
L Kern	IVp	Apr-Oct	8	123	297	part	3	1-2	75-198
Kings	III	Apr-Jul	12	205	226	part	8	1-2	80-190
Merced	IV-IVp	Apr-Jun	10	287	164	part	6	1-2	65-196
U Tuolumne	V+p	Apr-Oct	call	328	144	yes	1	1	185
Tuolumne	IV	Apr-Oct	10	318	133	yes	3	1-4	104-350
Stanislaus	Vp	will call	12	297	103	yes	1	1	40-50
Mokelumne	II	Apr-Oct	12	349	123	no	6	1	25
U EF-Carson	III	Apr-Jun	call	429	173	no	2	1	56
EF-Carson	II	Apr-Jun	5	420	164	yes	8	1-3	56-210
SF-American	III+	Mar-Oct	6	390	123	no	50	.5-5	35-285
MF-American	IV-Vp	May-Oct	7	400	130	yes	10	1-4	65-280
NF-American	IV+-V	Apr-Jun	10	410	133	yes	7	1-4	36-415
NF-Yuba	III-V	Apr-Jun	12	451	174	no	6	1-4	75-315
EB-NF-Feather	III-V	Apr-Jun	10	472	185	no	1	1	55
Pillsbury-Eel	III+	Jan-Apr	15	451	103	part	1	1	55
Main Eel	III	Apr-May	6	492	144	yes	1	3-6	215-350
MF-Eel	IV	Mar-May	6	513	164	yes	1	2-3	130-255
U Sacramento	III-IV	Apr-Jun	8	554	246	no	1	1-3	45-330
U Trinity	III	Mar-Nov	7	625	277	no	4	1-5	45-248
Burnt Ranch	V	Apr-Oct	15	615	267	part	1	2	185-230
SF-Trinity	V-Vp	Apr-Jun	12	625	277	yes	1	2-3	155-225
Cal Salmon	III-V	Apr-Jun	9	636	328	no	5	1-4	50-549
Scott	V	Apr-Jun	10	636	328	no	1	1-3	65-309
U Klamath	IV+	Apr-Sep	8	625	318	part	3	1-4	66-350
L Klamath	II-III	Mar-Oct	4	646	338	no	5	1-6	45-420
NF-Smith	IV	Apr-Jun	12	666	308	yes	1	1-2	65-180
SF-Smith	IV	Apr-Jun	7	676	318	part	1	1-2	75-135

Abbreviations

L	Lower
U	Upper
SF	South Fork
MF	Middle Fork
NF	North Fork
EF	East Fork
I	Class I (very easy)
II	Class II (easy)
III	Class III (moderate)
IV	Class IV (difficult)
V	Class V (extremely difficult)
p	portage
will call	season cannot be predicted
wild	yes = wilderness
	part = part of the run is in wilderness or has wilderness character
	no = not a wilderness run

Commercially serviced rivers by difficulty

*denotes a river with substantial commercial activity; other rivers may prove more difficult to book

Short, easy, first-time trips (for anyone)
  Mokelumne
*Powerhouse section of the Upper Kern

Beginner trips (suitable for young children)
*East Fork of the Carson
  Main Eel
*Lower Klamath

Advanced beginner trips (suitable for older, brave children)
*South Fork of the American
  Middle Fork of the Eel
  East Branch of the North Fork of the Feather (lower section)
*Kings
*Upper Trinity

Intermediate trips (suitable for teenagers)
*Middle Fork of the American
  Upper East Fork of the Carson
  Pillsbury Run of the Eel
*Lower Kern
*Merced
*Main Tuolumne
  Upper Sacramento
  South Fork of the Smith

Advanced trips (passengers must have rafting experience and be fit, healthy, and swim well)
*North Fork of the American (Chamberlain Falls section)
*California Salmon
*Upper Kern
*Upper Klamath
  Scott
  North Fork of the Smith
  Stanislaus
  South Fork of the Trinity
*North Fork of the Yuba

Expert trips (passengers should have taken an intermediate trip)
  North Fork of the American (Giant Gap section)
*Forks of the Kern
  Burnt Ranch Gorge
*Upper Tuolumne

—*Turtle River Rafting*
An inflatable kayak glides into a Class III hole on the Upper Sacramento

Chapter 2

Different Types of River Trips

Basic one-day trip. You and your fellow rafters gather at a specified "meet point" or at the trip's start point on the river, called the "put-in", usually between 8 and 10 a.m. You should have already had breakfast. Should you be told to gather at a meet point, be on time: the bus to the put-in won't wait long.

Once at the put-in, the guides will ready the rafts and other equipment for the river. Hint: If you volunteer to help, not only will everyone get on the river sooner, but you will feel more like a participant in a rafting expedition and less like a passenger on an amusement park ride. The guides will assemble all passengers, distribute life jackets, and deliver a safety talk. Pay attention, even if you already know it all; your lack of attention can be a poor example to other rafters, especially children. And if you have any questions, ask. Do not hesitate to ask a guide to demonstrate a move or a hold. Between readying equipment and hearing a safety talk, expect to spend 45 minutes to an hour on shore. And while you are there, if toilet facilities are available at the put-in, be sure to use them.

Then, when your anticipation peaks, you hit the river. Dreams of future goals fade in your enjoyment of the moment, shooting long rapids and absorbing scenic surroundings. On a typical day, you will raft about two hours in the morning and two hours in the afternoon. The duration of your trip, however, will depend on the speed of the water; this can vary from between 2 to 4 miles per hour. At higher water levels, the river moves faster, and your trip will take less time. Rafting trips short on river time will often be augmented by extensive scouting of rapids, visits to historic sites, and side hikes up canyons. You don't have to do any of these things: it is your cash-paying right to sleep on the beach if you so desire.

At lunchtime, all the rafts pull over and the guides break out first chips, vegetables, and dips and then sandwich materials. You make your own. If there are no facilities at the site where you stop, then a guide will set up a portable toilet (porta-potty) on request only.

At the end of the day, rafting equipment will have to be reloaded into the bus or van; once loading is complete, you will be shuttled back to your car and your normal boring existence. But there will be a smile on your face and satisfaction in your heart, which even the prospect of working the next day cannot diminish.

Basic overnight trip. Your trip follows the same pattern as a one-day, with the following additions. At the put-in or meet point you pack your gear into either a dry bag, if your campsite can be reached by river only, or a van, if your campsite has road access. Be sure to check with your outfitter before you leave home about camp access, as you won't be able to fit much gear in a dry bag, especially after packing your sleeping bag and pad.

Once at the campsite, the guides will again provide snacks before they start making dinner. Ask the guides if they need any help; you then have a free opportunity to learn river cookery, an art within an art.

While the guides are making dinner, most of the clients will be selecting a site for their sleeping bags. Unless you will be staying at a crowded campground, do yourself a favor and wait until the rowdy members of your group have picked out their spots. Then make claim on an area far, far away and unpack your gear.

Find yourself a private place and change out of your wet clothes. Then, when you are dry and warm, come back to camp and grab a cold drink or brewski. Sit around the campfire, make yourself useful, and tell lies.

Dinners I have had on commercial river trips have been fresh and of uniformly high quality. Meals are ranch-style, with entrees broiled or barbecued over an open fire (or campstove, in situations where an open fire may be a hazard). Over and over again, rafting companies serve steak: it's quick, easy, and generally makes a good impression. If you don't want steak, you have only to ask about the menu and request something else at least two weeks in advance. Many guides get so sick of steak they bring something different for themselves anyway. Of course, on a trip lasting more than two days, you will get steak one night and perhaps chicken the next, etc. Some outfitters indicated in their statements of philosophy (see Chapter 4) or in their trip descriptions that they break away from the steak tradition. Among the companies I have rafted with, Turtle River Rafting keeps red meat to a minimum, and Sierra Mac offers everyone a choice of entree at the time reservations are made.

Breakfast the next morning is also a hot meal: eggs and sausage, or pancakes, or french toast, etc. In an industry that emphasizes back to nature, this abundance of high-cholesterol cuisine is astonishing. If you have dietary limitations, tell your outfitter.

The consumption of all this food brings up an indelicate subject, toilet facilities. One male outfitter was appalled at the idea that I would include information on that here, because no one ever even asks about toilet facilities. Well, women who are sufficiently untraveled to be mortified by primitive toilet facilities do not just casually mention this to strange men. So take what follows as fair warning.

Most rafting in the state occurs on the South Fork of the American, with overnights usually in "improved" campgrounds. At such campgrounds you may find either running water and flush toilets or chemical toilets of the kind frequently seen at construction sites. On some other widely used rivers, such as the Lower Kern and the Kings, outfitters also maintain toilets at their campsites.

However, some campsites on the South Fork of the American and most riverside campsites elsewhere in the state have not been improved. At these sites, a guide will set up a porta-potty, which is most frequently a twelve inch by twelve inch by twelve inch ammunition can lined with several plastic garbage bags. On top of the porta-potty will be a toilet seat (provided that the guides didn't forget it). Keep the seat down, or the can lid closed, when the potty is not in use. Finally, the potty is used, by all, for solid waste only. It will be placed in a private or enclosed location, usually up-river of camp, and you will have to find another private place to urinate. Do not use the river for this purpose. Also, do not bury toilet paper; it takes years to decompose. Burn it in the campfire or throw it in a garbage bag. If you do in fact care about these things, the type of toilet used on a particular camping river tour is noted on the trip description.

Lodge trips. You may love whitewater but nevertheless prefer creature comforts to creature sleeping companions. No problem. Overnight trips at a lodge are offered by many outfitters on the South Fork of the American, the Lower Klamath, the Cal Salmon, the Merced, and the lower section of the North Fork of the American. In addition, if your group is large enough (usually six or more), and you will be rafting a river with good road access, an outfitter may be willing to arrange your delivery to a motel of your choice for a small fee. Ask. This option is obviously not available for the wilderness river trips on the Forks of the Kern, the Tuolumne, the Middle Fork of the American, the Eel river runs, the South Fork of the Trinity, and the North Fork of the Smith.

Bus trips. You love to go rafting but hate dealing with that Friday night traffic getting out of the city. Many companies have eliminated this headache for you, by arranging for buses from the San Francisco and Los Angeles areas. If your group is large enough to fill a bus, then a company will probably be able to arrange a bus any day of the week. Again, call the outfitter.

Cooperative trips. You love to raft, but it's too darn expensive. If your problem is money, then you can go for free by arranging a group tour (see Chapter 5). But, if all your friends' problems are money, then you may wish to consider a cooperative trip. These trips, conducted by the American River Touring Association (ARTA) on the South Fork of the American, the Main Tuolumne, and the Merced, are offered at a considerable discount. Group members must provide and prepare food for themselves and their guides.

Combination trips. You love to raft and you adore variety, but you live far from the mountains and have little time to arrange multiple tours. Have no fear. Many outfitters have stacked two or three river trips together to give you that four- or five-day totally planned vacation. Also, if you have just one weekend to spend on the water and would like to try two rivers, again, the outfitters will accommodate you. See the combination trips listing in Chapter 3.

Gourmet trips. Rafting, being such a physical pleasure, brings out the hedonist in many. And some outfitters are willing to cater to your pleasure by providing gourmet meals on the river. Gourmet is a key word in this book; outfitters who wanted to have their trips described as gourmet were required to submit sample menus. The following companies offer gourmet meals on one or all of their river trips: James Henry River Journeys on the Middle Fork of the Eel and the Middle Fork of the American; Libra Expeditions and Rubicon on the South Fork of the American; and Ouzel Outfitters on the Upper Klamath, Cal Salmon, and Lower Klamath. Any of these companies will provide menus on request.

Trips for the handicapped and persons with special needs. Several outfitters have indicated that they run tours for the handicapped. As described in Chapter 1, this is a special and rewarding activity for both passengers and guides. The reckless pursuit of adventure, excitement, and total wetness should be open to all. On the South Fork of the American, California Adventures, Gold Rush River Runners, River Mountain Action, Tributary Whitewater, and A Whitewater Connection offer tours for the handicapped. On the East Fork of the Carson, a somewhat easier but more scenic river, California Adventures and Tributary Whitewater will arrange your tours. On the Lower Klamath, bring your fishing pole and raft with Eagle Sun, Electric Rafting, Four Seasons Adventure, Headwaters, Noah's World of Whitewater, Ouzel Outfitters, Tributary Whitewater, or Turtle River Rafting. Finally, Electric Rafting will take you down the beautiful South Fork of the Smith, and Headwaters will carry you through the canyons of the Upper Trinity.

In addition to commercial outfitters, two non-profit organizations in San Francisco provide rafting tours for people with special needs.

Inner City Outings (associated with the Sierra Club) provides two-day tours on the South Fork of the American and the East Fork of the Carson for target organizations such as drug rehabilitation centers and halfway houses. They also provide trips for groups of the physically, developmentally, and hearing impaired. Groups interested in taking a tour with Inner City Outings have to meet the organization's guidelines and submit a request no later than April 30. Their address is 730 Polk Street, San Francisco, CA 94109.

Also, Environmental Traveling Companions (ETC.) provides tours for people with disabilities and for disadvantaged youth. For more information, write or call ETC. at Ft. Mason, Bldg. C, San Francisco, CA 94123,

(415) 474-7662. This organization is not associated with Friends of the River, although they do talk, being in the same building and all.

Family trips. Family trips offer real advantages for those with families. First, your child comes along at a substantial discount. Second, everyone else on the trip also has a child along, so you may receive more empathy and feel less embarrassment over your child's behavior. Third, guides are specially selected for this assignment and receive combat pay. ARTA offers family trips on the Lower Klamath, and Adventure Connection and Earthtrek Expeditions offer them on the South Fork of the American.

In a variation on the family trip, Adventure Connection conducts single parent and child trips on the South Fork of the American.

Women's trips. Let's be real here. You get a group of women together in a wilderness environment and the make-up disappears, the boozing declines to a trickle, and the truths of life come out over the campfire. This should not be interpreted to mean that it isn't possible to have mature, thought-provoking campfire discussions with a number of men. I have heard tales of such; I just cannot verify them from my own experience.

Should you prefer to raft in the company of women, Noah's World of Water offers all-woman trips on the Upper Klamath and the Lower Klamath, and Turtle River Rafting offers them on the Lower Klamath and the South Fork of the American.

Also, with any outfitter you have the option of gathering a full trip's complement of women and therefore custom chartering your own all-woman trip. Men likewise have the option of chartering an all-man trip.

Single adult trips. Rafting has many dimensions. In the novel *Almost Heaven* by Carole Halston, a young woman (a rafter) asks her newly-acquired lover (a rafting guide) "Has it occurred to you that making love feels a lot like going through a rapid?", to which he responds "I used to think that making love was the closest thing to going through a major rapid...the last couple of days I've revised that opinion." Well, isn't it amazing what a good woman can do.

Yet it is not the purpose of this book to discuss the similarities between running rapids and sex (the urge to merge with the surge, etc). These are in any event obvious, if not to you, then certainly to a salmon.

However, your interests may run less to spawning and more to spooning. In that case, you should not ignore the advantages of rafting with the man of your dreams. First, in a raft you are both excited, spirited adventurers: your hearts pound, your cheeks glow, and your eyes gleam, no matter how dull and lifeless you may be in your usual environment. Second, regardless of how different your backgrounds or how basically incompatible you may be, in a raft you always have something in common to discuss, namely, how to survive the next rapid. Third and most important, try as he might, he can't get away.

Finally, even if you arrive at the put-in with no partner, you should not underestimate the value of an opportunity to spread lotion over the body of a complete stranger, out of a totally altruistic concern for his (or her) well-being.

Yes, Adventure Connection is going to provide you this opportunity; they will offer single adult trips on the South Fork of the American in 1986. You read it here first.

And it may come to pass that you have designs on other rivers and other rafters. If so, recall that romance can be rather like fermentation; the presence of the products of romance (children) will often inhibit the reaction process. This, of course, is no secret to parents. If romance is your objective, you may wish to ask your outfitter about your fellow travelers (see Chapter 5).

Educationally oriented trips. River rafting is nothing if not mind-expanding. Some outfitters take advantage of this to fill your formerly rutted brain with new information and perspectives. James Henry River Journeys goes whole hog by offering a college-credit natural history trip on the Lower Klamath (check with your dean on the transferability of such credit).

Medical professionals can deduct the cost of their raft trips by taking a seminar on the river. James Henry conducts a seminar in sports medicine for doctors on the Lower Klamath. Check with your accountant on the applicability to your tax situation. Non-medical types may believe that it is tax deductions like these that make tax overhaul essential. Friends, the money involved here is peanuts. Wait until this book covers international river trips.

Finally, for those interested in learning for its own sake, several outfitters offer river trips where you will be exposed to more than just the sun. California Adventures teaches archaeology and natural history along the East Fork of the Carson. James Henry expounds on natural history on the Middle Fork of the Eel and provides guided imagery training on the Lower Klamath. Turtle River Rafting, also on the Lower Klamath, illuminates the culture, myths, and issues of local Indians.

Fishing. Though outfitters may raft the same river, some see only the surface, while others will look farther, to find the fish. The following companies recommended their trips for fishing: All-Outdoors, on the Main Tuolumne; Great Out of Doors, on the Upper Sacramento; Libra Expeditions, on the Middle Fork of the American; Sunshine River Adventures, on the Stanislaus; Noah's World of Water, on the Upper Klamath; and Klamath River Outdoor Experiences (KROE) and Noah's on the Lower Klamath.

Included and optional off-river tours. Some outfitters act as combination travel agent/guides in designing trips that will bring you more than just nature and the South Fork of the American. Earthtrek Expeditions does this in a big way, offering side trips to Lake Tahoe,

Yosemite, and the wine country. The last, I suppose, is for those rare folks who did not get enough alcohol on the river. Also, A Whitewater Connection will bus you off for sailing, horseback riding, and the vacuum-cleaner casinos at Lake Tahoe. Earthtrek, A Whitewater Connection, and OARS will let you see what you will get by offering optional hot air balloon rides with your South Fork of the American trip.

Lastly, should you doubt that every raft's a stage, Wilderness Adventures will book you on a combination Upper Klamath-Ashland Shakespeare Festival tour. Consider this trip the tempest as you like it.

Whitewater schools. And now for something completely different. Whitewater rafting schools serve two purposes: first, they train ordinary people who want to guide commercial or private rafting trips, and second, they provide a serious and intensive whitewater experience for people who take their rafting seriously.

Given the amount of time you spend rafting, whitewater school often represents an excellent value vis-a-vis other trips. But you will be expected to work, study, and practice, practice, practice.

If you are seriously interested in training for and becoming a guide, then call around to the various companies that offer schools. Ask about the hiring outlook. It would be a shame to take the course with a particular company and then discover there will be no openings.

—Water Colors

Class III+ "Surprise" rapid on the Lower Kern proves well-named

—Sierra Shutterbug/Paul Ratcliffe
A view from downstream of the tunnel of the Middle Fork of the American

Chapter 3

Selecting a California River Trip

Introduction. Well, now you've got an idea of what you're looking for in a river trip. Your new problem is finding that trip buried under the avalanche of alternatives and information that follows. Stiff upper lip, and let's go.

First, you don't have to read everything you always wanted to know about 29 different rivers. Instead, use the charts in Chapter 1 (perhaps in combination with the trip ideas in Chapter 2) to focus your search on just a few rivers.

Second, decide what time of year you want to raft. Put as many limitations on your trip choice as possible. For example, decide on the number of days you want the trip to last or the type of boat in which you want to raft.

Third, read the description of a river in which you are interested (later in this chapter). Does it sound like the river for you? Check the summary of the river between put-ins. Are you ready for that much whitewater, or do you want more?

Fourth, look at the trip descriptions (the tables which follow each river description). Note some of the differences between trips: types of rafts, location of put-ins and take-outs, comments, requirements, and prices. Make a list of up to 10 companies that offer a trip you want.

Fifth, go to Chapter 4 and read about the rafting companies. Selecting one may not be easy, as many excellent outfitters offer tours in California. Develop a final list of companies and tours that interest you. Rank them in order of preference.

Finally, read Chapter 5, which gives you some advice on booking your trip. When you phone your chosen outfitters, you will find that some tours are not available (a) when you would like to go, or (b) with your first choice of outfitter. That's why you made a list.

Since you will be spending, in all probability, some serious money on your trip, you may wish to obtain perspectives on some of these rivers written by men who have actually been down them all. Try to find *California White Water* (or see the order form on the last page), which has the advantage of concise, knowledgeable and lucid prose, not to mention river maps, and/or *A Guide to the Best Whitewater in the State of California*, which describes more rivers in less detail with somewhat more enthusiasm and somewhat less applicability to rafting.

Notes on the river descriptions

The river descriptions should contain all the information you need to decide (a) whether you would enjoy a trip on a river, and (b) what time of week or year is best to raft. The following notes may help you with the river descriptions.

Level of difficulty/water level concerns/flow information.

This section provides the International Whitewater Scale class of river difficulty as judged by Jim Cassady and Fryar Calhoun in their book *California White Water*. This is the rating to use in comparing rivers. In all cases, a one-number class rating (for example, IV) is applied to a particular section. If two numbers are provided, then the difficulty of the river depends on the section you choose to run. Of course, river ratings also vary with water level changes. For rivers where the level of difficulty changes during the commercial rafting season, the change is noted in the description. Recall that at higher water levels, rivers are substantially more difficult to run.

Next, this section talks about the source of the water, particularly whether the river is free-flowing or dam-controlled. Free-flowing rivers are fed from snow pack or rain; most precipitation occurs during the winter months, and the rivers dry up during the summer. Outfitters are frequently optimistic about the length of their seasons, so this book provides an estimated end of the season as reported in *California White Water*. If your rafting objective for the season is a free-flowing river, use the water level information sources identified in Chapter 1 to help select a time to raft.

Free-flowing rivers fed by snow melt (these are mostly the Sierra rivers) usually have a relatively long season. If weather conditions oblige, and they rarely do, the snow will melt steadily throughout the spring and feed the rivers at a fairly constant level. More often, however, the snow melts slowly in April, but more quickly in May, when the rivers rise. As the snow disappears from the mountains in June, so too do the rivers disappear from the river banks.

Rivers fed by rain, on the other hand, tend to respond quite radically to recent precipitation. They may become runnable with only one week's notice and may become unrunnable unseasonably early. If your objective is a rain-fed river, keep in especially close contact with both weather conditions and your outfitter.

Dam-controlled rivers rise and fall according to the desires of the dam authorities. In the springtime, their desires are usually to avoid the floods that may be caused by over-filling a reservoir. Thus, spring river levels usually remain high in spite of a dam. During the summer, however, dam releases determine the water level. The pattern of summer water releases is described is this section, for all dam-controlled rivers.

Finally, this section provides the minimum flow (water level in cubic feet per second) required to raft and also how to determine current water flows, again according to *California White Water*, except where noted.

Permit system/time to raft. This section describes the qualifications an outfitter must have or did have in order to receive a permit on this river. In many cases these were no qualifications at all, beyond having insurance and paying fees.

Next come any limits to the number of companies that can launch a trip on any one day (called the number of starts per day). This is the key factor in controlling the amount of commercial traffic on the river.

More common is a limit on the maximum number of people in a group. Sometimes these limits are on the total number of passengers and guides, sometimes only on passengers (in which case the limit coincides with the maximum group size). Large groups (over 25 passengers) make it difficult for a sense of community to develop among rafters. However, if you plan to hold your company's annual picnic on a rafting trip, you will need this information to select a river.

Then, taking into account water flow patterns, safety and crowding, I present a personal judgment about what may be the best time to raft the river.

Commercial rafting. This section provides any statistics available, either from a river authority or from outfitters, on the number of passengers rafting the river in 1985. Some river authorities report information only in "user days". One user day represents one person on the river one day.

Gear/safety/who can come. Again, this is my opinion only. You will observe that I am much more conservative than the average outfitter. People become anxious and sour when rafting a river that frightens them. Please do not select a river if you fear it may be too difficult. Your unhappiness may ruin your trip and diminish the pleasure of your fellow rafters. Review the appendices on *Safety* and on *What to Bring* for more information on gear, especially wetsuits.

Distinctive features. This section identifies what makes a river special. In some cases the river is compared with nearby rivers of the same level of difficulty.

River access. Roads or even railroads near the river can add an extra measure of safety by providing a means of rescue in an emergency. However, if you want to capture the inspiration of the wilderness, select a river with minimal access. Any excess of fishermen is also noted here.

Sites of interest. This section lists any historical sites or other special features along the river. This includes ruins, hot springs, swimming holes, etc.

Environment. In copious detail, this section provides: (a) a qualitative assessment of the depth and width of the river canyon (a canyon is narrower than a valley, but not as narrow as a gorge), (b) an indication of the water quality, especially if the water does or does not have a pleasing color or clarity, (c) types of vegetation that grow near the river during the rafting season, especially trees and wildflowers, and (d) any wildlife or large wild birds you may see on your trip.

Fishing. This section provides a list of the types of game fish in the stream during the rafting season. On some rivers with long seasons, the fish may not be running the river when you are. Check with your outfitter, who can tell you about the types of bait to bring, etc. If fishing is an important objective of your river tour, and the outfitter cannot answer fishing questions, perhaps you should select another outfitter. Be certain to obtain a California Fishing License. See the *Fishing trips* section in Chapter 2.

Summary of river between put-ins. This section lists numbers and difficulties of rapids that lie within different stretches of river. This section also locates all required and many potential portages. For some rafters, this may be an unnecessary level of detail. Me, I always like to know what I'm getting for my money.

Most outfitters don't include in their brochures information on where a trip starts and ends, or even the miles rafted. This is like an airline offering a "California plane flight, $79." How anyone can compare that with another airline's "California plane flight, $99" is difficult to understand. One can almost hear the confused consumer saying: "Gee, Martha, it must fly longer."

Another example of this is when an outfitter offers a two-day trip and also a three-day trip during which exactly the same section of river is rafted. Without the put-in and take-out information, you would never know that the extra day will get you more food instead of more river.

Some outfitters do provide put-ins, take-outs, and miles rafted in their brochures. More often than not, the miles reported by an outfitter do not match the miles reported in this book. This derives from the absence of odometers in rafts. For this book, all distances between put-ins and take-outs were standardized against a common reference, usually *California White Water*. Where that volume did not provide a detailed mileage guide, other published sources or Forest Service maps were used to determine rafting distances.

Information on how to obtain books cited in this section is included in the *Annotated Bibliography*.

River status. Finally, many of California's finest rafting runs may not be available for the next generation. The rivers may be flooded by dams and/or their waters diverted. Too often the expectation of a new dam causes the recommendation in this book to raft a river now, rather than next year. You, as a river runner, voter, and taxpayer, can affect the future of California's environment. This section tells you whom to contact with your concerns. If you don't know who your elected representatives are, your librarian can tell you. If you don't have time to write your congressional representative or senator, consider making a phone call.

Members of the House of Representatives maintain local offices; look up their names in the white pages of your phone book. Or, you can call Washington, DC before 8 a.m. for about 20 cents a minute.

Intermediate term protection for rivers comes from the 1968 wild and scenic rivers act. This act seeks to preserve outstanding rivers for the enjoyment of the public. Wild and scenic protection is provided at three different levels: (a) wild—the most restrictive—the river is treated as a wilderness area; (b) scenic—some timber harvest can take place, and (c) recreational—the river is protected for its recreational (boating or fishing) uses.

For a river to obtain wild and scenic status, several events must occur. First, the Forest Service or Bureau of Land Management must judge that a river is "eligible" for wild and scenic status, meaning that the river possesses "outstandingly remarkable scenic, recreational, geologic, fish and wildlife, historic, cultural, or other similar values."

In the event a river meets the several criteria for that status, the same river authority then balances the uses that would be continued if the river were protected (like fishing and river running) against uses that would be prohibited (like dams). If the benefits of river protection appear to outweigh the benefits of other uses of the river, the river is designated as "suitable" for wild and scenic status. Then the river's future lies with Congress, which must pass legislation to include the river under the wild and scenic act. For state-controlled rivers, the state legislature must pass similar legislation to protect a river.

Motels, lodges, and bed and breakfast inns. For each lodging, this section provides November, 1985 prices and directions (from Los Angeles for southern rivers and from San Francisco for northern rivers). Some outfitters have arranged discounts at local motels; be sure to ask. Your outfitter can also identify the motels or inns that are closest to your meet point. Abbreviations used in the directions are:

L, R = Turn left, Turn right
H = Highway
I = Interstate
N, S, E, W = North, South, East, West
n/p = price or service not provided
mi = miles

Campgrounds. For private campgrounds, this section lists price per site, unless otherwise noted. Also, many private campgrounds will permit you to take a shower for a fee, even if you do not stay in the campground. These fees are reported on a cost per person basis, unless otherwise noted.

Space at public campgrounds usually is available on a first-come first-served basis. Forest Service campgrounds most often cost between three to six dollars; Army Corps of Engineers campgrounds are free or cost six dollars. Again, ask your outfitter about which campgrounds are closest to your meet point.

Notes on the trip descriptions

A separate trip description is provided for every tour that has a different (a) outfitter, (b) number of days, (c) put-in point, or (d) take-out point. If an outfitter offers special options associated with one trip or another, these are noted in the Comments section.

Trip descriptions are sorted by the number of days in the trips. On trips that last less than one day, no food is provided. One rafting day includes approximately four river hours: a one-quarter day trip lasts about one hour. However, the amount of time you will spend on the river varies tremendously from tour to tour: be sure to check the miles listing.

Name. See the company descriptions in Chapter 4 for more information about each outfitter.

Maximum cubic feet per second (max. cfs). The highest water level at which a company will run a trip, or no max, meaning there is no level at which the company will not run (or that the company was unwilling to specify a level). On many rivers, rafting at high levels is far riskier than rafting when the waters are lower. The max. cfs figure offers an indication of an outfitter's attitude towards that risk.

Starting. The dates or days that a trip will start. Specific dates are provided on rivers with Forest Service or Bureau of Land Management mandated limited start dates. Pay attention; it gets tricky here. Even on rivers with assigned start dates, the outfitters can trade dates among themselves. However, for some rivers with limited start dates, companies may have difficulty obtaining Saturday start dates. See the river descriptions, under *Permit systems.*

Where you see "D", this means 'daily'. However, despite this designation, the outfitter will not in fact start on every day. The outfitter will run only if a certain minimum number of people want to raft. For trips run by small outfitters and for trips by any outfitter on a weekday, you may have to supply a minimum group in order for the trip to run. See below.

On rivers that do not have limited start dates, some outfitters have provided limited days or dates on which they expect to start, as a service to individuals, couples, and small groups. These "identified" start dates serve as a focus to bring very small groups together, especially for weekday starts. As an example, three dozen outfitters may offer "daily" trips on the Lower Klamath, but only three may actually run on any given Monday. The company most likely to be running on the Monday is the company that lists a Monday start.

Raft type. See Chapter 1 for a discussion of the advantages and disadvantages of different types of rafts. The following abbreviations are used:

ob	Oar boat
o/pa	Oar boat with paddle assist

pb	Paddle boat
ik	Inflatable kayak
s/b	Self-bailing (see appendix on Boat Types)
op	Optional (you must request this type of raft)
ia	If available or if appropriate (the outfitter cannot guarantee you would get this type of raft, even if you request it)

If you have a strong preference for one type of raft, be sure to tell your outfitter.

Put-ins and take-outs. The put-in is the river location where the trip starts, and the take-out is the river location where the trip ends. Whenever possible, location names have been standardized with the names used in *California White Water*. This permits you to use that book in evaluating river tours.

On most multi-day trips, the put-in on the second day is the same as the take-out on the first day, and so on for the subsequent days. However, on some multi-day trips (and some single day trips on the Upper Kern), the trip is not run continuously down one stretch of water. Where this occurs, two or three put-ins and take-outs are listed. For example, a combination trip that runs the first day on the South Fork of the American and the second day on the Middle Fork of the American may have a listing of: "Camp Lotus-Salmon Falls; Oxbow Bend-Greenwood Br". This would mean that on the first day you would raft the South Fork of the American from Camp Lotus to Salmon Falls, while on the second day you would raft the Middle Fork from Oxbow Bend to the Greenwood Bridge.

Miles. Distance between put-ins and take-outs, in miles.

Camp. Provided for overnight trips only. On-river means you will spend the night at a campsite beside the river. Off-river means you will spend the night at a campground away from the river. Lodge means you will spend the night at a lodge or motel. Optional overnight sites are noted in the Comments section.

Facilities. Provided for overnight camping trips only. See Chapter 2. Flush means the campground has flush toilets. Chem means the campground has chemical toilets or outhouses. Porta means your group travels with a porta-potty or lime can, used for solid waste only.

Recommendations (Rec). These are recommendations from the outfitter on wetsuits (see *What to Bring*) or passenger qualifications. Note the common abbreviation "exp" means rafting experience. "Pb exp" refers to paddle boat experience. "Exp for paddlers" is subtly different: it means that those who wish to be in a paddle boat should have rafted before. Temperature and cfs limits refer to water temperature and water levels.

Requirements (Req). Abbreviations are the same as those used in the recommendations. Every rafter is required to sign a statement releasing the outfitter from liability for a rafting injury. Life jackets are required at all times. Helmets are required on Class V rivers and at the discretion of the outfitter on other rivers. Life jackets and helmets are always provided by the outfitter. For tests, see the appendix *River Fitness Tests.*

Minimum age (Age). This is the age of the youngest child an outfitter will take on the river. If you feel that your child is particularly large and mature and also swims well for his or her age, then consult with your outfitter. In many cases, an outfitter reported that the minimum age varies according to the water level. If the minimum age may change due to the water level or other circumstances, this is noted as "call", which means you should call the outfitter and ask about the minimum age.

I strongly recommend that, at least for their first trip, you select an easy river for your children. A river that excites an adult may terrify a child, and then that young person will never return to the sport. Also, once you're on the river, you and your child are committed.

Cost. The price for one adult to raft on a trip starting on a Saturday. Note discounts, below. Prices for the same stretch of river vary widely, for several reasons.

(1) Many outfitters operate their rafting businesses out of their homes, with the owners serving as guides. These outfitters have substantially lower overhead and payroll expenses than do outfitters with full-fledged professional operations. However, all outfitters pay the same fees and insurance premiums.

(2) Some outfitters pay their guides more, especially on Class IV or V rivers. Also, some companies operate with a higher guide-to-customer ratio; this becomes obligatory on trips with a number of oar boats, which do not carry as many passengers as paddle boats do.

(3) Outfitters with equipment and personnel based far from particular rivers face higher transportation costs than outfitters located close to a river.

(4) Advertising and promotion in this industry is difficult and expensive; the cost of this activity, as well as the cost of printing and distributing four-color brochures, is reflected in a company's prices.

(5) Some outfitters spend more money on food and other details.

(6) Some outfitters operate with higher profit margins.

(7) Information on who offers what trip where and for what price has been nearly impossible to locate. Congratulations: You have located it.

When you are trying to determine which outfitter is offering you the best price, do not forget (a) your phone bills, (b) your transportation costs, (c) your wetsuit costs, and (d) discounts, below. Also, some outfitters cover the cost of camping the night before the trip.

Maximum group size. (Max. Grp.) This is the largest number of passengers that an outfitter will take on the river on one day. Frequently regulations dictate this limit. Occasionally, outfitters have some flexibility in the matter of maximum group size. If they do, this is noted in the river description under *Permit system*. By calling around, you may find an outfitter willing to increase his or her maximum group size. Recall that as a group gets larger, the rafting experience becomes less intimate, and waiting times increase.

Minimum group size. (Min. Grp.) Unlike an airline, where a plane flies empty or full, rafting trips run only when sufficient people want to raft on a particular date. In addition, even if an outfitter provided specific start dates, then the outfitter will also run on other dates with a large enough group. So, either (a) you have to assemble a group or (b) you have to hope that someone else has assembled a minimum group that you can join. Read Chapter 5 for caveats. If an outfitter does not list a minimum group, the trip will not start on dates other than those listed.

Discounts. Now is the time to get your teenager into the act. If he or she can figure out the trip discounts, then college admission is in the bag. Rafting trip discounts are almost as confusing as airline discounts. The one advantage of rafting discounts is that they don't change every week or so.

Free trips. This book lists two major types of discounts. The first is a 100% discount, otherwise known as a free trip. This is abbreviated as "F", for 'free'. (note also "w/", for 'with'). Many outfitters offer one free trip with a large group trip arranged by one person. Examples of free trip discounts are: "1Fw/10"—you will receive one free trip with at least ten paying customers in your group (your total group size, then, could be 11 people or more), or "2Fw/24"—you receive two free trips with 24 paying customers in your group (your group size could be 26 people or more).

Dollar and percentage discounts. The second type of discount is something less than 100%. Here the policies of outfitters fluctuate madly, and you can get a headache trying to figure them out. This is why you handed the chore to your teenager in the first place. There are again two subsets of the discount. An outfitter may choose to reduce prices (a) by a dollar amount, noted in this section as "less $", or (b) by a percentage of the trip price, noted as "less %".

Now you have to decipher why an outfitter offers a particular discount.

Weekday discounts. The most common reason for a discount is that a trip starts on a weekday. Look for "wd", for 'weekday'. Example: "Less $5 wd" means that the outfitter will reduce the cost of a trip by $5 if you raft on a trip that starts on a weekday. Alternatively, the outfitter may have reported "less 5% wd." This means that the outfitter will reduce the cost of a trip by 5% if you raft on a weekday. So, here you have to multiply the cost of the trip by .05 and subtract the product from the cost (alternatively, you could multiply the cost by .95, but what the heck). For a concrete example, a trip with a cost of $200 and a discount of "less

$5 wd" will cost you $200 for trips starting on Saturday and Sunday and $195 for trips starting on the weekdays. The same $200 trip with a discount of "less 5% wd" will cost you $190 for trips starting on the weekdays. Important: Weekday discounts almost always do not apply to holidays.

Specific start day discounts. Sometimes weekday savings depend on the specific day you start. Days are abbreviated by the first two letters of the day, so "Mo" is Monday, etc. "Mo-Th" is Monday through Thursday, which is again, fine, but then "FrSu" is Friday and Sunday, but not Saturday.

Group discounts. Outfitters commonly provide discounts for groups (instead of, or in addition to, a free trip). Example: "Less $10 w/6 +" means everybody in the group saves ten dollars if you gather a group of six or more. It's policies like these that make your teenager's repulsive buddies somewhat less repulsive. Important: Only one person in your group can phone or write the outfitter. One of the reasons for the group discount is that a pre-organized group creates less work for an outfitter's staff.

Youth discounts. Many outfitters offer a youth discount. This is noted as "y", for 'youth'. Because outfitters are an independent group of folks, they all have different ideas of what age is worthy of a discount. In these listings, "y16" means 'youth, age 16 or under'. Therefore, a discount of "less $10 y16", means that your 16-year-old gets $10 off the cost, while your 17-year-old pays full fare.

Senior citizen discounts. Sometimes outfitters offer discounts to seniors. This is noted as "s" for 'senior'. The abbreviation here is the reverse of the youth discount. So, "s65" means 'senior, 65 years old or older'.

Special discounts. Sometimes outfitters offer discounts to other categories of rafters. Here, the same format is continued. Example: "less 30% handicapped" means the price for handicapped people is 30% less than the quoted cost.

Combination discounts. Admit it. You got this far, and you didn't even need help from your teenager. Well, rafting companies *combine* discounts in a manner that even the airlines avoid. What makes this particularly difficult is that Company A may permit two different discounts to apply to one person, while Company B allows only one discount to apply to one person. If your teenager can understand the following discussion, then he or she is ready for graduate business school. If not, call up the outfitter and have him or her work out the price for your particular group.

If two discounts can apply to the same person, then the discounts are linked with the word "and". Example: "Less $20 wd *and* less $10 y16" means you, as an adult, pay $20 less than the quoted cost to raft on a weekday, and your 16-year-old pays $30 less.

However, if only one of two discounts can apply to the same person, then the discounts are linked with the word "or". Example: "Less $20 wd *or* less $10 y16" means that your 16-year-old pays only $20 less than the individual cost, because both discounts cannot apply to the same person.

Friends, Californians, and fellow rafters, it gets worse. Sometimes three or more discounts apply to the same trip. Here, again, "and" and "or" are used to identify whether two discounts can apply at the same time. Use common rules of arithmetic to determine the total discount applicable to your group. Again, if you have trouble deciphering the discounts, call your outfitter.

Call. The discount policy is so complicated that it could not fit in the space available. Call the outfitter and ask.

Transportation. Your outfitter will almost always provide shuttle transportation, that is, take you from a meet point to the river and from the river back to the meet point. If the outfitter does not provide shuttle transportation, it is noted here.

Also, an outfitter may provide transportation from a major city (and its local airport) to the river. If this transportation is included at no extra cost, then the transportation listing will read, for example: "Inc from SF", for 'transportation from San Francisco is included at no additional charge.' If transportation is available at an additional charge, then the listing will read, for example: "Avail from SF", for 'transportation is available from San Francisco, at an additional charge.' The cost of that transportation will be noted under comments.

Comments. This section identifies (a) special features offered by the outfitter, (b) any charges associated with trip options, such as lodging or transportation, and (c) any nonstandard additions to the trip, such as the outfitter providing alcoholic beverages. Also, if the outfitter requires a gear weight limit, that is noted in this section (# = pound; 35# = 35 pounds)

—River Country Rafting

Ukonom Falls, the highlight of a side hike from the Lower Klamath

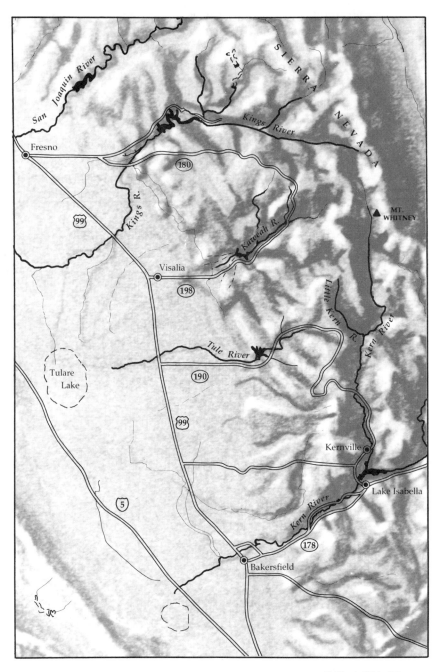

Rivers of the Southern Sierra Nevada

—California White Water

Forks of the Kern

Introduction. The so-called "Forks" section of the Kern river offers one of the finest wilderness rafting experiences in the country, yet it is located only a few hours north of Los Angeles. Because of the difficulty (Class V) of the Forks as well as the poor road access, this section should be attempted only by the experienced, fit, and healthy rafter.

Level of difficulty/water level concerns/flow information. Class V. The Forks is a free-flowing section; no dams lurk upstream to extend the season. Water levels tend to rise rather slowly and maintain dependable levels throughout the spring. Expect high water in May; the season usually ends in July. The minimum water flow to run the Forks is about 600 cfs. For up-to date flow information, call (916) 322-3327. Listen for the flow at Kernville and subtract five percent.

Permit system/time to raft. See the Lower Kern for a discussion of the selection process for permittees. In addition, the Forest Service has requested you be informed that Chuck Richards' Whitewater Inc. and Chuck Richards' Sequoia Outdoor Center hold different permits for the Kern sections. This book combines the tours offered by those two permittees, because they are under the same management.

—Water Colors
A "controlled" oar boat run through Class V + Carson Falls on the Forks of the Kern

Abbreviations

Mo,Tu,We	Monday, Tuesday, Wednesday, etc.	porta	Porta-potty or lime can at camp
D	Daily	exp	(Rafting) experience
will call	Outfitter will call you to arrange dates	Camping exp	Camping experience
ob	Oar boat	F	Free
o/pa	Oar boat with paddle assist	w/	With
pb	Paddle boat	wd	Weekday
ik	Inflatable kayak	we	Weekend
s/b	Self-bailing	y	Youth
op	Optional	y16	Youth, age 16 and under
ia	If available or if appropriate	s	Senior
on-river	Camp is beside the river	s65	Senior, age 65 and over
off-river	Camp is not beside the river	inc	Included
lodge	Overnight at a lodge or motel	avail	Available
flush	Flush toilets at camp	#	pound
chem	Chemical toilets or outhouse at camp		

Name– Max. cfs	Starting	Raft type	Put-in– Take-out	Miles Camp Facilities
FORKS OF THE KERN—2 DAYS				
Chuck Richards' WW/SOC No max	May 1, 2, 6, 7, 11, 12, 16, 17, 21, 22, 26, 27, 31; Jun 1, 5, 6, 10, 11, 15, 16, 20, 21, 25, 26, 30; Jul 1	ob, pb op ia, ik op exp ia	Little Kern Conf- Fairview Dam	19 On-river Porta
Kern River Tours 4,000	Apr 19, 24, 29; May 4, 14, 19; Jun 3	ob, pb op exp	Little Kern Conf- Fairview Dam	19 On-river Porta
Whitewater Voyages 4,000	May 13, 18, 23, 28	ob s/b, pb s/b op	Little Kern Conf- Fairview Dam	19 On-river Porta
FORKS OF THE KERN—3 DAYS				
Chuck Richards' WW/SOC No max	May 1, 2, 6, 7, 11, 12, 16, 17, 21, 22, 26, 27, 31; Jun 1, 5, 6, 10, 11, 15, 16, 20, 21, 25, 26, 30; Jul 1	ob, pb op ia, ik op exp ia	Little Kern Conf- Fairview Dam	19 On-river Porta
Kern River Tours 4,000	May 9, 24, 29; Jun 8, 13, 18, 23, 28; Jul 3, 8, 13, 18, 23, 28	ob, pb op exp	Little Kern Conf- Fairview Dam	19 On-river Porta
Whitewater Voyages 4,000	May 3, 8; Jun 2, 7, 12, 17, 22, 27; Jul 2, 7, 12, 22	ob s/b, pb s/b op ia	Little Kern Conf- Fairview Dam	19 On-river Porta
FORKS OF THE KERN—4 DAYS				
Chuck Richards' WW/SOC No max	May 1, 2, 6, 7, 11, 12, 16, 17, 21, 22, 26, 27, 31; Jun 1, 5, 6, 10, 11, 15, 16, 20, 21, 25, 26, 30; Jul 1	ob, pb op ia, ik op exp ia	Little Kern Conf- Fairview Dam	19 On-river Porta

Because of the poor access to this section of the Kern, companies are required to bring an Emergency Medical Technician on each trip.

Commercial rafting is limited to one start per day by any outfitter, with a maximum group size of 15 passengers. This policy provides for equal seclusion for weekdays and weekends, although weekends trips are more likely to be full and will more likely attract private boaters (also limited to one start per day). As with any Class V river, prudence indeed would dictate waiting until after high water to raft—try June. As this is a river for the expert only, you probably won't be able to gather a group to go with you. Keep in close contact with your outfitter about available dates and reservations.

Recom. Require. Min. Age	Cost Max. Grp. Min. Grp.	Discounts	Transportation	Comments
Rec: Lean, wiry, fit. Req: Wetsuit; Class V paddle test for paddlers. Age: 15	$360 15	Less $20wd and 1 Fw/14		
Rec: Good physical condition. Req: Wetsuit; exp. Age: 13	$315 15			May 4, Jun 3, add $25
Req: Exp; Class V paddle test; wetsuit. Age: 15	$372 15 15	Less 10%w/12 + or less 10%y16		Cocktails inc; 30# gear limit
Rec: Lean, wiry, fit. Req: Wetsuit; Class V paddle test for paddlers. Age: 15	$430 15	Less $32wd and 1 Fw/14		
Rec: Good physical condition. Req: Wetsuit; exp. Age: 13	$425 15	Less $25 Mo-We		Side hikes inc
Req: Exp; Class V paddle test; wetsuit. Age: 14	$462 15 15	Less 10%w/12 + or less 10%y16		Cocktails inc; 30# gear limit
Rec: Lean, wiry, fit. Req: Wetsuit; Class V paddle test for paddlers. Age: 15	$470 15	1 Fw/14		

Commercial rafting. In 1985, four outfitters took 479 intrepid adventurers down the Forks of the Kern.

Gear/safety/who can come. Wetsuit always. No one who has not already rafted a Class IV river should select the Forks, because if you can't take it, you won't be able to quit and hike to the road. Obviously, if you have any type of medical problem or chronic condition, you should choose another river.

Distinctive features. But if you're ready for the Forks, you'll find there an intense and incomparable whitewater experience. The river is so isolated that you will have to travel two miles to the put-in by horseback. For much of its length, the Kern carves a deep granite canyon that will delight the geologists in your party. Most striking of all is the lonely wilderness that evokes the experiences of early California explorers.

River access. Extremely difficult, even by helicopter. Road access along the last two miles of the run only.

Sites of interest. Several streams feed into the Kern, forming waterfalls and swimming holes along its banks.

Environment. The granite canyon of the Kern is home to assorted wildflowers in the spring: look for flannel brush, buck brush, and popcorn flowers. Near the put-in, pine trees (mainly Jeffrey pine) grow on both banks, but as you float downstream the forests change, to oak and chaparral. The river also moves through part of the Kern river deer herd belt, so keep an eye peeled for mule deer. Also bear. Red-tailed hawks, quail, owls, and blue heron call the Kern river home.

Fishing. Wild rainbow and brown trout. A great way to relax after a day when your adrenalin has run faster than the river.

Summary of river between put-ins. Summarized with permission from the extensive mile by mile guide in *California White Water*.

Little Kern Confluence to Fairview Dam (19 miles)—Five Class V rapids, eight Class IV + s.

River status. The Forest Service has declared this portion of the Kern river eligible for wild and scenic status, and Congress will be considering it in 1986. To express your support for wild and scenic status for the Kern, write your congressional representative at the House Office Building, Washington, DC, 20515, and ask for passage of HR 3934.

See Lower Kern for lodgings and campgrounds.

Upper Kern

Introduction. The Upper Kern alone among commercially rafted rivers in California offers sections of every level of difficulty. Anyone, regardless of experience, can find challenging and exciting whitewater on the Upper Kern.

Level of difficulty/water level concerns/flow information. Class II-V, depending on the section rafted. While a small diversion dam (Fairview Dam) sits just above this section, its reservoir is too small to lengthen the rafting season. Water flows taper off in July, depending on the snow pack. Minimum water flow to raft is about 800 cfs. For flow information, call (916) 322-3327. Listen for the flow at Kernville, and subtract 500 cfs for sections other than the "Powerhouse" run. If flows for the Class IV and V sections become too low, the outfitters will probably bus you upstream to the Class IV Johnsondale Bridge to Fairview Dam section (the "Limestone" run), which also has that extra 500 cfs.

Permit system/time to raft. See the discussion of the permitting system under the Lower Kern. On this river, each outfitter is permitted to start one trip each day with a maximum of 25 passengers per trip. You may wish to book on weekdays, not to avoid crowding on the river, which is unusual, but to miss the weekend fishermen.

The Class II "Powerhouse" section, running from the Powerhouse to Riverside Park, has much higher limits on rafting groups. Chuck Richards' Sequoia Outdoor Center, Kern River Tours, and some small, local companies run several trips per day there. This easy section serves as an excellent introduction to rafting. Try it, you'll like it, and if you don't, it's only about $15 anyway.

Commercial rafting. In 1985, outfitters took 3,130 passengers down the Upper Kern.

Gear/safety/who can come. The "Powerhouse" section is suitable for young and old. Persons running the Class V section should be swimmers and should have rafting experience. Spring rafters on all the upper sections should wear wetsuits.

Abbreviations

Mo,Tu,We	Monday, Tuesday, Wednesday, etc.	porta	Porta-potty or lime can at camp
D	Daily	exp	(Rafting) experience
will call	Outfitter will call you to arrange dates	Camping exp	Camping experience
ob	Oar boat	F	Free
o/pa	Oar boat with paddle assist	w/	With
pb	Paddle boat	wd	Weekday
ik	Inflatable kayak	we	Weekend
s/b	Self-bailing	y	Youth
op	Optional	y16	Youth, age 16 and under
ia	If available or if appropriate	s	Senior
on-river	Camp is beside the river	s65	Senior, age 65 and over
off-river	Camp is not beside the river	inc	Included
lodge	Overnight at a lodge or motel	avail	Available
flush	Flush toilets at camp	#	pound
chem	Chemical toilets or outhouse at camp		

Name— Max. cfs	Starting	Raft type	Put-in— Take-out	Miles Camp Facilities
UPPER KERN—¼ DAY				
Chuck Richards' WW/SOC No max	D Apr 1—Jul 15	pb, ik, op	Powerhouse-Riverside Park	2
Kern River Tours No max	D Apr 1—Aug 31	pb, ob op, ik op	Powerhouse-Riverside Park	2
UPPER KERN—½ DAY				
Chuck Richards' WW/SOC No max	D Apr 1—Jul 15	pb, ik, op	River Kern Bch-Riverside Park	3
Kern River Tours 6,000	D Apr 1—Aug 31	pb, ob op	Powerhouse-Riverside Park; Camp 3-Riverside Park	7
Kern River Tours No max	D Apr 1—Aug 31	pb, ob op, ik op	Powerhouse-Riverside Park; Powerhouse-Riverside Park	4
UPPER KERN—¾ DAY				
Kern River Tours 6,000	D Apr 1—Aug 31	ob, pb op exp	Ant Canyon-Riverside Park	12
UPPER KERN—1 DAY				
Chuck Richards' WW/SOC No max	We, Fr Apr 15—Jun 15	ob, pb s/b op	Ant Canyon-Riverside Park	12
Chuck Richards' WW/SOC No max	D Apr 1—Jul 15	pb, ik op	River Kern Bch-Riverside Park	3
Kern River Tours 6,000	D Apr 1—Aug 31	ob, pb op exp	Ant Canyon-Riverside Park	12
Whitewater Voyages 3,000	D Apr 1—Aug 31	pb s/b, ob s/b op	Ant Canyon-Riverside Park	12
Whitewater Voyages 8,000	D Apr 1—Sep 30	pb, ob op	Powerhouse-Riverside Park; Fairview Dam-Calkins Flat; Camp 3-Powerhouse	8
UPPER KERN—2 DAYS				
Whitewater Voyages 3,000	D Apr 1—Aug 31	pb s/b, ob s/b op	Fairview Dam-Riverside Park	17 On-river Chem

Recom. Require. Min. Age	Cost Max. Grp. Min. Grp.	Discounts	Transportation	Comments
Age: 6	$15 50 6	1 Fw/24 and less 10%w/12 + wd		
Age: 8	$16 50 6	Less 10%w/12 +		Ik op, add $4
Age: 6	$35 50 6	1 Fw/24 and less 10%w/12 + wd		
Age: 8	$45 25 6	Less 10%w/12 +		
Age: 8	$30 50 6	Less 10%w/12 +		
Req: Wetsuit. Age: 13	$59 25 10	Less 10%w/12 +		
Req: Wetsuit; Class V paddle test for paddlers. Age: 15	$95 25 6	1 Fw/24		
Rec: Wetsuit. Age: 8	$80 25 6	Less $12wd and 1 Fw/24 and less 10%w/12 + wd		
Age: 13	$95 25 10	Less $10wd and less 10%w/12 +		
Req: Exp; Class V paddle test; wetsuit. Age: 14	$107 25 25	1 Fw/24 and less $12wd and (less 10%w/12 + or less 10%y16)		Beer inc
Rec: Wetsuit Apr, May. Age: 12	$88 25 25	1 Fw/24 and less $16wd and (less $10%w/12 + or less 10%y16)		Beer inc
Req: Exp; Class V paddle test; wetsuit. Age: 14	$214 25 25	1 Fw/24 and less $12FrSu and less $30wd and (less 10%w/12 + or less 10%y16)		Cocktails inc

—*Water Colors*

A paddle boat bombs into a Class V rapid on the Upper Kern

Distinctive features. The Upper Kern is a natural for the truly custom-designed trip. The proximity of the road permits many put-ins and take-outs throughout the stretch. If you and your friends can make up a minimum group, and you would rather raft one section twice, or not raft another, then plan on a weekday for rafting and talk to an outfitter about creating a trip to your specifications. If some of your friends are queasy about the advanced sections of this river (a more than valid concern), then the nearness of the road makes scouting easy.

River access. Sierra Way runs adjacent to the river along much of its length. This permits easy access not only for you, but also for fishermen with trout bait. Watch out for the fishing lines.

Environment. The Upper Kern flows through an entrancing and attractive desert canyon. In spring, poppies, popcorn flowers, and owl's clover can be spotted on the chaparral-covered hills. Oaks and cottonwood add to the classic desert river environment.

Fishing. Wild rainbow and brown trout; stocked rainbows predominate.

Summary of river between put-ins. Summarized with permission from *California White Water*. See that book for excellent descriptions of these sections as well as a river map.

Fairview Dam to Calkins Flat (3 miles)—Class III rapids only.

Calkins Flat to Ant Canyon (2 miles)—Two Class IV+ rapids.

Ant Canyon to Camp 3 (7 miles)—Three Class V rapids, two Class IVs.

Camp 3 to River Kern Beach (2 miles)—Two Class IV rapids, two Class IIIs.

River Kern Beach to Powerhouse (.5 miles)—One long Class III+ rapid.

Powerhouse to Riverside Park (2 miles)—Two Class II+ rapids.

At low water, you may raft the "Limestone" run instead of one of the more advanced sections.

Johnsondale Bridge to Fairview Dam (2 miles)—Two Class IV rapids.

River status. Although the Forest Service designated this section eligible for the recreational classification of wild and scenic status, the North Fork Kern environmental impact statement did not recommend the Upper Kern for official wild and scenic designation. The lack of protection for the Upper Kern leaves this widely utilized trout stream and whitewater resource open for the expansion of the Southern California Edison power project and the resulting partial inundation of the Upper Kern, as well as tungsten mining and ore processing. If you feel that the Upper Kern should be nominated for wild and scenic river status along with the Forks of the Kern, then write your congressional representative at the House Office Building, Washington, DC 20515, and say so.

See Lower Kern for lodgings and campgrounds.

Lower Kern

Introduction. This rugged, narrow, intermediate-level river offers excellent whitewater only three hours from Los Angeles. As a result of the limited number of permittees, weekend trips may be booked solid several months in advance.

Level of difficulty/water level concerns/flow information. Class IVp. The portage is easy: the Kern outfitters have constructed a cement and stone walkway that resembles an ancient Roman road around the unrunnable rapid. Water levels are controlled by the Lake Isabella Dam, the primary purpose of which is irrigation. Water levels remain constant throughout the week. The highest water levels frequently occur in July. Minimum flow for rafting is about 900 cfs. For flow information, call (916) 322-3327. Listen for the release from Isabella Dam.

Permit system/time to raft. Companies rafting the three Kern river sections were chosen by a bid prospectus system in 1979 and 1983. Selection criteria for the current outfitters were experience on difficult whitewater, safety record, and financial ability. The Forest Service limited the number of permittees to ensure that the rafting companies chosen would develop substantial experience on the Kern river sections and would also become part of the community. Each company is required to provide a minimum of 2000 user days per year.

A company may start only one trip per day, each with no more than 25 passengers. The (a) low number of permittees and therefore low river traffic, in combination with (b) many, many challenging rapids and (c) good water flow throughout the summer season makes this river my choice for the best summer weekend run in the state. As a result, weekend bookings must be obtained months in advance; you may have to plan for a weekend next year or book on a weekday.

Commercial rafting. In 1985, four companies took 11,958 people down the Lower Kern.

Gear/safety/who can come. The Lower Kern attracts first time rafters despite its many Class IV rapids. Recall that if you paddle this river, you stand a good chance of falling out and swimming a rapid. Participants will probably enjoy this river more with some Class III experience behind them. With that in mind, the Lower Kern is suitable for anyone ready for excitement, including the handicapped. But remember the recent country-western song in which the singer loses his love to the river, and don't even go near Kern river without your life jacket on.

Distinctive features. This river offers everything for the Angeleno: easy access to the city, availability all summer, and a feeling of solitude in a scenic and natural canyon.

River access. Highway 178 runs near the river for the entire rafting section, but the traffic is always out of sight and usually cannot be heard.

Sites of interest. Miracle Hot Springs and Remington Hot Springs gurgle within walking distance of the river. On my 1985 trip, the group had plans to stop at Remington, but we spotted some nude sunbathers from the river and decided to stay wet and cool. There were wide-eyed children in our group.

Your guide can also point out Indian petroglyphs on the first day of your tour.

Environment. For the first six rafting miles, the river carries you under a canopy of cottonwoods. Later, the cottonwoods recede up the sides of the valley and are replaced with oaks on golden hills. During the spring, fields of poppies, popcorn flowers, and owl's clovers draw your attention off-river. Keep yours eyes open also for prairie falcons and ospreys; in the spring you may even see a bald eagle.

—*Water Colors*

Paddlers relax in a Lower Kern "pool"

Fishing. Stocked rainbow trout.

Summary of river between put-ins. Summarized with permission from *California White Water*. See that volume for excellent descriptions of the rapids along the stretch as well as a detailed river map.

Isabella Dam to Hwy 155 Bridge (1 mile)—Flat water.

Hwy 155 Bridge to Miracle Hot Springs (7 miles)—Four Class III rapids.

Miracle Hot Springs to Democrat Picnic Area (11 miles)—Five Class IV rapids, five Class IIIs. Easy portage.

River status. Despite the extensive recreational use of this beautiful and accessible river, the Lower Kern is not listed in the National Rivers Inventory, which is a required first step in its protection. Friends of the River is requesting a study of this river for that purpose by Sequoia National Forest. This river needs all the shields it can acquire, for in 1984 a preliminary permit was issued for the construction of a hydroelectric dam that would inundate a portion of this run and dewater the rest. To express your concern over this dam, referred to as the Hobo project, write to Sen. Alan Cranston at the Senate Office Building, Washington, DC 20510.

Motels and lodges. Abbreviations used in the following listings are: L, R = Turn left, Turn right; H = Highway; I = Interstate; N, S, E, W = North, South, East, West; mi = miles; n/p = price or service not provided.

Sierra South Lodge, #2 Sierra Way, P.O. Box 745, Kernville, CA 93238.

Name— Max. cfs	Starting	Raft type	Put-in— Take-out	Miles Camp Facilities
LOWER KERN—1 DAY				
Kern River Tours 7,000	Mo-Fr May 1—Jun 14, Sep 1—Sep 30	pb, ob op	Miracle Hot Spr- Democrat Picnic	11
LOWER KERN—2 DAYS				
Chuck Richards' WW No max	D May 1—Sep 30	pb, ik op exp, ob op ia	Isabella Dam- Democrat Picnic	19 On-river Chem
Kern River Tours 7,000	D May 1—Sep 30	pb, ob op	Hwy 155 Bridge- Democrat Picnic	18 On-river Chem
Whitewater Voyages 5,000	D Apr 1—Oct 31	pb, ob op	Hwy 155 Bridge- Democrat Picnic	18 On-river Chem

(619) 376-6019. Directions: I-5 to H-99 to Bakersfield; H-178E to H-155 to Kernville Rd, lodge on N end of Lake Isabella. Cost per room for one: $32; for two: $35; for three: $38; for four: $40.

Paradise Cove Lodge, Rt 1, Box 1, Lake Isabella, CA 93240. (619) 379-2719. Directions: I-5 to H-99 to Bakersfield; H-99 to H-178E to Lake Isabella; 3.5 mi E of dam. Cost per room for one: $25; for two: $25; for three: $30; for four: $30.

Lake Isabella Motel, P.O. Box 795, Lake Isabella, CA 93240-0795. (619) 379-2800. Directions: I-5 to H-99 to Bakersfield; H-99 to H-178E to Lake Isabella; at junction of H-178 and H-155. Cost per room for one: $20; for two: $22; for three: $26-28; for four: $28.

Sierra Vista Motel, 6617 Wofford Blvd, Wofford Heights, CA 93285. (619) 376-2250. Directions: I-5 to H-99 to Bakersfield; H-178E to H-155 to Wofford Heights. Cost per room for one: $25-30; for two: $25-40; for three: $30-45; for four: $35-50.

Abbreviations

Mo,Tu,We	Monday, Tuesday, Wednesday, etc.	porta	Porta-potty or lime can at camp
D	Daily	exp	(Rafting) experience
will call	Outfitter will call you to arrange dates	Camping exp	Camping experience
ob	Oar boat	F	Free
o/pa	Oar boat with paddle assist	w/	With
pb	Paddle boat	wd	Weekday
ik	Inflatable kayak	we	Weekend
s/b	Self-bailing	y	Youth
op	Optional	y16	Youth, age 16 and under
ia	If available or if appropriate	s	Senior
on-river	Camp is beside the river	s65	Senior, age 65 and over
off-river	Camp is not beside the river	inc	Included
lodge	Overnight at a lodge or motel	avail	Available
flush	Flush toilets at camp	#	pound
chem	Chemical toilets or outhouse at camp		

Recom. Require. Min. Age	Cost Max. Grp. Min. Grp.	Discounts	Transportation	Comments
Rec: Wetsuit until Jun 1. Age: 8	$98 25 10	Less 10%w/12 +		
Age: 8	$198 25 6	1 Fw/24 and (less $20SuMoTh and less 10%w/ 12SuMoTh) or less $39TuWe		May join trips for 1 day if space avail, day 1 = $75, day 2 = $88, take-out day 1 is just below Miracle Hot Springs
Age: 8	$198 25 10	(Less $23Mo-Th and less 10%w/ 12 + Mo-Th) or (less 5%w/ 12 + FrSu) and 1 Fw/24		
Req: Wetsuit Apr, May, Sep. Age: 12	$198 25 25	1 Fw/24 and (less $9FrSu or less $20wd) and (less 10%w/12 + Mo-Th or less 10%y16Mo-Th)		Cocktails inc

Whispering Pines Lodge, 13745 Sierra Way (Rt 1, Box 44), Kernville, CA 93238. (619) 376-2334. Directions: I-5 to H- 99 to Bakersfield; H-178E to H-155 to Kernville Rd; L on Sierra Way. Cost per room for one: $27.56; for two: $40.28; for three: n/p; for four: n/p.

Sequoia Motor Lodge, 16123 Sierra Way (Rt 1, Box 62), Kernville, CA 93238. (619) 376-2535. Directions: I-5 to H- 99 to Bakersfield; H-178E to H-155 to Kernville Rd; 3 mi N of Kernville on Sierra Way. Cost per room for one: $26-46; for two: $28-46; for three: $34-52; for four: $40-58.

Pine Cone Inn, 13383 Sierra Way (Box 553), Kernville, CA 93238. (619) 376-6669. Directions: I-5 to H-99 to Bakersfield; H-178E to H-155 to Kernville Rd; L on Sierra Way. Cost per room for one: $26-28; for two: $28-32; for three: $30-34; for four: $34-38.

Pala Ranches Motel, 11042 Kernville Rd (Box 838), Kernville, CA 93238. (619) 376-2222. Directions: I-5 to H-99 to Bakersfield; H-178E to H-155 to Kernville Rd. Cost per room for one: n/p; for two: $28-38; for three: $35-50; for four: $41-50.

McCambridge Lodge Motel, 13525 Sierra Way, Kernville, CA 93238. (619) 376-2288. Directions: I-5 to H-99 to Bakersfield; H-178E to H-155W to Kernville Rd; L on Sierra Way. Cost per room for one: $30-42; for two: $30-42; for three: $38-48; for four: $44-54.

Lazy River Lodge, Sierra Way (Star Route 1, Box 60), Kernville, CA 93238. (619) 376-2242. Directions: I-5 to H-99 to Bakersfield; H-178E to H-155 to Kernville Rd; 2.5 mi N of Kernville on Sierra Way. Cost per room for one: $26-52; for two: $26-52; for three: $32-58; for four: $52-64.

Kern Lodge Motel, P.O. Box 66, Kernville, CA 93238. (619) 376-2224. Directions: I-5 to H-99 to Bakersfield; H-178E to H-155 to Kernville; corner of Valley View and Sierra Dr. Cost per room for one: n/p; for two: $32-45; for three: $37- 50; for four: $42-55.

Western Motel, 132 Buena Vista, Kernville, CA 93238. (619) 376-3222. Directions: I-5 to H-99 to Bakersfield; H-178E to H-155 to Kernville Rd. Cost per room for one: $30; for two: $30; for three: $32; for four: $32.

Private campgrounds. Rivernook Campground. 14001 Sierra Way, Box 8, Kernville, CA 93238. (619) 376-2705. Open: All Year. Directions: I-5 to H-99 to Bakersfield; H-178E to H-155 to Kernville Rd; ¼ mi N of Kernville on Sierra Way. Cost for tenters: $6 for 2; for RVs: $10 for 2; for showers: free.

Public campgrounds. Main Dam (Army Corps of Engineers). Directions: I-5 to H-99 to Bakersfield; H-178E to 1 mi N of Lake Isabella.

Limestone (Forest Service). Directions: I-5 to H-99 to Bakersfield; H-178E to H-155 to Kernville Rd; 18 mi N of Kernville on Sierra Way.

Gold Ledge (Forest Service). Directions: I-5 to H-99 to Bakersfield; H-178E to H-155 to Kernville Rd; 10 mi N of Kernville on Sierra Way.

Fairview (Forest Service). Directions: I-5 to H-99 to Bakersfield; H-178E to H-155 to Kernville Rd; 17 mi N of Kernville on Sierra Way.

Hospital Flat (Forest Service). Directions: I-5 to H-99 to Bakersfield; H-178E to H-155 to Kernville Rd; 6 mi N of Kernville on Sierra Way.

Camp 3 (Forest Service). Directions: I-5 to H-99 to Bakersfield; H-178E to H-155 to Kernville Rd; 5 mi N of Kernville on Sierra Way.

Headquarters (Forest Service). Directions: I-5 to H-99 to Bakersfield; H-178E to H-155 to Kernville Rd; 4 mi N of Kernville on Sierra Way.

Many other Forest Service and Corps of Engineers campgrounds are available in the Kern river area.

Kings

Introduction. The secluded Kings river has a dual personality. Early in the season, it brings you the opportunity to raft waves up to ten feet high; later in the summer it calms to a Class III river suitable for novices.

Level of difficulty/water level concerns/flow information. Class III. The Kings is a free-flowing snow-melt fed river. High water (above 6,000 cfs) occurs from mid-May to mid-June. The river season ends in July or early August, depending on the snow pack. Minimum water to raft is about 1000 cfs. For flow information, call (916) 322-3327. Listen for the flow at Rodgers Crossing or the inflow into Pine Flat Reservoir.

Permit system/time to raft. Commercial rafting is limited to three companies, all of which have held permits for over ten years. Commercial trip starts are limited to four per day: one for each company, with the fourth allocated to one of the three based on usage in the previous year. Sierra National Forest imposes the most complicated trip regulations used on any river in the state: (1) no outfitter can put more than seven passengers in a raft; (2) no more than 10 boats can start at one time; and (3) no more than 60 persons, including guides, can come on one trip. This means that no more than 52 passengers can be on one start.

Abbreviations

Mo,Tu,We	Monday, Tuesday, Wednesday, etc.	porta	Porta-potty or lime can at camp
D	Daily	exp	(Rafting) experience
will call	Outfitter will call you to arrange dates	Camping exp	Camping experience
ob	Oar boat	F	Free
o/pa	Oar boat with paddle assist	w/	With
pb	Paddle boat	wd	Weekday
ik	Inflatable kayak	we	Weekend
s/b	Self-bailing	y	Youth
op	Optional	y16	Youth, age 16 and under
ia	If available or if appropriate	s	Senior
on-river	Camp is beside the river	s65	Senior, age 65 and over
off-river	Camp is not beside the river	inc	Included
lodge	Overnight at a lodge or motel	avail	Available
flush	Flush toilets at camp	#	pound
chem	Chemical toilets or outhouse at camp		

Name– Max. cfs	Starting	Raft type	Put-in– Take-out	Miles Camp Facilities
KINGS—1 DAY				
Kings River Expeditions 23,000	Sa, Su Apr 26—May 17; D May 18—Jul 31	pb	Garnet Dyke-Kirch Flat	10
Zephyr 20,000	D Apr 26—Aug 31	pb, ob op	Garnet Dyke-Kirch Flat	10
KINGS—2 DAYS				
Kings River Expeditions 23,000	Sa Apr 26—May 17; D May 18—Jul 31	pb	Garnet Dyke-Kirch Flat; Garnet Dyke-Kirch Flat	20 On-river Flush
Spirit Whitewater 20,000	D Apr 15—Aug 31	pb	Hermit's Hole-Kirch Flat; Garnet Dyke-Kirch Flat	18 On-river Chem
Zephyr 20,000	D Apr 26—Aug 31	pb, ob op	Garnet Dyke-Kirch Flat; Garnet Dyke-Kirch Flat	20 On-river Chem

This river attracts many private rafters, especially on the weekends. Also, because of the limits to commercial rafting, the beauty of this river, and its reasonable distance from Los Angeles (four to five hours), weekend trips may fill several months in advance. Finally, you should evaluate whether you are ready for the Class IV run that is the Kings at high water. Late June may find the water at your level and the weather warm enough to dispense with a wetsuit. Let your skills be your guide to when to raft.

Commercial rafting. In 1985, the three outfitters racked up 8400 user days on the Kings. As the majority of Kings trips last two days, I would estimate that about 5000 passengers rafted the Kings last year.

Gear/safety/who can come. Wetsuits always at high water. Even at lower levels, many rapids run together, so swims can be long. Children should not connect with the raging torrent that is the Kings at high water. The river changes character at lower water levels, and children will enjoy the river with their usual exhausting exuberance. This Jekyll and Hyde river behavior results in the appearance of "call" under minimum age in the trip listings. In my opinion, your offspring should be river-experienced, courageous, and weigh more than about 100 pounds to take on the high water.

Like the upper (Chili Bar) section of the South Fork of the American, the Kings has a major rapid just below the put-in. You may wish to paddle

Recom. Require. Min. Age	Cost Max. Grp. Min. Grp.	Discounts	Transportation	Comments
Age: Call	$88 52 20	Less $10Mo-Th and (less $7.50w/ 20 + or less $7.50y18 or less $7.50s65) and 1 Fw/20		
Rec: Wetsuit Apr, May, Jun or over 7,000 cfs. Age: 12	$80 50 6	1Fw/20 and less $15y15		Age restriction if cfs over 10,000, 15-55
Age: Call	$188 52 20	(Less $16FrSu or less $39Mo-Th) and (less $15w/ 20 + or less $15y18 or less $15s65) and 1 Fw/ 20		
Rec: Wetsuit until Jun 15. Age: Call	$190 50 12	Less $15w/15 + and less $15y15 and less $15wd and (1 Fw/20 or 2 Fw/40)		Breakfast day 1 inc
Rec: Wetsuit Apr, May, Jun or over 7,000 cfs. Age: 12	$185 50 6	1Fw/20 and less $10wd and less $25y15		Age restriction if cfs over 10,000, 15-55

something else, anything else, before taking on this monstrosity of waves.

Distinctive features. This section of the Kings River, which forms the border between the Sierra and the Sequoia National Forests, supplies its guests with some of the finest scenery in either forest.

River access. Access is by dead-end dirt road only; the deliberately poor quality of the road along the river effectively limits traffic to river runners.

Environment. In spring the hills, marked with oak and sycamore, turn prematurely golden with fields of California poppies. Wildflower enthusiasts will find 20 or 30 different varieties of lupine. The granite cliffs of the Kings River Canyon support golden eagles, and the rare bald eagle may soar above. Wood ducks have nesting sites along the river; you may also see mallards and mergansers swim by in the cold, clear water. And lest you think this river is only for the birds, white-tail deer winter in the area. The earlier you raft, the more likely you are to see them.

Fishing. Wild brown and wild rainbow trout.

Summary of river between put-ins. Provided by John Munger of Spirit Whitewater and Jim Cassady. See *California White Water* for a river map and alternate river description.

Garnet Dyke to Hermit's Hole (2 miles)—Above 6,000 cfs, one Class IV rapid and four Class IIIs; below 6,000 cfs, five Class IIIs.

Hermit's Hole to Kirch Flat (8 miles)—Above 6,000 cfs, three Class IV rapids, 19 class III rapids; below 6,000 cfs, 22 Class III rapids.

River status. At the November 1985 summit, President Reagan and General Secretary Gorbachev agreed to meet again in the United States in June 1986. The time of this meeting is significant, of course, because June is the peak of the rafting season. In addition, at this writing, students at Stanford University have invited Mr. Gorbachev to speak there during his visit. A well-planned California tour should allow Mr. Gorbachev time for a rafting trip in the Sierras. Such a trip, in the company of President Reagan, would offer both world leaders the opportunity to make an important political statement and have some fun, too. After all, Mayor Bradley did it (on the Lower Kern) in 1985. Imagine, if you will, a raft with Gorbachev (on the left) and Reagan (on the right) paddling together toward a goal of mutual survival. It would be the photo opportunity of the century.

Now then, if someone were to ask me which of the many California rivers Reagan and Gorbachev should raft, and of course no one has, then my choice would be the Kings. An excellent river for active beginners, the Kings offers exciting high waves with a minimum of hazards.

And perhaps a state visit is what it takes to get some visibility for the unique and irreplaceable Kings River, now threatened with obliteration by the Rodgers Crossing Project. This proposed dam would destroy six to thirteen miles of the river, depending on the size of dam the developers choose to build. A defense against this project would be the obtaining of wild and scenic status for the Kings, which must come from Congress. To express your views, write to Sen. Alan Cranston, Senate Office Building, Washington, DC 20510.

Motels and lodges. Abbreviations used in the following listings are: L, R = Turn left, Turn right; H = Highway; I = Interstate; N, S, E, W = North, South, East, West; mi = miles; n/p = price or service not provided.

Town House Motel, 1308 Church Ave, Sanger, CA 93657. (209) 875-5531. Directions: I-5 to H-99 to Fresno; H-180E to Sanger; take Jensen Rd until it ends at Academy Rd; motel at junction of Academy and Church. Cost per room for one: $29; for two: $32; for three: $38; for four: $43.

Wonder Valley Ranch Resort, 6450 Elwood Rd, Sanger, CA 93657. (209) 787-2551. Directions: I-5 to H-99 to Fresno; exit E on Belmont Ave; drive E for 25 mi; R on Piedra Ave, cross bridge, L on Elwood Rd; follow signs (6 mi). Cost per room for one: $63-81; for two: $63-81; for three: $73-82; for four: $83-92.

Public campgrounds. Mill Flat (Forest Service). Directions: I-5 to H-99 to Fresno; H-180E to Centerville; take Trimmer Springs Rd NE 36 mi.

Kirch Flat (Forest Service). Directions: I-5 to H-99 to Fresno; H-180E to Centerville; take Trimmer Springs Rd. NE 32 mi.

The Forest Service also maintains other campgrounds near the Kings.

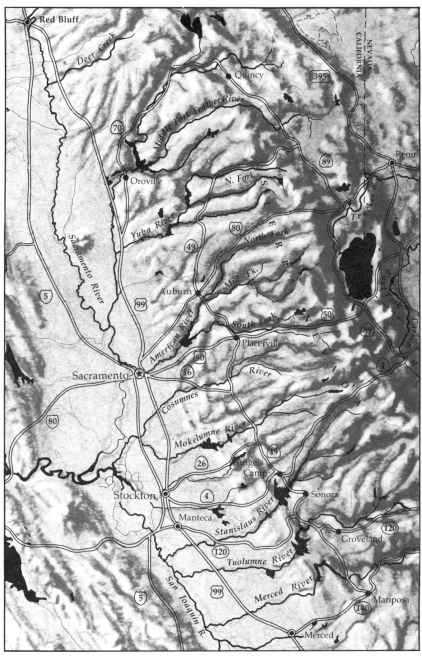

—*California White Water*

Rivers of the Central and Northern Sierra Nevada

Merced

Introduction. The Merced offers exciting intermediate-level white-water at the very gateway of Yosemite National Park.

Level of difficulty/water level concerns/flow information.
Class IV to IVp. Difficult portage in the lower section. The Merced is a free-flowing, snow-fed river; expect water levels sufficient for rafting to last only until June, except in high-water years. On the Merced, water levels are critical to safety. Should the water rise above about 5000 cfs, it becomes difficult to reach the shore above North Fork Falls, the location of the portage. At such water levels, outfitters will run the upper section of the river twice (a "double-upper") in place of the entire length of the river.

But don't shy away from moderate levels—above 3000 cfs this river supplies a wild ride in some sections. Keep a close watch on water levels, and stay in touch with your outfitter. Minimum water to raft is about 600 cfs. For flow information, call (916) 322-3327. Listen for the inflow to Lake McClure.

Permit system/time to raft. The Bureau of Land Management advertised for outfitters to run this river in 1976. At that time, the 13 outfitters who applied and who had Class III and IV experience became permit holders. Since that time, some permits have changed hands.

Commercial outfitters are limited to eight starts per day; start dates for each outfitter are based on a perpetual calendar that dates from 1976. Outfitters can trade start dates with approval from the Bureau of Land Management. Each start can have a maximum of 25 passengers.

Because of the number of people that these rules allow on the river on any one day (do not forget the "double-upper" trips), your escape from civilization may depend on selecting a weekday or early season trip. Campgrounds are few on the Merced, and they become crowded as the season progresses. The busiest time of the year is Memorial Day weekend.

Given that April is one of the least crowded and yet most beautiful months at Yosemite National Park, try stacking your trip on the Merced with your visit to the park. Few people raft in April, and even on the weekend you should have a delightful experience. Keep track of weather conditions.

Commercial rafting. In 1985, 13 outfitters took about 4500 passengers down the Merced. When you consider that the 1985 season ended about mid-June, this represents a rather high level of use.

Gear/safety/who can come. Wetsuits in spring, perhaps also with a wool sweater and windbreaker early in the season. If this is your first time on a river, put in at Cranberry Gulch to avoid the difficult whitewater immediately below the put-in at Red Bud. As noted above, be very conservative about rafting the lower section of this river at high water. Before booking a trip that takes out at Bagby, consider if you have the fitness for the difficult portage in the lower section.

Distinctive features. The Merced offers easy access not far from the Bay Area. At high water, portions of the river can rival the Tuolumne. But when you have given up hope for a weekend on the "T", you may nonetheless be able to find space on the Merced.

River access. Highway 140 runs about 20 feet above the Merced from Red Bud to Briceburg. A dirt road continues along the river down to Railroad Flat; below that, the only way out of the canyon is the river or an abandoned railroad line.

Sites of interest. That railroad line provided the only access to Yosemite in the twenties and thirties. Other artifacts along the river include a mining flume from the turn of the century and some prehistoric bedrock mortars used as mortars and pestles by the Indians of the region. Ned's Gulch (a rapid between Cranberry Gulch and Briceburg) is formed from the oldest rock in the Sierras.

Environment. The moss-green Merced river flows through a narrow canyon spotted with twisted oaks and digger pines. Did you take to heart my earlier recommendation to schedule your trip for April? In early spring the canyon's steep slopes are covered with shooting stars, baby blue eyes, golden poppies, and monkey flowers. Otter and beaver live on the river; you may also see deer, raccoon or bear. Ask your guide to point out the limestone salamander; it's an endangered species native to the area.

Fishing. Poor to moderate. Some rainbow trout; bass may swim upstream from the reservoir. Fishing improves on the lower section. Ask your outfitter for counsel on bringing your pole.

Summary of river between put-ins. Summarized with permission from *California White Water*. See that volume for further background on this river, especially the excellent descriptions of the major rapids. The river has a 9-mile Class II section, from 5 miles downstream of Cranberry Gulch to 3 miles upstream of Railroad Flat.

Abbreviations

Mo,Tu,We	Monday, Tuesday, Wednesday, etc.	porta	Porta-potty or lime can at camp
D	Daily	exp	(Rafting) experience
will call	Outfitter will call you to arrange dates	Camping exp	Camping experience
ob	Oar boat	F	Free
o/pa	Oar boat with paddle assist	w/	With
pb	Paddle boat	wd	Weekday
ik	Inflatable kayak	we	Weekend
s/b	Self-bailing	y	Youth
op	Optional	y16	Youth, age 16 and under
ia	If available or if appropriate	s	Senior
on-river	Camp is beside the river	s65	Senior, age 65 and over
off-river	Camp is not beside the river	inc	Included
lodge	Overnight at a lodge or motel	avail	Available
flush	Flush toilets at camp	#	pound
chem	Chemical toilets or outhouse at camp		

Name– Max. cfs	Starting	Raft type	Put-in– Take-out	Miles Camp Facilities
MERCED—1 DAY				
Action **Adventures** No max	May 3,4,24,25,29,30; Jun 19,20,21,22,26,27,28,29; Jul 3,4,6,7,8,9,12,13,18, 19,26,27,28,29	ob,pb op ia exp, ik s/b op ia exp	Red Bud-Briceburg	15
All- **Outdoors** 10,000	May 8,9,19,22,23; Jun 6, 7,8,9,20,21	o/pa, pb op ia	Cranberry Gulch- Railroad Flat	17
Kern River **Tours** No max	Apr 19,20,26,27; May 2,3, 4,5,30,31; Jun 1,2,3,4,5, 6,10,11,12,13; Jul 1,4,5, 12,13,19,20,21	pb,op op	Cranberry Gulch- Briceburg	12
Mariah 13,000	May 4,5,12,13,16,19; Jun 4,5,9-12,16-19,23-27; Jul 1-3,7-10,14-17	pb	Red Bud-Briceburg	15
OARS 10,500	May 14,21,22,26,27,28; Jun 3,9,10,11; Jul 1,15, 24; Aug 6	ob,pb op	Cranberry Gulch- Railroad Flat	17
Outdoors **Unlimited** No max	Apr 19; May 2-4,9-11,13, 16-18,22-26,30,31; Jun 1- 14,16,18,25-30; Jul 1-4,7, 9,12,14,15,25-27	ob,pb op	Cranberry Gulch- Briceburg	12
Wild River **Tours** 8,000	Apr 30; May 1,2,5,7,9,12, 14,15,19,21,23,27,29; Jun 4,7,9,12,13,15,16,17, 19,23,24,25,26,27,29,30	pb,ob op	Cranberry Gulch- Railroad Flat	17
Zephyr 13,000	Apr 25; May 9,11,12,20, 21,26,27,30; Jun 2,3,4,6, 9,17,18	pb,ob op	Cranberry Gulch- Railroad Flat	17
MERCED—2 DAY				
Action **Adventures** 6,000	May 3,24,29; Jun 19,21, 26,28; Jul 3,6,8,12,18,26, 28	ob,pb op ia exp, ik s/b op ia exp	Red Bud-Bagby	28 On-river Porta
Action **Adventures** No max	May 3,24,29; Jun 19,21, 26,28; Jul 3,6,8,12,18,26, 28	ob,pb op ia exp, ik s/b op ia exp	Red Bud-Briceburg; Red Bud-Briceburg	30 On-river Porta
All- **Outdoors** 10,000	May 1,13,15,17,19,25,28, 31; Jun 2,10,15,22,25,28; Jul 5,10,17,19,21,26,28, 30; Aug 2,9	o/pa; pb op ia	Cranberry Gulch- Railroad Flat; Red Bud-Briceburg	32 On-river Porta
ARTA 9,000	May 7,11,13,18,24,26; Jun 2,9,15,17,22,24	pb,ob op	Red Bud-Bagby	28 On-river Porta

Recom. Require. Min. Age	Cost Max. Grp. Min. Grp.	Discounts	Transportation	Comments
Rec: Wetsuit until Jul. Req: Exp for paddlers. Age: Call	$79 25 10	Less 10%w/11 +	Inc from Mariposa; avail from Sacramento	Van from Sacramento for 1-5, add $100
Rec: Exp. Req: Wetsuit until Jun 20. Age: 15	$87 25 25	1 Fw/12 and less $10wd		
Req: Wetsuit until Jun 15. Age: 10	$90 25 12	Less $10 Mo-Th and less 10%w/ 12 + and 1 Fw/24		
Age: 15	$85 25 12	1 Fw/16 and less $20wd and less 10%y16		
Rec: Wetsuit May and early Jun. Age: Call	$85 25 25	Less 10%w/11-24 or less 15%w/25		Groups of 12 + only; group minimum 12wd
Age: 10	$90 25 25	Less $20wd and 1 Fw/10 + or (less 10%w/25 and 1 Fw/24)		
Req: Exp; wetsuit until Jun 15. Age: 12	$65 50 6	Less 10%w/12 + and 1 Fw/24		
Req: Wetsuit until Jun 15. Age: 12	$90 25 6	Less $10wd		
Rec: Wetsuit until Jul. Req: Exp for paddlers. Age: Call	$149 25 10	Less 10%w/11 +	Inc from Mariposa; avail from Sacramento	Tow boat on reservoir; van from Sacramento for 1-5, add $100
Rec: Wetsuit until Jul. Req: Paddling exp. Age: Call	$149 25 10	Less 10%w/11 +	Inc from Mariposa and to lodge; avail from Sacramento	Van from Sacramento for 1-5, add $100
Rec: Exp. Req: Wetsuit until Jun 20. Age: 15	$196 25 25	1 Fw/12 and less $20wd		
Req: Wetsuit until Jun 20. Age: 10	$175 25 12	Less 10%w/10 + and 1Fw/20		

ARTA 9,000	May 7, 13, 26; Jun 2, 9, 17	pb	Red Bud-Bagby	28 On-river Porta
Kern River Tours No max	Apr 19, 26; May 2, 4, 30, 31; Jun 2, 3, 4, 5, 10, 12; Jul 4, 12, 19, 20	pb, op op	Cranberry Gulch-Briceburg; Cranberry Gulch-Briceburg	24 On-river Porta
Kern River Tours 6,000	Apr 19, 26; May 2, 4, 30, 31; Jun 2, 3, 4, 5, 10, 12; Jul 4, 12, 19, 20	pb, op op	Cranberry Gulch-Bagby	25 On-river Porta
Mariah 13,000	May 4, 10, 12, 17; Jun 4, 7, 9, 11, 13, 16, 18, 20, 23, 26, 29; Jul 1, 3, 7, 9, 11, 14, 16	pb	Red Bud-Bagby	28 On-river Porta
OARS 10,500	Apr 17, 19, 24, 26; May 9, 12, 16, 19, 23, 24, 25, 29, 31; Jun 5, 18, 21, 23, 30; Jul 2, 6, 8, 10, 13, 16, 20, 22, 25, 27, 29, 31; Aug 7, 16	ob, pb op	Cranberry Gulch-Bagby	25 On-river Porta
Outdoors Unlimited No max	Apr 19; May 2-4, 9-11, 13, 16-18, 22-26, 30, 31; Jun 1-14, 16, 18, 25-30; Jul 1-4, 7, 9, 12, 14, 15, 25-27	ob, pb op	Cranberry Gulch-Bagby	25 On-river Porta
Whitewater Voyages 5,000	Apr 26; May 2, 4, 8, 10, 11, 16, 18, 23, 27, 28, 30; Jun 1, 7, 13, 15, 20, 28; Jul 4, 10, 13, 17, 19, 21, 23, 29, 30; Aug 2, 6, 8	pb, ob op	Cranberry Gulch-Bagby	25 On-river Porta
Wild River Tours 8,000	May 3, 10, 17; Jun 14, 21, 28	pb, ob op	Cranberry Gulch-Railroad Flat	17 On-river Flush
Zephyr 13,000	May 3, 10, 17, 25, 26, 31; Jun 1, 3, 6, 7, 8, 14, 19, 22, 24, 27, 30; Jul 2, 4, 5, 6, 8, 12, 13, 14, 15, 21, 22, 23, 24	pb, ob op	Cranberry Gulch-Bagby	25 On-river Porta

Red Bud to Cranberry Gulch (3 miles)—Continuous Class IV, Class III rapids.

Cranberry Gulch to Briceburg (12 miles)—One Class IV rapid.

Briceburg to Railroad Flat (5 miles)—Two Class IV rapids.

Railroad Flat to Bagby (8 miles)—One Class IV+ rapid. Difficult portage. Class II rapids for the last 5 miles.

River status. The Merced's status is currently under review by Sierra National Forest; however, protection for the river in the form of wild and scenic legislation may come as soon as 1986. Representative Tony Coelho is believed to be planning to submit such legislation in the upcoming Congressional session. Again, the Merced needs that form of protection: a hydroelectric dam, the El Portal project, has been proposed that would dewater five miles of the rafting run. Construction on this project could begin as early as 1987. So, you have a couple of choices:

Age: 10	Com. 25 8		Coop; group provides and prepares own and guide's food. Group w/8-12, $1250; 13-18, $1800; 19-25, $2350
Req: Wetsuit until Jun 15. Age: 10	$185 25 12	Less $25 Mo-Th and less 10%w/ 12+ and 1 Fw/24	
Req: Wetsuit until Jun 15. Age: 10	$185 25 12	Less $25 Mo-Th and less 10%w/ 12+ and 1 Fw/24	
Age: 15	$185 25 12	1 Fw/16 and less $20wd and less 10%y16	
Rec: Wetsuit Apr, May, early Jun. Age: Call	$195 25 25	(Less $15y17 or less $25 wd or less $40wdy17) and (less 10%w/ 11-24 or less 15%w/25)	Lodge op, add $45; group minimum 12wd
Age: 10	$195 25 25	Less $20wd and 1 Fw/10+ or (less 10%w/25 and 1 Fw/24)	If water level is above 4,000 cfs OU runs a "double upper": Cranberry Gulch to Railroad Flat; Cranberry Gulch to Railroad Flat
Req: Wetsuit; exp for paddlers. Age: 12	$188 25 25	(Less $12FrSu or less $24wd) and 1 Fw/24 and less 10%w/12+ or less 10%y16	, Avail from LA, SF	Cocktails inc; bus from LA, add $55; bus from SF, add $45; bus trip inc breakfast day 1
Req: Exp; wetsuit until Jun 15. Age: 12	$175 50 6	Less 10%w/12+ and 1 Fw/24	Access to showers inc
Req: Wetsuit until Jun 15. Age: 12	$195 25 6	Less $20wd	

(a) you can raft the river in 1986, or (b) you can write to Sen. Alan Cranston (Senate Office Building, Washington, DC 20510) and express your feelings about the rush to replace recreation with electricity during an energy glut.

Motels and lodges. Abbreviations used in the following listings are: L, R = Turn left, Turn right; H = Highway; I = Interstate; N, S, E, W = North, South, East, West; mi = miles; n/p = price or service not provided.

E. C. Yosemite Motel, 5180 Jones St (Box 339), Mariposa, CA 95338. (209) 742-6800. Directions: I-5 to H-99 to Merced; H-140E to Mariposa; go through town to intersection of H-140 and H-49. Cost per room for one: $35; for two: $45; for three: $50; for four: $50.

Mariposa Lodge, Box 733, Mariposa, CA 95338. (209) 966-3607. Directions: I-5 to H-99 to Merced; H-140E to Mariposa; in center of town on H-140. Cost per room for one: n/p; for two: $50; for three: $55; for four: $60.

Mother Lode Lodge, 5051 Highway 140, P.O. Box 986, Mariposa, CA 95338. (209) 966-2521/374-3215. Directions: I-5 to H-99 to Merced; H-140E to downtown Mariposa. Cost per room for one: n/p; for two: $35; for three: $40; for four: $43.

Sierra View Motel, Seventh and Bullion, P.O. Box 1467, Mariposa, CA 95338. (209) 966-5793. Directions: I-5 to H-99 to Merced; H-140E to Mariposa. Cost per room for one: $30; for two: $38; for three: $40; for four: $45.

Also, five motels are available in El Portal, closer to the put-in and to Yosemite.

Bed and breakfast inns. Granny's Garden, 7333 Highway 49 N, Mariposa, CA 95338. (209) 377-8342. Directions: I-5 to H-99 to Merced; H-140E to Mariposa; H-49N to hotel (12 mi). Cost per room for one: $35; for two: $40; for three: n/p; for four: n/p.

Public campgrounds. Indian Flat (Forest Service). Directions: I-5 to H-99 to Merced; H-140E to 20 mi E of Mariposa.

Also, numerous campgrounds are available in Yosemite National Park. Be sure to obtain reservations for weekend campsites—to do so bring cash (not checks) to your local Ticketron office.

━━━━━━━━━━━━━━━━━━━━━━━━━━━━━━━━━━━━━━

Upper Tuolumne (Cherry Creek)

Introduction. The most difficult river section in this book, the Upper Tuolumne redefines the word awesome. Runnable on weekdays all summer long, this section causes professional river guides to shout in exultation. Suitable only for Class IV-experienced strong swimmers who have the facial musculature to support grinning for a week after the trip.

Level of difficulty/water level concerns/flow information. Class Vp. Moderate to difficult portage at Lumsden Falls. The river is dam-controlled: water levels are lower on the weekend than during the week. Runnable at low water only; I rafted this section in 1985 at 1150 cfs, and the river could have been 20% lower without any reduction whatsoever in fearsomeness. The minimum water to raft is about 600 cfs. For flow information, call (916) 322-3327. Listen for the flow at Meral's Pool.

Permit system/time to raft. In 1982, only one outfitter expressed interest in a permit and as a result, only one outfitter currently *has* a permit. A management plan for the Upper Tuolumne is scheduled to be completed in Fall, 1986, and this may recommend a change in the number of permittees or even the elimination of commercial rafting (see River status, below).

Commercial rafting. In 1985, 361 daring adventurers challenged the Upper Tuolumne with one outfitter.

Gear/safety/who can come. Wetsuit always (provided by the outfitter). Absolutely only for the courageous and experienced. Absolutely not for anyone who might freeze when faced with paddling through a Class V+ rapid.

Distinctive features. Miles of continuous Class V rapids. The trip may be expensive, but expert guides and first-class self-bailing equipment are absolutely necessary. On a dollar-to-whitewater basis, the Upper Tuolumne may be the best value in the state.

River access. A wilderness run with only three access points.

Environment. During the three or four minutes in the day when you are not putting 110% into your back paddle, you will see a clean, clear river bounded by craggy hills. Ponderosa pine, digger pine, and incense cedar stand well above the river.

Fishing. Trout, at the take-out only.

Summary of river between put-ins. Summarized with permission from *California White Water*. See that book for an extensive description of the rapids as well as a river map.

Cherry Creek Powerhouse to Meral's Pool (9 miles)—Eight Class V rapids, of which many are continuous rapids up to a mile long. Moderate to difficult portage at Lumsden Falls, (some crews may run it in September, but not me; I draw the line somewhere, and Lumsden Falls is it).

River status. The Upper Tuolumne has wild and scenic status. However, in the management plan for this river to be completed in Fall, 1986, the status and future of commercial rafting on this section will be reassessed. Persons interested in commenting on the draft plan can request information from: Forest Supervisor, Stanislaus National Forest, 19777 Greenly Road, Sonora, CA 95370.

See Main Tuolumne for lodgings and campgrounds.

Main Tuolumne

Introduction. The Main Tuolumne run (the river is pronounced Too-wal'-uhm-nee but affectionately known as the "T") is a California classic. Runnable all summer, the river pools and drops through eleven major rapids and many easier ones. Limited commercial passenger loads, required to minimize the effect of people on the wilderness environment, force rafters to book trips well in advance.

Level of difficulty/water level concerns/flow information.
Class IV. Dammed for power production. Runnable water levels are sustained throughout the summer but reduced somewhat on Saturday and even more on Sunday, so much so that the river often is too low to raft. Expect high water in mid-May. Very high levels will result in trip cancellations, as many rapids become difficult to run in control at high water. Also at high water, Clavey Falls may be portaged (a moderate portage). The minimum water to raft is about 600 cfs. For flow information, call (916) 322-3327. Listen for the flow at Meral's Pool.

Permit system/time to raft.
Current outfitters were selected by a bid-prospectus; the selection criteria included experience and guide training. Commercial activity on the river is limited to ten permittees (nine different outfitters). Only two starts per day are allowed with a limit of 25 passengers and guides per start.

This system means that on any day you chose, the Main Tuolumne will be uncrowded. For higher summer water levels, though, select an early week start. Do not select a date that will overlap with a Sunday, except during the high water season.

Commercial rafting.
In 1985, nine outfitters took 3800 commercial passengers down the Tuolumne, mostly on two-day trips. At summer weekday water levels (about 1200 cfs), the entire eighteen-mile trip takes about seven river hours.

Gear/safety/who can come.
Wetsuit until summer. Non-swimmers should note Class V Clavey Falls; get out and scout it with the guides. Although some first-time rafters do run the Tuolumne, if you have never rafted a river before, you should carefully review the description of Class IV rapids in Chapter 1 to make sure you are ready.

A steep Class V dirt road leads to the put-in. Persons suffering from acrophobia may wish to choose another river; at the very least they should sit on the right side of the bus or van and bring along moral support.

Distinctive features.
Like the South Fork of the American, the Tuolumne offers many challenging rapids of nearly equal level. Unlike the South Fork, this summer run offers wilderness isolation and inspiration, and Class IV rapids instead of Class IIIs. The Tuolumne is probably the best Class IV run in the state.

River access.
The only accesses are at put-in and take-out.

Environment.
The river offers classic California scenery: it runs through a canyon of oak savannah that turns golden in summer. In spring, look for Lemmon's paintbrush, shooting stars, and lupine flowering on the hills. If you habitually do extensive research before engaging in any activity, or if you ran the "T" in years past, you may be aware that log jams used to clog the river just above the take-out. They are gone now.

Fishing. Trout.

Summary of river between put-ins. Summarized with permission from *California White Water*. See that book for an extensive mile-by-mile guide to the rapids. See *Rocks and Rapids of the Tuolumne* for a large-scale river map and a 19-page river log, which describes (a) the geology of the river and the rapids, (b) historical sites along the river, and (c) how to run the rapids.

Meral's Pool to Ward's Ferry (18 miles)—One Class V rapid, ten Class IVs.

Ward's Ferry to Don Pedro Reservoir (10 miles)—Flat water.

River status. After a long battle, Congress awarded the Main Tuolumne wild and scenic status. However, a dam has been recently proposed for Clavey River, a major tributary of the Tuolumne. The dam would be located a little over a mile above the Clavey's confluence with the "T". This project is currently in the feasibility stage. Contact Friends of the River for further information.

Motels and lodges. Abbreviations used in the following listings are: L, R = Turn left, Turn right; H = Highway; I = Interstate; N, S, E, W = North, South, East, West; mi = miles; n/p = price or service not provided.

Sugar Pine Ranch, 21250 Highway 120, Groveland, CA 95321. (209) 962-7823. Directions: I-5 to H-99 to Manteca; H-120E to Groveland; 4 mi E of Groveland. Cost per room for one: $27; for two: $30; for three: $36; for four: $36.

Lee's Middle Fork Resort & Motel, 11399 Cherry Oil Rd, Groveland, CA 95321. (209) 962-7408. Directions: I-5 to H-99 to Manteca; H-120E to 14 mi E of Groveland; L on Cherry Oil Rd. Cost per room for one: $39; for two: $45; for three: $55; for four: $60-75.

Buck Meadows Lodge, 7647 Highway 120, Groveland, CA 95321. (209) 962-6366. Directions: I-5 to H-99 to Manteca; H-120E to 12 mi E of Groveland. Cost per room for one: $30; for two: $39-41; for three: $43; for four: $45.

Public campgrounds. The Pines (Forest Service). Directions: I-5 to H-99 to Manteca; H-120E to 8 mi E of Groveland.

Sweetwater (Forest Service). Directions: I-5 to H-99 to Manteca; H-120E to 10 mi E of Groveland.

Lost Claim (Forest Service). Directions: I-5 to H-99 to Manteca; H-120E to 10 mi E of Groveland.

Abbreviations

Mo,Tu,We	Monday, Tuesday, Wednesday, etc.	porta	Porta-potty or lime can at camp
D	Daily	exp	(Rafting) experience
will call	Outfitter will call you to arrange dates	Camping exp	Camping experience
ob	Oar boat	F	Free
o/pa	Oar boat with paddle assist	w/	With
pb	Paddle boat	wd	Weekday
ik	Inflatable kayak	we	Weekend
s/b	Self-bailing	y	Youth
op	Optional	y16	Youth, age 16 and under
ia	If available or if appropriate	s	Senior
on-river	Camp is beside the river	s65	Senior, age 65 and over
off-river	Camp is not beside the river	inc	Included
lodge	Overnight at a lodge or motel	avail	Available
flush	Flush toilets at camp	#	pound
chem	Chemical toilets or outhouse at camp		

Name– Max. cfs	Starting	Raft type	Put-in– Take-out	Miles Camp Facilities
UPPER TUOLUMNE—1 DAY				
Sierra Mac 2,000	Sa, Mo, We, Fr Jun 15—Oct 19	ob s/b, pb s/b op, o/pa s/b op	Cherry Creek PH- Meral's Pool	9
MAIN TUOLUMNE—1 DAY				
Action Adventures No max	Mar 15, 17, 20, 31; Apr 28	ob, pb s/b op exp	Meral's Pool-Ward's Ferry	18
All- Outdoors 10,000	May 8, 23	o/pa, pb op ia	Meral's Pool-Ward's Ferry	18
ARTA 4,000	Mar 13, 20, 24, 26, 27; Apr 1, 2, 3, 7, 10, 15, 24, 28, 30	pb	Meral's Pool-Ward's Ferry	18
ARTA 8,500	Mar 13, 20, 24, 26, 27; Apr 1, 2, 3, 7, 10, 15, 21, 24, 28, 30; May 6, 8, 13	pb, ob op	Meral's Pool-Ward's Ferry	18
ECHO 10,000	Mar 8, 9, 15, 18, 22, 23; Apr 5, 6, 7, 13, 25; May 1, 4	ob, pb op	Meral's Pool-Ward's Ferry	18
OARS 8,500	Apr 27	ob, pb op	Meral's Pool-Ward's Ferry	18
Sierra Mac 10,000	Apr 20; May 11, 16, 22; Jun 1, 5, 12, 19; Sep 6, 13, 26; Oct 4, 10, 11, 18, 25	ob s/b, pb s/b op, o/pa s/b op	Meral's Pool-Ward's Ferry	18
Zephyr 8,000	Apr 1, 8, 23, 29	ob, pb op, o/pa op	Meral's Pool-Ward's Ferry	18
MAIN TUOLUMNE—2 DAYS				
Action Adventures No max	May 5, 10, 12, 19, 21, 27, 30; Jun 3, 6, 14, 18, 21, 28, 30; Jul 6, 15, 20, 30; Aug 5, 13, 29; Sep 23; Oct 7, 20	ob, pb s/b op exp	Meral's Pool-Ward's Ferry	18 On-river Porta
All- Outdoors 10,000	May 11, 17, 24, 26, 30; Jun 1, 4, 11, 13, 15; Jul 4, 15, 17; Aug 8, 22; Sep 24; Oct 22	o/pa, pb op ia	Meral's Pool-Ward's Ferry	18 On-river Porta
ARTA 8,500	Apr 12; May 2, 16, 21, 28, 31; Jun 4, 7, 9, 11, 16, 23, 26, 29; Jul 30; Aug 11; Sep 1, 4, 9, 11, 18, 25; Oct 2, 4, 8, 15, 23	o/pa, pb op exp ia	Meral's Pool-Ward's Ferry	18 On-river Porta
ECHO 10,000	Mar 29, 30; Apr 4, 11, 18, 19, 22; May 9, 12, 18, 22, 25, 29; Jul 18; Aug 22; Sep 5, 12, 16, 19, 24, 26	ob, pb op	Meral's Pool-Ward's Ferry	18 On-river Porta

Recom. Require. Min. Age	Cost Max. Grp. Min. Grp.	Discounts	Transportation	Comments
Rec: Sierra Mac test; exp. Req: Swim test; wetsuit. Age: Call	$185 20 4	Less 5%w/10-19 or less 10%w/20		Breakfast, dinner inc
Rec: Extensive Class V exp. Req: Wetsuit. Age: 18	$129 20 10			Restaurant champagne-barbeque after trip; unqualified persons may be cancelled at high water
Req: Wetsuit until Jul 7, after Sep 15; exp. Age: 16	$104 20 20	1 Fw/19		
Req: Wetsuit. Age: 12	Com. 18 8			Coop; group provides own and guide's lunch. Group w/8-12, $720; 13-18, $1050
Rec: Exp for paddlers. Req: Wetsuit. Age: 12	$105 20 18	Less 10%w/10 + and 1Fw/19		No pb over 5,000 cfs
Rec: Exp. Age: 12	$120 20 20	1 Fw/19		
Rec: Wetsuit. Age: 12	$130 20 20	Less 10%w/11 +		2-day dates may be available to 12 +
Age: Call	$150 21 4	Less 5%w/10-19 or less 10%w/20-21 or less $20y17		
Req: Wetsuit. Age: 12	$125 20 10			No pb over 6,000 cfs
Rec: Wetsuit until Jul. Req: Exp; Class V paddle test. Age: 13	$222 20 10	Less 10%w/11 +	Avail from Sacramento, Modesto	35# gear limit; van from Sacramento for 1-5, add $100; van from Modesto for 1-5, add $50
Req: Wetsuit until Jul 7, after Sep 15; exp. Age: 16	$249 20 20	1 Fw/19		
Rec: Exp for paddlers. Req: Wetsuit until Jun 20. Age: 12	$235 20 18	Less 10%w/10 + and 1Fw/19		No pb over 5,000 cfs
Rec: Exp. Age: 12	$255 20 20	1 Fw/19 and less $30 Apr, Oct		

Name– Max. cfs	Starting	Raft type	Put-in– Take-out	Miles Camp Facilities
OARS 8,500	Mar 1, 8, 14, 19, 27; Apr 2, 5, 11, 13, 17, 21, 24, 26, 29; May 3, 6, 13; Jun 3, 7, 10, 15; Sep 15, 29; Oct 6, 13, 21; Nov 8, 15	ob, pb op	Meral's Pool-Ward's Ferry	18 On-river Porta
Outdoors Unlimited 8,500	Mar 25, 30; Apr 6, 10, 14, 17; May 1, 5, 7, 14, 18, 20, 26, 29; Jun 2, 5, 8; Jul 25; Aug 1, 8, 15, 18; Sep 2, 5, 8, 12, 16, 20, 25, 30; Oct 3, 6, 10, 14, 17, 22, 24, 28	ob, pb s/b op	Meral's Pool-Ward's Ferry	18 On-river Porta
Sierra Mac 10,000	Mar 14, 21, 28, 29, 31; Apr 3, 8, 14, 16, 19, 20, 26; May 14, 16, 17, 18, 19, 22, 24, 25, 27, 30; Jun 22, 25; Sep 13, 19, 22, 26; Oct 1, 4, 10, 11, 13, 17, 18, 25	ob s/b, pb s/b op, o/pa s/b op	Meral's Pool-Ward's Ferry	18 On-river Porta
Zephyr 8,000	May 15, 20; Jun 17, 22, 30; Jul 9, 23, 28; Sep 4, 8, 11	pb, ob op, o/pa op	Meral's Pool-Ward's Ferry	18 On-river Porta

MAIN TUOLUMNE—3 DAYS

Name– Max. cfs	Starting	Raft type	Put-in– Take-out	Miles Camp Facilities
Action Adventures No max	Jul 12, 26; Aug 2, 9, 23	ob, pb s/b op	Meral's Pool-Don Pedro Res.	28 On-river Porta
All- Outdoors 10,000	Jun 18; Jul 1, 10; Sep 18; Oct 9, 16, 24	o/pa, pb op ia	Meral's Pool-Ward's Ferry	18 On-river Porta
ARTA 8,500	Jul 3, 7, 10, 13, 18, 24, 27; Aug 3, 7, 14, 15, 20, 21, 27, 28	o/pa, pb op exp ia	Meral's Pool-Ward's Ferry	18 On-river Porta
ECHO 10,000	May 15, 18, 25, 29; Jun 12, 26; Jul 2, 9, 16, 18, 24, 28, 31; Aug 6, 13, 14, 19, 27; Sep 2, 6, 10, 17, 27	ob, pb op	Meral's Pool-Ward's Ferry	18 On-river Porta
OARS 8,500	Jun 23, 28; Jul 7, 13, 21, 31; Aug 4, 12, 18, 26; Sep 9, 16	ob, pb op	Meral's Pool-Ward's Ferry	18 On-river Porta
Outdoors Unlimited 8,500	May 10, 23; Jun 10, 14, 17, 21, 27; Jul 1, 5, 11, 16, 19, 22, 29; Aug 3, 11, 21, 25, 28	ob, pb s/b op	Meral's Pool-Ward's Ferry	18 On-river Porta
Sierra Mac 10,000	May 19, 24, 25, 30; Jun 2, 6, 9, 13, 16, 20, 22, 24, 25, 28, 29; Jul 3, 5, 8, 11, 14, 17, 22, 25, 26, 27, 29; Aug 1, 2, 5, 9, 12, 16, 19, 23, 30; Sep 3, 6, 27	ob s/b, pb s/b op, o/pa s/b op	Meral's Pool-Ward's Ferry	18 On-river Porta
Zephyr 8,000	Aug 4, 7, 25; Sep 15, 23, 29	pb, ob op, o/pa op	Meral's Pool-Ward's Ferry	18 On-river Porta

MAIN TUOLUMNE—4 DAYS

Name– Max. cfs	Starting	Raft type	Put-in– Take-out	Miles Camp Facilities
Action Adventures No max	Aug 30	ob, pb s/b op	Meral's Pool-Don Pedro Res.	28 On-river Porta

Recom. Require. Min. Age	Cost Max. Grp. Min. Grp.	Discounts	Transportation	Comments
Rec: Wetsuit Mar-May, Oct-Nov. Age: 12	$245 20 20	Less $20 until Apr 21, after Nov 1 and less 10%w/11+		Group minimum 12wd
Rec: Wetsuit for May, Jun. Req: Exp for paddlers. Age: 10	$249 21 21	1 Fw/10 or (less 10%w/21 and 1 Fw/20)		
Age: Call	$240 21 4	Less 5%w/10-19 or less 10%w/20-21 or less $20y17		
Req: Wetsuit until Jun 30. Age: 12	$245 20 10			No pb over 6,000 cfs
Rec: Wetsuit until Jul. Req: Exp; Class V paddle test. Age: 13	$333 20 10	Less 10%w/11+	Avail from Sacramento	Tow boat on reservoir; 35# gear limit; van from Sacramento for 1-5, add $100
Req: Wetsuit until Jul 7, after Sep 15; exp. Age: 16	$329 20 20	1 Fw/19		Fishing (trout) trips, Oct 9, 16, 24, group max 12, add $40
Age: 12	$335 20 18	Less 10%w/10+		No pb over 5,000 cfs
Age: 12	$345 20 20	1 Fw/19		
Age: 12	$350 20 20			Group minimum 12wd
Rec: Wetsuit in May, Jun. Req: Exp for paddlers. Age: 10	$319 21 21	1 Fw/10 or (less 10%w/21 and 1 Fw/20)		
Age: Call	$330 21 4	Less 5%w/10-19 or less 10%w/20-21 or less $20y17		
Age: 12	$325 20 10			No pb over 6,000 cfs
Rec: Wetsuit until Jul. Req: Exp; Class V paddle test. Age: 13	$333 20 10	Less 10%w/11+	Avail from Sacramento	Side stream and gold mine explorations; tow boat on reservoir; 35# gear limit; van from Sacramento for 1-5, add $100

Stanislaus (Goodwin Dam run)

Introduction. This four-mile run, located relatively near the Bay Area, offers some very difficult yet inexpensive summer Class V whitewater.

Level of difficulty/water level concerns/flow information. Class V. Probable portages. Highest flows occur in March. The water level is dam-controlled, but flows are not maintained at a predictable level. Minimum water to raft is about 600 cfs. For flow information, call (916) 322-3327. Listen for the flow at Orange Blossom Bridge.

Permit system/time to raft. No permits are required at this time. However, the Army Corps of Engineers is conducting a market study to determine whether a permit or licensing system is feasible and necessary.

Because the Bureau of Reclamation, which manages New Melones Dam, has ignored the government's promises vis-a-vis this stretch of river (see below), the water level cannot be counted on in advance, something required for a major commercial run. If you want to raft the Stanislaus, call an outfitter and ask that your name be placed on a will-call list for future trips. Expect such trips to be on a weekend.

Commercial rafting. Two companies took 200 people down this river in 1985.

Gear/safety/who can come. As ever with Class V runs, this section is for fit, healthy, good swimmers only. Wetsuits in spring. The river is choked with willows and cottonwoods, which create strainer hazards (see appendix on *Safety*).

Abbreviations

Mo,Tu,We	Monday, Tuesday, Wednesday, etc.	porta	Porta-potty or lime can at camp
D	Daily	exp	(Rafting) experience
will call	Outfitter will call you to arrange dates	Camping exp	Camping experience
ob	Oar boat	F	Free
o/pa	Oar boat with paddle assist	w/	With
pb	Paddle boat	wd	Weekday
ik	Inflatable kayak	we	Weekend
s/b	Self-bailing	y	Youth
op	Optional	y16	Youth, age 16 and under
ia	If available or if appropriate	s	Senior
on-river	Camp is beside the river	s65	Senior, age 65 and over
off-river	Camp is not beside the river	inc	Included
lodge	Overnight at a lodge or motel	avail	Available
flush	Flush toilets at camp	#	pound
chem	Chemical toilets or outhouse at camp		

Name– Max. cfs	Starting	Raft type	Put-in– Take-out	Miles Camp Facilities
STANISLAUS (GOODWIN DAM RUN)—1 DAY				
Great Valley 3,500	Will call	pb s/b	Goodwin Dam- Knights Ferry	4
Sunshine **River Adv.** 15,000	D Apr 1—Oct 15	pb	Goodwin Dam- Knights Ferry	4

—*Great Valley Canoe and Raft/Jim Sughrue*
A paddle boat in a Class IV rapid on the Stanislaus

Distinctive features. Very few short-length rivers are offered commercially in California.

River access. Wilderness run; three access points. The Army Corps of Engineers does the construction work for recreation facilities downstream of Goodwin Dam; here again, access points have not been developed as promised.

Environment. Oak trees enliven this craggy, granite canyon. In spring, Indian paintbrush, brodeia, and baby blue eyes visit the river along with you. Deer, raccoon and mountain lions roam the area (but don't expect to spot night animals on a day trip). Look overhead for red-tail hawks and turkey vultures.

Fishing. Steelhead trout and salmon in September; German brown and wild rainbow trout all year.

Recom. Require. Min. Age	Cost Max. Grp. Min. Grp.	Discounts	Transportation	Comments
Rec: Class IV exp; good swimmer. Age: 16	$40 34 12	Less 10%w/20 +		No food inc
Req: Good swimmer. Age: 12	$50 50 4	1Fw/12 + and less $5y16 and (less 10%w/10-19 or less 15%w/20 +)		Fishing for Rainbow, German Brown trout

Summary of river between put-ins. Summary provided by Jim Foust of Sunshine River Adventures and Jim Cassady. See also *California White Water* and the extensive discussion of this stretch in *A Guide to the Best Whitewater in the State of California*.

Goodwin Dam to Knights Ferry (4 miles)—Three difficult Class V rapids, two Class IVs.

River status. When your friends tell you they have rafted the Stanislaus, they almost certainly mean the extraordinarily scenic Class III (Camp 9) run that is now buried under the waters behind New Melones Dam. The failure of the Army Corps of Engineers to develop the Goodwin Dam run, and the failure of the Bureau of Reclamation to provide adequate flows for rafting, as promised in mitigation for the loss of the Camp 9 run in 1982, bodes badly indeed for promises made in association with future dams. It seems that the only way the Bureau and the Corps can be convinced to keep its word is by act of Congress. Should you wish your voice to be heard, write to your congressional representative and ask him or her to contact the Bureau and the Corps about this issue. Send a copy of your letter to: District Engineer, U.S. Army Engineer District, P.O. Box 1229, Oakdale, CA 95361-9510.

Motels and lodges. Abbreviations used in the following listings are: L, R = Turn left, Turn right; H = Highway; I = Interstate; N, S, E, W = North, South, East, West; mi = miles; n/p = price or service not provided.

Oakdale Motel, 828 East "F" St, Oakdale, CA 95361. (209) 847-9121. Directions: I-5 to H-99 to Manteca; H-120E to Oakdale; L on F St. Cost per room for one: $20-25; for two: $20-25; for three: $30; for four: $32-35.

Private campgrounds. Knights Ferry Resort, 17525 Sonora Rd, Knights Ferry, CA 95361. (209) 881-3349. Directions: I-5 to H-99 to Manteca; H-120E to 14 mi past Oakdale; go N on Kennedy Rd to Knights Ferry. Cost for tenters: $10-14; for RVs: $10-14.

Public camping is available at Caswell Memorial State Park.

Mokelumne

Introduction. The Mokelumne (Muh-kuhl'-uh-mee) run is most commonly used as (a) a whitewater training ground for kayakers and (b) a fun run for inner tubers. It is the easiest summer river described in this book. This run supplies first-time rafters with a quick, inexpensive, and low-fear introduction to the sport.

Level of difficulty/water level concerns/flow information. Class II. The difficulty level is such that young children navigate this stretch in inner tubes. Dam-controlled, this section is runnable all year, with high water in May. Demonstrate caution above 2000 cfs: the water will be swift and cold, and as on the Stanislaus, trees will form a strainer hazard (see appendix on *Safety*). The minimum water to raft is about 300 cfs. For flow information, call (916) 322-3327. Listen for the inflow into Pardee Reservoir.

Permit system/time to raft. Commercial permits are required for this river for any use of public lands. However, such use is not necessary on rafting trips, and no permits have been issued.

In selecting a time to raft, consider that the Mokelumne is used extensively by private boaters: you will find greater isolation on weekdays. However, on a weekday you would need to gather a minimum group of four to raft.

Commercial rafting. In 1985, one outfitter took 250 commercial passengers down the Mokelumne.

Gear/safety/who can come. Anyone. Wetsuits in spring, of course. If you inner-tube this river on your own, wear a life jacket.

Distinctive features. Among all the rivers in this book, this is the only one on which I would bring my mother.

River access. If it turns out my mother does not like rafting, a road leads right along the upper half of this river section. The lower half has road access only at the end of the run.

Environment. The Mokelumne runs through a typical Sierra Nevada river canyon: golden hills are dotted with oak and pine; some willow grow along the riverbanks. The water, which feeds into the East Bay water supply, runs extremely clean and clear, attracting black-tailed deer and white- tailed jack rabbits.

Fishing. Trout. Watch out you don't snag an inner tuber.

Summary of River between put-ins. Summary provided by Jim Foust of Sunshine River Adventures. His rapid ratings are somewhat higher than those in other guides. See *California White Water* for a river map covering the section from Electra to the Highway 49 Bridge.

Electra to Highway 49 Bridge (3 miles)—Above 1000 cfs (occurs in spring only), Two Class III rapids, six Class IIs. Below 1000 cfs (all summer and fall), eight Class IIs.

Highway 49 Bridge to Middle Bar Bridge (3 miles)—Two Class III rapids, three Class IIs.

River status. The East Bay Municipal Utility District (EBMUD) has proposed a dam, the Middle Bar-Railroad Flat Dam Project, that would flood the length of this run. Its purposes would be to generate power and to provide water for the East Bay, despite objections that the East Bay has alternative sources for power and no pressing need for that water. In 1986, the state legislature will vote on whether or not the Mokelumne will be protected as a recreational river. To let your voice be heard, write your assembly member (State Capitol, Sacramento, CA 95814).

Name– Max. cfs	Starting	Raft type	Put-in– Take-out	Miles Camp Facilities
MOKELUMNE—1 DAY				
Sunshine River Adv. 10,000	D Apr 1—Oct 15	pb, ik op	Electra-Middle Bar Br	6
Sunshine River Adv. 10,000	D Apr 1—Oct 15	pb, ik op	Electra-Hwy 49 Bridge	3

Abbreviations

Mo,Tu,We	Monday, Tuesday, Wednesday, etc.	porta	Porta-potty or lime can at camp
D	Daily	exp	(Rafting) experience
will call	Outfitter will call you to arrange dates	Camping exp	Camping experience
ob	Oar boat	F	Free
o/pa	Oar boat with paddle assist	w/	With
pb	Paddle boat	wd	Weekday
ik	Inflatable kayak	we	Weekend
s/b	Self-bailing	y	Youth
op	Optional	y16	Youth, age 16 and under
ia	If available or if appropriate	s	Senior
on-river	Camp is beside the river	s65	Senior, age 65 and over
off-river	Camp is not beside the river	inc	Included
lodge	Overnight at a lodge or motel	avail	Available
flush	Flush toilets at camp	#	pound
chem	Chemical toilets or outhouse at camp		

Motels and lodges. Abbreviations used in the following listings are: L, R = Turn left, Turn right; H = Highway; I = Interstate; N, S, E, W = North, South, East, West; mi = miles; n/p = price or service not provided.

Amador Motel, 12408 Kennedy Flat Rd, Jackson, CA 95642. (209) 223-0970. Directions: I-5 to Sacramento; H-16E to H-49S to Jackson. Cost per room for one: $22-37; for two: $31-37; for three: $37; for four: $42.

Bed and breakfast inns. Court Street Inn, 215 Court St, Jackson, CA 95642. (209) 223-0416. Directions: From Sacramento to H-16E to H-49S to Jackson; ½ block from gold church spire. Cost per room for one: $45-$65; for two: $50-$75; for three: $50-60; for four: $85-105.

Gate House Inn, 1330 Jackson Gate Rd, Jackson, CA 95642. (209) 223-3500. Directions: I-5 to Sacramento; H-16E to H-49S to Jackson; L on Jackson Gate Rd. Cost per room for one: $45-80; for two: $50-85; for three: n/p; for four: n/p.

Private campgrounds. Far Horizons 49er Trailer Village. Box 191, Plymouth, CA 95669. (209) 245-6981. Open: All Year. Directions: I-5 to Sacramento; H-16E to H-49N to Plymouth. Cost for tenters: no tents; for RVs: $16-20; for showers: free.

Lake Amador. 7500 Lake Amador Dr, Ione, CA 95640. (209) 274-2625. Open: Jan 31-Nov 30. Directions: I-5 to Stockton to 88E; R on Jackson Valley Rd for 4 mi; L on Lake Amador Dr. Cost for tenters: $8.75; for RVs: $8.75; for showers: $3.25/veh.

Recom. Require. Min. Age	Cost Max. Grp. Min. Grp.	Discounts	Transportation	Comments
Age: 12	$25 50 6	1Fw/12 and less $5y16 and (less 10%w/10-19 or less 15%w/20+)		Lunch op, add $4
Age: 12	$25 50 6	1Fw/12 and less $5y16 and (less 10%w/10-19 or less 15%w/20+)		Lunch op, add $4

Upper East Fork of the Carson

Introduction. Unlike rivers flowing down the west side of the Sierras, which are characterized by alternating sections of flat water and rapids (pool and drop), the East Fork of the Carson falls nearly constantly along its length. The upper section is challenging; the lower section is scenic.

Level of difficulty/water level concerns/flow information. Class III. More difficult than a typical Class III because of continuous rapids. The upper section season ends somewhat earlier than that of the lower section: look for water lasting only until June. Keep a close watch on snow levels, however; the season length varies dramatically from year to year. The Bureau of Land Management recommends a minimum water level of 750 cfs for rafting. For flow information, call (916) 322-3327. Listen for the flow near Gardnerville.

Permit system/time to raft. Any company with a permit on the lower section may raft the upper. Because of low rafting usage, there are no limits to group size.

This section's narrow chutes of challenging whitewater and its easy shuttle attract extensive use by kayakers, who may repeat the run two or three times in one day. Water moves more quickly in rapids than in pool sections; on this river with continuous rapids, about two river hours are required to complete the six-mile run.

If you are interested in rafting this section, contact an outfitter and have your name placed on a will-call list.

Commercial rafting. Companies do not report usage of this section separately from the much more heavily rafted lower section, so no statistics are available.

Gear/safety/who can come. The nearly continuous rapids make eddying out and/or swimming for shore difficult, so rafters contemplating this run should be experienced and should have confidence in their swimming skills. Full wetsuit always: this is a high-elevation run.

Distinctive features. In this section, the river runs through a narrow, rocky canyon, almost a gorge. The continuous rapids will keep you from an in-depth study of the geology, however.

River access. A highway lies about 30 feet above the river for the entire length of the run, providing an excellent opportunity for scouting the rapids.

Sites of interest. The river passes by Centerville Flats, a ghost town from the silver boom days. Rafters will also see ruins of other mining camps and dams.

Environment. On higher slopes, look for ponderosa, Jeffrey and pinyon pines; on the lower slopes, for brush and occasional wildflowers. For the most part, however, you will see rocks, many of them very, very close up.

Fishing. Cutthroat, rainbow, and brown trout, all stocked.

Summary of river between put-ins. Summarized with permission from *California White Water*. See that volume for a river map.

Silver Creek to Hangman's Bridge (6 miles)—Continuous Class III.

River status. The river's status is under review by Toiyabe National Forest; there are no active threats to this section.

See East Fork of the Carson (Wilderness Run) for lodgings and campgrounds.

Trip descriptions are also included under East Fork of the Carson (Wilderness Run).

East Fork of the Carson (Wilderness Run)

Introduction. This river runs through unspoiled Alpine County, appropriately named, for you will surely believe that your raft is voyaging through the mountain set of *The Sound of Music*. Though best-suited for beginners, the East Fork's outstanding scenery, in combination with its fast-moving, continuous Class II rapids, attracts rafters of all levels.

Level of difficulty/water level concerns/flow information. Class II. The East Fork is a free-flowing river fed by snow-melt. Expect the season to end in June, with high water around Memorial Day. In the short 1985 season, however, the river fell too low for rafting in May. The Bureau of Land Management recommends a minimum water level of about 700 cfs for rafting. For flow information, call (916) 322-3327. Listen for the flow near Gardnerville.

Permit system/time to raft. Permits are available to any outfitter, without any experience requirements, upon payment of a fee. For the 1986 season, there are 20 permitted outfitters. Start dates are required for weekends only; these are allocated using a complicated system based on previous usage. Commercial outfitters are limited to eight starts per weekend day with a limit of 30 passengers and guides per start. Unlike many rivers with start date limitations, East Fork weekend start dates are extensively traded among outfitters. Do not hesitate to book with an outfitter who does not have an official start for a particular weekend (except near Memorial Day weekend), as the outfitter will probably be able to obtain that start date from one of his or her buddies. Be sure to double check, though.

The East Fork becomes most crowded on the two Saturdays before and the one Saturday after Memorial Day. In estimating the extent of crowding from the figures below, consider that private boaters outnumber commercial passengers on the East Fork by about two to one. And as the weekend start date limitations do not really redirect passengers into the weekdays, come Monday morning the river is empty. If at all possible, book on a weekday.

Commercial rafting. In 1985, nine outfitters took 500 people down the East Fork. The low snow pack that year made the rafting season unusually short: in the average year of 1984, 44 outfitters took 8000 passengers down the river.

Gear/safety/who can come. The water runs cold, but your chances of getting wet are small. Wear a light wetsuit for safety. Children should not be afraid of the water and, for a two-day trip, should have camping experience. The county is alpine in altitude as well as beauty; for those nights at elevations above 5,000 feet bring along your heavy sleeping bag.

Distinctive features. The splendid environment. The pure, clear air. The peaceful, top-of-the-world landscape. The snow- and pine-covered mountains. The absence of punk rockers.

River access. A wilderness run: highway access only at put-in and take-out. Occasional dirt roads permit emergency egress.

Abbreviations

Mo,Tu,We	Monday, Tuesday, Wednesday, etc.	porta	Porta-potty or lime can at camp
D	Daily	exp	(Rafting) experience
will call	Outfitter will call you to arrange dates	Camping exp	Camping experience
ob	Oar boat	F	Free
o/pa	Oar boat with paddle assist	w/	With
pb	Paddle boat	wd	Weekday
ik	Inflatable kayak	we	Weekend
s/b	Self-bailing	y	Youth
op	Optional	y16	Youth, age 16 and under
ia	If available or if appropriate	s	Senior
on-river	Camp is beside the river	s65	Senior, age 65 and over
off-river	Camp is not beside the river	inc	Included
lodge	Overnight at a lodge or motel	avail	Available
flush	Flush toilets at camp	#	pound
chem	Chemical toilets or outhouse at camp		

Name– Max. cfs	Starting	Raft type	Put-in– Take-out	Miles Camp Facilities
EAST FORK OF THE CARSON—1 DAY				
ARR No max	Apr 26; May 3, 17; Jun 7, 21, 28; Jul 5	ik, ob op, pb op	Hangman's Br-BLM Boat Ramp	20
NOC No max	Apr 26; May 3, 9, 16, 25, 31; Jun 6, 14, 20, 28; Jul 5; Mo- Th Apr 1—Jul 5	ob, pb op	Hangman's Br-BLM Boat Ramp	20
NOC No max	Apr 26; May 3, 9, 16, 25, 31; Jun 6, 14, 20, 28; Jul 5; Mo- Th Apr 1—Jul 5	ob, pb op	Silver Creek- Hangman's Br	6
Nonesuch Whitewater No max	Mo-Fr May 1—Jun 30	pb	Hangman's Br-BLM Boat Ramp	20
OARS No max	Mo-Fr May 1—Jul 15	ob, pb op	Hangman's Br-BLM Boat Ramp	20
RAM River Expeditions No max	Mo-Fr Apr 1—Jul 15	ob, pb op, ik op	Hangman's Br-BLM Boat Ramp	20
Tributary Whitewater 3,500	Mo-Fr May 1—Jul 31	pb, ob op	Hangman's Br-BLM Boat Ramp	20
W.E.T. 4,500	Apr 26; May 10, 17, 25; Jun 8, 12, 15, 20, 22; Jul 5	ob, pb op, ik op	Hangman's Br-BLM Boat Ramp	20
Wild River Tours 6,000	Mo-Fr May 1—Jun 30	pb, ob op	Hangman's Br-BLM Boat Ramp	20
Zephyr No max	Mo-Fr Apr 1—Jun 30	pb, ob op	Hangman's Br-BLM Boat Ramp	20
EAST FORK OF THE CARSON—2 DAYS				
ARR No max	Apr 26; May 3, 17; Jun 7, 21, 28; Jul 5	ik, ob op, pb op	Hangman's Br-BLM Boat Ramp	20 On-river Porta
ARTA No max	May 9, 11, 16, 18; Jun 6, 8, 20, 22	pb, ob op	Hangman's Br-BLM Boat Ramp	20 On-river Porta
California Adventures 8,000	Apr 26; May 3, 17, 25, 31; Jun 7, 28; Jul 4	pb	Hangman's Br-BLM Boat Ramp	20 On-river Porta

Recom. Require. Min. Age	Cost Max. Grp. Min. Grp.	Discounts	Transportation	Comments
Rec: Wetsuit. Age: 8	$70 25 8	1 Fw/12		Beer, wine inc
Req: Wetsuit if water below 50 deg F. Age: Call	$58 25 6	1 Fw/12 and less $6w/12+ and .5 Fy14		Lunch op, add $5
Req: Wetsuit if water below 50 deg F. Age: Call	$56 25 6	1 Fw/12 and .5 Fy14		Lunch op, add $5
Rec: Booties until Jun 30, wetsuit until May 15. Age: 8	$70 24 8	Less 10%w/12+		
Rec: Wetsuit May. Age: 5	$85 20 12	Less 10%w/11+		
Rec: Wetsuit Apr-Jun; good health. Age: 6	$65 25 6	1 Fw/12 and (less 10%w/8+ or less 15%w/20+ or less $10y12)		
Req: Children must swim, like water. Age: 9	$75 20 6	Less $10wd and (less 10%w/10+ or 1 Fw/10 or less 30%y16 or less 30% handicapped or less 30%s65)		Handicapped; hot springs visit inc
Rec: Wetsuit. Req: Wetsuit for ik. Age: 6	$65 24 6	Less $10y12 and 1 Fw/12		
Req: Wetsuit. Age: 6	$125 25 6	Less 10%w/12+ or less 10%y16		
Age: 6	$75 25 20			
Rec: Wetsuit. Age: 8	$130 25 8	1 Fw/12		Beer, wine inc
Age: 7	$150 20 12	Less $20y17 and less 10%w/10+ and 1Fw/19		
Age: Call	$150 25 10	1 Fw/10 and less 20%UC Berkeley students	Inc from Berkeley	Study archeology, natural history of EF-Carson; handicapped; food not inc

Name– Max. cfs	Starting	Raft type	Put-in– Take-out	Miles Camp Facilities
Charter River Adv. No max	May 3, 10, 17; Jun 14; Jul 5	ob, pb op	Hangman's Br-BLM Boat Ramp	20 On-river Porta
James Henry 6,000	May 11, 16, 23, 25, 30; Jun 1, 6, 8, 13, 14, 15, 21, 22, 29	pb, ob op ia, ik op	Hangman's Br-BLM Boat Ramp	20 On-river Porta
NOC No max	Apr 26; May 3, 9, 16, 25, 31; Jun 6, 14, 20, 28; Jul 5; Mo- Th Apr 1—Jul 5	ob, pb op	Hangman's Br-BLM Boat Ramp	20 On-river Porta
Nonesuch Whitewater No max	Mo-Fr May 1—Jun 30	pb, ob op, o/pa op	Hangman's Br-BLM Boat Ramp	20 On-river Porta
OARS No max	May 10, 24; Jun 7, 21, 28; Jul 5; Mo-Fr May 1—Jul 15	ob, pb op	Hangman's Br-BLM Boat Ramp	20 On-river Porta
RAM River Expeditions No max	Mo-Fr Apr 1—Jul 15	ob, pb op, ik op	Hangman's Br-BLM Boat Ramp	20 On-river Porta
Tributary Whitewater 3,500	Mo-Fr May 1—Jul 31	pb, ob op	Hangman's Br-BLM Boat Ramp	20 On-river Porta
W.E.T. 4,500	Apr 26; May 10, 17, 25; Jun 8, 12, 15, 20, 22; Jul 5	pb, ob op, ik op	Hangman's Br-BLM Boat Ramp	20 On-river Porta
Whitewater Voyages 5,000	May 10, 31; Jun 7; Jul 5	pb, ob op	Hangman's Br-BLM Boat Ramp	20 On-river Porta
WW Rapid Transit No max	May 23, 25; Jun 7, 21, 28; Jul 4	ob s/b, pb s/b op	Hangman's Br-BLM Boat Ramp	20 On-river Porta
Zephyr No max	Mo-Fr Apr 1—Jun 30	pb, ob op	Hangman's Br-BLM Boat Ramp	20 On-river Porta

EAST FORK OF THE CARSON—3 DAYS

Name– Max. cfs	Starting	Raft type	Put-in– Take-out	Miles Camp Facilities
Nonesuch Whitewater No max	Mo-Fr May 1—Jun 30	pb, ob op, o/pa op	Hangman's Br-BLM Boat Ramp	20 On-river Porta
RAM River Expeditions No max	Mo-Fr Apr 1—Jun 15	ob, pb op	Silver Creek-BLM Boat Ramp	26 On-river Porta

Recom. Require. Min. Age	Cost Max. Grp. Min. Grp.	Discounts	Transportation	Comments
Req: Wetsuit May. Age: 12	$190 24 10	Less $15w/10 +		Beer, wine, sleeping pads, tents (weather demanding) inc
Age: 6	$150 24 12	Less $40y16 and (1 Fw/12-15 and less 5%w/12-15) or (1 Fw/16-23 and less 10%w/16-24)		Wine inc
Req: Wetsuit if water below 50 deg F. Age: Call	$143 25 6	Less $7wd or less $14w/12 + and 1 Fw/12 and .5 Fy14		
Rec: Booties until Jun 30, wetsuit until May 31. Age: 8	$160 24 8	Less 10%w/12 + and less $10wd		
Rec: Wetsuit May. Age: 5	$155 20 20	Less $10y17 and less 10%w/11-24		
Rec: Wetsuit Apr-Jun; good health. Age: 6	$130 25 6	1 Fw/12 and (less 10%w/8 + or less 15%w/20 +) or less $10y12		
Req: Children must swim, like water. Age: 9	$135 20 6	Less $10wd and (less 10%w/10 + or 1 Fw/10 or less 30%y16 or less 30% handicapped or less 30%s65)		Handicapped; hot springs visit inc
Rec: Wetsuit. Req: Wetsuit for ik. Age: 6	$140 24 6	Less $15y12 and 1 Fw/12		
Req: Wetsuit. Age: 8	$165 20 20	Less 20%w/12 + or less 10%y16	Avail from LA	Cocktails inc; bus from LA, add $55; bus trip inc breakfast day 1
Age: 6	$120 25 6	1Fw/12		Beer, wine inc
Age: 6	$155 25 20	Less $10wd		
Rec: Booties until Jun 30, wetsuit until May 31. Age: 8	$210 24 8	Less 10%w/12 + and less $15wd		Layover day near hot springs
Rec: Wetsuit Apr-Jun; good health. Age: 8	$190 25 6	1 Fw/12 and (less 10%w/8-19 or less 15%w/20 + or less $10y12)		

Sites of interest. The East Fork has its own hot spring; commercial rafters can visit but not spend the night. See the comments on the trip descriptions. Also, your guides will point out Young's Crossing, a toll road that dates from the 1860s. Other archaeological sites, some from pre-historic times, lie along the East Fork. Obtain *The Lore and Legend of the East Fork* for further details.

Environment. The hills are alive—with the sound of nesting geese and mergansers, jays and starlings. Mule deer winter in the valley through April. Later in the season, lupine, poppies, and irises add interest to the riverbanks. The broad valley of the East Fork permits a view of cold-stunted forests on distant snow-covered mountains. Downstream from the put-in, the river flows through a high desert canyon.

Finally, the cattle stand like statues. I bring this up because the Bureau of Land Management requested that rafters be asked not to get drunk and play cowboy. Watch out for the rattlesnakes, which have their own habitat about half-way down this section.

Fishing. Cutthroat, rainbow and brown trout, all stocked.

Summary of river between put-ins. Summarized with permission from *California White Water*. See that volume for a river map. See *The Lore and Legend of the East Fork* for an entertaining mile-by-mile historical guide, as well as topographical maps.

Hangman's Bridge to BLM Boat Ramp (20 miles)—Continuous Class II.

River status. This section's status is also under review by Toiyabe National Forest, and again, there are no active threats. The Bureau of Land Management will manage the East Fork as a "scenic area" until the Park Service decides if the river is worthy to enter the wild and scenic system.

Motels and lodges. Abbreviations used in the following listings are: L, R = Turn left, Turn right; H = Highway; I = Interstate; N, S, E, W = North, South, East, West; mi = miles; n/p = price or service not provided.

Woodfords Inn, P.O. Box 426, Markleeville, CA 96120. (916) 694-2410. Directions: I-5 to Sacramento to H-50E; H-89S to Woodfords. Cost per room for one: $28; for two: $33; for three: $39; for four: $45.

Sorensen's Resort, Highway 88, Hope Valley, CA 96120. (916) 694-2203. Directions: I-5 to Sacramento to H-50E; H-89S to H-88E. Cost per room for one: $35-110; for two: $35-110; for three: $50-110; for four: $55-110.

Public campgrounds. Grover State Park (State of California). Directions: I-5 to Sacramento to H-50E: H-89S to Markleeville; go 4 mi on Alpine Cty Rd E-1 (Hot Springs Rd).

Markleeville (Forest Service). Directions: I-5 to Sacramento; H-50E to H-89S to ½ mi S of Markleeville.

South Fork of the American

Introduction. The most popular rafting river in the western United States, the South Fork of the American offers (a) many excellent rapids suitable for the adventurous beginner, (b) runnable water levels throughout the summer, (c) proximity to the Bay Area, (d) scenic, and in some sections unspoiled, surroundings, and, last but not least, (e) competitive prices.

Level of difficulty/water level concerns/flow information. Class III +. Water levels are controlled by the Chili Bar powerhouse just upstream from the Chili Bar put-in. During the spring, additional water spills over the dam, and the river becomes more difficult (Class IV above 2500 cfs). In 1985, summer water levels were held relatively constant Monday through Saturday, with lower levels on Sunday. Minimum water to raft is about 800 cfs. For flow information, call (916) 322-3327. Listen for the release from Chili Bar.

Permit system/time to raft. The large number of outfitters and the large groups sizes permitted on the South Fork are due to a system based on 1980 levels of usage, revised in 1985. Unlike many rivers, where extensive commercial rafting began after regulations were in place, commercial use of the South Fork exploded before the limits began. Strict usage regulations could not be imposed without harming existing business. As a result, there are no limits to the number of companies that may start on any particular day.

The South Fork is the only river described in this book where maximum group sizes for different outfitters vary dramatically. If yours is a relatively small group of rafters, i.e. 20 or fewer, you may wish to book your trip with a company that has a low limit. You will then reap the benefits of a more intimate rafting group.

If yours is a large group, say, over 35 people, then your group's fees will represent a substantial chunk of change. Ignore the already low group prices provided in this book, because you will be able to negotiate lower ones. Call three or four outfitters with large maximum group sizes, and ask each for his or her best price for a group of (however large your group is) on (specify the date). You will be able to obtain an even better price for a weekday trip.

Professional river guides use several terms to describe the South Fork on a summer weekend. Printable ones include: "zoo", "carnival", and "Disneyland". In this context, friends and fellow rafters, these terms express contempt for the loss of a inspiring natural experience, namely rafting in peaceful surroundings. On land you will find lines everywhere. As one rafter told me: "you get in line first, ask questions later." On the river, above major rapids, you will have to pause over and over again to allow other groups to go through together.

If you must raft on a weekend day, choose a Saturday, when water levels are higher. Also, if you will be rafting the upper (Chili Bar) section, talk with your outfitter about starting in the afternoon. The overwhelming majority of rafters start in the late morning, creating considerable congestion at the put-in and on the river. As the upper section can easily be run in two to three river hours, there is little reason to suffer in the river's population explosion. Some companies offer the Chili Bar section as a half-day trip, which can save you money.

As noted over and over again in this book, the lack of real weekend passenger limits concentrates commercial demand on the weekends. You can still find a wilderness experience if you raft on a summer weekday, when (a) river usage run a mere 10% of weekend levels, (b) water releases are higher, (c) you raft with the more senior guides, and (d) you pay less. You can multiply the isolation of your river tour by rafting before Memorial Day or after Labor Day. My 1985 raft trip on a Thursday in late September found only 20 people on the entire river (and that included our party). An autumn trip has the further advantage of low water levels in Folsom Reservoir; rafters won't need to paddle though a mile of flat water to reach the take-out.

Commercial rafting. In 1985, 75,000 people took commercial rafting trips on the South Fork.

"Pirate" outfitters (see Chapter 4) are reported to be quite active on the South Fork of the American. Demonstrate caution in arranging a trip with a company that is not listed in this book.

The attributes of the South Fork also attract private boaters to the river—17,000 in 1985.

Gear/safety/who can come. A few of the rapids on the South Fork have more in common with Class IV rapids than with Class IIIs. I, for one, would not recommend bringing young children (under age 10) on this river. If they fall out of the boat, they face some difficult swims. A child's first river experience should make him or her water-happy, not water-shy. The Lower Klamath or even the Middle Fork of the American (if you portage the Tunnel Chute and take out above Ruck-a-Chucky) may be better for children.

Wetsuits should be worn in the spring; children under 12 should wait for the summer.

Distinctive features. Nature created very few river sections where the rapids come frequently and at a more or less similar level. Nature did very well indeed with the South Fork, doubling its value by forming advanced beginner rapids with enough excitement for anyone. So despite the crowds, people love the South Fork, and thousands return to the river year after year.

River access. Limited to certain areas between Marshall State Park and Greenwood Creek. Trespassing on private lands adjacent to the South Fork is forbidden. You will not be able to ask your guide to take you to shore whenever you feel the need (so use the facilities at the put-in, and make sure your children do also). There is a long "quiet zone" along the central part of the run where homes are visible from the river; please do not demonstrate your enthusiasm for water sports in that section.

Sites of interest. Sutter's Mill, the site of the original California gold discovery, sits river-left, just upstream from Marshall State Park.

Environment. Unlike many Sierra rivers that run through steep, deep canyons, the South Fork rolls through golden foothills dotted with oak and digger pine. In the final five miles, the so-called "gorge" section, the river passes through low rock walls that constrict the current and create rapids. In spring, California poppies, lilacs, shooting stars and lupine light the hills. Great blue herons and golden eagles may fly above. Geese and ducks may pay you a visit, especially during lunch. Please, don't feed the fowl.

Fishing. Feed the fish instead. The South Fork supports trout, bass, and catfish.

Summary of river between put-ins. The big rapids are concentrated in the first six miles and the last five miles of this run. There are several take-outs between those sections. Choosing one or the other does not get you more or less "real" whitewater.

However, because the rapids start fast and furious at Chili Bar, first-time paddlers should run the second half of the river first. This offers the chance to learn paddle skills before the river comes up to greet you. Experienced weekend paddlers may wish to start at Chili Bar on Saturdays, because that put-in is less crowded on Saturday than on Sunday.

The following is summarized from the *South Fork of the American Information Guide to Whitewater Boating*, with some input from other sources. See that pamphlet or *California White Water* for a river map. See *A Guide to Three Rivers* for an excellent historical guide to the South Fork of the American, as well as descriptions of plant and animal life in the canyon.

Gold Nugget to Chili Bar (0.5 miles)—Flat water.

Chili Bar to Marshall State Park (6 miles)—One Class III + rapid, three Class IIIs.

Marshall State Park to Beaver Point or Ponderosa Park (1.5 miles)—One Class II rapid.

Beaver Point or Ponderosa Park to Camp Lotus (1.5 miles)—One Class II rapid.

Camp Lotus to Baachi Ranch (1 mile)—Flat water.

Baachi Ranch to Greenwood Creek (1.5 miles)—One Class II rapid.

Greenwood Creek to Salmon Falls (9 miles) One Class III + rapid, three Class IIIs, three Class II + s.

The last mile of this stretch is usually through the flat water of Folsom Reservoir. It is difficult to paddle a raft across a lake. Some companies arrange for motorized towboats for that last mile; if this is important to you, ask your outfitter.

River status. See South Fork of the American (Kyburz run) in *New Commercial Rivers for 1986*. The dam proposed for the upstream run would reduce weekday flows to this widely used section.

Motels and lodges. Abbreviations used in the following listings are: L, R = Turn left, Turn right; H = Highway; I = Interstate; N, S, E, W = North, South, East, West; mi = miles; n/p = price or service not provided.

Gold Trail Motor Lodge, 1970 Broadway, Placerville, CA 95667. (916) 622-2906. Directions: I-5 to Sacramento; H-50 to Placerville; exit Pt. View Dr, L on Broadway. Cost per room for one: $33; for two: $38; for three: $42; for four: $47.

Mother Lode Motel, 1940 Broadway, Placerville, CA 95667. (916) 622-0895. Directions: I-5 to Sacramento; H-50 to Placerville; exit Pt. View Dr; L on Broadway. Cost per room for one: $35-37; for two: $40-42; for three: $50-52; for four: $55-57.

Stagecoach Motor Inn, 5940 Pony Express Trail (Box 628), Pollock Pines, CA 95726. (916) 644-2029. Directions: I-5 to Sacramento; H-50 to Pollock Pines exit; L at off-ramp, E on Pony Express Trail. Cost per room for one: $38-42; for two: $45; for three: $50; for four: $54.

El Dorado Motel, 1500 Broadway, Placerville, CA 95667. (916) 622-3884. Directions: I-5 to Sacramento; H-50 to Placerville to Schnell School Rd; L on Broadway. Cost per room for one: $28-31; for two: $31-34; for three: $38-41; for four: $41-45.

Best Western - Cameron Park Inn, 3361 Coach Lane, Cameron Park, CA 95682. (800) 528-1234 or (916) 677-2203. Directions: I-5 to Sacramento; H-50 to 10 mi W of Placerville; exit Cameron Park Dr. Cost per room for one: $39-49; for two: $47-57; for three: $52-72; for four: $57-77.

Bed and breakfast inns. Combellack Blair House, 3059 Cedar Ravine, Placerville, CA 95667. (916)-622-3764. Directions: I-5 to Sacramento; H-50 to Placerville; R at 3rd light; L on Main St; R on Cedar Ravine. Cost per room for one: $45-55; for two: $55; for three: n/p; for four: n/p.

Fleming Jones Homestead, 3170 Newtown Road, Placerville, CA 95667. (916) 626-5840. Directions: I-5 to Sacramento; H-50 to Placerville; exit Newtown Rd/Pt. View Dr; R at stop, L on Broadway, which becomes Newtown Rd Cost per room for one: $50-65; for two: $55-70; for three: $70-85; for four: $70-85.

James Blair House Bed & Breakfast, 2985 Clay St, Placerville, CA 95667. (916) 626-6136. Directions: I-5 to Sacramento; H-50 to Placerville; exit Bedford; L on Main St, L on Clay St Cost per room for one: $42.75; for two: $45-70; for three: $55-80; for four: n/p.

River Rock Inn, 1756 Georgetown Dr, Placerville, CA 95667. (916) 622-7680. Directions: I-5 to Sacramento; H-50 to Placerville; H-49N; R on H-193, cross bridge, L immediately, road ends at inn. Cost per room for one: $55-65; for two: $55-65; for three: n/p; for four: n/p.

Strawberry Lodge, Highway 50, Kyburz, CA 95720. (916) 659-7030. Directions: I-5 to Sacramento; H-50 to Kyburz (85 mi). Cost per room for one: $38-60; for two: same; for three: same; for four: same.

American River Inn Bed and Breakfast, P.O. Box 43, Georgetown, CA 95634. (916) 333-4499. Directions: I-5 to Sacramento; I-80 towards Auburn; H-49S to H-193E to Georgetown. Cost per room for one: $57-67; for two: $67-77; for three: $77-87; for four: $87-97.

Chichester House Bed & Breakfast, 800 Spring St, Placerville, CA 95667. (916) 626-1882. Directions: I-5 to Sacramento; H-50 to Placerville; go 1 block N on H-49. Cost per room for one: $45-55; for two: $55-60; for three: $65-70; for four: none.

Coloma Country Inn Bed & Breakfast, 2 High St, Coloma, CA 95613. (916) 622-6919. Directions: I-5 to Sacramento; take H-50E, exit Ponderosa Rd; follow signs to Coloma; R on H-49, R on Brewery, L on Back St, R on High St. Cost per room for one: $50-55; for two: $60-65; for three: $65-75; for four: n/p.

Private campgrounds. Camp Lotus. P.O. Box 460, Lotus, CA 95651. (916) 622-8672. Open: Feb 14—Oct 31. Directions: I-5 to Sacramento; H-50E to Shingle Spring exit; N on N. Shingle Rd; L on Lotus Rd; L on Bassi Rd, go 1 mi. Cost for tenters: $4; for RVs: $4; for showers: n/p.

Camp Coloma. Highway 49 S on Main St, Coloma, CA 95613. (619) 622-6700. Open: Apr 1—Oct 1. Directions: I-5 to Sacramento; H-50E to H-49N (8 mi NE of Placerville); to Main St, Coloma. Cost for tenters: $12; for RVs: $15; for showers: n/p.

Abbreviations

Mo,Tu,We	Monday, Tuesday, Wednesday, etc.	porta	Porta-potty or lime can at camp
D	Daily	exp	(Rafting) experience
will call	Outfitter will call you to arrange dates	Camping exp	Camping experience
ob	Oar boat	F	Free
o/pa	Oar boat with paddle assist	w/	With
pb	Paddle boat	wd	Weekday
ik	Inflatable kayak	we	Weekend
s/b	Self-bailing	y	Youth
op	Optional	y16	Youth, age 16 and under
ia	If available or if appropriate	s	Senior
on-river	Camp is beside the river	s65	Senior, age 65 and over
off-river	Camp is not beside the river	inc	Included
lodge	Overnight at a lodge or motel	avail	Available
flush	Flush toilets at camp	#	pound
chem	Chemical toilets or outhouse at camp		

Name— Max. cfs	Starting	Raft type	Put-in— Take-out	Miles Camp Facilities
SOUTH FORK OF THE AMERICAN—½ DAY				
Action Adventures No max	D Mar 22—Oct 5	pb, ik s/b op exp, ob op	Chili Bar-Marshall Park	6
Adventure Connection 10,000	Mo-Fr Apr 1—Sep 30	pb	Chili Bar-Marshall Park	6
OARS No max	D Apr 1—Oct 31	ob, pb op	Gold Nugget-Marshall Park	6.5
SOUTH FORK OF THE AMERICAN—1 DAY				
Action Adventures No max	D Mar 22—Oct 5	pb, ik s/b op exp, ob op	Beaver Point-Salmon Falls	13
Action Adventures No max	D Mar 22—Oct 5	pb, ik s/b op exp, ob op	Chili Bar-Beaver Point; Chili Bar-Beaver Point	15
Adventure Connection 10,000	Mo-Sa Apr 1—Oct 31	pb, ob op, o/pa op	Baachi Ranch-Salmon Falls	10
Adventure Connection 10,000	Su-Fr Apr 1—Oct 31	pb, ob op, o/pa op	Chili Bar-Marshall Park	6
All-Outdoors 10,000	D Apr 26—Oct 26	pb, o/pa op	Camp Lotus-Salmon Falls	11.5
All-Outdoors 10,000	D Apr 26—Oct 26	pb, o/pa op	Chili Bar-Camp Lotus	9
ARR No max	D Apr 1—Oct 31	pb, ob op	Chili Bar-Beaver Point	7.5
ARR No max	D Apr 1—Jun 30	pb, ob op	Chili Bar-Salmon Falls	20.5
ARR No max	D Apr 1—Oct 31	pb, ob op	Marshall Park-Salmon Falls	14.5
ARTA No max	D Apr 1—Sep 30	pb, ob op	Chili Bar-Camp Lotus	9

Recom. Require. Min. Age	Cost Max. Grp. Min. Grp.	Discounts	Transportation	Comments
Age: Call	$39 150 5		Avail from Sacramento	Guided tour of Gold Discovery site, State Park, Marshall Monument, lunch inc; van from Sacramento for 1-5, add $50
Rec: Wetsuit Apr, May, Sep. Age: 8	$35 50 12			
Rec: Wetsuit Apr, May, Oct. Age: 7	$49 25 6	Less 10%w/11 +		Operates w/1-day only
Age: Call	$59 150 5	Less 5%wd and less 10%w/11-25 or less 15%w/26-40 or less 20%w/41 + or less 20%y13		
Age: Call	$59 150 5	Less 5%wd and less 10%w/11-25 or less 15%w/26-40 or less 20%w/41 + or less 20%y13		
Rec: Wetsuit Apr, May, Sep, Oct. Age: 8	$60 90 12	1 Fw/12 and less $5w/24 + and less $15wd and less $5y15		
Rec: Wetsuit Apr, May, Sep, Oct. Age: 8	$60 90 20	1 Fw/12 and less $5w/24 + and less $15wd and less $5y15		
Wetsuit until May 15. Age: Call	$71 50 25	1 Fw/12 and less $5wd		
Wetsuit until May 15. Age: Call	$71 50 25	1 Fw/12 and less $5wd		
Rec: Wetsuit until Jun 30. Age: 12	$54 86 6	Less $5wd and 1 Fw/12 and less $5y16		Beer, champagne inc
Req: Wetsuit. Age: 12	$70 86 6	Less $5wd and 1 Fw/12 and less $5y16		Beer, champagne inc
Rec: Wetsuit until Jun 30. Age: 12	$59 86 6	Less $5wd and 1 Fw/12 and less $5y16		Beer, champagne inc
Age: 8	$75 36 20	Less $5wd and less 10%w/10 + and 1Fw/20		

Name– Max. cfs	Starting	Raft type	Put-in– Take-out	Miles Camp Facilities
ARTA No max	Mo-Fr Apr 1—Sep 30	pb	Chili Bar-Camp Lotus	9
A WW Connection 6,000	D Apr 1—Oct 31	pb, ob op, ik op	Marshall Park-Salmon Falls	14.5
California Adventures 7,000	Sa May 3—Aug 30	pb	Camp Lotus-Salmon Falls	11.5
California Adventures 7,000	Su May 4—Aug 31	pb	Chili Bar-Camp Lotus	9
California River 8,000	D Mar 22—Oct 26	pb, ob op	Chili Bar-Camp Lotus	9
California River 8,000	D Mar 22—Oct 26	pb, ob op	Camp Lotus-Salmon Falls	11.5
California River 8,000	D May 1—Jun 15	pb, ob op	Chili Bar-Salmon Falls	20.5
ECHO 10,000	D Apr 1—Oct 31	pb, ob op	Gold Nugget-Camp Lotus	9.5
Friends of the River 10,000	Apr 26; May 17; Jun 19; Jul 17; Aug 7; Sep 6; Oct 4	pb, ob op ia	Camp Lotus-Salmon Falls	11.5
Friends of the River 10,000	Apr 27; May 18; Jun 20; Jul 18; Aug 8; Sep 7; Oct 5	pb, ob op ia	Chili Bar-Camp Lotus	9
Gold Rush 8,000	Tu-Su May 1—Sep 30	pb, ob op	Beaver Point-Salmon Falls	13
Gold Rush 8,000	Tu-Su May 1—Sep 30	pb, ob op	Chili Bar-Beaver Point	7.5
Kern River Tours 10,000	D May 1—Sep 30	pb, ob op	Chili Bar-Beaver Point	7.5

Recom. Require. Min. Age	Cost Max. Grp. Min. Grp.	Discounts	Transportation	Comments
Req: Group of 8+. Age: 8	Com. 33 8			Coop; group provides and prepares own and guide's food. Group w/8-12, $525; 13-18, $750; 19-25, $950; 26-33, $1150
Age: Call	$65 75 4	Less 15%wd and 1 Fw/12 and less $5w/24+		Handicapped; balloon trip op, add $85
Age: Call	$54 30 10	1 Fw/10 and less 20%UC Berkeley students	Inc from Berkeley	Handicapped; food not inc; lunch op, add $4
Age: Call	$54 30 10	1 Fw/10 and less 20%UC Berkeley students	Inc from Berkeley	Handicapped; food not inc; lunch op, add $4
Rec: Wetsuit or wool and rain suit, Mar-May, Oct. Age: 7	$60 30 6	1 Fw/6 and less $10wd and less $5w/o lunch		
Rec: Wetsuit or wool and rain suit, Mar-May, Oct. Age: 7	$60 30 6	1 Fw/6 and less $10wd and less $5w/o lunch		
Rec: Wetsuit or wool and rain suit. Age: 8	$75 30 6	1 Fw/6 and less $10wd and less $5w/o lunch		
Age: 7	$77 35 25	1 Fw/25 and less $10wd and less $8y17 and less $8w/8+		
Req: Wetsuit over 2500 cfs. Age: 7	$42 35	Less $7/FOR members or less $5w/6+		Tow to take-out, add $1-2; make camping reservation 2-3 weeks in advance; not tax deductible; food not inc
Req: Wetsuit over 2500 cfs. Age: 7	$42 35	Less $7/FOR members or less $5w/6+		Not tax deductible; food not inc
Age: Call	$59 123 8	(1Fw/12 and less $10w/12+ and less $10wd) or (1Fw/7y16 and less $10y16)	Inc from Placerville for 8+	Handicapped
Age: Call	$59 123 8	(1Fw/12 and less $10w/12+ and less $10wd) or (1Fw/7y16 and less $10y16)	Inc from Placerville for 8+	Handicapped; tour of Marshall Gold Discovery State Park inc
Age: 8	$59 50 12	Less $10wd and less 10%w/12+ and 1 Fw/24		

Name— Max. cfs	Starting	Raft type	Put-in— Take-out	Miles Camp Facilities
Libra Expeditions No max	Mo-Fr Apr 1—Oct 5	pb	Chili Bar-Marshall Park	6
Libra Expeditions 4,000	Sa, Su Apr 1—Oct 5	ik s/b	Marshall Park-Salmon Falls	14.5
Libra Expeditions No max	Mo-Fr Apr 1—Oct 5	pb	Marshall Park-Salmon Falls	14.5
Mariah 10,000	D Apr 1—Sep 30	pb	Baachi Ranch-Salmon Falls	10.5
Mariah 10,000	D Apr 1—Sep 30	pb	Chili Bar-Baachi Ranch	10
NOC 9,000	D Mar 1—Oct 30	ob, pb op	Chili Bar-Marshall Park	6
NOC 9,000	D Mar 1—Oct 30	ob, pb op	Marshall Park-Salmon Falls	14.5
Nonesuch Whitewater No max	D Mar 1—Oct 31	pb, ob op, ik op	Chili Bar-Marshall Park	6
Nonesuch Whitewater No max	D Mar 1—Oct 31	pb, ob op, ik op	Marshall Park-Salmon Falls	14.5
OARS No max	D Apr 1—Oct 31	ob, pb op	Camp Lotus-Salmon Falls	11.5
Outdoor Adv./UCD 8,000	Sa, Su Apr 19—Nov 1	pb	Chili Bar-Marshall Park	6
Outdoor Adv./UCD 8,000	Sa, Su Apr 19—Nov 1	pb	Marshall Park-Salmon Falls	14.5
River Riders 10,000	D May 1—Sep 30	pb, ob op, ik op	Chili Bar-Marshall Park	6
River Riders 10,000	D May 1—Sep 30	pb, ob op, ik op	Marshall Park-Salmon Falls	14.5

Recom. Require. Min. Age	Cost Max. Grp. Min. Grp.	Discounts	Transportation	Comments
Age: 8	$60 254 8	Call		
Rec: Good health; not overweight. Req: Libra test. Age: 14	$70 20 8	Less 10%w/20+		
Age: 8	$60 254 8	Call		
Age: 7	$65 90 12	1 Fw/16 and less $20wd and less 10%y16		Breakfast inc
Age: 7	$65 90 12	1 Fw/16 and less $20wd and less 10%y16		Breakfast, prior night camping inc
Req: Wetsuit if water below 50 deg F. Age: Call	$51 75 6	1 Fw/12+ and (less $5w/12+ or less $5wd or less $9w/12+wd) and .5 Fy14		Lunch op, add $5
Req: Wetsuit if water below 50 deg F. Age: Call	$63 75 6	1 Fw/12+ and less $6wd and (less $6w/12+ or less $9w/18+) and .5 Fy14		Lunch op, add $5
Rec: Wetsuit until May 31. Age: Call	$60 27 8	Less 10%w/12+		
Rec: Wetsuit until May 31. Age: Call	$60 27 8	Less 10%w/12+		
Rec: Wetsuit Apr, May, Oct. Age: 7	$75 25 25	Less $10wd and less $10y17 and (less 10%w/11-24 or less 15%w/25)		1 night lodge and hot air balloon flight op, add $190; group minimum 12wd
Req: Wetsuit Apr, May. Age: 8	$36 60 12		Shuttle not inc	Food not inc
Req: Wetsuit Apr, May. Age: 8	$36 60 12		Shuttle not inc	Food not inc
Age: 10	$55 24 10	Less $10w/6+ and 1 Fw/10		Beer, wine inc
Age: 10	$55 24 10	Less $10w/6+ and 1 Fw/10		Beer, wine inc

Name– Max. cfs	Starting	Raft type	Put-in– Take-out	Miles Camp Facilities
River Runners, Inc. 8,000	D Apr 1—Sep 30	pb, ob op	Chili Bar-Ponderosa Park	7.5
River Runners, Inc. 8,000	D Apr 1—Sep 30	pb, ob op	Ponderosa Park-Salmon Falls	13
Rollinson 7,500	D May 1—Sep 30	pb	Camp Lotus-Salmon Falls	11.5
Rollinson 7,500	D May 1—Sep 30	pb	Chili Bar-Camp Lotus	9
Rubicon 10,000	D Mar 1—Oct 31	pb, ik op, ob op	Camp Lotus-Salmon Falls	11.5
Rubicon 10,000	D Mar 1—Oct 31	pb, ik op, ob op	Chili Bar-Camp Lotus	9
Tributary Whitewater No max	D Mar 1—Oct 31	pb, ob op	Chili Bar-Marshall Park	6
Tributary Whitewater No max	D Mar 1—Jun 15	pb, ob op	Chili Bar-Salmon Falls	20.5
Tributary Whitewater No max	D Mar 1—Oct 31	pb, ob op	Marshall Park-Salmon Falls	14.5
Turtle River 10,000	Apr 13, 16, 18, 20; May 11, 14, 16, 18; Jun 8, 11, 13, 15; Jul 20, 23, 25, 27; Aug 17, 20, 22, 24; Sep 14, 17, 19, 21	pb, ik s/b op exp	Camp Lotus-Salmon Falls	11.5
Turtle River 10,000	Apr 12, 15, 17, 19; May 10, 13, 15, 17; Jun 7, 10, 12, 14; Jul 19, 22, 24, 26; Aug 16, 19, 21, 23; Sep 13, 16, 18, 20	pb	Chili Bar-Camp Lotus	9
W.E.T. 8,000	D Apr 15—Oct 15	ob, pb op, o/pa op, ik op	Camp Lotus-Salmon Falls	11.5

Recom. Require. Min. Age	Cost Max. Grp. Min. Grp.	Discounts	Transportation	Comments
Req: Wetsuit Apr, May, if cfs over 4,000. Age: Call	$70 84 20	Less $10wd and less $10w/12 + and 1 Fw/20	Avail from LA	Bus from LA, add $45 or $40w/12 + or $1100 for 39; breakfast inc; group minimum 4wd
Req: Wetsuit Apr, May, if cfs over 4,000. Age: Call	$80 84 20	Less $10wd and less $10w/12 + and 1 Fw/20	Avail from LA	Bus from LA, add $45 or $40w/12 + or $1100 for 39; breakfast, dinner, live evening entertainment inc; group minimum 4wd
Req: Wetsuit over 2500 cfs. Age: 12	$65 24 8	Less $10wd and less $5w/12 + and .5 Fw/12		
Req: Wetsuit over 2500 cfs. Age: 12	$65 24 8	Less $10wd and less $5w/12 + and .5 Fw/12		
Age: Call	$60 27 6	1 Fw/12 and less 10%w/20 +		
Age: Call	$60 27 6	1 Fw/12 and less 10%w/20 +		
Rec: Wetsuit until Jun 1. Req: Children must swim, like water. Age: 8	$57 32 10	Less $12wd and (less 10%w/10 + or 1 Fw/10 or less 30%y16 or less 30% handicapped or less 30%s65)	Avail from LA for groups of 22 +	Handicapped; bus from LA, add $40-60
Rec: Wetsuit until Jun 1. Req: Children must swim, like water. . Age: 9	$78 32 6	Less $13wd and (less 10%w/10 + or 1 Fw/10 or less 30%y16 or less 30% handicapped or less 30%s65)	Avail from LA for groups of 22 +	Handicapped; bus from LA, add $40-60
Rec: Wetsuit until Jun 1. Req: Children must swim, like water. Age: 9	$67 32 6	Less $12wd and (less 10%w/10 + or 1 Fw/10 or less 30%y16 or less 30% handicapped or less 30%s65)	Avail from LA for groups of 22 +	Handicapped; bus from LA, add $40-60
Age: 10	$60 20 6	(1 Fw/10 or .5 Fw/ 6) and less 25% before May 15 and less 20%y12	Shuttle is coop style	All-woman trips May 18; Jun 15; Jul 27; Aug 24
Age: 10	$60 20 6	(1 Fw/10 or .5 Fw/ 6) and less 25% before May 15 and less 20%y12	Shuttle is coop style	All-woman trips May 17; Jun 14; Jul 26; Aug 23
Rec: Good health. Req: Wetsuit over 4000 cfs. Age: Call	$65 48 6	Less $20y12 and 1 Fw/12 and less $20wd	Avail from LA, Sacramento Airport	Bus from Sacramento Airport, add $25; bus from LA for 35-40, add $50

Name– Max. cfs	Starting	Raft type	Put-in– Take-out	Miles Camp Facilities
W.E.T. 8,000	D Apr 15—Oct 15	ob, pb op, o/pa op, ik op	Chili Bar-Camp Lotus	9
Whitewater Excitement 10,000	D Apr 1—Oct 31	pb	Chili Bar-Baachi Ranch	10
Whitewater Excitement 10,000	D Apr 1—Oct 31	pb	Marshall Park- Salmon Falls	14.5
Whitewater Voyages 10,000	D Apr 1—Oct 1	pb, ob op	Beaver Point-Salmon Falls	13
Whitewater Voyages 10,000	D Apr 1—Oct 1	pb, ob op	Chili Bar-Beaver Point	7.5
Wild River Tours 8,000	D Apr 1—Oct 31	pb, ob op	Baachi Ranch- Salmon Falls	10.5
Wild Water West, Ltd. No max	D May 1—Oct 31	pb	Camp Lotus-Salmon Falls	11.5
Wild Water West, Ltd. No max	D May 1—Oct 31	pb	Chili Bar-Camp Lotus	9
Zephyr No max	D Apr 1—Sep 15	pb, ob op	Beaver Point-Salmon Falls	13

SOUTH FORK OF THE AMERICAN—2 DAY

Name– Max. cfs	Starting	Raft type	Put-in– Take-out	Miles Camp Facilities
Action Adventures No max	D Mar 22—Oct 5	pb, ik s/b op exp, ob op	Chili Bar-Salmon Falls	20.5 On-river Chem
Adventure Connection 10,000	D Apr 1—Oct 31	pb, ob op, o/pa op	Baachi Ranch- Salmon Falls; Chili Bar-Marshall Park	16.5 On-river Chem

Recom. Require. Min. Age	Cost Max. Grp. Min. Grp.	Discounts	Transportation	Comments
Rec: Good health. Req: Wetsuit over 4000 cfs. Age: Call	$65 48 6	Less $20y12 and 1 Fw/12 and less $20wd	Avail from LA, Sacramento Airport	Bus from Sacramento Airport, add $25; bus from LA for 35-40, add $50
Age: 7	$70 90 24	Less $10wd and 1 Fw/12		
Age: 7	$60 90 24	Less $10wd and 1 Fw/12		
Rec: Wetsuit Apr, May, Oct. Age: 7	$70 48 48	(1 Fw/25 or 2 Fw/ 47) and less $6wd and (less 10%w/ 12 + or less 10%y16)		Beer inc
Rec: Wetsuit Apr, May, Oct. Age: 7	$70 48 48	(1 Fw/25 or 2 Fw/ 47) and less $6wd and (less 10%w/ 12 + or less 10%y16)		Beer inc
Req: Wetsuit until Jun 1. Age: 8	$65 50 6	1 Fw/15		
Age: 8	$67 55 10	(1 Fw/12 or 2 Fw/ 20 or 3 Fw/30, etc.) and less $10wd		
Age: 8	$67 55 10	(1 Fw/12 or 2 Fw/ 20 or 3 Fw/30, etc.) and less $10wd		
Age: 7	$70 30 6	Less $15wd		
Age: Call	$129 150 5	Less 5%wd and less 10%w/11-25 or less 15%w/26-40 or less 20%w/ 41 + or less 20%y13	Avail from Sacramento	No extra cost to run lower section first, upper on day 2; van from Sacramento for 1-5, add $50
Rec: Wetsuit Apr, May, Sep, Oct. Age: 8	$150 90 12	1 Fw/12 and less $10w/24 + and less $20wd and less $10y15	Avail from LA, SF	2 nights' camping (hot tub), breakfast day 1, beer, wine inc; bus from LA, add $45; plane from LAX for 10 +, add $135; family trips Jun 17, Jul 1, 22, Aug 5, 19, less $90y15 w/ adult; single parent & child trips Jun 24, Jul 15, Aug 12, less $90y15 w/ adult; single adult trips Jun 10, Jul 29, Aug 26, less $30; lodge op, add $60/night for 2

Name– Max. cfs	Starting	Raft type	Put-in– Take-out	Miles Camp Facilities
All- Outdoors 10,000	D Apr 26—Oct 26	pb, o/pa op	Camp Lotus-Salmon Falls; Chili Bar-Camp Lotus	20.5 On-river Porta
ARR No max	D Apr 1—Oct 31	pb, ob op	Chili Bar-Salmon Falls	20.5 On-river Chem
ARTA No max	Su, Tu, Th Apr 1—Sep 30	pb	Chili Bar-Salmon Falls	20.5 On-river Flush
ARTA No max	D Apr 1—Sep 30	pb, ob op	Chili Bar-Salmon Falls	20.5 On-river Chem
A WW Connection 6,000	D Apr 1—Oct 31	pb, ob op, ik op	Chili Bar-Salmon Falls	20.5 On-river Flush
A WW Connection 3,000	D Apr 1—Oct 31	pb, ob op, ik op	Marshall Park- Salmon Falls	14.5 On-river Flush
California Adventures 7,000	Sa May 3—Aug 30	pb	Camp Lotus-Salmon Falls; Chili Bar-Camp Lotus	20.5 On-river Flush
California River 8,000	D Mar 22—Oct 26	pb, ob op	Chili Bar-Salmon Falls	20.5 On-river Flush
Earthtrek Expeditions 10,000	Tu, Th, Sa Apr 5—Oct 12	pb, ob op	Marshall Park- Salmon Falls; Chili Bar-Marshall Park	20.5 On-river Chem
Earthtrek Expeditions 10,000	Mo, Fr Apr 4—Oct 11	pb, ob op	Marshall Park- Salmon Falls; Chili Bar-Marshall Park	20.5 On-river Chem
ECHO 10,000	D Apr 1—Oct 31	ob, pb op	Chili Bar-Salmon Falls	20.5 On-river Porta
Gold Rush 8,000	Tu, Th, Sa May 1—Sep 30	pb, ob op	Chili Bar-Salmon Falls	20.5 On-river Chem

Recom. Require. Min. Age	Cost Max. Grp. Min. Grp.	Discounts	Transportation	Comments
Req: Wetsuit until May 15. Age: Call	$149 50 25	1 Fw/12 and less $10wd		Lodge op, add $30; off-river op, flush
Rec: Wetsuit until Jun 30. Age: 12	$137 86 6	Less $10wd and 1 Fw/12 and less $10y16		Beer, champagne inc
Req: Group of 8+. Age: 8	Com. 33 8			Coop; group provides and prepares own and guide's food. Group w/8-12, $1050; 13-18, $1500; 19-25, $1900; 26-33, $2300
Age: 8	$150 36 20	Less $10wd and less 10%w/10+ and 1Fw/20		Lodge op, add $48
Age: Call	$155 75 6	Less 15%wd and 1 Fw/12 and less 10%w/24+	Avail from LA, SF	Handicapped; balloon trip op, add $85; bus from LA, add $45; from SF, add $40
Age: Call	$165 45 12	Less $20wd and 1 Fw/12 and less $10w/24+	Avail from LA, SF	Handicapped; balloon trip op, add $85; bus from LA, add $50; from SF for 10+, add $45; sailing, horseback riding at Lake Tahoe inc
Age: Call	$108 30 10	1 Fw/10 and less 20%UC Berkeley students	Inc from Berkeley	Handicapped; food not inc
Rec: Wetsuit or wool and rain suit, Mar-May, Oct. Age: 7	$130 30 6	1 Fw/6 and less $20Su-Th or less $10Fr and less $20w/o food		On-river op, porta
Req: Wetsuit Apr, Oct and above 3000 cfs. Age: 8	$155 110 6	Less $20wd and 1 Fw/15 and less $10y16		Family trips .5Fy16w/adult Jun 26, Jul 8, 22, Aug 5, 26
Req: Wetsuit Apr, Oct and above 3000 cfs. Age: 8	$199 110 12	Less $20wd and 1 Fw/15 and less $10y16	Inc from Santa Ana, San Fernando Valley	Lodge op for 16+, add $70
Age: 7	$153 30 25	1 Fw/25 and less $8wd and less $7y17 and less $7w/8+		
Age: Call	$149 123 8	1Fw/12 and (less $15w/12+ we or less $30w/ 12+wd)	Inc from Placerville for 8+, avail from LA, Orange Cty	Bus from LA, Orange Cty, add $30

Name– Max. cfs	Starting	Raft type	Put-in– Take-out	Miles Camp Facilities
Kern River Tours 10,000	D May 1—Sep 30	pb, ob op	Chili Bar-Salmon Falls	20.5 On-river Flush
Libra Expeditions 4,000	Sa-Th Apr 1—Oct 5	ik s/b	Marshall Park- Salmon Falls; Chili Bar-Marshall Park	20.5 Off-river Flush
Libra Expeditions 4,000	Mo-Th, Sa Apr 1—Oct 5	pb	Marshall Park- Salmon Falls; Chili Bar-Marshall Park	20.5 Off-river Flush
Mariah 10,000	D Apr 1—Sep 30	pb	Baachi Ranch- Salmon Falls; Chili Bar-Baachi Ranch	20.5 On-river Porta
NOC 9,000	D Mar 1—Oct 31	ob, pb op	Chili Bar-Salmon Falls	20.5 On-river Chem
Nonesuch Whitewater No max	D Apr 1—Oct 31	pb, ob op	Chili Bar-Salmon Falls	20.5 On-river Porta
OARS No max	D Apr 1—Oct 31	ob, pb op	Gold Nugget- Salmon Falls	21 On-river Chem
River Mountain 4,500	D May 1—Sep 30	pb, ob op ia	Marshall Park- Salmon Falls; Chili Bar-Marshall Park	20.5 On-river Flush
River Riders 10,000	D May 1—Sep 30	pb, ob op, ik op	Chili Bar-Salmon Falls	20.5 On-river Porta
River Runners, Inc. 8,000	D Apr 1—Sep 30	pb, ob op	Chili Bar-Salmon Falls	20.5 On-river Flush
Rollinson 7,500	D May 1—Sep 30	pb	Chili Bar-Salmon Falls	20.5 On-river Flush
Rubicon 10,000	Jul 13	pb, ik op, ob op	Chili Bar-Salmon Falls	20.5 On-river Flush
South Bay No max	D Apr 1—Oct 31	pb	Ponderosa Park- Salmon Falls; Chili Bar-Ponderosa Park	20.5 On-river Flush

Recom. Require. Min. Age	Cost Max. Grp. Min. Grp.	Discounts	Transportation	Comments
Age: 8	$149 50 12	Less $20wd and (less 10%y12 or less 10%w/12+) and 1 Fw/24	Avail from LA	Bus from LA for 40+, add $30
Rec: Good health; not overweight. Req: Libra test. Age: 14	$165 20 8	Less $10wd and less $10w/14+	Avail from Anaheim, Irvine, Torrance, San Fernando Valley	Bus from Anaheim, Irvine, Torrance, San Fernando Valley, add $45
Age: 6	$150 254 8	Less $10wd and less $10w/14+	Avail from Anaheim, Irvine, Torrance, San Fernando Valley	Bus from Anaheim, Irvine, Torrance, San Fernando Valley, add $45; gourmet trip, 30-person max, off-river, add $20
Age: 7	$150 90 12	1 Fw/16 and less $20wd and less 10%y16		Breakfast day 1, prior night camping inc
Req: Wetsuit if water below 50 deg F. Age: Call	$158 75 6	1 Fw/12+ and (less $15w/12+ or less $15wd or less $28w/12+wd) and .5 Fy14		On-river op, flush
Rec: Wetsuit until May 31. Age: Call	$160 27 8	Less 10%w/12+		
Rec: Wetsuit Apr, May, Oct. Age: 7	$160 25 25	Call	Avail from LA	1 night lodge op, add $50; 3 nights lodge op, add $115; bus from LA, add $40; group minimum 12wd
Req: Not in excess of 280 lbs. Age: 10	$160 108 4	Less $25wd and (less $5w/10-39 or less $10w/40+) and 1 Fw/20	Avail from LA, Orange Cty on Fr or for 20+	Breakfast day 1 inc; draft beer, wine inc; bus from LA, add $45; bus from Orange Cty, add $48; handicapped
Age: 10	$125 24 10	Less $10w/6+ and 1 Fw/10		Beer, wine inc
Req: Wetsuit Apr, May, if cfs over 4000. Age: Call	$150 84 20	Less $25wd and less $10w/12+ and 1 Fw/20	Avail from LA	Bus from LA, add $45 or $40w/12+ or $1100 for 39; breakfast day 1, live evening entertainment inc; group minimum 4wd
Req: Wetsuit over 2500 cfs. Age: 12	$140 24 8	Less $10wd and less $10w/12+ and .5 Fw/12		
Age: Call	$229 27 25			Gourmet; wine inc
Rec: Wetsuit Apr, May. Age: Call	$205 84 6	Less $45wd (no bus) and (1 Fw/45 or 1 Fw/25wd) and less $5w/25	Bus from LA inc	Breakfast day 1 inc

Name– Max. cfs	Starting	Raft type	Put-in– Take-out	Miles Camp Facilities
Tributary **Whitewater** No max	D Mar 1—Oct 31	pb, ob op	Chili Bar-Salmon Falls	20.5 On-river Flush
Turtle River 10,000	Apr 12, 15, 17, 19; May 10, 13, 15, 17; Jun 7, 10, 12, 14; Jul 19, 22, 24, 26; Aug 16, 19, 21, 23; Sep 13, 16, 18, 20	pb, ik s/b op exp	Chili Bar-Salmon Falls	20.5 On-river Chem
W.E.T. 8,000	D Apr 15—Oct 15	ob, pb op, o/pa op, ik op	Chili Bar-Salmon Falls	20.5 On-river Porta
Whitewater **Excitement** 10,000	D Apr 1—Oct 31	pb	Chili Bar-Salmon Falls	20.5 On-river Flush
Whitewater **Voyages** 10,000	D Apr 1—Oct 31	pb, ob op	Beaver Point-Salmon Falls; Chili Bar- Beaver Point	20.5 On-river Chem
Whitewater **Voyages** 10,000	D Apr 1—Oct 31	pb, ob op	Chili Bar-Salmon Falls	20.5 On-river Chem
Wild River **Tours** 8,000	D Apr 1—Oct 31	pb, ob op	Chili Bar-Salmon Falls	20.5 On-river Chem
Wild Water **West, Ltd.** No max	D May 1—Oct 31	pb	Chili Bar-Salmon Falls	20.5 On-river Flush
Zephyr No max	D Apr 1—Sep 15	pb, ob op	Chili Bar-Salmon Falls	20.5 On-river Porta

SOUTH FORK OF THE AMERICAN—3 DAYS

Name– Max. cfs	Starting	Raft type	Put-in– Take-out	Miles Camp Facilities
Adventure **Connection** 10,000	Jul 4	pb, ob op, o/pa op	Marshall Park- Salmon Falls; Chili Bar-Marshall Park	20.5 On-river Chem
A WW **Connection** 3,000	D Apr 1—Oct 31	pb, ob op, ik op	Chili Bar-Salmon Falls	20.5 On-river Flush

SOUTH FORK OF THE AMERICAN—5 DAYS

Name– Max. cfs	Starting	Raft type	Put-in– Take-out	Miles Camp Facilities
Earthtrek **Expeditions** 10,000	Will call Apr 5—Oct 12	pb, ob op	Marshall Park- Salmon Falls; Chili Bar-Marshall Park	20.5 Com. Chem

Recom. Require. Min. Age	Cost Max. Grp. Min. Grp.	Discounts	Transportation	Comments
Rec: Wetsuit until Jun 1. Req: Children must swim, like water. Age: 9	$138 32 6	Less $26wd and (less 10%w/10+ or 1 Fw/10 or less 30%y16 or less 30% handicapped or less 30%s65)	Avail from LA for groups of 22+	Handicapped; bus from LA, add $40-60; on-river op, porta
Age: 10	$120 20 6	(1 Fw/10 or .5 Fw/ 6) and less 25% before May 15 and less 20%y12	Shuttle is coop style	All-woman trips May 17; Jun 14; Jul 26; Aug 23
Rec: Good health; camping exp. Req: Wetsuit over 4000 cfs. Age: Call	$160 48 6	Less $15y12 and 1 Fw/12 and less $20wd	Avail from LA, Sacramento Airport	Bus from Sacramento Airport, add $25; bus from LA for 35-40, add $50; wine, cocktails inc
Age: 7	$135 60 24	Less $10wd and 1 Fw/12		
Rec: Wetsuit Apr, May, Oct. Age: 7	$150 48 48	(1 Fw/25 or 2 Fw/ 46) and (less $12FrSu or less $24wd) and (less 10%w/12+ or less 10%y16)	Avail from LA	Cocktails inc; bus from LA, add $40; bus trip inc breakfast day 1
Rec: Wetsuit Apr, May, Oct. Age: 7	$150 48 48	(1 Fw/25 or 2 Fw/ 46) and (less $12FrSu or less $24wd) and (less 10%w/12+ or less 10%y16)		Cocktails inc
Req: Wetsuit until Jun 1. Age: Call	$145 50 6	1 Fw/15		
Age: 8	$145 55 10	(1 Fw/12 or 2 Fw/ 20 or 3 Fw/30 etc.) and (less $15wd or less $10FrSu)		Beer, wine inc
Req: Wetsuit until Jun 15. Age: 7	$155 30 6	Less $15wd		
Rec: Wetsuit Apr, May, Sep, Oct. Age: 8	$220 90 12	1 Fw/12 and less $10w/24+ and less $20wd and less $10y15	Inc from LA	Breakfast day 1, 3 nights' camping (hot tub), beer, wine tasting trip day 3 inc
Age: Call	$215 45 12	Less $20wd and 1 Fw/12 and less $10w/24+	Avail from LA, SF	Handicapped; balloon trip op, add $85; bus from LA, add $50; from SF, for 10+, add $45; sailing, horseback riding at Lake Tahoe inc
Req: Group of 16+. Age: 8	$285 22 16	1 Fw/15	Inc from Santa Ana, San Fernando Valley	Inc 2 days in wine country; no food inc in wine country; only days 1 and 2 on river, 2 nights at hotel inc

Name– Max. cfs	Starting	Raft type	Put-in– Take-out	Miles Camp Facilities
Earthtrek Expeditions 10,000	Jul 9, Aug 6	pb, ob op	Marshall Park- Salmon Falls; Chili Bar-Marshall Park	20.5 On-river Chem
Earthtrek Expeditions 10,000	Jul 23, Aug 13, Aug 20, Sep 10	pb, ob op	Marshall Park- Salmon Falls; Chili Bar-Marshall Park	20.5 On-river Chem

Middle Fork of the American

Introduction. The beautiful Middle Fork of the American attracts many rafters because of its proximity to the Bay Area, the good water levels all summer long, and the ready availability of weekend trips. However, its long, flat stretches may disappoint experienced rafters, while its few major rapids may be too difficult for beginners.

Level of difficulty/water level concerns/flow information. Class IV-Vp. Difficult portage at Ruck-a-Chucky (even the teenagers complain). There are only two Class IV rapids on the river; the vast majority of the rapids are Class II and easier. Water levels are dam-controlled, with releases for power generation, but levels remain rather constant throughout the week. Spring high water brings safety concerns; it becomes impossible to eddy out (leave the main current and go to the shore of the river) above the hazardous Tunnel Chute rapid. Running the Tunnel Chute becomes considerably more difficult at higher water levels. At very high water levels, the tunnel will fill with water. At low water levels, boats in the Tunnel Chute may be ripped by sharp rocks. Keep in touch with your outfitter about water levels.

The minimum water level for rafting is about 700 cfs. For flow information, call (916) 322-3327. Listen for the release from Oxbow powerhouse.

Permit system/time to raft. Before taking passengers down the Middle Fork, all commercial guides must complete three training trips. Outfitters are limited to 14 starts per day, and to five boats per start. This system, in addition to the portage (where baggage boats are prohibited), encourages the use of paddle boats. The high limit of 14 starts per day is effectively no limit: as a result, demand is concentrated on the weekends, when you may see 30 boats on the river. On a weekday, you may find one or two, so try to pull a minimum group size together and go for a weekday, especially if your objective is to enjoy a wilderness experience.

Some companies have two permits on this river: this enables them to take twice as many people down river. However, a group of more than

Recom. Require. Min. Age	Cost Max. Grp. Min. Grp.	Discounts	Transportation	Comments
Age: 8	$249 22 16	1 Fw/15 and less $10y16	Inc from Santa Ana, San Fernando Valley	Inc 2 days in Yosemite (nights in tent cabins); only days 1 and 2 on river
Age: 8	$245 45 16	1 Fw/15 and less $10y16	Inc from Santa Ana, San Fernando Valley	Inc 2 days in Lake Tahoe; camp (food inc) at Tahoe Jul 23, Aug 20; hotel at Tahoe Aug 13, Sep 10, add $20 (food not inc); only days 1 and 2 on river

five boats must be divided for running the river.

You should choose summer to run this river; in spring many far superior runs are available nearby, notably the North Fork of the American, the North Fork of the Yuba, and the Merced.

On the weekend of July 19-20, 1986, the river will be closed to rafting because of a horse race. Don't ask.

Commercial rafting. A recent study commissioned by the Bureau of Reclamation estimated that 6600 commercial passengers and 160 private boaters ran the Middle Fork of the American in 1985. Passenger volume figures reported to the State Department of Parks and Recreation by outfitters were significantly higher. It is expected that in the very near

—*Rapid Shooters*

The author (in the dark glasses) backpaddles under the spray at the top of the Class V Tunnel Chute rapid of the Middle Fork of the American

future, perhaps even in 1986, the State Department of Parks and Recreation will make significant changes in the permit system for both the Middle and North Forks of the American.

Five of the largest rafting outfitters on the Middle and North Forks of the American in 1985, in user-day volume as reported to the Department of Parks and Recreation, were Libra Expeditions, Whitewater Voyages, Adventours Unlimited, American River Recreation, and Wild River Tours.

Gear/safety/who can come. Absolutely everyone who is considering running the Tunnel Chute should get out of the raft and watch other boats run it first. Persons who contemplate running the Chute should be over 16, strong and confident swimmers, with no history of heart disease, and with no brittle bone conditions. Your insurance should be up to date. Wear tennis shoes rather than booties, as the former would provide superior protection for your feet should you exit the boat.

If you have any qualms about rafting the Tunnel Chute, don't. If you would be embarrassed to demonstrate wisdom when others in your boat are demonstrating folly, you may wish to book your trip with one of the outfitters that has a policy of always portaging the Tunnel Chute. See the comments in the trip descriptions.

The portage around Ruck-a-Chucky rapid taxes even the young and agile. Remember that you will have to carry your share of equipment around the rapid, even if it is just a paddle. This portage is suitable only for what outfitters call "healthy, rugged" types.

Distinctive features. Yes, you've got it figured out by now. The highlight and hazard of this trip is the notorious Class V Tunnel Chute rapid. In the 1800's, gold miners decided to reroute the river by carving a ninety-foot tunnel through a hill around which the river meandered. In addition, the miners dynamited a chute leading down into the tunnel. This recently created rapid (in river years) still has sharp, jagged walls.

The chute is justifiably advertised as the highlight of a raft trip: it provides a wild, steep, rushing ride that will have you moaning at the top and cheering at the bottom (soaked to the skin, too).

Yet, more than almost all California rapids, the Tunnel Chute has a dark history of unverifiable unpleasantness. One very experienced guide, whose company does run the Tunnel Chute, says that when he takes private trips, he portages out of concern for the hazards. On my 1985 trip (water level 1300 cfs), we had four swimmers through this rapid, including one guide. One strong young man fell out at the top of the rapid and came up later with several scratches on his helmet. The fellow next to me in the bow of the boat and I both were ejected at the huge hole at the bottom of the rapid; he was held under water for about 45 feet. I came up earlier and bounced against the wall of the tunnel along all of its 90-foot length. This rather inelegant passage was substantially facilitated by my long-neglected lifeguard skills.

So, if you want to run the Tunnel Chute, be sure to (a) hang on tight at the "hold on" command and (b) position yourself low in the raft. As always, do not tie yourself to the boat. It's infinitely superior to swim the Tunnel Chute than to be tied to a flipped boat.

River access. Wilderness run; occasional access by dirt road. More than other rivers, the Middle Fork brings first-time rafters to wilderness campsites. Some people without backpacking experience may be unsuited to the toilet arrangements. See Chapter 2.

Sites of interest. Remnants of old mining operations, including rusted iron equipment, still remain in the river canyon. You will also see the sites of old bridges, reminders of 1964, when the river rose up and washed out a dam, sending floodwaters far downstream.

Environment. Among all commercially rafted rivers in the Sierras, the Middle Fork of the American may offer the most beautiful and idyllic scenery (after the first five miles, where mining scars are visible). The river runs in a deep, green canyon, heavily forested with sugar, ponderosa, and Jeffrey pine, white and red fir, oak, and alpine willow. You would break out into song but for the concern that your fellow passengers would toss you from the boat. Wild berries grow along the river, and predators such as turkey vultures, hawks and eagles fly overhead.

Fishing. Trout. Some grow to trophy size.

Summary of river between put-ins. Summarized with permission from *California White Water*, with some additions.

Oxbow Bend to Ruck-a-Chucky (14 miles)—One Class V rapid (Tunnel Chute), one Class IV.

Ruck-a-Chucky to Greenwood Bridge (2 miles)—One Class IV rapid, two Class IIIs. Difficult portage.

Greenwood Bridge to Mammoth Bar (7 miles)—Class II rapids.

Mammoth Bar to North Fork Confluence (2 miles)—One Class V rapid.

River status. You may get the impression from reading about recent California water management that the more accessible and scenic a wild river, the more likely it is to be dammed. The Middle Fork of the American, which qualifies on both counts yet lacks wild and scenic status, would be flooded in its entirety by the proposed $2.2 + billion Auburn Dam. Before construction can begin on this outstanding misuse of taxpayers' money, Congress must reauthorize the dam. You may wish to write to Sen. Alan Cranston (Senate Office Building, Washington, DC 20510) with your suggestions on how to reduce the federal budget deficit.

Should the Middle Fork survive the upcoming battle over Auburn dam, still other projects have been proposed to generate hydroelectricity from its waters. One, the Horseshoe Bar project, would destroy the Tunnel Chute and flood the river upstream.

As all of the lands around both the North Fork of the American and the Middle Fork have been purchased or optioned by the state, a different

Abbreviations

Mo,Tu,We	Monday, Tuesday, Wednesday, etc.	porta	Porta-potty or lime can at camp
D	Daily	exp	(Rafting) experience
will call	Outfitter will call you to arrange dates	Camping exp	Camping experience
ob	Oar boat	F	Free
o/pa	Oar boat with paddle assist	w/	With
pb	Paddle boat	wd	Weekday
ik	Inflatable kayak	we	Weekend
s/b	Self-bailing	y	Youth
op	Optional	y16	Youth, age 16 and under
ia	If available or if appropriate	s	Senior
on-river	Camp is beside the river	s65	Senior, age 65 and over
off-river	Camp is not beside the river	inc	Included
lodge	Overnight at a lodge or motel	avail	Available
flush	Flush toilets at camp	#	pound
chem	Chemical toilets or outhouse at camp		

Name— Max. cfs	Starting	Raft type	Put-in— Take-out	Miles Camp Facilities
MIDDLE FORK OF THE AMERICAN—1 DAY				
Action Adventures 5,000	D May 15-Sep 15	pb, ob op, ik s/b op exp	Oxbow Bend-Ruck-a-chucky	14
Adventours Unlimited No max	D Apr 5—Sep 28	pb, ik op	Oxbow Bend-Ruck-a-chucky	14
All- Outdoors 3,000	D May 1—Oct 26	pb	Oxbow Bend-Ruck-a-chucky	14
ARR No max	D Jun 1—Sep 30	pb, ob	Oxbow Bend-Ruck-a-chucky	14
A WW Connection 3,000	D May 1—Sep 30	ob, pb op	Oxbow Bend-Greenwood Br	16
California River 3,000	D Jun 7—Sep 28	pb, ob op	Oxbow Bend-Ruck-a-chucky	14
Libra Expeditions No max	Mo-Th, Sa Apr 1—Oct 5	pb	Oxbow Bend-Greenwood Br	16
NOC 2,500	D May 1—Jun 30	ob, pb op	Oxbow Bend-Greenwood Br	16
RAM River Expeditions 6,000	D May 1—Sep 30	ob, pb op	Oxbow Bend-Ruck-a-chucky	14
River Riders 3,000	D May 1—Sep 30	pb, ob op, ik op	Oxbow Bend-Ruck-a-chucky	14

future for these rivers could be a state-protected recreation area, created where Auburn Dam would have left flooded lands. Contact Friends of the River for information.

See North Fork of the American for lodgings and campgrounds.

Recom. Require. Min. Age	Cost Max. Grp. Min. Grp.	Discounts	Transportation	Comments
Req: Wetsuit until Jun 1. Age: Call	$75 25 10	Less 10%w/11 +	Avail from Sacramento	Van from Sacramento for 1-5, add $50
Rec: Wetsuit in Apr. Age: 13	$80 40 6	1 Fw/7-17 or 2 Fw/18-27 or 3 Fw/ 28-35 or 4 Fw/36	Avail from LA, Orange Cty	Bus from LA, Orange Cty (beer, wine, off-river flush camp inc), add $35
Req: Wetsuit until Jun 1. Age: Call	$74 30 25	1 Fw/12 and less $5wd		Portage Tunnel Chute
Rec: Wetsuit until Jun 30. Age: 12	$75 30 8	1 Fw/12		Beer, champagne inc
Rec: Hardy paddlers. Age: Call	$85 35 12	Less $20wd and 1 Fw/12 and less $5w/18 +	Avail from LA, SF	Bus from LA, add $50; bus from SF, for 12 +, add $25
Req: Exp. Age: 12	$75 24 12	1 Fw/6 and 1ess $10wd		
Rec: Wetsuit in Apr, May; good health; exp. Age: 14	$85 70 12	Less $10wd and 1 Fw/14 and less $10w/20 +		Client evaluation for Tunnel Chute; portage Tunnel Chute above 2,500 cfs
Rec: Above avg health; exp. Req: Wetsuit if water below 50 deg F. Age: 16	$80 24 6	Less $8wd or (1 Fw/12 + and less $8w/12 + or less $15w/12 + wd) and .5 Fy14		Portage Tunnel Chute; lunch op, add $5
Rec: Wetsuit May, Jun; good health. Age: 12	$75 50 6	1 Fw/12 and (less 10%w/8-19 or less 15%w/20 +) or less $10y12		
Age: 10	$65 18 10	Less $10w/6 + and 1 Fw/10		Beer, wine inc; ik op after Tunnel Chute only; age 16 w/ adult to raft Tunnel Chute

Name– Max. cfs	Starting	Raft type	Put-in– Take-out	Miles Camp Facilities
Rollinson 2,500	D Jun 1—Aug 31	pb	Oxbow Bend-Ruck- a-chucky	14
Tributary Whitewater 2,500	D Mar 1—Oct 31	pb, ob op	Oxbow Bend-Ruck- a-chucky	14
W.E.T. 2,500	D Jun 1—Oct 31	ob, pb op, o/pa op, ik op exp	Oxbow Bend-Ruck- a-chucky	14
Whitewater Excitement 2,800	D May 1—Oct 31	pb	Oxbow Bend- Greenwood Br	16
Whitewater Voyages 3,000	D May 1—Oct 31	pb	Oxbow Bend-Ruck- a-chucky	14

MIDDLE FORK OF THE AMERICAN—2 DAYS

Name– Max. cfs	Starting	Raft type	Put-in– Take-out	Miles Camp Facilities
Action Adventures 5,000	D May 15-Sep 15	pb, ob op, ik s/b op exp	Oxbow Bend-Ruck- a-chucky	14 On-river Porta
Adventours Unlimited No max	D Apr 5—Sep 28	pb	Oxbow Bend- Mammoth Bar	23 Off-river Flush
Adventure Connection 3,500	D May 1—Oct 31	pb, ob op, o/pa op	Oxbow Bend- Greenwood Br	16 On-river Porta
All- Outdoors 3,000	D May 1—Oct 26	pb	Oxbow Bend- Greenwood Br	16 On-river Porta
ARR No max	D Jun 1—Sep 30	pb, ob op	Oxbow Bend- Greenwood Br	16 On-river Porta
ARTA 4,000	Th, Sa Jun 1—Aug 31	pb, ob op	Oxbow Bend-Ruck- a-chucky	14 On-river Porta
A WW Connection 3,000	D May 1—Sep 30	ob, pb op	Oxbow Bend- Greenwood Br	16 On-river Porta
California River 3,000	D Jun 7—Sep 28	pb, ob op	Oxbow Bend-Ruck- a-chucky	14 On-river Porta
Charter River Adv. 2,500	Sa Jun 1—Aug 31	ob, pb op	Oxbow Bend-Ruck- a-chucky	14 On-river Porta

Recom. Require. Min. Age	Cost Max. Grp. Min. Grp.	Discounts	Transportation	Comments
Req: Wetsuit over 2500 cfs. Age: 12	$75 24 8	Less $10wd and less $7.50w/12+ and .5 Fw/12+		
Rec: Wetsuit until Jun 1. Req: Children must swim, like water. Age: 12	$74 35 6	Less $14wd and (less 10%w/10+ or 1 Fw/10 or less 30%y16)	Avail from LA for groups of 22+	Bus from LA, add $40-60
Req: Exp paddlers only through Tunnel Chute. Age: 12	$75 24 6	Less $20wd		Under 16 must walk around Tunnel Chute; ik op only after Tunnel Chute; client evaluation for running Tunnel Chute
Req: Healthy; active. Age: 12	$75 30 24	Less $10wd and 1 Fw/12		
Rec: Wetsuit May, Sep, Oct. Req: Exp. Age: 16	$91 33 33	1 Fw/25 and less $11wd and (less 10%w/12+ or less 10%y16)		Beer inc
Req: Wetsuit until Jun 1. Age: Call	$139 25 10	Less 10%w/11+	Avail from Sacramento	35# gear limit; van from Sacramento for 1-5, add $50
Rec: Wetsuit in Apr. Age: 13	$170 40 6	1 Fw/7-17 or 2 Fw/18-27 or 3 Fw/ 28-35 or 4 Fw/36	Avail from LA, Orange Cty	Bus from LA, Orange Cty (beer, wine inc), add $35; breakfast on day 1 inc; on-river op, porta
Rec: Wetsuit May, Oct. Age: 14	$175 70 12	1 Fw/12 and less $10w/24+ and less $10wd and less $10y15	Avail from LA	Breakfast day 1, 2 nights' camping, beer, wine inc; bus from LA, add $45; may portage Tunnel Chute
Req: Wetsuit until Jun 1. Age: Call	$169 30 25	1 Fw/12 and less $10wd		Portage Tunnel Chute
Rec: Wetsuit until Jun 30. Age: 12	$150 30 8	1 Fw/12		Beer, wine inc
Req: Paddling exp. Age: 12	$175 20 12	Less $20wd and less 10%w/10+ and 1Fw/20		
Age: Call	$175 35 12	Less $20wd and 1 Fw/12 and less $10w/24+	Avail from LA, SF	Bus from LA; add $50; bus from SF for 12+, add $40
Req: Exp. Age: 12	$165 24 12	1 Fw/6 and (less $10Fr or less $20Su-Th)		
Age: 12	$190 24 10	Less $15w/10+		Beer, wine, sleeping pads, tents (weather demanding) inc

River/Days/ Name	Starting	Raft type	Put-in– Take-out	Miles Camp Facilities
Earthtrek Expeditions 3,000	Sa May 24—Sep 13; Tu Jun 24—Aug 26	pb	Oxbow Bend-Greenwood Br	16 On-river Porta
James Henry 4,000	D May 1—Jul 31	pb	Oxbow Bend-Greenwood Br	16 Off-river Porta
Libra Expeditions No max	Mo-Th, Sa Apr 1—Oct 5	pb	Oxbow Bend-Greenwood Br	16 On-river Porta
Mariah 3,000	D Jun 1—Sep 30	pb	Oxbow Bend-Greenwood Br	16 On-river Porta
Nonesuch Whitewater 3,500	D May 1—Oct 31	pb, ob op, o/pa op	Oxbow Bend-Greenwood Br	16 On-river Porta
Pacific Adventures No max	D May 15—Sep 3	pb, ob op ia	Oxbow Bend-Ruck-a-chucky	14 On-river Porta
OARS 4,000	Th, Sa Jun 12—Sep 13	ob, pb op	Oxbow Bend-Ruck-a-chucky	14 On-river Porta
RAM River Expeditions 6,000	D May 1—Sep 30	ob, pb op, ik op	Oxbow Bend-Greenwood Br	16 On-river Porta
River Riders 3,000	D May 1—Sep 30	pb, ob op, ik op	Oxbow Bend-NF Confluence	25 On-river Porta
Rollinson 2,500	D Jun 1—Aug 31	pb	Oxbow Bend-Ruck-a-chucky	14 On-river Porta
Tributary Whitewater 2,500	D Mar 1—Oct 31	pb, ob op	Oxbow Bend-Ruck-a-chucky	14 On-river Porta
W.E.T. 2,500	D Jun 1—Oct 31	ob, pb op, o/pa op, ik op exp	Oxbow Bend-Ruck-a-chucky	14 On-river Porta
Whitewater Excitement 2,800	D May 1—Oct 31	pb	Oxbow Bend-Greenwood Br	16 On-river Porta

Recom. Require. Min. Age	Cost Max. Grp. Min. Grp.	Discounts	Transportation	Comments
Rec: Paddling exp. Age: 14	$175 40 12	Less $25wd and 1 Fw/15	Avail from Santa Ana, San Fernando Valley	Bus from Santa Ana, San Fernando Valley, add $54; 1 night motel inc
Req: Paddling exp; wetsuit until Jun 15. Age: 14	$170 24 6	Less $25wd and less 15%y16 and (1 Fw/12-15 and less 5%w/12-15) or (1 Fw/16- 24 and less 10%w/ 16-24)		Wine inc; gourmet; portage Tunnel Chute
Rec: Wetsuit Apr, May; good health; exp. Age: 14	$175 70 12	Less $10wd and 1 Fw/14 and less $10w/20 +	Avail from Anaheim, Irvine, Torrance, San Fernando Valley	Bus from Anaheim, Irvine, Torrance, San Fernando Valley, add $45; client evaluation for Tunnel Chute; portage Tunnel Chute above 2,500 cfs
Age: 15	$175 40 12	1 Fw/16 and less $20wd and less 10%y16		Breakfast day 1, prior night camping inc
Rec: Paddling exp. Age: 10	$160 24 8	Less 10%w/12 +		Portage Tunnel Chute above 2,700 cfs
Req: Active, healthy. Age: 12	$165 20 8	1 Fw/12		Orientation, night prior, at Coloma Country Inn op
Rec: Shorty wetsuit early Jun. Age: Call	$170 20 20	Less 10%w/11 +		Group minimum 12Th
Rec: Wetsuit May, Jun; good health. Age: 12	$145 30 6	1 Fw/12 and (less 10%w/8 + or less 15%w/20 +) or less $10y12		
Req: Good physical condition. Age: 10	$145 18 10	Less $10w/6 + and 1 Fw/10		Beer, wine inc
Req: Wetsuit over 2500 cfs. Age: 12	$155 24 8	Less $10wd and less $7.50w/12 + and .5 Fw/12 +		
Req: Children must swim, like water. Age: 12	$165 35 6	Less $35wd and (less 10%w/10 + or 1 Fw/10 or less 30%y16)	Avail from LA for groups of 22 +	Bus from LA, add $40-60
Req: Exp paddlers only through Tunnel Chute. Age: 12	$185 24 6	Less $20wd		Under 16 must walk around Tunnel Chute; ik op only after Tunnel Chute; client evaluation for running Tunnel Chute; wine, cocktails inc
Req: Healthy; active. Age: 12	$145 30 24	Less $10wd and 1 Fw/12		

River/Days/ Name	Starting	Raft type	Put-in— Take-out	Miles Camp Facilities
Whitewater Voyages 3,000	D May 1—Oct 31	pb	Oxbow Bend-Greenwood Br	16 On-river Porta
Wild River Tours 6,000	D May 1—Sep 30	pb	Oxbow Bend-Ruck-a-chucky	14 On-river Porta
Wild Water West, Ltd. No max	D Jun 1—Sep 30	pb	Oxbow Bend-Greenwood Br	16 On-river Porta
WW Rapid Transit 4,000	D Jun 1—Aug 30	ob s/b, pb s/b op	Oxbow Bend-Ruck-a-chucky	14 On-river Porta
Zephyr 2,500	D Jul 1—Sep 30	pb, ob op	Oxbow Bend-Ruck-a-chucky	14 On-river Porta

MIDDLE FORK OF THE AMERICAN—3 DAYS

River/Days/ Name	Starting	Raft type	Put-in— Take-out	Miles Camp Facilities
All-Outdoors 3,000	D May 1—Oct 26	pb	Oxbow Bend-Mammoth Bar	23 On-river Porta
James Henry 4,000	Mo-Fr May 1—Jul 31	pb	Oxbow Bend-NF Confluence	25 On-river Porta
Libra Expeditions No max	Mo-We Apr 1—Oct 5	pb	Oxbow Bend-NF Confluence	25 On-river Porta
RAM River Expeditions 6,000	D May 1—Sep 30	ob, pb op, ik op	Oxbow Bend-NF Confluence	25 On-river Porta
Tributary Whitewater 2,500	D Mar 1—Oct 31	pb, ob op	Oxbow Bend-NF Confluence	25 On-river Porta
W.E.T. 2,500	D Jun 1—Oct 31	ob, pb op, o/pa op, ik op exp	Oxbow Bend-Mammoth Bar	23 On-river Porta
Whitewater Voyages 3,000	D May 1—Oct 31	pb	Oxbow Bend-NF Confluence	25 On-river Porta

MIDDLE FORK OF THE AMERICAN—4 DAYS

River/Days/ Name	Starting	Raft type	Put-in— Take-out	Miles Camp Facilities
Libra Expeditions No max	Mo, Tu Apr 1—Oct 5	pb	Oxbow Bend-NF Confluence	25 On-river Porta

Recom. Require. Min. Age	Cost Max. Grp. Min. Grp.	Discounts	Transportation	Comments
Rec: Wetsuit May, Sep, Oct. Req: Exp. Age: 16	$184 33 33	1 Fw/25 and less $22wd and (less 10%w/12+ or less 10%y16)	Avail from LA	Cocktails inc; bus from LA, add $55; bus trip inc breakfast day 1
Age: 7	$155 24 6	Less 10%w/12+		Portage Tunnel Chute
Age: 12	$170 24 10	1 Fw/12 or 2 Fw/ 20		Beer, wine inc
Age: 12	$130 20 6	1Fw/12		
Age: 7	$185 30 10	Less $15wd		
Req: Wetsuit until Jun 1. Age: Call	$239 30 25	1 Fw/12 and less $15wd		Portage Tunnel Chute
Req: Paddling exp; wetsuit until Jun 15. Age: 14	$250 24 6	Less $40Mo-Th and less 15%y16 and (1 Fw/12-15 and less 5%w/12-15) or (1 Fw/16-24 and less 10%w/16-24)		Wine inc; gourmet; portage Tunnel Chute
Rec: Wetsuit Apr, May; good health; exp. Age: 14	$250 70 12	Less $10wd and 1 Fw/14 and less $10w/20+	Avail from LA area for 25+	Fishing for trout; bring gold pan; bus from LA area, add $50
Rec: Wetsuit May, Jun; good health. Age: 12	$210 30 6	1 Fw/12 and (less 10%w/8+ or less 15%w/20+) or less $10y12		
Req: Children must swim, like water. Age: 12	$220 35 6	Less $25wd and (less 10%w/10+ or 1 Fw/10 or less 30%y16)	Avail from LA for groups of 22+	Bus from LA, add $40-60
Rec: Camping exp. Req: Exp paddlers only through Tunnel Chute. Age: 12	$215 24 6	Less $20wd		Under 16 must walk around Tunnel Chute; ik op only after Tunnel Chute; client evaluation for running Tunnel Chute; wine, cocktails inc
Rec: Wetsuit May, Sep, Oct. Req: Exp. Age: 16	$260 33 33	1 Fw/25 and less $14wd and (less 10%w/12+ or less 10%y16)	Avail from LA	Cocktails inc; bus from LA, add $55; bus trip inc breakfast day 1
Rec: Wetsuit Apr, May; good health; exp. Age: 14	$280 70 12	Less $10wd and 1 Fw/14 and less $10w/20+		Layover, hiking day inc; fishing for trout; portage Tunnel Chute above 2,500 cfs

North Fork of the American

Introduction. The North Fork of the American is divided into two parts. The upper (Giant Gap) section, which will be commercially rafted for the first time in 1986, is an isolated, multi-day Class V expert run. The popular lower (Chamberlain Falls) section provides an exciting Class IV+ one-day trip.

Level of difficulty/water level concerns/flow information. Class IV+-V. A free-flowing, snow-melt fed, low-elevation river. Expect high water in May. The rafting season ends in June. High water on this river is especially hazardous. The minimum water to raft is about 500 cfs. For flow information, call (916) 322-3327. Listen for the inflow to Lake Clementine.

Permit system/time to raft. Commercial guides must complete three training trips on the river. Starts are limited to 18 companies per day; the outfitters are supposed to work together to ensure that this limit is not exceeded. Each outfitter may launch four boats per start, and each company has an assigned put-in time.

As the extremely difficult upper section will be new to many guides, rafters may wish to wait until after high water for their tours.

On the Chamberlain Falls section, demand follows the same pattern as that observed on the South and Middle Forks of the American. Ten times more rafters run on weekend days than on weekdays. Enough said. Chamberlain Falls also attracts large numbers of private rafters and kayakers, although they tend to run early in the season.

Commercial rafting. A recent study commissioned by the Bureau of Reclamation estimated that 2400 commercial passengers and 1000 private boaters ran the North Fork in the short 1985 season.

Gear/safety/who can come. Wetsuit, always, for both runs. Giant Gap requires a two-mile hike to the put-in; that section is suitable only for fit, healthy, and experienced rafters who can pass a swimming test. Chamberlain Falls rafters should have paddle rafting experience and some swimming ability.

Distinctive features. The North Fork of the American offers isolated, unspoiled river canyons only one hour from Sacramento. Easy access for outfitters as well as extensive competition keeps the cost of rafting low, especially in view of the need for well-qualified guides.

River access. Limited to the put-in and take-out points. The deep canyons make hiking out nearly impossible.

Environment. When you raft the North Fork, you voyage through deep, occasionally craggy canyons. Far above the river grow stands of ponderosa and sugar pine; you will also see several varieties of oak where the canyons widen.

—*Sierra Shutterbug/Paul Ratcliffe*
An oar boat with paddle assist prepares to run the Class IV + Chamberlain Falls of the North Fork of the American

Fishing Trout.

Summary of river between put-ins. Summarized with permission from *California White Water*. See that volume for two river maps and detailed descriptions of the rapids. See *A Guide to the Best Whitewater in the State of California* for the histories of several kayaking adventures in these waters.

Euchre Bar to Iowa Hill Road (Giant Gap section, 14 miles)—Several Class V rapids. Two-mile hike to the put-in.

Iowa Hill Road to Shirttail Canyon Creek (Chamberlain Falls section, 5 miles)—Four Class IV rapids, three Class IIIs.

Shirttail Canyon Creek to Ponderosa Way (4 miles)—Class II rapids.

Ponderosa Way to Lake Clementine (6 miles)—Class II rapids.

River status. The Chamberlain Falls section would be entirely flooded if the proposed $2.2 + billion Auburn Dam were built downstream (see the Middle Fork of the American). Also, some smaller hydroelectric

Abbreviations

Mo,Tu,We	Monday, Tuesday, Wednesday, etc.	porta	Porta-potty or lime can at camp
D	Daily	exp	(Rafting) experience
will call	Outfitter will call you to arrange dates	Camping exp	Camping experience
ob	Oar boat	F	Free
o/pa	Oar boat with paddle assist	w/	With
pb	Paddle boat	wd	Weekday
ik	Inflatable kayak	we	Weekend
s/b	Self-bailing	y	Youth
op	Optional	y16	Youth, age 16 and under
ia	If available or if appropriate	s	Senior
on-river	Camp is beside the river	s65	Senior, age 65 and over
off-river	Camp is not beside the river	inc	Included
lodge	Overnight at a lodge or motel	avail	Available
flush	Flush toilets at camp	#	pound
chem	Chemical toilets or outhouse at camp		

Name— Max. cfs	Starting	Raft type	Put-in— Take-out	Miles Camp Facilities
NORTH FORK OF THE AMERICAN—1 DAY				
Action Adventures 6,000	D May 15—Jul 1	pb, ob op, ik op ia exp	Iowa Hill Rd-Lake Clementine	15
Adventours Unlimited No max	D Apr 5—Jun 8	pb	Iowa Hill Rd-Shirttail Canyon	5
Adventure Connection 5,000	D Apr 1—Jun 30	pb ia, ob op, o/pa op	Iowa Hill Rd- Ponderosa Way	9
All- Outdoors 4,000	Apr 19, 20, 26, 27; May 3, 4, 10, 11, 17, 18, 24, 25, 26, 31; Jun 1, 7, 8, 14, 15	o/pa, pb op ia	Iowa Hill Rd- Ponderosa Way	9
ARR 6,000	D Apr 1—Jun 30	pb s/b, o/pa op	Iowa Hill Rd- Ponderosa Way	9

projects have been proposed for this river. Contact Friends of the River for further information.

Motels and lodges. Abbreviations used in the following listings are: L, R = Turn left, Turn right; H = Highway; I = Interstate; N, S, E, W = North, South, East, West; mi = miles; n/p = price or service not provided.

Best Western Golden Key Motel, 13450 E. Lincoln Way, Auburn, CA 95603. (916) 885-8611. Directions: I-5 to Sacramento; I-80 to Auburn; exit Foresthill Rd; R at 1st light, L on Lincoln Way. Cost per room for one: $32-38; for two: $36-42; for three: $40-42; for four: $42-44.

Bed and breakfast inns. Dry Creek Inn Bed and Breakfast, 13740 Dry Creek Rd, Auburn, CA 95603. (916) 878-0885. Directions: I-5 to Sacramento; I-80 to Auburn; exit Bell Rd; cross freeway, R on Haines Rd, L on Dry Creek Rd. Cost per room for one: $40-50; for two: $45-55; for three: n/p; for four: $100.

Private campgrounds. Morning Star Lake Resort. P.O. Box 119, Foresthill, CA 95631. (916) 367-2129. Open: Apr 25—Nov 1. Directions: I-5 to Sacramento; I-80 to Auburn; New Auburn-Foresthill Rd to 9.5 mi past Foresthill; take Rd 10 (Sugar Pine Rd) to Rd 24 to Rd 21, go ½ mi on Rd 21. Cost for tenters: $8; for RVs: $8; for showers: $1.50.

Public campgrounds. Bear River (Placer Cty Parks Dept). Directions: I-5 to Sacramento; I-80E to Colfax; Tokayana Way to Milk Ranch Rd (3 mi SW of Colfax).

Recom. Require. Min. Age	Cost Max. Grp. Min. Grp.	Discounts	Transportation	Comments
Rec: Exp 1986 season. Req: Wetsuit. Age: 13	$75 25 10	Less 10%w/11 +	Avail from Sacramento	Van from Sacramento for 1-5, add $50
Rec: Paddling exp. Req: Wetsuit. Age: 13	$80 32 6	1 Fw/7-17 or 2 Fw/18-27 or 3 Fw/ 28	Avail from LA, Orange Cty	Bus from LA, Orange Cty (beer, wine, off-river flush camp inc), add $35
Rec: Exp; good physical condition. Req: Wetsuit. Age: 14	$80 50 12	1 Fw/12 and less $10w/24 + and less $10wd		
Req: Wetsuit; exp. Age: 16	$78 21 21	1 Fw/12 and less $5wd		
Req: Wetsuit. Age: 16	$70 30 8	1 Fw/12		Beer, champagne inc

River/Days/ Name	Starting	Raft type	Put-in– Take-out	Miles Camp Facilities
ARTA 6,000	Sa, Su May 1—Jun 30	pb, o/pa op	Iowa Hill Rd- Ponderosa Way	9
A WW Connection 2,500	D Apr 1—Jul 15	ob, pb op, o/pa op	Iowa Hill Rd- Ponderosa Way	9
California River 5,500	D Apr 19—Jun 15	pb s/b, ob op	Iowa Hill Rd- Ponderosa Way	9
ECHO 7,000	D Apr 1—Jun 30	ob, pb op	Iowa Hill Rd- Ponderosa Way	9
Libra Expeditions 2,000	Apr 8, 10, 14, 17, 21, 23, 28; May 5, 12, 15, 18, 20, 25; Jun 1, 4, 7, 9, 11, 15, 17, 20, 25, 27	pb s/b	Euchre Bar-Iowa Hill Rd	14
Libra Expeditions 4,000	Mo-Th, Sa Apr 1—Jun 30	pb	Iowa Hill Rd-Shirttail Canyon	5
Mariah 5,000	D Apr 1—Jun 30	pb	Iowa Hill Rd- Ponderosa Way	9
NOC 2,500	D May 1—Jun 30	ob, pb op	Iowa Hill Rd- Ponderosa Way	9
Nonesuch Whitewater 3,500	D Apr 1—Jul 15	pb, o/pa op	Iowa Hill Rd- Ponderosa Way	9
OARS 3,000	Fr, Sa, Su, We May 2—Jul 30	ob, pb op	Iowa Hill Rd- Ponderosa Way	9
Outdoor Adv./UCD 3,500	Apr 19, 20, 26, 27; May 3, 4, 17, 18, 24, 25, 31; Jun 1, 7, 8	pb, o/pb op	Iowa Hill Rd- Ponderosa Way	9
Pacific Adventures No max	D Apr 15—Jun 15	pb s/b, ob s/b op	Iowa Hill Rd- Ponderosa Way	9
RAM River Expeditions No max	D Apr 1—Jun 30	ob, pb op	Iowa Hill Rd- Ponderosa Way	9
River Riders 3,000	D Apr 1—Jul 31	pb ia, ob op, o/pa op	Iowa Hill Rd- Ponderosa Way	9

Recom. Require. Min. Age	Cost Max. Grp. Min. Grp.	Discounts	Transportation	Comments
Req: Wetsuit; paddling exp. Age: 12	$80 24 12	Less 10%w/10 + and 1Fw/20		
Req: Exp for paddlers. Age: 12	$79 24 6	Less 15%wd and 1 Fw/12 and less $5w/18 +	Avail From SF	Beer, wine inc; bus from SF, add $25
Req: Wetsuit; exp. Age: 12	$70 24 6	1 Fw/6 and less $10wd and less $5w/o lunch		
Rec: Exp. Age: 12	$82 20 20	1 Fw/19 and less $7y17 and less $7w/8 +		
Req: Exp; wetsuit; Class V paddle test. Age: 16	$150 20 10	Less $20wd and 1 Fw/14 and less 10%w/20 +		
Rec: Exp. Req: Wetsuit; good health. Age: 14	$75 50 8	Less $10wd and 1 Fw/14 and less $10w/20 +		
Age: 15	$75 25 12	1 Fw/16 and less $20wd and less 10%y16		Breakfast inc
Rec: Above avg health; exp. Req: Wetsuit if water below 50 deg F. Age: 16	$70 24 6	(Less $5wd or less $5w/12 + or less $11w/12 + wd) and .5 Fy14		Lunch op, add $5
Req: Wetsuit until May 31; Class III paddling exp. Age: 12	$80 24 8	Less 10%w/12 +		
Rec: Shorty wetsuit until Jun 15. Age: 12	$85 20 20	Less $10wd and less 10%w/11 +		Group minimum 12 Fr, Su, We
Rec: Pb exp; good physical condition; able to swim. Req: Wetsuit. Age: 15	$36 24 10		Shuttle not inc	Food not inc
Req: Active, healthy. Age: 12	$75 20 8	1 Fw/12		Orientation, night prior, at Coloma Country Inn op
Rec: Wetsuit May, Jun; good health. Age: 12	$65 50 6	1 Fw/12 and (less 10%w/8-19 or less 15%w/20 +) or less $10y12		
Age: 10	$65 18 10	Less $10w/6 + and 1 Fw/10		Beer, wine inc; hike to Indian Falls

Name– Max. cfs	Starting	Raft type	Put-in– Take-out	Miles Camp Facilities
River Runners, Inc. 5,000	D Apr 1—Jul 15	pb, ob op	Iowa Hill Rd- Ponderosa Way	9
Rollinson 3,000	D May 1—Jun 30	pb	Iowa Hill Rd- Ponderosa Way	9
Rubicon 3,000	D Mar 1—Jun 15	pb	Iowa Hill Rd- Ponderosa Way	9
Tributary Whitewater 4,500	D Mar 1—Jun 30	pb, o/pa op	Iowa Hill Rd- Ponderosa Way	9
W.E.T. 4,500	D Apr 1—Jun 30	o/pa, pb op	Iowa Hill Rd- Ponderosa Way	9
Whitewater Excitement 4,000	D Apr 1—Jun 30	pb	Iowa Hill Rd- Ponderosa Way	9
Whitewater Voyages 5,000	D Apr 1—Jul 31	pb, ob op	Iowa Hill Rd- Ponderosa Way	9
Wild River Tours 4,000	D Apr 15—Jun 15	pb, ob op, o/pa op	Iowa Hill Rd- Ponderosa Way	9
Wild Water West, Ltd. 3,500	D Apr 26—Jun 30	pb	Iowa Hill Rd- Ponderosa Way	9
WW Rapid Transit 5,000	D Apr 1—Jun 15	ob s/b, pb s/b op	Iowa Hill Rd- Ponderosa Way	9

NORTH FORK OF THE AMERICAN—2 DAYS

Name– Max. cfs	Starting	Raft type	Put-in– Take-out	Miles Camp Facilities
Action Adventures 6,000	D May 15—Jul 1	pb, ob op, ik op ia exp	Iowa Hill Rd-Lake Clementine; Iowa Hill Rd-Ponderosa Way	24 On-river Chem
Adventours Unlimited No max	D Apr 5—Jun 8	pb	Iowa Hill Rd- Ponderosa Way	9 Off-river Flush
Adventure Connection 5,000	D Apr 1—Jun 30	pb ia, ob op, o/pa op	Iowa Hill Rd- Ponderosa Way; Iowa Hill Rd- Ponderosa Way	18 Off-river Porta
All- Outdoors 4,000	Apr 26; May 10, 17, 24, 31; Jun 7, 14	o/pa, pb op ia	Iowa Hill Rd- Ponderosa Way; Iowa Hill Rd- Ponderosa Way	18 Off-river Flush

Recom. Require. Min. Age	Cost Max. Grp. Min. Grp.	Discounts	Transportation	Comments
Req: Exp; wetsuit. Age: 12	$80 24 6	Less $5wd and less $10w/12+ and 1 Fw/20	Avail from LA	Dinner, live evening entertainment inc
Req: Wetsuit. Age: 14	$75 24 8	Less $10wd and less $7.50w/12+ and .5 Fw/12		
Rec: Exp. Req: Wetsuit. Age: 12	$70 25 10	1 Fw/12		
Rec: Wetsuit. Req: Children must swim, like water. Age: 12	$72 24 6	Less $12wd and (less 10%w/10+ or 1 Fw/10 or less 30%y16)	Avail from LA for groups of 22+	Bus from LA, add $40-60
Rec: Exp. Req: Wetsuit; exp for paddlers. Age: 16	$75 20 6	1 Fw/12		Client evaluation at put-in
Rec: Healthy; active. Req: Wetsuit. Age: 14	$70 24 24	Less $10wd and 1 Fw/12		
Req: Wetsuit; exp. Age: 14	$84 24 24	Less $10wd and (less 10%w/12+ or less 10%y16)		Beer inc
Rec: Wetsuit. Req: Exp. Age: 18	$75 25 6	Less 10%w/12+		
Req: Wetsuit. Age: 13	$77 28 10	(1 Fw/12 or 2 Fw/ 20) and less $10wd		
Rec: Wetsuit; exp. Age: 12	$65 20 6	1Fw/12	Inc from Sacramento	
Rec: Exp 1986 season. Req: Wetsuit. Age: 13	$139 25 10	Less 10%w/11+	Avail from Sacramento	Van from Sacramento for 1-5, add $50
Rec: Paddling exp. Req: Wetsuit. Age: 13	$180 32 6	1 Fw/7-17 or 2 Fw/18-27 or 3 Fw/ 28	Avail from LA, Orange Cty	Bus from LA, Orange Cty (beer, wine inc), add $35; breakfast on day 1 inc; on-river op, porta
Rec: Exp; good physical condition. Req: Wetsuit. Age: 14	$175 50 12	1 Fw/12 and less $10w/24+ and less $10wd	Avail from LA	Breakfast day 1, 2 nights' camping, beer, wine inc; bus from from LA, add $45; plane from LA for 10+, add $135
Req: Wetsuit; exp. Age: 16	$169 21 21	1 Fw/12 and less $10wd		

Name– Max. cfs	Starting	Raft type	Put-in– Take-out	Miles Camp Facilities
ARR 6,000	D Apr 1—Jun 30	pb s/b, o/pa op	Iowa Hill Rd- Ponderosa Way; Iowa Hill Rd- Ponderosa Way	18 On-river Porta
A WW **Connection** 2,500	D Apr 1—Jul 15	ob, pb op, o/pa op	Iowa Hill Rd- Ponderosa Way; Iowa Hill Rd- Ponderosa Way	18 Off-river Chem
Earthtrek **Expeditions** 5,000	Sa Apr 5—Jun 28	pb, o/pa op	Iowa Hill Rd- Ponderosa Way; Iowa Hill Rd- Ponderosa Way	18 Off-river Chem
Libra **Expeditions** 2,000	Apr 8, 10, 14, 17, 21, 23, 28; May 5, 12, 15, 18, 20, 25; Jun 1, 4, 7, 9, 11, 15, 17, 20, 25, 27	pb s/b	Euchre Bar-Iowa Hill Rd	14 On-river Porta
Libra **Expeditions** 4,000	Mo-Th, Sa Apr 1—Jun 30	pb	Iowa Hill Rd-Shirttail Canyon; Iowa Hill Rd-Shirttail Canyon	10 Off-river Flush
Mariah 5,000	D Apr 1—Jun 30	pb	Iowa Hill Rd- Ponderosa Way; Iowa Hill Rd- Ponderosa Way	18 Off-river Flush
Outdoors **Unlimited** No max	Apr 1, 7, 11, 19, 23, 30; May 8, 11, 13, 17, 19, 24, 26; Jun 2, 3, 5, 8, 10, 13, 15, 17, 19, 21, 23, 25	pb s/b	Euchre Bar-Iowa Hill Rd	14 On-river Porta
Outdoors **Unlimited** No max	Sa May 10—Jun 29	pb s/b	Iowa Hill Rd- Ponderosa Way; Iowa Hill Rd- Ponderosa Way	18 On-river Porta
River Riders 5,000	D Apr 1—Jul 31	pb, ob op, o/pa op	Iowa Hill Rd- Ponderosa Way; Iowa Hill Rd- Ponderosa Way	18 On-river Porta
Tributary **Whitewater**	D Mar 1—Jun 30	pb	Euchre Bar-Iowa Hill Rd	14 On-river Porta
Tributary **Whitewater** 4,500	D Mar 1—Jun 30	pb, o/pa op	Iowa Hill Rd- Ponderosa Way; Iowa Hill Rd- Ponderosa Way	18 Off-river Flush
W.E.T. 4,500	D Apr 1—Jun 30	o/pa, pb op	Iowa Hill Rd- Ponderosa Way; Iowa Hill Rd- Ponderosa Way	18 Off-river Porta
Whitewater **Excitement** 4,000	D Apr 1—Jun 30	pb	Iowa Hill Rd- Ponderosa Way; Iowa Hill Rd- Ponderosa Way	18 Off-river Flush

Recom. Require. Min. Age	Cost Max. Grp. Min. Grp.	Discounts	Transportation	Comments
Req: Wetsuit. Age: 16	$150 30 6	1 Fw/12		Beer, wine inc; off-river op, flush
Req: Exp for paddlers. Age: 12	$170 24 6	Less 15%wd and 1 Fw/12 and less $10w/24 +	Avail from SF	Beer, wine inc; bus from SF, add $40
Rec: Paddling exp. Req: Wetsuit. Age: 16	$175 20 12	Less $25wd and 1 Fw/15	Avail from Santa Ana, San Fernando Valley	Bus from Santa Ana and San Fernando Valley, add $54
Req: Exp; wetsuit; Class V paddle test. Age: 16	$285 20 10	Less $20wd and 1 Fw/14 and less 10%w/20 +		
Rec: Exp. Req: Good health; wetsuit. Age: 14	$175 50 8	Less $15wd and 1 Fw/14 and less $10w/20 +	Avail from Anaheim, Irvine, Torrance, San Fernando Valley	Bus from Anaheim, Irvine, Torrance, San Fernando Valley, add $45
Age: 15	$175 24 12	1 Fw/16 and less $20wd and less 10%y16		Breakfast day 1 inc
Rec: Wetsuit. Req: Paddling exp. Age: 10	$265 20 20	Less $20wd and 1 Fw/10 or (less 10%w/25 and 1 Fw/24)		Sleeping gear inc
Age: 10	$170 25 25	Less $20wd and 1 Fw/10 or (less 10%w/25 and 1 Fw/24)		
Rec: Wetsuit until Jun. Age: 10	$145 18 10	Less $10w/6 + and 1 Fw/10		Beer, wine inc; pb only below 4,000 cfs; pb subject to client evaluation
Rec: Wetsuit. Req: Children must swim, like water; wetsuit. Age: 12	$260 20 6	Less 10%w/10 + or 1 Fw/10 or less 30%y16	Avail from LA for groups of 22 +	Bus from LA, add $40-60
Rec: Wetsuit. Req: Children must swim, like water. Age: 12	$155 24 6	Less $30wd and (less 10%w/10 + or 1 Fw/10 or less 30%y16)	Avail from LA for groups of 22 +	Bus from LA, add $40-60
Rec: Fit, alert. Req: Class III exp; wetsuit. Age: 16	$175 20 6	1 Fw/12		Client evaluation at put-in
Rec: Healthy; active. Req: Wetsuit. Age: 14	$140 24 24	Less $10wd and 1 Fw/12		

Name– Max. cfs	Starting	Raft type	Put-in– Take-out	Miles Camp Facilities
Whitewater Voyages 2,000	Apr 4, 8, 11, 18, 25, 29; May 1, 9, 12, 13, 16, 22, 24, 26, 28, 31; Jun 6, 12, 14, 16, 19, 21, 26, 28	pb	Euchre Bar-Shirttail Canyon	19 On-river Porta
Whitewater Voyages 5,000	D Apr 1—Jul 31	pb, ob op	Iowa Hill Rd- Ponderosa Way; Iowa Hill Rd- Ponderosa Way	18 On-river Porta
Wild River Tours 4,000	D Apr 15—Jun 15	pb, ob op, o/pa op	Iowa Hill Rd- Ponderosa Way; Iowa Hill Rd- Ponderosa Way	18 Off-river Flush
Wild Water West, Ltd. 2,500	Apr 5, 18, 26; May 3, 10, 31; Jun 6, 7, 14, 21, 28	pb	Euchre Bar-Iowa Hill Rd	14 On-river Porta

NORTH FORK OF THE AMERICAN—3 DAYS ———

Name– Max. cfs	Starting	Raft type	Put-in– Take-out	Miles Camp Facilities
Libra Expeditions 2,000	Apr 8, 10, 14, 17, 21, 23, 28; May 5, 12, 15, 18, 20, 25; Jun 1, 4, 7, 9, 11, 15, 17, 20, 25, 27	pb s/b	Euchre Bar-Iowa Hill Rd	14 On-river Porta
Tributary Whitewater 2,000	D Mar 1—Jun 30	pb	Euchre Bar- Ponderosa Way	23 On-river Porta

NORTH FORK OF THE AMERICAN—4 DAYS ———

Name– Max. cfs	Starting	Raft type	Put-in– Take-out	Miles Camp Facilities
Libra Expeditions 2,000	Apr 8, 10, 14, 17, 21, 23, 28; May 5, 12, 15, 18, 20, 25; Jun 1, 4, 7, 9, 11, 15, 17, 20, 25, 27	pb s/b	Euchre Bar- Ponderosa Way	23 On-river Porta

North Fork of the Yuba

Introduction. The North Fork of the Yuba, which flows high in Tahoe National Forest, offers both Class V and Class III rafting in an all-green environment. Real limits on commercial passenger volume keep river traffic relatively low.

Level of difficulty/water level concerns/flow information.
Class III-V. A free-flowing, snow-melt fed river. High water (in May) creates rafting hazards in the section above Downieville. The season usually ends in June; the minimum water to raft is about 700 cfs. For flow information, call (916) 322-3327. Listen for the inflow into Bullard's Bar Reservoir: for the sections above Downieville, divide the flow by three; for the sections below Downieville, divide the flow by two.

Recom. Require. Min. Age	Cost Max. Grp. Min. Grp.	Discounts	Transportation	Comments
Req: Exp; Class V paddle test. Age: 16	$244 20 20	Less $20 Fr and less $46wd and (less 10%w/12+ or less 10%y16)	Avail from LA	Cocktails inc; 30# gear limit; camp gear inc; bus from LA, add $55; bus trip inc breakfast day 1
Req: Wetsuit; exp. Age: 14	$172 24 24	Less $5FrSu and less $30wd and (less 10%w/12+ or less 10%y16)	Avail from LA	Cocktails inc; bus from LA, add $55; bus trip inc breakfast day 1
Rec: Wetsuit. Req: Exp. Age: 18	$175 25 6	Less 10%w/12+		Lodge op, add $45
Req: Paddling exp; wetsuit. Age: 15	$250 20 10	1 Fw/12 or 2 Fw/ 18		Beer, wine inc
Req: Exp; wetsuit; Class V paddle test. Age: 16	$350 20 10	Less $20wd and 1 Fw/14 and less 10%w/20+		
Req: Children must swim, like water; wetsuit. Age: 12	$260 20 6	Less 10%w/10+ or 1 Fw/10 or less 30%y16	Avail from LA for groups of 22+	Bus from LA, add $40-60
Req: Exp; wetsuit; Class V paddle test. Age: 16	$415 20 10	Less $20wd and 1 Fw/14 and less 10%w/20+		

Permit system/time to raft. The three outfitters operating on the North Fork of the Yuba were selected by the Forest Service in 1982 using a bid prospectus system. Companies were evaluated on experience and professionalism. The three outfitters may carry commercial passengers within the following limits: each may have (a) only one start per day on each section, (b) a maximum of six rafts per start, and (c) no more than 700 rafters per season. The rafting season can be extended beyond July 1 only by permission of the Forest Service. However, it is not expected that any conflicts will arise requiring cancellation of July rafting (presuming that the water level allows July rafting).

The limits may cause weekend trips to fill early; contact the outfitters for information. If you raft on a weekend, you may have difficulty locating a campground or even hotel space for the night prior to your trip. The Yuba attracts many tourists and fishermen in addition to other river runners.

Abbreviations

Mo,Tu,We	Monday, Tuesday, Wednesday, etc.	porta	Porta-potty or lime can at camp
D	Daily	exp	(Rafting) experience
will call	Outfitter will call you to arrange dates	Camping exp	Camping experience
ob	Oar boat	F	Free
o/pa	Oar boat with paddle assist	w/	With
pb	Paddle boat	wd	Weekday
ik	Inflatable kayak	we	Weekend
s/b	Self-bailing	y	Youth
op	Optional	y16	Youth, age 16 and under
ia	If available or if appropriate	s	Senior
on-river	Camp is beside the river	s65	Senior, age 65 and over
off-river	Camp is not beside the river	inc	Included
lodge	Overnight at a lodge or motel	avail	Available
flush	Flush toilets at camp	#	pound
chem	Chemical toilets or outhouse at camp		

Name— Max. cfs	Starting	Raft type	Put-in— Take-out	Miles Camp Facilities
NORTH FORK OF THE YUBA—1 DAY				
Tributary **Whitewater** 3,000	D Apr 1—Jul 15	pb, ob op	Union Flat- Downieville	6
Tributary **Whitewater** 8,000	D Apr 1—Jul 15	pb, ob op	Goodyear's Bar- Indian Valley	7
Tributary **Whitewater** 8,000	D Apr 1—Jul 15	pb, ob op	Indian Valley- Bullard's Bar	13
Whitewater **Voyages** 8,000	D Apr 1—Jul 31	pb, ob op	Goodyear's Bar- Fiddle Creek	8
Whitewater **Voyages** 3,000	D Apr 1—Jun 30	pb, ob op	Union Flat- Goodyear's Bar	10
Wild Water **West, Ltd.** No max	D Apr 5—Jun 30	pb	Fiddle Creek- Bullard's Bar	12
Wild Water **West, Ltd.** No max	D Apr 5—Jun 30	pb	Goodyear's Bar- Fiddle Creek	8
Wild Water **West, Ltd.** 3,500	D Apr 5—Jun 30	pb	Union Flat- Goodyear's Bar	10
NORTH FORK OF THE YUBA—2 DAYS				
Tributary **Whitewater** 3,000	D Apr 1—Jul 15	pb, ob op	Union Flat-Indian Valley	17 On-river Porta
Tributary **Whitewater** 8,000	D Apr 1—Jul 15	pb, ob op	Goodyear's Bar- Bullard's Bar	20 On-river Porta

Commercial rafting. In 1985, three outfitters carried 1400 rafters down the North Fork of the Yuba.

Gear/safety/who can come. Yuba water runs extremely cold, and the air, too, is cold due to the river's high elevation. Rafters should therefore wear wetsuits the entire season. The multiple and in some areas continuous Class V rapids above Indian Valley require that rafters (a) be experienced, (b) be in excellent health, and (c) swim well. The Class III section below Indian Valley can be rafted by bold, adventuresome beginners.

Recom. Require. Min. Age	Cost Max. Grp. Min. Grp.	Discounts	Transportation	Comments
Req: Children must swim, like water; wetsuit. Age: 12	$75 42 6	Less $12wd and (less 10%w/10+ or 1 Fw/10 or less 30%y16)	Avail from LA for groups of 22+	Bus from LA, add $40-60
Req: Children must swim, like water; wetsuit. Age: 12	$75 42 6	Less $12wd and (less 10%w/10+ or 1 Fw/10 or less 30%y16)	Avail from LA for groups of 22+	Bus from LA, add $40-60
Req: Children must swim, like water; wetsuit. Age: 12	$75 42 6	Less $12wd and (less 10%w/10+ or 1 Fw/10 or less 30%y16)	Avail from LA for groups of 22+	Bus from LA, add $40-60
Rec: Wetsuit. Age: 12	$84 36 36	Less $10wd and (less 10%w/12+ or less 10%y16) and 1 Fw/25		Beer inc
Req: Exp; Class V paddle test; wetsuit. Age: 16	$98 36 36	Less $8wd and 1 Fw/25 and (less 10%w/12+ or less 10%y16)		Beer inc
Req: Wetsuit. Age: 12	$77 42 10	(1 Fw/12 or 2 Fw/ 20 or 3 Fw/30) and less $10wd		
Req: Wetsuit. Age: 12	$77 42 10	(1 Fw/12 or 2 Fw/ 20 or 3 Fw/30) and less $10wd		
Req: Wetsuit. Age: 14	$77 36 10	(1 Fw/12 or 2 Fw/ 20 or 3 Fw/30) and less $10wd		
Req: Children must swim, like water; wetsuit. Age: 12	$168 42 6	Less $33wd and (less 10%w/10+ or 1 Fw/10 or less 30%y16)	Avail from LA for groups of 22+	Bus from LA, add $40-60
Req: Children must swim, like water; wetsuit. Age: 12	$168 42 6	Less $33wd and (less 10%w/10+ or 1 Fw/10 or less 30%y16)	Avail from LA for groups of 22+	Bus from LA, add $40-60

Name– Max. cfs	Starting	Raft type	Put-in– Take-out	Miles Camp Facilities
Whitewater Voyages 8,000	D Apr 1—Jul 31	pb, ob op	Goodyear's Bar- Bullard's Bar	20 On-river Porta
Whitewater Voyages 3,000	D Apr 1—Jul 31	pb, ob op	Goodyear's Bar- Fiddle Creek; Union Flat-Goodyear's Bar	18 On-river Porta
Wild Water West, Ltd. No max	D Apr 5—Jun 30	pb	Goodyear's Bar- Bullard's Bar	20 On-river Porta
Wild Water West, Ltd. 3,500	D Apr 5—Jun 30	pb	Union Flat-Fiddle Creek	18 On-river Porta

NORTH FORK OF THE YUBA—3 DAYS ————————

Name– Max. cfs	Starting	Raft type	Put-in– Take-out	Miles Camp Facilities
Tributary Whitewater 3,000	D Apr 1—Jul 15	pb, ob op	Union Flat-Bullard's Bar	30 On-river Porta
Whitewater Voyages 3,000	D Apr 1—Jul 31	pb, ob op	Goodyear's Bar- Bullard's Bar; Union Flat-Goodyear's Bar	30 On-river Porta
Wild Water West, Ltd. 3,500	D Apr 5—Jun 30	pb	Union Flat-Bullard's Bar	30 On-river Porta

NORTH FORK OF THE YUBA—4 DAYS ————————

Name– Max. cfs	Starting	Raft type	Put-in– Take-out	Miles Camp Facilities
Wild Water West, Ltd. 2,500	D Apr 5—Jun 30	pb	Loganville-Bullard's Bar	35 On-river Porta

Distinctive features. The North Fork of the Yuba is only slightly farther from population centers than the North Fork of the American, yet the Yuba is relatively unknown and uncrowded.

River access. Highway 49 runs parallel to the river except below Fiddle Creek. Between Downieville and Indian Valley the road rises well above the river and is unobtrusive. Below Fiddle Creek the river diverges from the highway, and there is essentially no road access until the reservoir. In the other sections the road, campgrounds, and homes are all nearby.

Environment. The Yuba sports all shades of green. The river itself may run emerald, jade or kelly. The forests on both sides of the river include several varieties of pine, cedar, fir, and oak. To complete the effect, dark moss clings to the south shore trees, while olive-colored brush grows high on the north side of the canyon. Wild strawberries may be ripe during the rafting season, but you won't see them from the river.

Recom. Require. Min. Age	Cost Max. Grp. Min. Grp.	Discounts	Transportation	Comments
Rec: Wetsuit. Age: 12	$167 36 36	Less $10FrSu and less $40wd and 1 Fw/25 and (less 10%w/12 + or less 10%y16)	Avail from LA	Cocktails inc; bus from LA, add $55; bus trip inc breakfast day 1
Req: Class V paddle test; wetsuit. Age: 16	$180 36 36	Less $6FrSu and less $40wd and 1 Fw/25 and (less 10%w/12 + or less 10%y16)	Avail from LA	Cocktails inc; bus from LA, add $55; bus trip inc breakfast day 1
Req: Wetsuit. Age: 12	$165 42 10	(1 Fw/12 or 2 Fw/ 20 or 3 Fw/30) and less $15wd		Beer, wine inc
Req: Wetsuit. Age: 14	$165 36 10	(1 Fw/12 or 2 Fw/ 20 or 3 Fw/30) and less $15wd		Beer, wine inc
Req: Children must swim, like water; wetsuit. Age: 12	$230 42 6	Less $35wd and (less 10%w/10 + or 1 Fw/10 or less 30%y16)	Avail from LA for groups of 22 +	Bus from LA, add $40-60
Req: Wetsuit; Class V paddle test for paddlers. Age: 16	$255 36 36	Less $45Mo-We and 1 Fw/25 and (less 10%w/12 + or less 10%y16)	Avail from LA	Cocktails inc; bus from LA, add $55; bus trip inc breakfast day 1
Req: Wetsuit. Age: 14	$240 36 10	1 Fw/12 or 2 Fw/ 20 or 3 Fw/30		Beer, wine inc
Req: Wetsuit. Age: 14	$315 24 10	1 Fw/12 or 2 Fw/ 20		Beer, wine inc

What you may just see are some bald eagles; they nest around Bullard's Bar. Bring your binoculars or you may mistake a turkey vulture for our national symbol.

Fishing. Rainbow trout.

Summary of river between put-ins. Summarized with permission from *California White Water*, with further information from the Forest Service. See *California White Water* for some rapid descriptions as well as a river map from Union Flat to Fiddle Creek. To locate the river above and below that section, send $1 in check or money order, made out to USDA Forest Service, to USDA Forest Service, Office of Information, 630 Sansome Street, Room 529A, San Francisco, CA 94111. Request a Tahoe National Forest map.

Loganville to Union Flat (5 miles)—Class V rapids.

Union Flat to Downieville (6 miles)—Continuous Class IV - V rapids.

Downieville to Goodyear's Bar (4 miles)—A one-mile long set of Class V rapids.

Goodyear's Bar to Indian Valley (7 miles)—One Class V rapid (extremely hazardous: weak swimmers should walk around), three Class IV rapids.

Indian Valley to Fiddle Creek (1 mile)—Class III rapids.

Fiddle Creek to Bullard's Bar (12 miles)—Two Class IV rapids, many Class III rapids. Includes six miles (being towed) on the reservoir.

River status. The lower portion of this run is threatened by the Wambo Bar project, which would provide hydroelectricity and water storage. The project is currently in the feasibility stage. Political pressure could render this project infeasible. The person to contact is Sen. Alan Cranston (Senate Office Building, Washington, DC 20510).

Motels and lodges. Abbreviations used in the following listings are: L, R = Turn left, Turn right; H = Highway; I = Interstate; N, S, E, W = North, South, East, West; mi = miles; n/p = price or service not provided.

Herrington's Sierra Pines, Box 235 (Highway 49), Sierra City, CA 96125. (916) 862-1151. Directions: I-5 to Sacramento; I-80 to Auburn; H-49N to Sierra City (85 mi). Cost per room for one: $39-52; for two: $39-52; for three: $44-57; for four: $49-62.

Bed and breakfast inns. Murphy's Inn, 318 Neal St, Grass Valley, CA 95945. (916) 273-6873. Directions: I-5 to Sacramento; I-80 to Auburn; H-49N to Grass Valley (24 mi); exit Colfax-174; L at stop sign, L at Neal for 3 blocks. Cost per room for one: $38-78; for two: $48-88; for three: n/p; for four: n/p.

Flume's End Bed & Breakfast Inn, 317 S. Pine St, Nevada City, CA 95959. (916) 265-9665. Directions: I-5 to Sacramento; I-80 to Auburn; H-49N to Nevada City; exit Broad St; L on Pine. Cost per room for one: $40-50; for two: $65-85; for three: $95; for four: $130.

Annie Hooran's, 415 W Main St, Grass Valley, CA 95945. (916) 272-2418. Directions: I-5 to Sacramento; I-80 to H-49N; exit Central Grass Valley; L on S. Auburn, L on Main St. Cost per room for one: $54-81; for two: $54-81; for three: n/a; for four: n/a.

Sierra Shangri-La, Highway 49, Downieville, CA 95936. (916) 289-3455. Directions: I-5 to Sacramento; I-80 to Auburn; H-49N to Downieville. Cost per room for one: $55-100; for two: $55-100; for three: $65-110; for four: $75-120.

Private campgrounds. Sierra Skies RV Park. Highway 49, Sierra City, CA 96125. (916) 862-1166. Open: Apr 25—Oct 31. Directions: I-5 to Sacramento; I-80E to Auburn; H-49N to Sierra City. Cost for tenters: no tents; for RVs: $11; for showers: free.

Public campgrounds. Union Flat (Forest Service). Directions: I-5 to Sacramento; I-80E to Auburn; H-49N to 4 mi N of Downieville.

Indian Valley (Forest Service). Directions: I-5 to Sacramento; I-80E to Auburn; H-49N to 48 mi N of Nevada City.

Fiddle Creek (Forest Service). Directions: I-5 to Sacramento; I-80E to Auburn; H-49N to 46 mi N of Nevada City.

East Branch of the North Fork of the Feather

Introduction. This stretch of spring river includes two dramatically different river sections. The stark Class V upper section is suited for experienced rafters and self-confident swimmers, while the more scenic Class III lower section is suited for the isolation-seeking novice.

Level of difficulty/water level concerns/flow information. Upper section, Class V (below 2500 cfs, Class IV); lower section, Class III. The river is generally runnable until mid-June, with high water in late April and early May. For flow information, keep in contact with the outfitter.

Permit system/time to raft. At present, only one outfitter has a permit on this section. Because this river is underutilized, even by kayakers, the weekend is a fine time to raft.

Commercial rafting. In 1985, one outfitter took 50 passengers down the East Branch.

Gear/safety/who can come. Wetsuits always in the spring. Upper section rafters should be experienced, strong swimmers, capable of smiling through continuous Class V rapids. The lower section offers rapids easy enough for most beginners.

Distinctive features. The East Branch is the least-rafted snow-melt fed river in this book. This permits you to plan ahead for a rafting expedition, even on a weekend, and find that yours is the only party on the river.

River access. A highway runs along the length of the river, although in the lower section access to the road is sometimes difficult.

Sites of interest. A reopened nineteenth-century gold mine in the lower section.

Environment. The upper section of this run broke the rule that I never saw a free-flowing river I didn't like. Here both walls of a narrow and rocky river canyon have been carved out by man; a road runs along one wall and a railroad runs along the other, both a mere 20 feet above the river. Indeed, rocks that have fallen from the new walls appear to be responsible for many of the rapids. Only the barest minimum of vegetation survives near the river, although shrubs and some pine grow at the higher elevations.

In the lower section, however, the canyon widens and both the road and railroad rise about 100 feet. Ponderosa and yellow pines, willows, and oaks shade the yellow canyon walls, giving the area a resemblance to Yellowstone National Park.

Fishing. Rainbow and brown trout.

Summary of river between put-ins. Summary provided by Andrew Price of Trinity Wilderness Travel. For a brief description of the run, see *A Guide to the Best Whitewater in the State of California.* No river maps available; for a large-scale local map, send $1 in check or money order, made out to USDA Forest Service, to USDA Forest Service, Office of Information, 630 Sansome Street, Room 529A, San Francisco, CA 94111. Request a Plumas National Forest map.

Virgilia to Mill Creek (5 miles)—Above 2500 cfs, Two Class V rapids, many Class IVs. Below 2500 cfs, five Class IV rapids. Rapids generally continuous.

Mill Creek to Belden (5 miles)—One Class IV rapid, 15 Class IIIs.

River status. This section is unprotected, and there are no current threats to the river. However, on driving to the East Branch, river runners will observe a string of diversion dams and small reservoirs that have blocked and battered what must have been a beautiful canyon and fantastic kayaking run on the downstream North Fork. This section provides a

Abbreviations

Mo,Tu,We	Monday, Tuesday, Wednesday, etc.	porta	Porta-potty or lime can at camp
D	Daily	exp	(Rafting) experience
will call	Outfitter will call you to arrange dates	Camping exp	Camping experience
ob	Oar boat	F	Free
o/pa	Oar boat with paddle assist	w/	With
pb	Paddle boat	wd	Weekday
ik	Inflatable kayak	we	Weekend
s/b	Self-bailing	y	Youth
op	Optional	y16	Youth, age 16 and under
ia	If available or if appropriate	s	Senior
on-river	Camp is beside the river	s65	Senior, age 65 and over
off-river	Camp is not beside the river	inc	Included
lodge	Overnight at a lodge or motel	avail	Available
flush	Flush toilets at camp	#	pound
chem	Chemical toilets or outhouse at camp		

Name– Max. cfs	Starting	Raft type	Put-in– Take-out	Miles Camp Facilities
EAST BRANCH OF THE NORTH FORK OF THE FEATHER—1 DAY				
Trinity Wilderness No max	D Apr 5—Jun 8	pb, ob op	Mill Creek-Belden; Mill Creek-Belden	10
Trinity Wilderness 4,500	D Apr 5—Jun 8	ob, pb op exp ia	Virgilia-Belden	10

vision of what the Kyburz run of South Fork of the American (see *New Commercial Rivers for 1986*) may look like in the very near future.

Motels and lodges. Abbreviations used in the following listings are: L, R = Turn left, Turn right; H = Highway; I = Interstate; N, S, E, W = North, South, East, West; mi = miles; n/p = price or service not provided.

Pine Hill Motel, Highway 70, P.O. Box 3289, Quincy, CA 95971-3289. (916) 283-1670. Directions: I-5 to Sacramento; H-99N to H-70E to Quincy. Cost per room for one: $22-30; for two: $26-33; for three: $30-35; for four: $32-37.

Spanish Creek Motel, 233 Crescent-Highway 70, Quincy, CA 95971. (916) 283-1200. Directions: I-5 to Sacramento; H-99N to H-70E to Quincy. Cost per room for one: $28; for two: $34-38; for three: $43; for four: $60.

Bed and breakfast inns. The Feather Bed, 542 Jackson St, P.O. Box 3200, Quincy, CA 95971. (916) 283-0102. Directions: I-5 to Sacramento; H-99N to H-70E to Quincy. Cost per room for one: n/p; for two: $50-65; for three: n/p; for four: n/p.

Public campgrounds. Queen Lily (Forest Service). Directions: I-5 to Sacramento; H-99N to H-70E; 2 mi NE of Belden, take Caribou Rd N 2 mi.

North Fork (Forest Service). Directions: I-5 to Sacramento; H-99N to H-70E; 2 mi NE of Belden, take Caribou Rd N 2 mi.

Gansner Bar (Forest Service). Directions: I-5 to Sacramento; H-99N to H-70E; 2 mi NE of Belden, take Caribou Rd N ½ mi.

Belden (Forest Service). Directions: I-5 to Sacramento; H-99N to H-70E to Belden.

Recom. Require. Min. Age	Cost Max. Grp. Min. Grp.	Discounts	Transportation	Comments
Age: 10	$55 24 12	Less 10% for returnees or less 10%w/12 + or less 10%y16		
Rec: Exp. Req: Wetsuit. Age: 14	$55 16 8	Less 10% for returnees or less 10%w/12 +		Group max 24 in pb

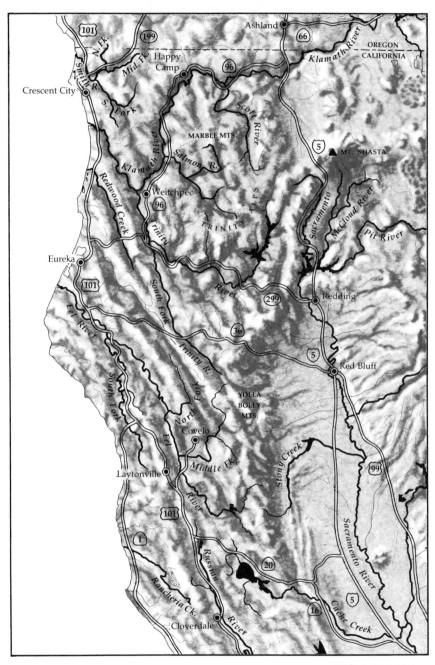

—California White Water

Rivers of the Coast Ranges

Eel (Pillsbury run)

Introduction. In the dark days of the winter, while snow still falls in the Sierras, the Eel can relieve your case of rafting fever.

Level of difficulty/water level concerns/flow information. Class III + (Class IV at the water level rafted by the one outfitter on this run). Dam-controlled, but releases sufficient for rafting come only when the reservoir is full. High water in December to March, depending on rain levels; raft in February and March. The outfitter reports that his company only rafts when the water level is above 2000 cfs. For flow information, call (916) 322-3327. Listen for the release from Lake Pillsbury.

Permit system/time to raft. No permits required.

Weekends are the best time to raft, as nearby roads are used extensively by noisy logging trucks during the week. Kayakers run this section all year—I saw a dozen die-hards on the river one Saturday last December.

Unless you have a minimum group size for rafting, contact the outfitter and ask to be placed on a will-call list.

Commercial rafting. In 1985, one outfitter took 30 people down this river.

Gear/safety/who can come. Full winter rafting gear: a heavy wetsuit, booties, gloves and mittens, wool sweater, windbreaker, and wool hat. This run is suitable only for the cold-proof, experienced rafter dressed for the weather. Some sections of continuous rapids make good swimming ability essential.

Distinctive features. A challenging winter run, a portion of which has substantial wilderness character.

River access. Poor-quality dirt roads run along both sides of the river. However, for the first five river miles the roads are high above the river and out of sight. For the last three miles of the run, the left-bank road sits about 30 feet above the river.

Environment. In this section, the Eel runs through a narrow green canyon, with sizable stands of fir on the south (left) bank, and oaks, willows, and more fir on the north bank. Deer, beaver, and otter may join you at the river; hawks, golden eagles and turkey vultures own the sky.

Fishing. Trout. Expect to see fishermen near the road access points at any season.

Summary of river between put-ins. Summary provided by Jim Cassady. See *California White Water* for a river map.

Elk Mountain Road Bridge to Eel River Road (8 miles)—Two Class IV rapids, six Class IIIs.

River status. This section has wild and scenic status.

See Main Eel for the trip description, lodgings, and campgrounds.

—*Rubicon Whitewater Adventures*

Paddlers exult in Class IV water on the Pillsbury run of the Eel

Main Eel

Introduction. This isolated, early spring river offers a wilderness experience suitable for beginners. If you want to show your scouts a wild river, and not just a wild ride, the Main Eel should be your choice.

Level of difficulty/water level concerns/flow information. Class III. Water levels vary dramatically depending on rainfall. The river will usually become too low to run sometime in May. Minimum water to raft is about 800 cfs. For flow information, call (916) 322-3327. Listen for the flow at Fort Seward.

Permit system/time to raft. No permits required.

You may find it difficult to book a tour without having a group of people who want to raft. Call the outfitter of your choice and ask how reservations are running. Be prepared to put your name on a will-call list.

The earlier in the season you plan your trip, the more likely you are to find sufficient water. Be prepared for rain. On the Main Eel, you have to consider time of day in addition to time of week and time of year. High upstream winds in the late spring afternoons can overpower both the current and a raft full of paddlers. So cooperate with the guides and get an early start in the morning, because you will want to leave the river by 2 p.m. Plan some activities for those long, well-lit afternoons (such as visiting some swimming holes).

Commercial rafting. No statistics available. Believed to be rafted in very small numbers.

Gear/safety/who can come. A river for all rafters, the Main Eel is comparable to the Lower Klamath but has fewer rafters, no roads, and no fishermen (except at the put-in). Bring your wetsuit, rain gear, and tent. The more adventurous may wish to travel by inflatable kayak.

Distinctive features. This river makes for an expedition far from the madding crowd. The valley and watershed are, geologically speaking, rather young. Persons with a strong interest and background in geology may wish to see *Rivers of the West* for more on the geology of the river and the region.

River access. No road access, except at put-in and take-out. However, a railroad runs along the river, which permits an easy way out in case of an emergency.

Sites of interest. Along your route you can still see evidence of the 1964 flood, during which the river went fifteen rounds with the trappings of civilization and won. Ask your guide to show you.

Environment. The emerald-green Main Eel flows through a broad valley of oak woodland. Numerous wildflowers blossom in spring, not only the more common ones, but also acacia, farmer's foxtails, hemlock, and buttercups. From time to time, you may see deer, otter, wild pigs, or rabbits. Hawks, ospreys, herons, and golden eagles will be on the look out for chow.

At night, you will settle in on broad, flat, sandy beaches. And so what if the coyotes howl. Who is the bigger coward, you or a coyote? Well, you're right. It depends on the coyote.

Summary of river between put-ins. Summarized with permission from *California White Water.* See that volume for a river map and river description.

Dos Rios to Alderpoint (47 miles)—Five Class III rapids, many Class IIs.

River status. The Main Eel has wild and scenic status.

Abbreviations

Mo,Tu,We	Monday, Tuesday, Wednesday, etc.	porta	Porta-potty or lime can at camp
D	Daily	exp	(Rafting) experience
will call	Outfitter will call you to arrange dates	Camping exp	Camping experience
ob	Oar boat	F	Free
o/pa	Oar boat with paddle assist	w/	With
pb	Paddle boat	wd	Weekday
ik	Inflatable kayak	we	Weekend
s/b	Self-bailing	y	Youth
op	Optional	y16	Youth, age 16 and under
ia	If available or if appropriate	s	Senior
on-river	Camp is beside the river	s65	Senior, age 65 and over
off-river	Camp is not beside the river	inc	Included
lodge	Overnight at a lodge or motel	avail	Available
flush	Flush toilets at camp	#	pound
chem	Chemical toilets or outhouse at camp		

Name– Max. cfs	Starting	Raft type	Put-in– Take-out	Miles Camp Facilities
PILLSBURY RUN OF THE EEL—1 DAY				
Rubicon 12,000	D Jan 1—Apr 30	pb, ob op, ik op ia	Elk Mtn Rd Br-Eel River Rd	8
MAIN EEL—3 DAYS				
River Country 3,000	Fr Apr 4—May 30	ob, pb op, ik op ia	Dos Rios-Alderpoint	47 On-river Porta
MAIN EEL—4 DAYS				
Orange Torpedo 7,000	May 1, 8	ik s/b, ob op	Dos Rios-Alderpoint	47 On-river Porta
Rubicon 25,000	D Apr 1—May 31	ik, ob op, pb op	Dos Rios-Alderpoint	47 On-river Porta
Trinity Wilderness No max	Apr 26; May 17	pb, ik op, ob op	Dos Rios-Alderpoint	47 On-river Porta
MAIN EEL—6 DAYS				
Action Adventures No max	D Jun 1—Aug 31	ik s/b	Dos Rios-Alderpoint	47 On-river Porta

Motels and lodges. Abbreviations used in the following listings are: L, R = Turn left, Turn right; H = Highway; I = Interstate; N, S, E, W = North, South, East, West; mi = miles; n/p = price or service not provided.

Skunk Train Motel, 500 S Main St, Willits, CA 95490. (707) 459-2302. Directions: H-101 to Willits; in center of town. Cost per room for one: $30-40; for two: $38-45; for three: $35-40; for four: $45-60.

Johnston's Motel, 839 Redwood Dr, Garberville, CA 95440. (707) 923-3327. Directions: H-101 to Garberville; exit opposite Beacon Gas Station sign. Cost per room for one: $25; for two: $27; for three: $34; for four: $36.

Best Western Humboldt House Inn, 701 Redwood Dr, Garberville, CA 95440. (707) 923-2771. Directions: H-101, exit Garberville. Cost per room for one: $34-43; for two: $39-48; for three: $43-53; for four: $48-58.

Motel Garberville, 948 Redwood Dr, Garberville, CA 95440. (707) 923-2422. Directions: H-101 to Garberville. Cost per room for one: n/p; for two: n/p; for three: n/p; for four: n/p.

Sherwood Forest Motel, 814 Redwood Dr, Garberville, CA 95440. (707) 923-2721. Directions: H-101 to Garberville. Cost per room for one: $30-38; for two: $32-62; for three: $36-60; for four: $40-62.

Private Campgrounds. Giant Redwoods RV & Campground. Avenue of the Giants, P.O. Box 222, Myers Flat, CA 95554. (707) 943-3198. Open: Apr-Nov. Directions: H-101 to Myers Flat; exit Avenue of the Giants; ¼ mi W at Myers Ave. Cost for tenters: $11 for 2; for RVs: $11-14 for 2; for showers: free.

Recom. Require. Min. Age	Cost Max. Grp. Min. Grp.	Discounts	Transportation	Comments
Rec: Wetsuit hood. Req: Full wetsuit; gloves; booties. Age: 15	$55 18 8	Less 10%w/12		
Age: 12	$215 15 5	1 Fw/10		
Age: 12	$350 12 8		Inc from Grants Pass, Eureka	Beer, wine inc; groups of 24 w/ 2 weeks' advance notice
Rec: Wetsuit. Age: 6	$280 30 8	1 Fw/10		Train shuttle from Willits for 20+ op, dinner inc, add $120
Age: 8	$245 25 12	Less 10% for returnees or less 10%w/12+ or less 10%y16		
Rec: Camping exp. Age: Call	$300 25 10	Less 10%w/11+ or less 25% w/ own canoe or kayak	Avail from Sacramento	35# gear limit; van from Sacramento for 1-5, add $100

Thompson's Campground. P.O. Box 672, Richardson's Grove, Garberville, CA 95440. (707) 247-3344. Open: Jun 1-Sep 15. Directions: 5 mi S of Garberville on H-101, .5 mi N of Richardson's Grove. Cost for tenters: $6; for RVs: $6; for showers: free.

Dean Creek Resort. P.O. Box 157, Redway, CA 95560. (707) 923-2555. Open: All Year. Directions: H-101 to Garberville; take Redwood Dr/Redway exit 3 mi N of city. Cost for tenters: $4 for 2; for RVs: $5 for 2; for showers: $2.50.

Ukiah-Willits KOA. Box 946, Willits, CA 95490. (707) 459-6179/(800) 551-CAMP. Open: All Year. Directions: H-101 to Willits; H-20W for 1.5 mi. Cost for tenters: $11.50 for 2; for RVs: $14.50 for 2; for showers: free.

Public campgrounds are available at Standish-Hickey State Recreation Area and at Richardson Grove State Park (both on H-101).

Middle Fork of the Eel

Introduction. In a truly remote wilderness area, your acute senses are not overwhelmed by the sounds and the smells of civilization and the highway. You can distinguish the calls of different birds, notice the noises of crickets, and breathe in the scent of wild grasses. The Middle Fork of the Eel carries you into just such a wilderness.

Level of difficulty/water level concerns/flow information. Class IV. May include one difficult portage. The free-flowing Middle Fork receives both snow-melt and rainwater: the abrupt appearance of the latter tends to cause the swift melting and therefore equally abrupt appearance of the former. Middle Fork flows are thus characterized by large, swift and unpredictable changes in water levels. The river peaks during the rainy season, sometime between December and March. The minimum water to raft is about 700 cfs. For flow information, call (916) 322-3327; the Middle Fork flows are approximately 50% of the flow at Fort Seward in the winter and 95% of the flow at Fort Seward in May. Keep in close contact with your outfitter about water levels.

Permit system/time to raft. No permits are required.

While commercial trips are rare, many private boaters are attracted by the beauty of the Middle Fork. Try a weekday to guarantee total isolation. Unless you have a minimum group yourself, contact your outfitter of choice and ask to be placed on a will-call list.

This river run is 30 miles long and includes a difficult potential portage: I strongly recommend running it over three days rather than two.

Commercial rafting. No statistics available.

Gear/safety/who can come. Rain may arrive at any time: take along your backpacking tent. Bring cold weather gear: wetsuit and wool sweater, gloves and wool mittens, wool hat, and booties. Bring sneakers, too, as you may have to walk around the Class V rapid (Coal Mine Falls), even if the boats go through. Important: Coal Mine Falls is a notorious consumer of equipment. If you bring a camera on the trip, carry it around the rapid. Finally, no matter what your outfitter's policy is on running Coal Mine Falls (and you should ask), a change in the water level may require a time-consuming, all-equipment portage. Therefore, only strong, healthy, rugged, wilderness lovers should be on this river.

Coal Mines Falls is a more hazardous rapid than the Tunnel Chute of the Middle Fork of the American. See that river description for extensive warnings on who should navigate such a rapid.

Distinctive features. Like the Middle Fork of the American, the Middle Fork of the Eel, at a superficial level, seems appropriate for no one level of rafter. For its first 26 miles, the river offers nothing more difficult than Class II rapids, suitable for beginners. However, the final four miles supply several major rapids and one very difficult potential portage.

Unlike the Middle Fork of the American, however, the Middle Fork of the Eel offers true immersion into the wilderness. Here no thousands of rafters float each year; no roads bring vans to the campgrounds; no cables help you around the portage; no photographers wait above the rapids. The peace one can find in such wilderness immersion is deserved by and suitable for anyone.

Should you require more action in the Class II section, ask your outfitter to bring along some inflatable kayaks; these can be deflated, rolled up, and stored in the raft for the final four miles.

River access. Forget it. Put-in and take-out only.

Environment. For this run's first 26 miles, the green, silt-filled river rolls through a broad valley of mixed firs and pines. An incredible array of wildflowers coats the hills: look especially for monkey flowers, lupines, and irises. Deer roam the area; otter and bear feed off the spawning salmon. In the final four miles, the valley narrows to a gorge. Side streams entering the gorge form bright waterfalls on both walls.

Summary of river between put-ins. Summary provided by Bill Mashek of Rubicon Whitewater Adventures. See *California White Water* for a river map.

Black Butte to Dos Rios (30 miles)—One Class V rapid, six Class III + s. Difficult potential portage.

River status. The Middle Fork of the Eel has wild and scenic status.

See Main Eel for lodgings and campgrounds.

Abbreviations

Mo,Tu,We	Monday, Tuesday, Wednesday, etc.	porta	Porta-potty or lime can at camp
D	Daily	exp	(Rafting) experience
will call	Outfitter will call you to arrange dates	Camping exp	Camping experience
ob	Oar boat	F	Free
o/pa	Oar boat with paddle assist	w/	With
pb	Paddle boat	wd	Weekday
ik	Inflatable kayak	we	Weekend
s/b	Self-bailing	y	Youth
op	Optional	y16	Youth, age 16 and under
ia	If available or if appropriate	s	Senior
on-river	Camp is beside the river	s65	Senior, age 65 and over
off-river	Camp is not beside the river	inc	Included
lodge	Overnight at a lodge or motel	avail	Available
flush	Flush toilets at camp	#	pound
chem	Chemical toilets or outhouse at camp		

Name– Max. cfs	Starting	Raft type	Put-in– Take-out	Miles Camp Facilities
MIDDLE FORK OF THE EEL—2 DAYS				
Nonesuch Whitewater 10,000	D Mar 1—May 15	pb, ob op, o/pa op	Black Butte-Dos Rios	30 On-river Porta
Rubicon 12,000	D Apr 1—May 15	pb, ob op	Black Butte-Dos Rios	30 On-river Porta
Turtle River 10,000	D Apr 1—May 3/will call	pb, o/pa op	Black Butte-Dos Rios	30 On-river Porta
WW Rapid Transit No max	D Apr 1—May 31/will call	pb s/b	Black Butte-Dos Rios	30 On-river Porta
MIDDLE FORK OF THE EEL—3 DAYS				
James Henry 4,000	D Apr 1—May 31	pb, ob op	Black Butte-Dos Rios	30 On-river Porta
Nonesuch Whitewater 10,000	D Mar 1—May 15	pb, ob op, o/pa op	Black Butte-Dos Rios	30 On-river Porta
Turtle River 10,000	Apr 18, D Apr 1—May 3/ will call	pb, o/pa op	Black Butte-Dos Rios	30 On-river Porta
Rubicon 12,000	D Apr 1—May 15	pb, ob op	Black Butte-Dos Rios	30 On-river Porta
WW Rapid Transit No max	D Apr 1—May 31/will call	pb s/b	Black Butte-Dos Rios	30 On-river Porta

Upper Sacramento

Introduction. When next you drive Interstate 5, where the highway hugs the mountains just north of Lake Shasta, glance frequently to your right. Every so often, through a break in the oak trees, you may see some of the finest underutilized intermediate whitewater in California. Yes, there, under your very nose.

Recom. Require. Min. Age	Cost Max. Grp. Min. Grp.	Discounts	Transportation	Comments
Rec: Wetsuit; rain gear, camping exp. Age: 10	$160 24 8	Less 10%w/12 +		
Rec: Good physical condition. Req: Wetsuit. Age: 14	$130 15 6	Less 10%w/12 +		
Age: 10	$130 20 6	(1 Fw/10 or .5 Fw/ 6) and less 25% before May 15 and less 20%y12		
Rec: Wetsuit; rain gear. Age: 6	$130 20 6	1 Fw/12		
Age: 7	$255 24 12	(Less 10%y16 or less 25%y12) and (1 Fw/12-15 and less 5%w/12-15) or (1 Fw/16 and less 10%w/16-24) and (less 20%y16 or less 25%y12)		Wine inc; natural history; gourmet
Rec: Wetsuit; rain gear, camping exp. Age: 10	$220 24 8	Less 10%w/12 +		
Age: 10	$195 20 6	(1 Fw/10 or .5 Fw/ 6) and less 25% before May 15 and less 20%y12		
Rec: Good physical condition. Req: Wetsuit. Age: 15	$200 15 6	Less 10%w/8 +		
Rec: Wetsuit; rain gear. Age: 6	$195 20 6	1Fw/12		

Level of difficulty/water level concerns/flow information.

Class III-IV. The dam upstream of this section destroyed a beautiful canyon but is too small to extend the rafting season (the dam did not even prove effective in its stated goal of flood prevention, but being a dam-builder means never having to say you're sorry). Expect high water in May and water too low for rafting by the end of June. For flow information, call (916) 322-3327. Listen for the release from Lake Siskiyou. The minimum water level for rafting occurs when the release from Lake Siskiyou is 400 cfs (the water level in the rafting run, downstream, will be higher)

Abbreviations

Mo,Tu,We	Monday, Tuesday, Wednesday, etc.	porta	Porta-potty or lime can at camp
D	Daily	exp	(Rafting) experience
will call	Outfitter will call you to arrange dates	Camping exp	Camping experience
ob	Oar boat	F	Free
o/pa	Oar boat with paddle assist	w/	With
pb	Paddle boat	wd	Weekday
ik	Inflatable kayak	we	Weekend
s/b	Self-bailing	y	Youth
op	Optional	y16	Youth, age 16 and under
ia	If available or if appropriate	s	Senior
on-river	Camp is beside the river	s65	Senior, age 65 and over
off-river	Camp is not beside the river	inc	Included
lodge	Overnight at a lodge or motel	avail	Available
flush	Flush toilets at camp	#	pound
chem	Chemical toilets or outhouse at camp		

Name– Max. cfs	Starting	Raft type	Put-in– Take-out	Miles Camp Facilities
UPPER SACRAMENTO—1 DAY				
Great Out of Doors 3,000	D Apr 1—Jun 30	pb, ob op, o/pa op, ik s/ b op	Sims Flat-La Moine	9
Wilderness Adventures No max	Sa, Su Apr 1—Jul 31	ob, pb op	Sims Flat-Dog Creek	14
UPPER SACRAMENTO—2 DAYS				
Great Out of Doors 3,000	D Apr 1—Jun 30	pb, ob op, o/pa op, ik s/ b op	Sims Flat-Dog Creek	14 On-river Porta
Headwaters No max	D Apr 1—Jul 15	pb, ob op, s/b op, o/pa op	Castle Crags-Dog Creek	23 On-river Porta
Turtle River No max	Apr 12, 19, 26; May 3, 10, 24	pb, ik s/b op, ob op, o/ pa op	Sims Flat-Dog Creek	14 Off-river Porta
Wilderness Adventures No max	Sa Apr 1—Jun 21	ob, pb op	Castle Crags-Dog Creek	23 On-river Porta
Wilderness Adventures No max	Apr 6, 13, 20, 27; May 4, 11, 18, 25, 26; Jun 1, 8, 15, 22	ob	Castle Crags-Dog Creek	23 On-river Porta
UPPER SACRAMENTO—3 DAYS				
Wilderness Adventures No max	Fr-Su Apr 4—Jun 15	ob	Castle Crags-Shasta Lake	32 On-river Porta

Permit system/time to raft. Permits are required, but there are no commercial limits to rafting. So, once your scout troop has mastered the Klamath or the Main Eel, here's an intermediate river that will take all of them.

Go ahead, select a weekend. No one else will be there.

Commercial rafting. In 1985, only 120 savvy commercial passengers rafted the Upper Sacramento. The rest of us chose crowded rivers with fewer rapids.

Gear/safety/who can come. Wetsuit all season. Non-swimmers should note the Class V rapid in the upper section. Beginners should consider rafting the lower section, from Sim's Flat to Dog Creek.

Distinctive features. This river offers fifty rapids of Class III or better, available with the easiest road access and the fastest shuttle of any river in the state. Not only is the whitewater extensive, but it's technical whitewater that requires twists, turns, and quick maneuvering on the part of the crew.

River access. Although Interstate 5 runs parallel to the river, vehicle

Recom. Require. Min. Age	Cost Max. Grp. Min. Grp.	Discounts	Transportation	Comments
Req: Wetsuit; rain gear. Age: 8	$55 25 10	Less 10%y12 and (1 Fw/12 or 2 Fw/ 23)		Fishing for trout
Age: 8	$45 50 6	1 Fw/12 or 2 Fw/ 20		
Req: Wetsuit; rain gear. Age: 8	$110 25 10	Less 10%y12 and (1 Fw/12 or 2 Fw/ 23)		Fishing for trout; off-river, flush op, add $7
Rec: Wetsuit. Age: 12	$150 25 15	Less 10%w/10 + and 1 Fw/20 or less 10%y16	Avail from Medford for 8 +	Bus from Medford, add $30
Req: Exp for ik. Age: 10	$120 25 6	(1 Fw/10 or .5 Fw/ 6) and less 25% before May 15 and less 20%y12	Shuttle is coop style	
Age: 12	$120 24 6	1 Fw/12 or 2 Fw/ 20		
Age: 16	$220 20 6	1 Fw/12		You-oar
Age: 16	$330 20 6	1 Fw/12		You-oar

access is limited to areas around some exits, where your may see fishermen and gold panners. In the event of an emergency, one could climb to the interstate for help. Rafters will be surprised by the apparent distance of the highway, as it hides behind a wall of oak for most of the length of the river. Sounds will carry, however, especially at night.

Sites of interest. Railroad trestles, dating from 1902, stand by the river. Trains to and from the Pacific Northwest still use the nearby tracks.

Environment. This is another river with a dual personality. On one side, the valley has been slashed by the interstate and the railroad, while on the other side the land survives in a nearly natural state. Expect to see deer and otter enjoying the clear, clean water. Goshawks and ospreys may fly by. You may even see a turkey (but be careful where you point when you shout, "Look Ma, a turkey!").

Unlike most California whitewater rivers, the Upper Sacramento supports forests of deciduous trees, such as black oak, willow, and canyon maple, in addition to the ubiquitous pines and Douglas fir. Dogwood trees blossom in spring, joining the wildflowers of the season—Indian rhubarb, violets, mustard grass, and rhododendra.

Fishing. And how. Rainbow and brown trout.

Summary of river between put-ins. Summary provided by Dean Munroe of Wilderness Adventures. See *California White Water* for a river map.

Castle Crags to Sims Flat (9 miles)—One Class V rapid (potential portage: ask your outfitter), one Class IV, 30 Class IIIs.

Sims Flat to La Moine (9 miles)—Ten Class III rapids.

La Moine to Dog Creek (5 miles)—Ten Class III rapids.

Dog Creek to Shasta Lake (9 miles)—Class II rapids. Includes eight miles on the reservoir (flat water).

River status. The river is not protected, but there are no current threats.

Motels and lodges. Abbreviations used in the following listings are: L, R = Turn left, Turn right; H = Highway; I = Interstate; N, S, E, W = North, South, East, West; mi = miles; n/p = price or service not provided.

Swiss Holiday Lodge Motel, Box 335, Mount Shasta, CA 96067. (916) 926-4587. Directions: I-5N past Dunsmuir to junction of I-5 and H-89. Cost per room for one: $21.95; for two: $25.95; for three: $31.95; for four: $34.95.

El Rancho Motel, 6604 Dunsmuir Ave, Dunsmuir, CA 96025. (916) 235-2884. Directions: I-5N to Dunsmuir; take first Dunsmuir exit. Cost per room for one: n/a; for two: $22; for three: $24; for four: $28.

Private Campgrounds. Lake Siskiyou Campground RV Park & Marina. W.A. Barr Rd, P.O. Box 276, Mt. Shasta, CA 96067. (916) 926-

2618/(800) 822-CAMP. Open: Apr-Oct. Directions: I-5N to Mt. Shasta; take Central Mt. Shasta exit; W to Old Stage Rd, S to fork of W.A. Barr Rd, bear right to entrance. Cost for tenters: $4 per person; for RVs: $6 per person; for showers: free.

Cave Springs Motel. 4727 Dunsmuir, Dunsmuir, CA 96025. (916) 235-2721. Open: All Year. Directions: I-5 to Dunsmuir; visible from freeway, N of ballpark. Cost for tenters: no tents; for RVs: $10; for showers: free.

Rustic Trailer Park. 910 Crag View, Dunsmuir, CA 96025. (916) 235-4330. Open: All Year. Directions: I-5 to Dunsmuir; exit Cragview Dr-Railroad Park; camp is ¼ mi N on Cragview Dr. Cost for tenters: no tents; for RVs: $9; for showers: $2.

KOA Mount Shasta. 900 N Mt. Shasta Blvd., Mt. Shasta, CA 96067. (916) 926-4029. Open: All Year. Directions: I-5 to Mt. Shasta; take Central Mt. Shasta exit; E 3 blocks, N .5 mi on N Mt. Shasta Blvd. Cost for tenters: $5.50 per person; for RVs: $5.50 per person; for showers: free.

Antlers Trailer Resort & Campground. P.O. Box 127, Lakehead, CA 96051. (916) 238-2322. Open: May-Sep. Directions: I-5 to Lakehead; take Antler's Lakeshore Exit; 1.5 mi S on Antler's Rd. Cost for tenters: $3.50 per person; for RVs: $6.25 per person; for showers: free.

Public Campgrounds. Pollard Flat (Forest Service). Directions: I-5N; 6 mi N of Lakehead.

Sims Flat (Forest Service). Directions: I-5N; 13 mi N of Lakehead.

Upper Trinity

Introduction. This scenic river, suitable for the adventure-seeking beginner, provides an attractive alternative to the South Fork of the American, one that is usually available all summer long.

Level of difficulty/water level concerns/flow information. Class III. The river is dam-controlled; daily releases are designed to provide sufficient water levels for fish. The river is raftable all summer long, but summer water levels may require small rafts. The minimum water to raft is about 500 cfs. For flow information, call (916) 322-3327. Listen for the flow at Hoopa, and take 60% of that amount.

Abbreviations

Mo,Tu,We	Monday, Tuesday, Wednesday, etc.	porta	Porta-potty or lime can at camp
D	Daily	exp	(Rafting) experience
will call	Outfitter will call you to arrange dates	Camping exp	Camping experience
ob	Oar boat	F	Free
o/pa	Oar boat with paddle assist	w/	With
pb	Paddle boat	wd	Weekday
ik	Inflatable kayak	we	Weekend
s/b	Self-bailing	y	Youth
op	Optional	y16	Youth, age 16 and under
ia	If available or if appropriate	s	Senior
on-river	Camp is beside the river	s65	Senior, age 65 and over
off-river	Camp is not beside the river	inc	Included
lodge	Overnight at a lodge or motel	avail	Available
flush	Flush toilets at camp	#	pound
chem	Chemical toilets or outhouse at camp		

Name– Max. cfs	Starting	Raft type	Put-in– Take-out	Miles Camp Facilities
UPPER TRINITY—1 DAY				
Great Out of Doors 8,000	D Mar 1—Sep 30	pb, ob op, ik s/b op	Pigeon Point-Big Flat	5
O.R.E. Inc. 20,000	D May 1—Aug 15	ob, pb op	Junction City-Big Flat	10
Rubicon 6,000	D Jun 1—Jul 31	ik, pb op	Pigeon Point-Big Bar	8
Trinity Wilderness No max	D Apr 5—Jun 29	pb, ik op, ob op	Pigeon Point-White's Bar	10
Wilderness Adventures No max	Sa, Su May 1—Nov 30	pb, ob op	Elkhorn Lodge-Big Flat	8
UPPER TRINITY—2 DAYS				
Great Out of Doors 8,000	D Mar 1—Sep 30	pb, ob op, ik s/b op	Junction City-Big Flat	10 On-river Flush
Headwaters 8,000	D Apr 1—Oct 31	pb, ob op, s/b op, o/pa op	Pigeon Point-Cedar Flat	24 On-river Porta
O.R.E. Inc. 20,000	D May 1—Aug 15	ob, pb op	Junction City-Hayden Flat	22 On-river Porta
Rubicon 6,000	D Jun 1—Jul 31	ik, pb op	Pigeon Point-Hayden Flat	17 On-river Chem
Tributary Whitewater No max	D Apr 1—Oct 31	pb, o/pa op, ob op	Pigeon Point-Cedar Flat	24 On-river Chem
Trinity River Raft 3,000	D May 15—Sep 13	pb, ik op	Junction City-French Creek	18 On-river Chem
Trinity Wilderness No max	D Apr 5—Jun 29	pb, ik op, ob op	Pigeon Point-Cedar Flat	24 On-river Porta
Wilderness Adventures No max	Sa Apr 5—Oct 25	ob	Pigeon Point-Cedar Flat	24 On-river Chem

Recom. Require. Min. Age	Cost Max. Grp. Min. Grp.	Discounts	Transportation	Comments
Age: 7	$45 50 12	Less $5y12 and 1 Fw/12 or 2 Fw/24 or 3 Fw/36		Bring gold pan
Req: Group of 12 +. Age: 8	$45 25 12	(Less 10%w/12 + and 1Fw/12) or less 10%w/3 immediate family members	Shuttle not inc	You-oar; Asian cooking; wine inc
Age: Call	$65 30 12	1 Fw/12 and less 10%w/20		
Age: 8	$55 25 12	Less 10% for returnees or less 10%w/12 + or less 10%y16		
Age: 12	$50 50 6	1 Fw/12 or 2 Fw/ 20		
Age: 7	$90 50 12	Less $10y12 and 1 Fw/12 or 2 Fw/24 or 3 Fw/36		Bring gold pan
Rec: Good health. Age: 8	$150 30 15	Less 10%w/10 + and 1 Fw/20 or less 10%y16		Handicapped
Age: 8	$170 25 12	(Less 10%w/12 + and 1Fw/12) or less 10%w/3 immediate family members	Shuttle not inc	You-oar; Asian cooking; wine inc
Age: Call	$90 30 12	1 Fw/12 and less 10%w/20		
Req: Children must swim, like water. Age: 12	$130 36 6	Less $20wd and (less 10%w/10 + or 1 Fw/10 or less 30%y16)		
Req: Exp if cfs over 800. Age: 7	$120 40 12	1 Fw/12 and less 20%w/20 + and (less 10% w/ payment 60 days in advance or less 5% w/ payment 30 days in advance)		Lodge op, add $30
Age: 8	$125 25 12	Less 10% for returnees or less 10%w/12 + or less 10%y16		
Age: 16	$245 20 6	1 Fw/15		You-oar

Permit system/time to raft. Like the Upper Sacramento, there are no usage limits, as demand has been rather limited. To raft an empty river, pick a weekday. [I will be rafting the Upper Trinity, along with some seniors, on a special charter tour with Great Out of Doors starting Monday, August 4. Call that company if you want to join us].

Commercial rafting. In 1985, 612 commercial passengers rafted the Upper Trinity, down from about 1000 in 1984. Most are multiple-day trips.

Gear/safety/who can come. Anyone can come. The more conservative boaters may wish to request the downstream portions of the river (see the summary of the river between put-ins, below). The more adventuresome may prefer an inflatable kayak. As the water runs rather cold, bring a wool sweater and a windbreaker, particularly if you will be traveling in an inflatable kayak.

Name– Max. cfs	Starting	Raft type	Put-in– Take-out	Miles Camp Facilities
UPPER TRINITY—3 DAYS				
Great Out of Doors 8,000	D Mar 1—Sep 30	pb, ob op, ik s/b op	Junction City-French Creek	18 On-river Flush
O.R.E. Inc. 20,000	D May 1—Aug 15	ob, pb op	Junction City-Cedar Flat	29 On-river Porta
Rubicon 6,000	D Jun 1—Jul 31	ik, pb op	Pigeon Point-Cedar Flat	24 On-river Chem
Tributary Whitewater No max	D Apr 1—Oct 31	pb, o/pa op, ob op	Pigeon Point-Cedar Flat	24 On-river Chem
Trinity River Raft 3,000	D May 15—Sep 13	pb, ik op	Junction City-Cedar Flat	29 On-river Chem
Wilderness Adventures No max	Fr, Sa May 1—Nov 30	ob, pb op	Pigeon Point-Cedar Flat	24 On-river Chem
UPPER TRINITY—4 DAYS				
Great Out of Doors 8,000	D Mar 1—Sep 30	pb, ob op, ik s/b op	Junction City-Cedar Flat	29 On-river Flush
UPPER TRINITY—5 DAYS				
Great Out of Doors 8,000	D Mar 1—Sep 30	pb, ob op, ik s/b op	Douglas City-Cedar Flat	39 On-river Flush

Distinctive features. Like the Lower Klamath, this is an all-season river suitable for novices. Compared with the Klamath, the Upper Trinity is somewhat more difficult in one (the upper) section, is more scenic, has cleaner water, and receives much less rafting traffic. On the other hand, the highway along the Upper Trinity comes closer to the river, and rafters will see more evidence of civilization, not to mention more fishermen.

River access. Highway 299 runs alongside the river, except between Douglas City and Junction City.

Sites of interest. Rafters can visit gold mining operations, both modern and historical. Better yet, bring along your gold pan. Unlike the lottery, it's free.

Environment. On some rivers you raft in a forest, on some in a canyon, and on others in a flower garden. Along the Upper Trinity, you will find all three environments along one river. Like the Upper Sacramento,

Recom. Require. Min. Age	Cost Max. Grp. Min. Grp.	Discounts	Transportation	Comments
Age: 7	$135 50 12	Less $10y12 and 1 Fw/12 or 2 Fw/24 or 3 Fw/36		Bring gold pan
Age: 8	$248 25 12	(Less 10%w/12 + and 1Fw/12) or less 10%w/3 immediate members	Shuttle not inc	You-oar; Asian cooking; wine inc
Age: Call	$135 30 12	1 Fw/12 and less 10%w/20		Handicapped
Req: Children must swim, like water. Age: 12	$185 36 6	Less $10wd and (less 10%w/10 + or 1 Fw/10 or less 30%y16)		
Req: Exp if cfs over 800. Age: 7	$180 40 12	1 Fw/12 and less 20%w/20 + and (less 10% w/ payment 60 days in advance or less 5% w/ payment 30 days in advance)		Lodge op, add $60
Age: 8	$210 30 8	1 Fw/12 or 2 Fw/ 20		
Age: 7	$180 50 12	Less $10y12 and 1 Fw/12 or 2 Fw/24 or 3 Fw/36		Bring gold pan
Age: 7	$225 50 12	Less $10y12 and 1 Fw/12 or 2 Fw/24 or 3 Fw/36		Bring gold pan

willows, alders, oaks and maples join the pine and fir. Black-tail deer visit the river, as do otter and bear (they like the fishing), egrets, kingfishers, and blue heron.

Fishing. In summer, king and silver salmon. In fall, steelhead trout join the salmon.

Summary of river between put-ins. Summary provided by Julie Buer of Great Out of Doors. A river map in *California White Water* covers the run from Pigeon Point to Cedar Flat.

Douglas City to Junction City (10 miles)—Flat water.

Junction City to Elkhorn Lodge (2 miles)—Flat water.

Elkhorn Lodge to Pigeon Point (3 miles)—Flat water.

Pigeon Point to Big Flat (5 miles)—Two Class III + rapids, five Class III rapids.

Big Flat to Big Bar (3 miles)—Class II rapids.

Big Bar to White's Bar (2 miles)—Class II rapids.

White's Bar to French Creek (3 miles)—Class II rapids.

French Creek to Hayden Flat (4 miles)—One Class II rapid.

Hayden Flat to Cedar Flat (7 miles)—Three Class II rapids.

River status. The Upper Trinity has wild and scenic status, under the "recreational" classification.

Motels and lodges. Abbreviations used in the following listings are: L, R = Turn left, Turn right; H = Highway; I = Interstate; N, S, E, W = North, South, East, West; mi = miles; n/p = price or service not provided.

Red Hill Motel, Box 234, Weaverville, CA 96093. (916) 623-4331. Directions: H-101 to H-299E to Weaverville; or I-5 to Redding to H-299W to Weaverville. Cost per room for one: $30; for two: $35; for three: $39; for four: $42.

Adams Motel Homes & Apartments, 304 Center St, Weaverville, CA 96093. (916) 623-4112. Directions: I-5 to Redding; H-299 for 42 mi; R on H-3 1 block. Cost per room for one: $25; for two: $25-30; for three: $30-35; for four: $30-40.

Hocker-Bartlett House, 807 Main St, Weaverville, CA 96093. (916) 623-4403. Directions: I-5 to Redding; H-299W to Weaverville. Cost per room for one: $40; for two: $46; for three: n/p; for four: n/p.

Private campgrounds. Elkhorn Motel & Trailer Park. P.O. Box 51, Helena, CA 96042. (916) 623-6318. Open: All Year. Directions: I-5 to Redding; H-299W for 65 mi; or H-101 to H-299E for 100 mi. Cost for tenters: $6; for RVs: $12; for showers: free.

Fantasy Mobile Home & RV Park. P.O. Box 68, Douglas City, CA 96024-0068. (916) 623-6640. Open: All Year. Directions: I-5 to Redding; H-299W for 37 mi; or H-101 to H-299E for 100 mi. Cost for tenters: $7; for RVs: $9.50; for showers: $2.50.

Indian Creek Trailer Park. P.O. Box 8, Douglas City, CA 96024-0008.

(916) 623-6332. Open: All Year. Directions: I-5 to Redding; H-299W for 35 mi; or H-101 to H-299E for 100 mi. Cost for tenters: no tents; for RVs: $10 for two; for showers: free.

Lazy Double "B" Park. Highway 299, Box 527, Salyer, CA 95563-0527. (916) 629-2156. Open: May-Nov. Directions: I-5 to Yreka; H-299W for 93 mi; or H-101 to H-299E for 46 mi. Cost for tenters: $10 for two; for RVs: $12; for showers: $2.

Public Campgrounds. Pigeon Point (Forest Service). Directions: I-5 to Redding; H-299W to 13 mi W of Weaverville.

Big Flat (Forest Service). Directions: I-5 to Redding; H-299W to 18 mi W of Weaverville.

Big Bar (Forest Service). Directions: I-5 to Redding; H-299W to 21 mi E of Weaverville.

Hayden Flat (Forest Service). Directions: I-5 to Redding; H-299W to 30 mi W of Weaverville.

Burnt Ranch (Forest Service). Directions: I-5 to Redding; H-299W to 41 mi W of Weaverville.

Gray's Falls (Forest Service). Directions: I-5 to Redding; H-299W to 44 mi W of Weaverville.

Burnt Ranch Gorge

Introduction. This section of the Trinity river, which is usually runnable all summer, provides one of the top paddle rafting challenges in the state.

Level of difficulty/water level concerns/flow information. Class V. Potential portages, a Class V hike to the campground, and Class IV scouting. The river is dam-controlled, with releases throughout the summer designed to meet the spawning needs of the native salmon (so the water levels are not lowered on the weekends). Burnt Ranch Gorge is too dangerous to run at high water, so you won't see rafters or even gonzo kayakers there until the flows get down to reasonable levels in the summer. The minimum water to raft is about 500 cfs. For flow information, call (916) 322-3327. Listen for the flow at Hoopa.

Permit system/time to raft. The Forest Service plans to limit rafting on Burnt Ranch Gorge to about five outfitters. Given the current volume of commercial traffic, this may not be too difficult. At present, only three companies have permits. The Forest Service does not evaluate companies that apply for permits on Burnt Ranch Gorge, but the outfitters must submit a plan outlining physical, skill, and experience requirements for passengers.

Commercial companies raft this section whenever an outfitter can scrape together enough people who want to make the run. If you are interested, call the outfitter of your choice and provide a range of weekends when you would be available. Let the outfitter put the group together; do not drag along one of your drinking buddies in order to make up a large enough group (See who can come, below). [I'm going to be rafting this section starting on August 2 with Wild Water West, so that's a definite start date. Call that outfitter if you want to come along.]

Ask your outfitter about the equipment that will be used on this section. (Review the appendix on boat types first.) On a river such as this, I prefer a self-bailing raft with foot cuffs or foot loops. The firmer floor of a self-bailer, combined with the cuffs or loops, helps prevent you from losing your footing, even while paddling down steep rapids. If you have done a lot of rafting in conventional boats (and you should have, if you are considering this river), you will recognize the problem of your feet sliding out from underneath you at the least desirable time.

Commercial rafting. In 1985, 74 optimists ran this river with two outfitters (Wild Water West and Whitewater Voyages). Of the 74, 16 took a one-day trip and the remainder took two-day trips. Outfitters do not advertise one-day trips.

Abbreviations

Mo,Tu,We	Monday, Tuesday, Wednesday, etc.	porta	Porta-potty or lime can at camp
D	Daily	exp	(Rafting) experience
will call	Outfitter will call you to arrange dates	Camping exp	Camping experience
ob	Oar boat	F	Free
o/pa	Oar boat with paddle assist	w/	With
pb	Paddle boat	wd	Weekday
ik	Inflatable kayak	we	Weekend
s/b	Self-bailing	y	Youth
op	Optional	y16	Youth, age 16 and under
ia	If available or if appropriate	s	Senior
on-river	Camp is beside the river	s65	Senior, age 65 and over
off-river	Camp is not beside the river	inc	Included
lodge	Overnight at a lodge or motel	avail	Available
flush	Flush toilets at camp	#	pound
chem	Chemical toilets or outhouse at camp		

Name– Max. cfs	Starting	Raft type	Put-in– Take-out	Miles Camp Facilities
BURNT RANCH GORGE—2 DAYS				
Headwaters 2,000	D Jun 1—Oct 31	pb	Cedar Flat-Hawkins Bar	8 Off-river Chem
Tributary Whitewater 2,000	D Jun 1—Oct 31	pb	China Slide-Hawkins Bar	9 Off-river Chem
Whitewater Voyages 3,000	D Jun 15—Sep 30	pb	Cedar Flat-Hawkins Bar	8 Off-river Porta
Wild Water West, Ltd. 2,500	D Jun 1—Sep 30	pb	Cedar Flat-Hawkins Bar	8 Off-river Chem

Gear/safety/who can come. Rafters should be mature, calm, fit, and good swimmers. You will have to take some kind of fitness test before getting on the river. Once you choose to raft, you're committed: your paddle team will need you, and the gorge won't let you out anyway. This is the home of paddle or die.

A couple of notes on gear: Whitewater Voyages recommends tennis shoes instead of booties on this run. This makes sense (a) because of the difficult hike to the campground, and (b) because when you spend two days running an eight-mile river, you are spending a lot of time out of the boat, looking at the river, instead of rafting it.

Also, the trail to the campground passes through what appears to be a poison oak farm. If you do not wear a full-length wetsuit, long pants may be a smart choice.

Distinctive features. This is one tough river. Burnt Ranch Gorge rapids are classical pool and drop, in contrast to the more technical continuous rapids of the Upper Tuolumne. However, no oar boats can be used in Burnt Ranch Gorge, because many of the chutes that must be navigated are too narrow for oar power. Oar boats with paddle assist have run this section, but they are not offered for 1986. If you have a strong preference for this option, discuss it with your outfitter.

River access. Good river access at put-in and take-out only. The highway may look close on a map, but it's an illusion. The road will be hundreds of feet up and out of sight by the time you realize you may not be ready for this run.

Environment. In this section, the Trinity passes through a deep gorge of rock and sand. Pine and fir grow well above the river. In some of the pool sections, you may see deer, otter, or bear.

Recom. Require. Min. Age	Cost Max. Grp. Min. Grp.	Discounts	Transportation	Comments
Req: Class V paddle test; wetsuit; pb exp on 2 Class IV + rivers. Age: 18	$230 15 10	Less 10%w/10 +		
Req: Class IV pb exp; physically active; good condition. Age: 18	$230 24 6	Less $40wd and (less 10%w/10 + or 1 Fw/10)		May portage Lower Burnt Ranch Falls or other rapids
Req: Exp; wetsuit; Class V paddle test. Age: 16	$198 20 20	(Less $16Mo-We and less $20Mo-We inc on-river) and (less 10%w/ 12 + or less 10%y16)	Avail from LA, SF	Cocktails inc; bus from LA, add $80; bus from SF, add $45; bus trip inc breakfast day 1; camp in gorge, on-river, add $44
Req: Paddling exp. Age: 15	$185 24 10	1 Fw/12 or 2 Fw/ 20	Avail from SF	Beer, wine inc; bus from SF, add $30

Fishing. Excellent. See Upper Trinity.

Summary of river between put-ins. Summarized with permission from *California White Water*. See that book for both the detailed descriptions of the rapids and the many caveats for river runners.

Cedar Flat to China Slide (1 miles)—Flat water.

China Slide to Hawkins Bar (8 miles)—Six Class V rapids, five Class IVs. Potential portage at one or more rapids.

River status. This section of the Trinity also has wild and scenic status.

See Upper Trinity for lodgings and campgrounds.

South Fork of the Trinity

Introduction. This rarely rafted wilderness river offers a Class V adventure. However, you will have to be flexible about your start times, because the South Fork of the Trinity is runnable for only a short time in the spring and after major storms.

Level of difficulty/water level concerns/flow information. Class V - Vp. Difficult portage. As water levels depend on recent rainfall, you won't have a lot of advance notice about when the river is runnable (usually in April and May). The minimum water to raft is about 600 cfs. For flow information, call (916) 322-3327. Listen for flow at Hoopa and divide it by four.

Permit system/time to raft. Outfitters on this river face no performance or experience requirements, no limits to group size and, indeed, no limits of any kind. For the two companies listed here, permits to run the river are attached as riders to their Upper Trinity permits.

The time to raft is really up to the river. If you are interested in this run, call one of the outfitters and put your name on a will-call list.

Commercial rafting. There were no commercial trips on this river in 1985, due to low water conditions. In 1984, 17 paying rafters took this trip with Great Out of Doors.

Gear/safety/who can come. Wetsuit. Experience is required, preferably Class V experience. On a trip such as this you are a full participant, not just a client or passenger. Bring along strength, stamina, and the need to participate.

Distinctive features. There are wilderness runs, and there are wilderness runs. See Middle Fork of the Eel. The South Fork of the Trinity is to the Middle Fork of the Eel as the Middle Fork of the Eel is to the Middle Fork of the American. You won't see anyone else on the South Fork of the Trinity, no matter when you run. Jim Cassady terms this river "remote and exotic", and that just about sums it up.

River access. You wanted an adventure, you've got it. No access except at put-in and take-out points.

Environment. The clear, blue-green waters of the South Fork pass through isolated meadows and rugged, deep canyons. Depending on the river section, you will find digger pine, Douglas fir, maple, and oak along the river, as well as (of course) assorted Coast Range wildflowers. Because of the good fishing, don't be surprised to see ospreys, blue heron, or even a bear.

Fishing. Salmon and steelhead trout. Ask your outfitter about when they will be running.

Summary of river between put-ins. Summary provided by Andrew Price of Trinity Wilderness Travel. See *California White Water* for a river map and an excellent river description.

Big Slide Campground to Underwood Creek (5 miles)—Above 2500 cfs, three Class V rapids, four Class IVs. Below 2500 cfs, seven Class IV rapids. Difficult portage.

Underwood Creek to Low Water Bridge (12 miles)—Above 2500 cfs, two Class V rapids, six Class IVs. Below 2500 cfs, eight Class IV rapids.

Low Water Bridge to Main Trinity (8 miles)—Class I rapids.

River status. This section also has wild and scenic status.
See Upper Trinity for lodgings and campgrounds.

Abbreviations

Mo,Tu,We	Monday, Tuesday, Wednesday, etc.	porta	Porta-potty or lime can at camp
D	Daily	exp	(Rafting) experience
will call	Outfitter will call you to arrange dates	Camping exp	Camping experience
ob	Oar boat	F	Free
o/pa	Oar boat with paddle assist	w/	With
pb	Paddle boat	wd	Weekday
ik	Inflatable kayak	we	Weekend
s/b	Self-bailing	y	Youth
op	Optional	y16	Youth, age 16 and under
ia	If available or if appropriate	s	Senior
on-river	Camp is beside the river	s65	Senior, age 65 and over
off-river	Camp is not beside the river	inc	Included
lodge	Overnight at a lodge or motel	avail	Available
flush	Flush toilets at camp	#	pound
chem	Chemical toilets or outhouse at camp		

Name– Max. cfs	Starting	Raft type	Put-in– Take-out	Miles Camp Facilities
SOUTH FORK OF THE TRINITY—2 DAYS				
Great Out of Doors 4,000	Will call	ob s/b, o/pa s/b op	Underwood Creek- Main Trinity	20 On-river Porta
Trinity Wilderness 4,000	D Apr 5—Jun 14	ob, pb op exp ia	Big Slide-Low Water Br	17 On-river Porta
SOUTH FORK OF THE TRINITY—3 DAYS				
Trinity Wilderness 4,000	D Apr 5—Jun 14	ob, pb op exp ia	Big Slide-Main Trinity	25 On-river Porta

California Salmon

Introduction. The Salmon (often referred to as the Cal Salmon to distinguish it from the Salmon river in Idaho) is one of the most popular Class V runs in the state, notorious for its big, exhilarating rapids.

Level of difficulty/water level concerns/flow information. Class III-V. Free-flowing. Fed by snow-melt and occasionally rain; the latter can cause water levels to change radically overnight. Expect high water in April and May.

The Salmon is hazardous at any water level and more so at high water. The Forest Service, which administers a start date allocation system based on historical use, does not penalize an outfitter for failing to start a trip if the water level exceeds 5000 cfs. I urge you to be conservative about the water levels at which you choose to raft this river.

The minimum water level for rafting is about 500 cfs, although again, the Forest Service will not penalize an outfitter for failure to start below 1000 cfs. For flow information, call (707) 443-9305. Listen for the Salmon river flow, provided during the season only.

Permit system/time to raft. Each company must complete two certification runs with Forest Service personnel to demonstrate boat-handling competency, safety techniques, the put-in talk, and equipment quality. At this time, dozens of outfitters have permits on this river, although many are not active.

Commercial groups are limited to 25 passengers and guides, and starts are limited to five per day, with the following exceptions: (a) any company may start on Monday, Tuesday, and Wednesday, and (b) during the busy period around Memorial Day, starts are limited to four per day.

Many private boaters and kayakers run this river, especially on weekends (Saturday is the busiest day) and from May 22 to June 2.

As previously noted, start dates are allocated on a historical use basis: companies with many Thursday through Sunday start dates have usually had the earliest and highest use of the river.

Recom. Require. Min. Age	Cost Max. Grp. Min. Grp.	Discounts	Transportation	Comments
Req: Wetsuit; rain gear. Age: 12	$175 20 8	1 Fw/12		
Req: Wetsuit. Age: 14	$155 16 12	Less 10% for returnees or less 10%w/12 +		Group max 24 in pb
Req: Wetsuit. Age: 14	$225 16 12	Less 10% for returnees or less 10%w/12 +		Group max 24 in pb

Commercial rafting. In 1985, 26 outfitters reported 2000 user days on this river. Because most trips are two days, this translates to approximately 1000 passengers. As these figures make obvious, many outfitters offered only one or two trips all season.

However, one thing you should be getting when you pay for a commercial rafting tour, especially on a Class V river, is a guide who is familiar with the vagaries of the river. The Salmon rearranges its rapids each spring, requiring a guide to relearn it every year. On the Salmon, I would not choose to join an outfitter's first trip of the season.

Contrast the experience of and challenge facing a guide on the Salmon with that of a guide on the Upper Tuolumne. Only one company runs the latter river, and the same guides lead trips four days a week all summer long. The upstream sections are dammed, so the water levels are relatively constant throughout the season. The run is not offered at high water.

On the Salmon, however, a guide may have the opportunity to run the river only once, twice, or thrice a year—a river that rearranges itself every spring and whose flows vary widely over the season.

The five largest rafting outfitters on the Salmon in 1985, in user-day volume as reported to the Klamath National Forest, were Ouzel Voyages, ECHO, Whitewater Voyages, Noah's, and Sierra Whitewater. Be aware that outfitters have the opportunity to overreport their passenger loads. That practice has certain advantages in a system where start date allocation depends on historical usage.

Gear/safety/who can come. Wetsuit always. Experienced rafters only. Do not consider this run unless you have real confidence in your swimming ability, as the big, powerful rapids on this river frequently flip boats. I have heard of trips run by three different outfitters where every single raft flipped. Before taking a tour on this river, be sure to carefully read the safety appendix to this book.

The Salmon is often the first advanced river attempted by commercial rafting passengers. This is appropriate, as the Salmon is easier and less technical than many other Class V rivers in the state (but on other rivers, boats flip less frequently). If this is your first Class V river, be cautious. Wait until after high water to raft. In addition, if the river will be your first this season, choose a tour that puts in well above Nordheimer Creek. This will give you the opportunity to review your paddling skills before facing the big rapids. Finally, you may wish to request an oar boat with paddle assist, so that if your desire to paddle is overcome by the difficulty of the river, the absence of your paddling power will not cause major maneuvering problems.

Abbreviations

Mo,Tu,We	Monday, Tuesday, Wednesday, etc.	porta	Porta-potty or lime can at camp
D	Daily	exp	(Rafting) experience
will call	Outfitter will call you to arrange dates	Camping exp	Camping experience
ob	Oar boat	F	Free
o/pa	Oar boat with paddle assist	w/	With
pb	Paddle boat	wd	Weekday
ik	Inflatable kayak	we	Weekend
s/b	Self-bailing	y	Youth
op	Optional	y16	Youth, age 16 and under
ia	If available or if appropriate	s	Senior
on-river	Camp is beside the river	s65	Senior, age 65 and over
off-river	Camp is not beside the river	inc	Included
lodge	Overnight at a lodge or motel	avail	Available
flush	Flush toilets at camp	#	pound
chem	Chemical toilets or outhouse at camp		

Name– Max. cfs	Starting	Raft type	Put-in– Take-out	Miles Camp Facilities
CAL SALMON—1 DAY				
All- Outdoors 5,000	May 1, 10, 17, 25; Jun 6, 8, 12, 14, 21, 24, 26, 29; Jul 3, 6, 12	o/pa	Nordheimer Crk- Butler Creek	7
ARR 5,000	Mo-We May 1—Jun 14; will call Apr, Jul	pb, o/pa op	Butler Creek-Dolan's Bar	13
Eagle Sun 5,000	Apr 26; May 3, 11, 17, 31	ob, pb op, o/pa op	Butler Creek-Dolan's Bar	13
Electric Rafting Co 5,000	May 4, 8, 15, 30; Jun 13, 20; Mo-We May 1—Jun 30	ob, pb op, o/pa op	Butler Creek-Ike Falls	10
Noah's 5,000	May 11, 18, 31; Jun 8, 15, 22, 29	o/pa s/b, pb s/b op exp ia	Nordheimer Crk- Wooley Creek	10
Ti Bar 6,000	Mo-We May 5—Jul 2; May 3, 8, 15, 18, 26, 29; Jun 1, 29, 30; Jul 4	o/pa	Butler Creek-Oak Bottom	7
Tributary Whitewater 4,500	May 3-7	pb, o/pa op, ob op	Nordheimer Crk-Oak Bottom	12
W.E.T. 5,000	Mo, Tu Apr 21-Jun 24; Jul 2, 8	o/pa	Nordheimer Crk-Oak Bottom	12

Distinctive features. This river features big, big rapids leading down into huge holes. If your idea of rafting is experiencing a wild ride, this is your river.

River access. A road sits well above the Salmon. Access is available at several points.

Sites of interest. Old mining claims.

Environment. The Salmon runs through a deep canyon walled with sheer granite cliffs. Look for black and tan oaks, Pacific madrone, Douglas and white fir, and pines.

Fishing. When they name a river the Salmon, and they call a rapid Steelhead Falls, you might be justified in thinking you should bring along your pole. Wrong again. For fishing, return in the fall, long after the rafting season is over.

Recom. Require. Min. Age	Cost Max. Grp. Min. Grp.	Discounts	Transportation	Comments
Req: Wetsuit; exp. Age: 16	$104 20 20	1 Fw/12 and less $7wd		
Rec: Wetsuit. Age: 16	$80 25 12	1 Fw/12		Beer, wine inc
Req: Class III exp. Age: 14	$100 24 6	Less 10%w/6 + and 1 Fw/8	Inc from Medford, Ashland	
Rec: Wetsuit; booties. Age: 14	$75 20 8	Less 10%w/12 + or less 10%s65 or less 10%y18	Inc from Eureka, Arcata	
Rec: Good health. Req: Wetsuit; excellent health for pb. Age: 14	$66 20 6	(Less 10%w/8 + or less 25%y17) and 1 Fw/12		
Rec: Exp; wetsuit. Age: 16	$50 25 4	1 Fw/6		
Req: Children must swim, like water. Age: 12	$85 25 6	Less $5wd and (less 10%w/10 + or 1 Fw/10 or less 30%y16)		
Req: Exp; wetsuit; hardy; fit; alert. Age: 16	$85 20 8	1 Fw/12		On-site client evaluation

Name— Max. cfs	Starting	Raft type	Put-in— Take-out	Miles Camp Facilities

CAL SALMON—2 DAYS ──────────────

Name— Max. cfs	Starting	Raft type	Put-in— Take-out	Miles Camp Facilities
Action Adventures 6,500	Fr, Sa, Su May 15, 22; Jun 1, 7; Mo-We May 12—Jun 18	ob, pb op, ik s/b op exp, o/pa op	Nordheimer Crk-Oak Bottom	12 On-river Porta
All- Outdoors 5,000	May 1, 10, 17, 25; Jun 3, 6, 8, 12, 14, 18, 21, 24, 26, 29; Jul 3, 6, 12	o/pa, pb op ia	Nordheimer Crk-Oak Bottom	12 Off-river Chem
ARR 5,000	Mo-We May 1—Jun 14; will call Apr, Jul	pb, o/pa op	Forks of Salmon-Oak Bottom	16 On-river Chem
Eagle Sun 5,000	Apr 26; May 3, 11, 17, 31	ob, pb op, o/pa op	Nordheimer Crk-Dolan's Bar	20 On-river Porta
Electric Rafting Co 5,000	May 4, 8, 15, 30; Jun 13, 20; Mo-We May 1—Jun 30	ob, pb op, o/pa op	Nordheimer Crk-Ike Falls	17 On-river Porta
Headwaters 4,200	Mo-We Apr 1—Jul 31; May 17, 24, 26, 30, 31; Jun 5, 26, 28; Jul 4	pb, ob op, s/b op, o/pa op	Nordheimer Crk-Orleans	21 On-river Porta
Great Out of Doors 6,000	Mo-We May 1—Jul 6; May 3, 5, 11, 17, 25, 27; Jun 7, 22, 29; Jul 1	ob s/b, o/pa s/b op	Butler Creek-Orleans	14 On-river Porta
KROE No max	Mo-We Apr 15—Jun 15	ob, pb op, o/pa op	Butler Creek-Dolan's Bar	13 On-river Porta
Noah's 5,000	May 11, 18, 24, 31; Jun 8, 11, 15, 18, 22, 25, 27, 29	o/pa s/b, pb s/b op exp ia	Nordheimer Crk-Dolan's Bar	20 On-river Porta
OARS 6,000	May 8, 15; Jun 9	ob, pb op	Nordheimer Crk-Orleans	21 On-river Porta
Outdoor Adv./UCD 5,000	Apr 26; May 10; Jul 3	pb, o/pb ob	Nordheimer Crk-Dolan's Bar	20 On-river Chem
Ouzel Outfitters 6,000	May 27, 28; Jun 20	ob, o/pa op, pb op ia	Nordheimer Crk-Oak Bottom	12 On-river Porta
Ouzel Voyages 5,600	May 3, 10, 17, 23, 24, 27, 30; Jun 5, 7, 19, 27; Jul 4; Mo-We May 1—Jul 2	o/pa, pb op exp ia	Nordheimer Crk-Orleans	21 On-river Porta

Recom. Require. Min. Age	Cost Max. Grp. Min. Grp.	Discounts	Transportation	Comments
Rec: Extensive exp. Req: Wetsuits. Age: 13	$199 25 10	Less 10%w/11+	Inc from Happy Camp; avail from Yreka	Van from Yreka for 1-5, add $50
Req: Wetsuit; exp. Age: 16	$219 20 20	1 Fw/12 and less $25wd		pb day 2 only
Req: Wetsuit. Age: 16	$170 25 12	1 Fw/12		Beer, wine inc
Req: Class III exp. Age: 14	$150 24 6	Less 10%w/6+ and 1 Fw/8	Inc from Medford, Ashland	Lodge op, add $25
Rec: Wetsuit; booties. Req: Strong swimmer; exp. Age: 14	$150 20 8	Less 10%w/12+ or less 10%s65 or less 10%y18	Inc from Eureka, Arcata	Lodge (dinner inc) op, add $40
Rec: Good physical condition; wetsuit. Req: Pb exp for paddlers. Age: 14	$200 20 15	Less 10%w/10+ and 1 Fw/19 or less 10%y16	Avail from Medford for 8+	Bus from Medford, add $40; lodge op, add $25
Req: Wetsuit. Age: 12	$175 20 8	1 Fw/12		
Req: Class IV exp; good physical condition; wetsuit. Age: 14	$200 25 3	Less 10%w/6-14 or less 15%w/ 15+		
Rec: Good health. Req: Wetsuit; excellent health for pb. Age: 14	$138 20 6	(Less 10%w/8+ or less 25%y17) and 1 Fw/12	Inc from Medford, Ashland, Yreka	Lodge w/ hot tub, May 11, 18, 24 or op, add $20
Rec: Wetsuit. Age: 12	$215 16 12	Less 10%w/11+		Lodge op, add $30
Rec: Pb exp; able to swim; good physical condition. Req: Wetsuit. Age: 15	$72 24 10		Shuttle not inc	Food op, add $10
Req: Exp for paddlers. Age: 16	$200 25 6	Less 10%w/12-17 or 1 Fw/12 or less 20%w/18+ or 2 Fw/18		Gourmet; Oregon wines inc
Rec: Class III exp. Req: Adventure exp; wetsuit or pile until Jun 15. Age: 16	$195 20 4	1 Fw/19 and (less 10%w/10+ or less 15%y15)		Lodge op, add $40

Name— Max. cfs	Starting	Raft type	Put-in— Take-out	Miles Camp Facilities
Sierra Whitewater 6,000	May 3, 17, 24, 25, 31; Jun 7, 27, 28; Jul 3, 4, 5, 6, 12	o/pa, pb op exp ia s/b	Butler Creek-Dolan's Bar	13 On-river Porta
Ti Bar 6,000	Mo-We May 5—Jul 2; May 3, 8, 15, 18, 26, 29; Jun 1, 29, 30; Jul 4	o/pa	Nordheimer Crk-Oak Bottom	12 On-river Chem
Tributary Whitewater 4,500	May 3-7	pb, o/pa op, ob op	Nordheimer Crk- Orleans	21 On-river
Trinity River Raft 3,330	May 22; Jun 7, 16, 30	pb	Nordheimer Crk-Oak Bottom	12 On-river Chem
Turtle River 5,000	May 8; Jun 6, 21; Mo-We Apr 1—Jun 30	pb s/b, o/pa op, ob op	Nordheimer Crk-Ike Falls	17 Off-river Chem
W.E.T. 5,000	Mo, We Apr 21-Jun 30; May 9; Jul 1, 7, 9	o/pa	Nordheimer Crk- Orleans	21 On-river Porta
Whitewater Excitement 3,500	May 3, 4, 19, 26, 27	pb s/b, ob op s/b	Forks of Salmon- Wooley Creek	14 On-river Porta
Whitewater Voyages 5,000	May 1, 2, 9, 10, 16, 24, 29, 30; Jun 5, 6, 13, 19, 20, 28; Jul 4, 7; Mo-We May 5—Jul 2	pb, ob op	Nordheimer Crk- Orleans	21 Off-river Porta
Wilderness Adventures No max	Apr 5, 12, 19, 26; May 5, 12, 17, 19, 25, 31; Jun 7, 9, 21, 23, 25, 28; Jul 3	o/pa	Methodist Creek- Oak Bottom	22 On-river Chem
Wild Water West, Ltd. 7,000	May 3, 23; Jun 7, 13, 21; Jul 5	pb	Nordheimer Crk- Orleans	21 On-river Porta

CAL SALMON—3 DAYS

Name— Max. cfs	Starting	Raft type	Put-in— Take-out	Miles Camp Facilities
Action Adventures 6,500	May 15, 22; Jun 1, 7; Mo- We May 12—Jun 18	ob, pb op, ik s/b op exp, o/pa op	Forks of Salmon- Orleans	25 On-river Porta
All- Outdoors 5,000	May 1, 10, 25; Jun 8, 14, 18, 26, 29; Jul 3, 6, 12	o/pa	Nordheimer Crk- Dolan's Bar	20 Off-river Chem
ARR 5,000	Mo-We May 1—Jun 14; will call Apr, Jul	pb, o/pa op	Forks of Salmon- Dolan's Bar	24 On-river Chem
ARTA 5,000	May 12, 24, 30; Jun 3, 13, 17, 20, 25; Jul 2, 11	o/pa, pb op ia, ob op	Nordheimer Crk- Dolan's Bar	20 Off-river Chem

Recom. Require. Min. Age	Cost Max. Grp. Min. Grp.	Discounts	Transportation	Comments
Rec: Wetsuit until Jun 15. Req: Wetsuit in May. Age: 12	$185 20 8	1 Fw/12 and less $20wd and (less 10%w/10+ or less 20%w/20 or less 20%y16)	Avail from Medford	Van from Medford, add $5
Rec: Exp; wetsuit. Age: 16	$150 25 4	1 Fw/6		Lodge op, add $45; on-river op, porta
Req: Children must swim, like water. Age: 12	$180 25 6	Less $15wd and (less 10%w/10+ or 1 Fw/10 or less 30%y16)		Lodge op, add $100
Rec: Exp; excellent swimmer. Req: Wetsuit. Age: 14	$120 20 8			
Rec: Exp. Age: 16	$130 20 6	(1 Fw/10 or .5 Fw/ 6) and less 25% before May 15 and less 20%y12	Shuttle is coop style	
Req: Exp; wetsuit; hardy; fit; alert. Age: 16	$175 20 8	1 Fw/12		On-site client evaluation
Rec: Healthy; active; exp. Req: Wetsuit. Age: 14	$170 20 20	1 Fw/12		
Req: Wetsuit; Class V paddle test for paddlers; exp. Age: 14	$226 20 20	Less $19Mo-We and (less 10%w/ 12+ or less 10%y16)	Avail from LA, SF	Cocktails inc; bus from LA, add $80; bus from SF, add $45; bus trip inc breakfast day 1; on-river, add $30; lodge w/ sauna, hot tub, add $40
Req: Wetsuit. Age: 16	$190 24 8	Less 10%w/12+ or 1 Fw/12		
Req: Wetsuit. Age: 15	$185 24 10	1 Fw/12 or 2 Fw/ 20	Avail from SF	Beer, wine inc; bus from SF, add $30
Rec: Extensive exp. Req: Wetsuit. Age: 13	$259 25 10	Less 10%w/11+	Inc from Happy Camp; avail from Yreka	Van from Yreka for 1-5, add $50
Req: Wetsuit; exp. Age: 16	$309 20 20	1 Fw/12 and less $25wd		
Req: Wetsuit. Age: 16	$235 30 12	1 Fw/12		Beer, wine inc
Req: Wetsuit in May, Jun. Age: 12	$290 20 12	Less 10%w/10+ and 1Fw/20		Lodge op Jun 3, 13, add $85

Name– Max. cfs	Starting	Raft type	Put-in– Take-out	Miles Camp Facilities
Electric Rafting Co 5,000	May 4, 8, 15, 30; Jun 13, 20; Mo-We May 1—Jun 30	ob, pb op, o/pa op	Methodist Creek-Ike Falls	27 On-river Porta
Get Wet River Trips 2,000	Jun 27, will call	ik s/b	Methodist Creek-Ike Falls	27 Off-river Flush
Great Out of Doors 6,000	Mo-We May 1—Jul 6; May 3, 5, 11, 17, 25, 27; Jun 7, 22, 29; Jul 1	ob s/b, o/pa s/b op	Nordheimer Crk- Orleans	21 On-river Porta
Headwaters 4,200	Mo-We Apr 1—Jul 31; May 17, 24, 26, 30, 31; Jun 5, 26, 28; Jul 4	pb, ob op, s/b op, o/pa op	Methodist Creek- Orleans	31 On-river Porta
Nonesuch Whitewater 5,000	May 9, 11; Jun 27, 28; Jul 5	pb	Methodist Creek- Oak Bottom	22 Off-river Chem
OARS 6,000	May 4, 11, 19, 23, 30; Jun 3, 6, 12, 14, 17, 21, 25, 30; Jul 3, 9	ob, pb op	Methodist Creek- Orleans	31 On-river Porta
Ouzel Outfitters 6,000	May 27, 28; Jun 20	ob, o/pa op, pb op ia	Methodist Creek- Orleans	31 On-river Porta
Ouzel Voyages 5,600	May 3, 10, 17, 23, 24, 27, 30; Jun 7, 19, 27; Mo-We May 1—Jul 2	o/pa, pb op exp ia	Methodist Creek- Orleans	31 On-river Porta
Rivers West 5,000	May 1, 2; Jun 27, Jul 6	pb, o/pa, ik s/b op exp	Methodist Creek- Nordheimer Crk; Butler Creek-Dolan's Bar	23 On-river Porta
Rubicon 10,000	Jun 7, 13, 20, 21, 23, 27; Jul 1, 6, 8	ob, pb op, ik op ia	Nordheimer Crk- Orleans	21 Off-river Chem
Sierra Whitewater 6,000	May 16, 23, 24, 30; Jun 6, 27; Jul 3, 4, 11	o/pa, pb op exp ia s/b	Forks of Salmon- Dolan's Bar	24 On-river Porta
Ti Bar 6,000	Mo-We May 5—Jul 2; May 3, 8, 15, 18, 26, 29; Jun 1, 29, 30; Jul 4	o/pa	Methodist Crk; Nordheimer Crk- Forks of Salmon; Oak Bottom	18 On-river Chem
Tributary Whitewater 4,500	May 3-7	pb, o/pa op, ob op	Methodist Creek- Orleans	31 On-river Chem

Recom. Require. Min. Age	Cost Max. Grp. Min. Grp.	Discounts	Transportation	Comments
Rec: Wetsuit; booties. Req: Strong swimmer; exp. Age: 14	$225 20 8	Less 10%w/12+ or less 10%s65 or less 10%y18	Inc from Eureka, Arcata	Lodge (meals inc) op, add $40; wine tasting trip May 30, add $30
Req: Ik exp; physically fit. Age: 12	$549 15 9	Less 5%w/8-11 or less 10%w/12+	Inc from Medford, Eureka	Boutique varietal wines, beer, sport shirts inc; lodge op, add $155
Req: Wetsuit. Age: 12	$225 20 8	1 Fw/12		
Rec: Good physical condition; wetsuit. Req: Pb exp for paddlers. Age: 14	$280 20 15	Less 10%w/10+ and 1 Fw/20 or less 10%y16	Avail from Medford for 8+	Bus from Medford, add $40; lodge op, add $50
Rec: Class IV paddling exp; wetsuit. Age: 12	$240 24 8	Less 10%w/12+		
Rec: Wetsuit May and early Jun. Age: 12	$295 16 16	Less 10%w/11+		Lodge op, add $60; group minimum 12wd
Req: Exp for paddlers. Age: 16	$275 25 6	Less 10%w/12-17 or 1 Fw/12 or less 20%w/18+ or 2 Fw/18		Gourmet; Oregon wines inc
Rec: Class III exp. Req: Wetsuit or pile until Jun 15; good health; active. Age: 16	$270 20 4	1 Fw/20 and (less 10%w/10+ or less 15%y15)		Lodge op, add $80
Age: 9	$265 12 6	Less 10%w/12+ and .75 Fw/12 or less 10% w/3 same family or less 10%y16		Gold panning avail w/ 3 wks advance notice
Rec: Exp. Req: Wetsuit; exp for paddlers. Age: 12	$259 24 8			1 night lodge op, add $55
Rec: Wetsuit until Jun 15. Req: Wetsuit in May. Age: 12	$270 20 8	(1 Fw/12 or 2 Fw/20) and less $20wd and (less 10%w/10+ or less 20%w/20 or less 20%y16)	Avail from Medford	Van from Medford, add $5
Rec: Exp; wetsuit. Age: 16	$195 25 4	1 Fw/6		Lodge op, add $90; on-river op, porta
Req: Children must swim, like water. Age: 12	$300 25 6	Less $50wd and (less 10%w/10+ or 1 Fw/10 or less 30%y16)		Lodge op, add $200

Name– Max. cfs	Starting	Raft type	Put-in– Take-out	Miles Camp Facilities
Whitewater **Voyages** 5,000	May 1, 2, 9, 10, 16, 24, 29, 30; Jun 5, 6, 13, 19, 20, 28; Jul 4, 7; Mo-We May 5—Jul 2	o/pa	Forks of Salmon- Orleans	25 Off-river Porta
Wild Water **West, Ltd.** 7,000	May 3, 23; Jun 7, 13, 21; Jul 5	pb	Methodist Creek- Orleans	31 On-river Porta

CAL SALMON—4 DAYS ─────────

Name– Max. cfs	Starting	Raft type	Put-in– Take-out	Miles Camp Facilities
Headwaters 4,200	Mo-We Apr 1—Jul 31; May 17, 24, 26, 30, 31; Jun 5, 26, 28; Jul 4	pb, ob op, s/b op, o/pa op	Methodist Creek- Orleans	31 On-river Porta
Rubicon 10,000	Jun 6, 12, 19, 20, 22, 26, 31; Jul 5, 7	ob, pb op, ik op ia	Forks of Salmon- Orleans	25 Off-river
Whitewater **Voyages** 5,000	May 1, 2, 9, 10, 16, 24, 29, 30; Jun 5, 6, 13, 19, 20, 28; Jul 4, 7; Mo-We May 5—Jul 2	pb, ob op	Methodist Creek- Orleans	31 Off-river Porta
Wild Water **West, Ltd.** 7,000	May 3, 23; Jun 7, 13, 21; Jul 5	pb	Methodist Creek- Orleans	31 On-river Porta

Summary of river between put-ins. Salmon river summary provided by Dean Munroe of Wilderness Adventures and Jim Cassady. Klamath river rapids summarized with permission from the *Handbook to the Klamath River Canyon*. See *California White Water* for rapid descriptions and for a river map from Forks of Salmon to Orleans.

Methodist Creek to Forks of Salmon (6 miles)—Class III rapids.

Forks of Salmon to Nordheimer Creek (4 miles)—15 Class II + rapids.

Nordheimer Creek to Butler Creek (7 miles)—Two Class V rapids, six Class IV + s.

Butler Creek to Wooley Creek (3 miles)—Six Class IV rapids. The actual take-out is just below Wooley Creek.

Wooley Creek to Oak Bottom (2 miles)—Class III rapids.

Oak Bottom to Ike Falls (5 miles)—One Class IV rapid, one Class III.

Ike Falls to Dolan's Bar (3 miles)—Three Class III rapids.

Dolan's Bar to Orleans (1 mile)—Class I rapids.

River status. The Salmon has wild and scenic status, under the "scenic" and "recreational" classifications.

Recom. Require. Min. Age	Cost Max. Grp. Min. Grp.	Discounts	Transportation	Comments
Req: Wetsuit; Class V paddle test for paddlers; exp. Age: 14	$277 25 20	Less $15MoTu and (less 10%w/12+ or less 10%y16)	Avail from LA, SF	Cocktails inc; bus from LA, add $80; bus from SF, add $45; bus trip inc breakfast day 1; on-river op, add $45; lodge w/ sauna, hot tub, add $81
Req: Wetsuit. Age: 15	$260 24 10	1 Fw/12 or 2 Fw/ 20	Avail from SF	Beer, wine inc; bus from SF, add $30
Rec: Good physical condition; wetsuit. Req: Pb exp for paddlers. Age: 14	$360 20 15	Less 10%w/10+ and 1 Fw/20 or less 10%y16	Avail from Medford for 8+	Bus from Medford, add $40; lodge op, add $75
Rec: Exp. Req: Wetsuit; exp for paddlers. Age: 12	$354 24 8			1 night lodge op, add $55; above 1500 cfs, put-in at Methodist Creek
Req: Wetsuit; Class V paddle test for paddlers; exp. Age: 14	$376 25 20	Less $34MoTu and (less 10%w/12+ or less 10%y16)		Cocktails inc; on-river op, add $60; lodge w/ sauna, hot tub op, add $120
Req: Wetsuit. Age: 15	$335 24 10	1 Fw/12 or 2 Fw/ 20	Avail from SF	Beer, wine inc; bus from SF, add $30

Motels and lodges. Abbreviations used in the following listings are: L, R = Turn left, Turn right; H = Highway; I = Interstate; N, S, E, W = North, South, East, West; mi = miles; n/p = price or service not provided.

Otter Bar Lodge, Forks of Salmon, CA 96031. (707) 444-3044. Directions: H-101 to H-299E; H-96 to Somes Bar; take Salmon River Rd for 15 mi; lodge is on right, 2 mi from Forks of Salmon. Cost per room for one: $100; for two: $200; for three: $300; for four: $400.

See also motels and lodges on the Lower Klamath.

Public campgrounds. Matthews Creek (Forest Service). Directions: I-5 or H-101 to H-299 to H-96N to Somes Bar; Salmon River Rd SE 28 mi.

Hotelling (Forest Service). Directions: I-5 or H-101 to H-299 to H-96N to Somes Bar; Salmon River Rd SE 22 mi.

Oak Bottom (Forest Service). Directions: I-5 or H-101 to H-299 to H-96N to Somes Bar; Salmon River Rd SE 3 mi.

—Turtle River Rafting

A paddle boat maneuvers through a Class V rapid on the Scott

Scott

Introduction. This underutilized river, called by one outfitter "a sister to the Salmon", has a slightly shorter season than its much more popular sibling. Experienced rafters will appreciate both the solitude and technical Class V challenge.

Level of difficulty/water level concerns/flow information. Class V. High water in late April and early May. The river is not always runnable in June. The minimum water level for rafting is about 600 cfs. For flow information, call (707) 443-9305. Listen for the Scott River flow.

Permit system/time to raft. Permittees on the Scott are required to complete the same on-river certification process as on the Salmon. However, as all current outfitters were Salmon-certified when they received their permits, that process was not repeated for the Scott.

There are no start date limitations for the Scott; groups are limited to 30 passengers and guides.

Go ahead and book for a weekend. Given the small numbers of passengers that have rafted the Scott in the past, be sure to ask the outfitter about how many reservations have already been made by others. See Chapter 5. Be prepared to change your start date or call several outfitters in order to find a group to join.

Commercial rafting. Only 100 user days were reported for the short 1985 season, or about 70 passengers.

Gear/safety/who can come. Wetsuit throughout the season. Experienced rafters and strong swimmers only.

Distinctive features. In contrast to the Salmon, the Scott has smaller, more technical rapids. Crews will be required to pivot and spin the boats through multiple boulder gardens.

River access. A road runs along the river, except through the canyon section between Kelsey Creek and McGuffy Creek.

Sites of interest. Gold mining flumes, dating from the 1850's.

Environment. Many sections of the Scott run through a broad

Abbreviations

Mo,Tu,We	Monday, Tuesday, Wednesday, etc.	porta	Porta-potty or lime can at camp
D	Daily	exp	(Rafting) experience
will call	Outfitter will call you to arrange dates	Camping exp	Camping experience
ob	Oar boat	F	Free
o/pa	Oar boat with paddle assist	w/	With
pb	Paddle boat	wd	Weekday
ik	Inflatable kayak	we	Weekend
s/b	Self-bailing	y	Youth
op	Optional	y16	Youth, age 16 and under
ia	If available or if appropriate	s	Senior
on-river	Camp is beside the river	s65	Senior, age 65 and over
off-river	Camp is not beside the river	inc	Included
lodge	Overnight at a lodge or motel	avail	Available
flush	Flush toilets at camp	#	pound
chem	Chemical toilets or outhouse at camp		

Name– Max. cfs	Starting	Raft type	Put-in– Take-out	Miles Camp Facilities
SCOTT—1 DAY				
All- Outdoors 4,500	Apr 26; May 3, 6, 15, 20, 23, 27, 30, 31; Jun 2, 4, 16	o/pa, pb op ia	Kelsey Creek-Scott Bar	10
Noah's 3,000	Apr 6, 20; May 17, 26, 30; Jun 7, 14	o/pa s/b, pb s/b op exp ia	Canyon Creek-Scott Bar	12
Rubicon 3,500	D May 1—May 31	ob, pb op	Kelsey Creek-Scott Bar	10
Tributary Whitewater 3,000	D Apr 1—Jul 15	pb, o/pa op, ob op	Kelsey Creek-Scott Bar	10
Turtle River 3,000	Sa, Su Apr 1—Jun 30	pb s/b, ob op, o/pa op	Kelsey Creek-Scott Bar	10
SCOTT—2 DAYS				
All- Outdoors 4,500	Apr 26; May 3, 6, 15, 20, 23, 27, 31; Jun 2, 4, 16	o/pa, pb op ia	Kelsey Creek-Sarah Totten	14 On-river Porta
Eagle Sun 3,000	Fr, Sa Apr 1—Jul 31	ob, pb op, o/pa op	Gaging Station- Sarah Totten	22 On-river Porta
Headwaters 3,000	D Apr 1—Jul 15	pb, ob op, s/b op, o/pa op	Canyon Creek-Sarah Totten	16 On-river Porta
Nonesuch Whitewater 3,500	D May 1—Jun 30	pb, o/pa op	Gaging Station- Scott Bar	18 On-river Chem
Ouzel Voyages 3,000	Jun 14, Jun 21	o/pa	Gaging Station- Klamath Conf	21 On-river Chem
Rubicon 3,500	D May 1—May 31	ob, pb op	Kelsey Creek-Scott Bar; Kelsey Creek- Scott Bar	20 On-river Chem
Tributary Whitewater 3,000	D Apr 1—Jul 15	pb, o/pa op, ob op	Indian Scotty-Sarah Totten	17 On-river Chem
Turtle River 3,000	Apr 26; May 10, 24; Jun 14, 28	pb s/b, ob op, o/pa op	Kelsey Creek-Scott Bar; Kelsey Creek- Scott Bar	20 Off-river Chem

Recom. Require. Min. Age	Cost Max. Grp. Min. Grp.	Discounts	Transportation	Comments
Req: Wetsuit; exp. Age: 10	$104 25 25	1 Fw/12 and less $7wd		
Rec: Good health. Req: Wetsuit; excellent health for pb. Age: 14	$66 16 6	(Less 10%w/8 + or less 25%y17) and 1 Fw/12	Inc from Medford, Ashland, Yreka	
Req: Wetsuit; exp. Age: 15	$85 15 8			
Req: Children must swim, like water. Age: 12	$85 25 6	Less $5wd and (less 10%w/10 + or 1 Fw/10 or less 30%y16)		
Rec: Exp. Age: 16	$65 20 6	(1 Fw/10 or .5 Fw/ 6) and less 25% before May 15 and less 20%y12		
Req: Wetsuit; exp. Age: 16	$219 25 25	1 Fw/12 and less $25wd		
Req: Class III exp. Age: 14	$150 24 6	Less 10%w/6 + and 1 Fw/8	Inc from Medford, Ashland	
Rec: Good physical condition; wetsuit. Req: Pb exp for paddlers. Age: 14	$200 20 15	Less 10%w/10 + and 1 Fw/19 or less 10%y16	Avail from Medford for 8 +	Bus from Medford, add $30
Req: Class IV paddling exp. Age: 12	$180 24 8	Less 10%w/12 +		
Rec: Good swimmer. Req: Class IV exp; wetsuit or pile. Age: 16	$195 20 4	1 Fw/19 and less 10%w/10 +		
Req: Wetsuit; exp. Age: 15	$170 15 8			
Req: Children must swim, like water. Age: 12	$180 25 6	Less $15wd and (less 10%w/10 + or 1 Fw/10 or less 30%y16)		
Rec: Exp. Age: 16	$130 20 6	(1 Fw/10 or .5 Fw/ 6) and less 25% before May 15 and less 20%y12		

Name– Max. cfs	Starting	Raft type	Put-in– Take-out	Miles Camp Facilities
W.E.T. 4,000	D Apr 1—Jun 30	o/pa	Indian Scotty-Sarah Totten	17 On-river Porta
Whitewater Voyages 3,000	D Apr 1—Jul 31	pb, ob op	Gaging Station- Scott Bar	18 On-river Porta
Wilderness Adventures No max	Sa Apr 5—Jun 21	ob, o/pa op	Indian Scotty- Klamath Conf	16 On-river Porta
Wild Water West, Ltd. 3,000	May 10, 17; Jun 7	pb	Gaging Station- Klamath Conf	21 On-river Chem
WW Rapid Transit 4,000	D May 1—Jun 30	pb s/b, ob s/b op	Kelsey Creek- Klamath Conf	13 On-river Porta

SCOTT—3 DAYS

Name– Max. cfs	Starting	Raft type	Put-in– Take-out	Miles Camp Facilities
All-Outdoors 4,500	May 6, 20, 30; Jun 2, 16	o/pa, pb op ia	Gaging Station- Sarah Totten	22 On-river Porta
Tributary Whitewater 3,000	D Apr 1—Jul 15	pb, o/pa op, ob op	Indian Scotty-Sarah Totten	17 On-river Chem
Turtle River 3,000	Apr 25; May 9, 23; Jun 13, 27	pb s/b, ob op, o/pa op	Gaging Station- Indian Scotty; Kelsey Creek-Scott Bar; Kelsey Creek-Scott Bar	25 On-river Chem

valley forested with fir and madrone. Acres of wild azaleas grow in the canyon: you will smell their sweet aroma from miles away. Ospreys, geese, bald eagles, and black-tail deer also visit the river.

Fishing. Come back in the fall.

Summary of river between put-ins. Summarized with permission from *California White Water* with further information from Jim Cassady. See that book for a river map and description of the major rapids.

Scott Gaging Station to Jones Beach (4 miles)—Class III rapids.
Jones Beach to Indian Scotty (1 mile)—Class IV rapids.
Indian Scotty to Canyon Creek (1 mile)—One Class V rapid, one Class IV.
Canyon Creek to Kelsey Creek (2 miles)—Class IV rapids.
Kelsey Creek to McGuffy Creek (7 miles)—Three Class V rapids.
McGuffy Creek to Scott Bar (3 miles)—Class III rapids.
Scott Bar to Klamath Confluence (3 miles)—Class III rapids.
Klamath Confluence to Sarah Totten (1 mile)—One Class III rapid.

River status. The Scott has wild and scenic status.

Recom. Require. Min. Age	Cost Max. Grp. Min. Grp.	Discounts	Transportation	Comments
Rec: Good health. Req: Class IV exp; wetsuit. Age: 16	$175 20 12	1 Fw/12		Client evaluation at put-in
Req: Wetsuit; exp; Class V paddle test. Age: 14	$200 20 20	Less $25wd and (less 10%w/12 + or less 10%y16)	Avail from LA, SF	Cocktails inc; bus from LA, add $80; bus from SF, add $45; bus trip inc breakfast day 1
Req: Wetsuit. Age: 16	$170 20 6	1 Fw/12		
Req: Wetsuit. Age: 15	$185 24 10	1 Fw/12 or 2 Fw/ 20		Beer, wine inc
Rec: Wetsuit. Age: 12	$170 20 6	1 Fw/12	Avail from Sacramento	Van from Sacramento, add $10
Req: Wetsuit; exp. Age: 16	$309 25 25	1 Fw/12 and less $25wd		
Req: Children must swim, like water. Age: 12	$300 25 6	Less $50wd and (less 10%w/10 + or 1 Fw/10 or less 30%y16)		
Rec: Exp. Age: 16	$195 20 6	(1 Fw/10 or .5 Fw/ 6) and less 25% before May 15 and less 20%y12		

Motels and lodges.
Abbreviations used in the following listings are: L, R = Turn left, Turn right; H = Highway; I = Interstate; N, S, E, W = North, South, East, West; mi = miles; n/p = price or service not provided.

Marble View Motel, P.O. Box 159, Ft. Jones, CA 96032. (916) 468-2394. Directions: I-5 to Yreka; H-3SW for 15 mi. Cost per room for one: $18; for two: $25; for three: $30; for four: $35.

Klamath River Lodge, 17931 Highway 96, Klamath River, CA 96050. (916) 465-2234. Directions: I-5 to H-96W, go 17 mi. Cost per room for one: $25; for two: $32.50; for three: $40; for four: $47.50.

See also Yreka motels listed in Upper Klamath.

Public campgrounds.
Spring Flat (Forest Service). Directions: I-5 to Yreka; H-3SW to Ft. Jones; W on Scott River Rd 16 mi.

Indian Scotty Campground (Forest Service). Directions: I-5 to Yreka; H-3SW to Ft. Jones; W on Scott River Rd for 14 mi.

Bridge Flat Campground (Forest Service). Directions: I-5 to Yreka; H-3SW to Ft. Jones; W on Scott River Rd for 17 mi.

Upper Klamath

Introduction. The Klamath is dammed and diverted through a two-turbine power plant just above this run. Releases from this facility allow rafting almost all year on this stretch of advanced whitewater.

Level of difficulty/water level concerns/flow information. Class IV+ when water is released from one generator (most of the summer); Class V when water is released from both generators. Higher flows, caused by spring spill-off from the dam, make running the river extremely hazardous. For flow information, call (800) 547-1501. Listen for the flow at John Boyle Power Plant.

Permit system/time to raft. The Upper Klamath operates on a simple permit system: outfitters only have limits on group size (20 people starting at one time, or 30 people starting at two times). Again, this system acts to concentrate demand on the weekends. On a typical summer weekend you will find four or five outfitters starting trips, with only one or two tours starting during the week.

The limitations of the John Boyle Power Plant mean that river levels do not decline on weekends as they do on some other summer rivers. Releases are also maintained at virtually the same level throughout the summer, making any time fine for rafting the Upper Klamath. An exception is from July 7 to July 25, 1986, when the power plant will be closed for annual maintenance and releases will be halted. In past years, releases have continued on the second weekend of this shut-down period. Check with your outfitter for updated information.

In 1985, I ran the entire river in one day (at 1600 cfs), in about 4.5 river hours. Such a trip makes a long day—don't plan on attending the Ashland Shakespeare Festival in the evening.

Commercial rafting. In 1985, 23 companies had permits for the Upper Klamath, and 1217 people rafted the river on 140 commercial trips. Of the 140 trips, 52 lasted one day and 86 two days. The leading outfitters on the Upper Klamath in 1985, in user-day volume as reported to the Bureau of Land Management, were Whitewater Voyages, All-Outdoors, Headwaters, Wilderness Adventures, Noah's, and Wild Water West.

Gear/safety/who can come. Even at summer water levels, this river has two relatively easy but long Class V rapids that are difficult to walk around. Rafters should have previously rafted a Class III+ or IV river. As the water is rather warm in the summer, wetsuits may not be necessary. However, they are definitely indicated at other times of the year.

Distinctive features. The Upper Klamath run includes a series of long, difficult rapids, each resembling a continuous quilt of whitewater. At high water, the rapids tend to run into one another, leaving few, if any, places to swim or pull for an eddy. But if you seek continuous whitewater thrills, the Upper Klamath is for you. In addition, on a cost-to-whitewater basis, the Upper Klamath offers some excellent values, especially from local companies. Check the trip descriptions.

River access. River access is by dirt road only.

Sites of interest. Originally settled in the last century, the shores of the Upper Klamath display ruins of nineteenth century buildings and signs of the early Indian population.

Environment. In Oregon, the Upper Klamath rolls though a canyon green with ponderosa pine, cedar, tan oak and juniper. The landscape flattens out as the river reaches the state border, and classic California scenery appears—golden hills dotted with oak. You expect to see a stagecoach coming over the hills at any moment or, at the very least, the cast of *Silverado*.

Upstream of the rafting run, the Klamath travels along phosphate beds. The combination of these phosphates, high water temperatures in the summer, and standing water above the Klamath's dams, creates a river that is high in algae and whose aeration in rapids forms piles of foam. If your ideal river is pristine, you may wish to raft further south or in the spring, when lower water temperatures reduce the solubility of the phosphates and inhibit the growth of algae.

The river canyon is home to deer (sightings are more common in winter), falcons, ospreys, blue heron, and even bald eagles. Bring along binoculars.

Fishing. Wild trout, hook and release only.

Summary of river between put-ins. The following section is summarized with permission from the *Handbook to the Klamath River Canyon*. See that excellent book for (a) dozens of photographs of the Upper and Lower Klamath, (b) an extensive mile-by-mile guide to the rapids and the river's history, and (c) detailed river maps.

John Boyle to Bridge Meadow—(5 miles) One Class III rapid, nine Class IIs.

Bridge Meadow to Rainbow Rock—(4 miles) Two easy Class V rapids, three Class IV rapids. Frain Ranch site.

Rainbow Rock to BLM Access—(2 miles) Six Class III rapids, several Class IIs.

BLM Access to Access Point 1—(6 miles) Two Class III rapids, seven Class IIs. Beswick Hot Springs site. Indian caves site.

Access Point 1 to Copco Lake—(0.5 miles) Flat water.

River status. The City of Klamath Falls currently plans to locate a new hydroelectric facility, the Salt Caves dam, square in the middle of the Upper Klamath section. This project would destroy an excellent rafting run, eliminate one of the best wild trout streams on Oregon, and substantially deteriorate river water quality, all to produce electricity for which there is no market at its true cost.

Recognizing that the loss of this $20 million recreational resource cannot be mitigated by the production of another stagnant, man-made algae pond, the dam's supporters have proposed the development of a ski resort (for which they have neither a permit nor the land). For more on the mitigation promises of dam builders, see the Stanislaus.

1986 will be a key year in the expensive legal struggle to stop the dam. Friends of the River accepts tax-deductible donations directed toward the battle against this dam, but they prefer general contributions. Also, members of the Klamath Canyon River Outfitters (KCRO) contribute a small portion of their Upper Klamath revenues toward the legal fees required to confront an opposition with a $250,000 litigation budget. Mary Gray Holt, attorney for both the Sierra Club and KCRO, has remarked: "If this dam is built, they're going to be able to build dams anywhere. This project is very poorly conceived." To put on the record your conception of the Salt Caves Dam, write to Sen. Mark Hatfield, 322 Hart Senate Office Building, Washington, DC 20510.

Motels and lodges. Abbreviations used in the following listings are: L, R = Turn left, Turn right; H = Highway; I = Interstate; N, S, E, W = North, South, East, West; mi = miles; n/p = price or service not provided.

Curl Up Motel, 50 Lowe Rd, Ashland, OR 97520. (503) 482-4700 or 1-800-482-4701 outside OR. Directions: I-5 to Ashland, take Exit 19. Cost per room for one: $27-30; for two: $30-34; for three: $34-38; for four: $38-42.

Valley Entrance Motel, 1193 Siskiyou Blvd, Ashland, OR 97520. (503)

—Turtle River Rafting
An oar boat with paddle assist on the Upper Klamath's Hell's Corner Rapid

482-2641. Directions: I-5 to Ashland; 3 mi from Exits 14 or 19. Cost per room for one: $38-44; for two: $38-48; for three: $52-56; for four: $58-62.

Yreka Motel, 336 N Main St, Yreka, CA 96097. (916) 842-2655. Directions: I-5 to Yreka; take center exit; N at light, N 2 blocks. Cost per room for one: $18; for two: $21; for three: $24; for four: $26.

Heritage Inn, 306 N Main St, Yreka, CA 96097. (916) 842-6835. Directions: I-5 to Yreka; 3 blocks N of central off-ramp. Cost per room for one: $20; for two: $25; for three: $30; for four: $37.50.

Thompson Creek Lodge, Star Route, Seiad Valley, CA 96086. (916) 496-3657. Directions: I-5 to Yreka; H-96W for 55 mi. Cost per room for one: $35-55; for two: $35-55; for three: $40-60; for four: $45-65.

Thunderbird Lodge, 526 S Main St, Yreka, CA 96097. (916) 842-4405. Directions: I-5 to Yreka; take center exit; L on S. Main, go 3 blocks. Cost per room for one: $24; for two: $30-34; for three: $36-40; for four: $38-40.

Motel Orleans, 1806 B Fort Jones Ave, Yreka, CA 96097. (916) 842-1612. Directions: I-5 to Yreka; exit Ft. Jones Rd; L under freeway, L on Ft. Jones, L into motel driveway. Cost per room for one: $23; for two: $25-27; for three: $29; for four: $31-33.

Best Western Miner's Inn, 122 E. Miner St., Yreka, CA 96097. (916) 842-4355/(800) 528-1234. Directions: I-5 to Yreka; take central off-ramp. Cost per room for one: $33; for two: $36-43; for three: $46; for four: $49.

Bed and breakfast inns. The Spiridon House, 353 Hargadine, P.O. Box 3030, Ashland, OR 97520. (503) 488-1362. Directions: I-5 to Ashland; 2nd Ashland exit; L at off-ramp; R on Siskiyou Blvd; L. on Gresham; R on Hargadine. Cost per room for one: n/p; for two: $50-95; for three: $60-105; for four: $80-125.

The Winchester Inn, 35 S Second St, Ashland, OR 97520. (503) 488-1113. Directions: I-5 to Ashland; exit Main St; Second is off Main St. Cost per room for one: $43-67; for two: $48-72; for three: $58-82; for four: $68-92.

Private campgrounds. Glenyan KOA. 5310 Highway 66, Ashland, OR 97520. Phone: (503) 482-4138. Directions: I-5 to Ashland; take Exit 14; go 3.5 mi SE on H-66. Price for tenters: $10 for 2; for RVs: $12.50 for 2; for showers: $2.

See Lower Klamath for more campgrounds.

Abbreviations

Mo,Tu,We	Monday, Tuesday, Wednesday, etc.	porta	Porta-potty or lime can at camp
D	Daily	exp	(Rafting) experience
will call	Outfitter will call you to arrange dates	Camping exp	Camping experience
ob	Oar boat	F	Free
o/pa	Oar boat with paddle assist	w/	With
pb	Paddle boat	wd	Weekday
ik	Inflatable kayak	we	Weekend
s/b	Self-bailing	y	Youth
op	Optional	y16	Youth, age 16 and under
ia	If available or if appropriate	s	Senior
on-river	Camp is beside the river	s65	Senior, age 65 and over
off-river	Camp is not beside the river	inc	Included
lodge	Overnight at a lodge or motel	avail	Available
flush	Flush toilets at camp	#	pound
chem	Chemical toilets or outhouse at camp		

Name– Max. cfs	Starting	Raft type	Put-in– Take-out	Miles Camp Facilities
UPPER KLAMATH—1 DAY				
All-Outdoors 4,500	Jun 28; Jul 5, 26; Aug 2, 9, 16, 23; Sep 6, 13, 27	o/pa	John Boyle-Copco Lake	17
ARR No max	D Apr 1—Oct 31	pb, o/pa op	Bridge Meadow- Copco Lake	12
Eagle Sun 3,500	D May 1—Oct 31	ob, pb op, o/pa op	John Boyle-BLM Access	11
Headwaters 3,000	D Apr 1—Oct 31	pb, ob op, s/b op, o/pa op	John Boyle-BLM Access	11
Noah's 4,500	Apr 5, 19; May 3, 16, 26, 29; Jun 1, 7, 14, 21, 28; and Fr- Mo Jun 3—Oct 5	o/pa s/b, pb s/b op exp ia	John Boyle-Copco Lake	17
Smith's River Adv. No max	D May 15—Sep 15	ob, pb op	John Boyle-Access Point 1	17
Tributary Whitewater 4,500	D May 1—Oct 31	pb, ob op	John Boyle-BLM Access	11
Whitewater Excitement 3,500	D Jun 1—Sep 30	pb s/b	John Boyle-Copco Lake	17
Whitewater Voyages 5,000	D Apr 1—Oct 31	pb, ob op	Bridge Meadow- Access Point 1	12
WW Rapid Transit 3,500	D Jun 1—Sep 30	pb s/b, ob s/b op	John Boyle-Copco Lake	17
UPPER KLAMATH—2 DAYS				
All-Outdoors 4,500	Jun 28; Jul 5, 26, 30; Aug 2, 9, 16, 23, 30; Sep 6, 13, 27	o/pa, pb op	John Boyle-Copco Lake	17 On-river Porta
ARR No max	D Apr 1—Oct 31	pb, o/pa op	John Boyle-Copco Lake	17 On-river Porta
ARTA 4,000	Jul 26; Aug 2, 9, 16, 23	o/pa, pb exp ia	John Boyle-Copco Lake	17 On-river Porta
A WW Connection 3,000	D Jun 1—Sep 30	o/pa, pb op exp	John Boyle-Copco Lake	17 On-river Porta

Recom. Require. Min. Age	Cost Max. Grp. Min. Grp.	Discounts	Transportation	Comments
Req: Wetsuit until Jun 10, after Sep 7. Age: 16	$104 25 25	1 Fw/12 and less $7wd		
Rec: Wetsuit. Age: 16	$80 30 12	1 Fw/12	Avail from Yreka, Ashland	Beer, wine inc; van from Yreka, Ashland, add $5
Rec: Class III exp. Age: 14	$75 24 4	Less 10%w/6+ and 1 Fw/8	Inc from Medford, Ashland	
Rec: Healthy, active; wetsuit Apr, May, Sep, Oct; exp for paddlers. Age: 14	$78 25 15	Less 10%w/10+ and 1 Fw/20 or less 10%y16	Inc from Ashland; avail from Medford	Bus from Medford, add $15; above 3200 cfs, take-out at Copco Lake
Rec: Good health; wetsuit. Req: Wetsuit in pb; excellent health in pb. Age: 14	$66 25 4	(Less 10%w/8+ or less 25%y17) and 1 Fw/12	Inc from Medford, Ashland	Side trip to Frain Ranch ruins
Rec: Good physical condition; Class III exp. Age: 12	$85 20 6	1 Fw/8 or less 10%w/6-14 or less 20%w/15+	Inc from Medford, Ashland	Beer inc
Req: Exp for paddlers; children must swim, like water. Age: 12	$95 20 6	Less $15wd and (less 10%w/10+ or 1 Fw/10 or less 30%y16)		
Rec: Healthy; exp. Req: Wetsuit. Age: 14	$75 24 24	1 Fw/12		
Rec: Wetsuit. Req: Exp for paddlers. Age: 12	$84 20 20	Less $6wd and (less 10%w/12+ or less 10%y16)		Beer inc
Req: Exp. Age: 12	$85 20 6	1 Fw/12	Inc from Sacramento	
Req: Wetsuit until Jun 10, after Sep 7. Age: 16	$219 23 23	1 Fw/12 and less $25wd		pb day 1 only
Rec: Wetsuit. Age: 16	$165 30 12	1 Fw/12	Avail from Yreka, Ashland	Beer, wine inc; van from Yreka, Ashland, add $5
Age: 12	$190 20 12	Less $15y17 and less 10%w/10+	Inc from Yreka	
Req: Wetsuit. Age: Call	$190 24 8	Less 10%wd and 1 Fw/12 and less 20%w/15+	Avail from Oakland	Beer, wine inc; train from Oakland, add $135

Name– Max. cfs	Starting	Raft type	Put-in– Take-out	Miles Camp Facilities
Eagle Sun 3,500	Mo, We, Fr May 1—Oct 31	ob, pb op, o/pa op	John Boyle-Copco Lake	17 On-river Porta
Great Out of Doors 4,000	D Mar 1—Sep 30	ob, pb op ia, o/pa op, ik op ia	John Boyle-Copco Lake	17 On-river Porta
Headwaters 3,000	D Apr 1—Oct 31	pb, ob op, s/b op, o/pa op	John Boyle-Copco Lake	17 On-river Porta
Noah's 4,500	May 25; Jun 21, 28; Jul 4, 19, 26; Aug 2, 9, 31	o/pa s/b, pb s/b op exp ia	John Boyle-Rainbow Rock; Bridge Meadow-Copco Lake	21 On-river Porta
Ouzel Outfitters 3,000	May 31; Jun 21, 28; Jul 2, 5; Aug 2, 9, 16, 23, 30	o/pa s/b, pb s/b op, ob s/b op	John Boyle-Copco Lake	17 On-river Porta
Ouzel Voyages No max	D Jun 10—Sep 30	o/pa, pb op	John Boyle-Copco Lake	17 On-river Porta
Rubicon 5,000	D Jun 1—Sep 30	ob, pb op	John Boyle-Access Point 1	17 On-river Porta
Sierra Whitewater No max	Th, Sa May 15—Jul 5, Jul 26—Oct 15	o/pa, pb s/b op exp ia	John Boyle-Copco Lake	17 On-river Porta
Smith's River Adv. No max	Mo, We, Fr May 15—Sep 15	ob, pb op	John Boyle-Access Point 1	17 On-river Porta
Tributary Whitewater 4,500	D May 1—Oct 31	pb, ob op	John Boyle-Copco Lake	17 On-river Porta
Turtle River No max	Jun 28; Jul 26; Aug 2, 9, 23; Sep 6, 27	pb, ob op, o/pa op	John Boyle-Copco Lake	17 On-river Porta
Whitewater Voyages 5,000	D Apr 1—Oct 31	pb, ob op	John Boyle-Copco Lake	17 On-river Porta
Whitewater Excitement 3,500	D Jun 1—Sep 30	pb s/b	John Boyle-Copco Lake	17 On-river Porta

Recom. Require. Min. Age	Cost Max. Grp. Min. Grp.	Discounts	Transportation	Comments
Rec: Class III exp. Age: 14	$150 24 6	Less 10%w/6+ and 1 Fw/8	Inc from Medford, Ashland	
Req: Wetsuit; rain gear until Jul 1. Age: 12	$175 20 8	Less $10y12 and 1 Fw/12		
Rec: Healthy, active; wetsuit Apr, May, Sep, Oct; exp for paddlers. Age: 14	$170 25 15	Less 10%w/10+ and 1 Fw/20 or less 10%y16	Inc from Ashland; avail from Medford	Bus from Medford, add $15
Rec: Good health; wetsuit. Req: Wetsuit in pb; excellent health in pb. Age: 14	$138 25 6	(Less 10%w/8+ or less 25%y17) and 1 Fw/12	Inc from Medford, Ashland	Side trips to Indian encampments, Frain Ranch ruins, Beswick/Klamath hot springs resort ghost town; fishing for native wild rainbow trout (hook and release); all-woman trip (age 16+) Aug 16
Age: 16	$185 30 6	Less 10%w/12+ or 1 Fw/12 or less 20%w/18+ or 2 Fw/18	Inc from Ashland; avail from Medford	Gourmet; Oregon wines inc.
Rec: Class III exp. Req: Good health. Age: 12	$180 20 4	Less 10%w/10+ or less 15%y15		
Req: Wetsuit until Jun 30. Age: 12	$220 30 15	1 Fw/12	Inc from Yreka	
Rec: Wetsuit May, Oct. Age: 8	$185 20 8	1 Fw/12 and less $20wd and (less 10%w/10+ or less 20%w/20 or less 20%y16)	Inc from Medford	
Rec: Good physical condition; Class III exp. Age: 12	$165 20 6	1 Fw/8 or less 10%w/6-14 or less 20%w/15+	Inc from Medford, Ashland	
Req: Exp for paddlers; children must swim, like water. Age: 12	$188 20 6	Less $28wd and (less 10%w/10+ or 1 Fw/10 or less 30%y16)		
Age: 16	$155 25 6	(1 Fw/10 or .5 Fw/6) and less 25% before May 15 and less 20%y12		
Rec: Wetsuit. Req: Exp for paddlers. Age: 12	$180 20 20	Less $14wd and (less 10%w/12+ or less 10%y16)	Avail from LA, SF	Cocktails inc; bus from LA, add $80; bus from SF, add $45; bus trip inc breakfast day 1
Rec: Healthy; exp. Req: Wetsuit. Age: 14	$170 24 24	1 Fw/12		

Name– Max. cfs	Starting	Raft type	Put-in– Take-out	Miles Camp Facilities
Wilderness Adventures No max	Sa May 3—Oct 25 except Jul 12; Jul 4	ob, pb op	John Boyle-Copco Lake	17 On-river Porta
Wild River Tours 4,000	D Jun 1—Aug 31	pb, ob op, o/pa op	John Boyle-Copco Lake	17 On-river Porta
Wild Water West, Ltd. No max	D Jun 1—Oct 30	pb	John Boyle-Copco Lake	17 On-river Porta
WW Rapid Transit 3,500	D Jun 1—Sep 30	pb s/b, ob s/b op	John Boyle-Copco Lake	17 On-river Porta

UPPER KLAMATH—3 DAYS

Name– Max. cfs	Starting	Raft type	Put-in– Take-out	Miles Camp Facilities
Ouzel Voyages No max	D Jun 10—Sep 30	o/pa, pb op exp ia	John Boyle-Copco Lake	17 On-river Porta
Wilderness Adventures No max	Aug 1	ob, pb op	John Boyle-Copco Lake	17 On-river Porta
Wilderness Adventures No max	Fr, Su Aug 1—Sep 7; Fr Sep 12—Oct 26	ob	John Boyle-Copco Lake	17 On-river Porta

UPPER KLAMATH—4 DAYS

Name– Max. cfs	Starting	Raft type	Put-in– Take-out	Miles Camp Facilities
Wilderness Adventures No max	Aug 14	ob, pb op	John Boyle-Copco Lake	17 On-river Porta

Lower Klamath

Introduction. The relatively easy waters and green vistas of the Klamath offer an excellent introduction to rafting. In addition, the river serves as the fall site for some of the finest steelhead and salmon fishing in the state,

Level of difficulty/water level concerns/flow information. Class III. Dam-controlled, but the water level does not fall on the weekends. However, the water gradually falls as summer progresses. Outfitters report that they have never had to stop rafting due to high water. The minimum water for rafting is 500 cfs. For flow information, call 322-3327; listen for the flow at Orleans.

Permit system/time to raft. The Lower Klamath operates on a simple permit system: the only requirement is that groups have 30 or fewer members, including guides. This requirement can be waived for

Recom. Require. Min. Age	Cost Max. Grp. Min. Grp.	Discounts	Transportation	Comments
Age: 12	$190 30 4	1 Fw/12 or 2 Fw/ 20		
Age: 16	$195 24 12	Less 10%w/12 +		
Age: 13	$175 30 10	1 Fw/12 or 2 Fw/ 20	Avail from SF for 6 +	Beer, wine inc; bus from SF, add $30
Rec: Wetsuit. Req: Exp. Age: 12	$170 20 6	1 Fw/12	Inc from Sacramento	
Rec: Class III exp. Req: Good health. Age: 12	$250 20 4	Less 10%w/10 + or less 15%y15		25 min hike to day 2 camp
Age: 12	$270 30 6	1 Fw/15 or 2 Fw/ 28		Shakespeare play inc
Req: You-oar exp. Age: 16	$350 20 6			You-oar
Age: 12	$340 30 6	1 Fw/15 or 2 Fw/ 28	Inc from Ashland	2 Shakespeare plays inc

groups such as students, scouts, etc. Your selection of when to raft depends on what you want from the river: for high water, choose May; to introduce young children to rafting, wait for July or August; for good fishing, float in September.

Commercial rafting. In 1985, 35 companies took 3400 passengers down the Lower Klamath (a total of approximately 10,000 user days). Of the 3400 passengers, 2800 camped out on the river, and 600 stayed in lodges.

Gear/safety/who can come. The Lower Klamath offers a whitewater experience suitable for anyone, including children, the handicapped, and senior citizens. Do not fail to bring your rain gear in the spring and fall or, for overnighters, your mosquito repellent.

If you are in the mood for a challenge, request an inflatable kayak.

Distinctive features. The Lower Klamath permits the longest river trips in the state. If you have six or more people who wish to raft for more than seven days, many companies will be willing to arrange it. You need not go all the way to Arizona for a week on the water.

River access. Frequent access from Highway 96. Although the highway is often located well above the river, it is never far away.

Sites of interest. For those rafting between Independence Creek and Coon Creek, outfitters often offer a side hike to Ukonom Falls, a double waterfall on Ukonom Creek. This is a difficult hike, and the trail tends to deteriorate as the season progresses. Get the latest on path conditions from your guide.

Environment. The buffalo may no longer roam, but black-tailed deer still swim the Klamath, maintaining, of course, a discreet distance from the rafts. Otters and turtles show off their paddling skills. You will also see blue herons, mergansers, ospreys, hawks, golden eagles, and bald eagles. You may even spot a black bear who knows where the good fishing is. There are better times to teach your children about the virtues of sharing.

The water runs warm and brown; there has been extensive clear cutting of timber in the Klamath watershed. However, you won't see evidence of recent logging along the river itself, where alder, ash, sugar and ponderosa pine, oak, cottonwood, bay laurel, and Douglas and white fir provide shelter for many attractive campsites.

Fishing. King and silver salmon; rainbow and steelhead trout. See the *Handbook to the Klamath River Canyon* for details on the best time to fish, or ask your outfitter.

Summary of river between put-ins. Summarized with permission from the *Handbook to the Klamath River Canyon*. That volume provides river maps as well as a mile-by-mile guide to the rapids and history of the Lower Klamath. Educational groups, in particular, should not miss the book. The following ratings run about ½ to 1 full class higher than other ratings in this guide.

Iron Gate Dam to Tree of Heaven (18 miles)—Three Class III rapids, eight Class IIs.

Tree of Heaven to Beaver Creek (11 miles)—Three Class III rapids, twelve Class IIs.

Beaver Creek to Klamath River (1 mile)—Class I rapids.

Klamath River to Horse Creek (13 miles)—Two Class II rapids, many Class Is.

Horse Creek to Sarah Totten (5 miles)—One Class III rapid, one Class II.

Sarah Totten to Walker Creek (9 miles)—One Class III rapid, seven Class IIs.

Walker Creek to Seiad Vly Bridge (0.5 miles)—Flat water.

Seiad Vly Bridge to Seiad Valley (2 miles)—One Class II rapid, three Class Is.

Seiad Valley to Grider Creek (1 mile)—Class I rapids.

Grider Creek to Fort Goff (3 miles)—One Class III rapid, two Class IIs.

—Turtle River Rafting

An inflatable kayaker in a Class III rapid on the Lower Klamath

Fort Goff to Thompson Creek (4 miles)—Two Class IIIs.

Thompson Creek to Seattle Creek (2 miles)—One Class III rapid.

Seattle Creek to China Creek (3 miles)—Two Class II rapids, many Class I rapids.

China Creek to Happy Camp (11 miles)—Class I rapids.

Happy Camp to Ferry Point (11 miles)—Three Class III rapids, nine Class IIs.

Ferry Point to Independence Creek (2 miles)—One Class IV rapid, one Class III.

Independence Creek to Coon Creek (6 miles)—Three Class III rapids, five Class IIs. Class IV+ hike to Ukonom Falls.

Coon Creek to Cottage Grove (1 mile)—One Class III rapid, two Class IIs.

Cottage Grove to Dillon Creek (4 miles)—Four Class II rapids.

Dillon Creek to Presidio Bar (2 miles)—Two Class II rapids, many Class Is.

Presidio Bar to Ti Bar (1 mile)—Two Class II rapids.

Ti Bar to Green Riffle (10 miles)—Two Class III rapids.

—Portage—

Oak Bottom (Cal Salmon) to Somes Bar (2 miles)—Class III rapids.

Somes Bar to Dolan's Bar (6 miles)—One Class IV rapid, four Class IIIs.

Dolan's Bar to Orleans (1 mile)—Class I rapids.

Abbreviations

Mo,Tu,We	Monday, Tuesday, Wednesday, etc.	porta	Porta-potty or lime can at camp
D	Daily	exp	(Rafting) experience
will call	Outfitter will call you to arrange dates	Camping exp	Camping experience
ob	Oar boat	F	Free
o/pa	Oar boat with paddle assist	w/	With
pb	Paddle boat	wd	Weekday
ik	Inflatable kayak	we	Weekend
s/b	Self-bailing	y	Youth
op	Optional	y16	Youth, age 16 and under
ia	If available or if appropriate	s	Senior
on-river	Camp is beside the river	s65	Senior, age 65 and over
off-river	Camp is not beside the river	inc	Included
lodge	Overnight at a lodge or motel	avail	Available
flush	Flush toilets at camp	#	pound
chem	Chemical toilets or outhouse at camp		

Name— Max. cfs	Starting	Raft type	Put-in— Take-out	Miles Camp Facilities
LOWER KLAMATH—1 DAY				
All- Outdoors No max	D May 15—Sep 15	pb, o/pa op, ik op	Happy Camp-Ferry Point	11
All- Outdoors No max	D May 15—Sep 15	pb, o/pa op, ik op	Ferry Point-Coon Creek	8
Four Seasons Adv No max	D Jun 15—Oct 15	pb, ik s/b op	Tree of Heaven- Klamath River	12
Headwaters No max	D Apr 1—Oct 31	pb, ob op, s/b op, o/pa op	Seiad Valley-Seattle Creek	10

Orleans to Weitchpec (12 miles)—Two Class III rapids.
Weitchpec to Pacific Ocean (17 miles)—Flat water.

River status. The Lower Klamath has wild and scenic status.

Motels and lodges. Abbreviations used in the following listings are: L, R = Turn left, Turn right; H = Highway; I = Interstate; N, S, E, W = North, South, East, West; mi = miles; n/p = price or service not provided.

Steelhead Bend Motel, 36309 Highway 96, Hamburg, CA 96045. (916) 496-3256. Directions: I-5 to H-96W; go 36 mi. Cost per room for one: $30; for two: $35; for three: $40; for four: $45.

Forest Lodge Motel, 63712 Highway 96, Happy Camp, CA 96039. (916) 493-5424. Directions: I-5 to H-96W to Happy Camp. Cost per room for one: $29; for two: $36-45; for three: $42-52; for four: $52-55.

Anglers Motel, 61700 Highway 96, P.O. Box 483, Happy Camp, CA 96039. (916) 493-2735. Directions: I-5 to H-96W; go for 64 mi; 2 mi E of Happy Camp on left. Cost per room for one: $28-32; for two: $30-36; for three: $32-38; for four: $34-40.

Private campgrounds. Steelhead Bend Motel and Riverfront RV Park. 36309 Highway 96, Hamburg, CA 96045. (916) 496-3256. Open: All Year. Directions: I-5 to H-96W; go 36 mi. Cost for tenters: $2.50; for RVs: $8; for showers: n/p.

Elk Creek Campground. 921 Elk Creek Rd, Happy Camp, CA 96039. (916) 493-2208. Open: All Year. Directions: I-5 to H-96W to Happy Camp. Cost for tenters: $5 per person; for RVs: $10; for showers: $3.

Hawk's Roost R.V. Park. Box 707 - 44701 Highway 96, Seiad Valley, CA 96086. (916) 496-3400. Open: All Year. Directions: I-5 to H-96W to 18 mi E of Happy Camp. Cost for tenters: $6; for RVs: $8; for showers: $1.

Public campgrounds. Fort Goff (Forest Service). Directions: I-5 to H-96W to 4 mi NW of Seiad Valley.

O'Neil Creek (Forest Service). Directions: I-5 to H-96W; go 30 mi.

Sarah Totten (Forest Service). Directions: I-5 to H-96W; go 25 mi.

Recom. Require. Min. Age	Cost Max. Grp. Min. Grp.	Discounts	Transportation	Comments
Req: Wetsuit until Jun 20. Age: Call	$79 25 25	1 Fw/12 and less $5wd		
Req: Wetsuit until Jun 20. Age: Call	$79 25 25	1 Fw/12 and less $5wd		
Age: 5	$45 25 6	Less 10%w/10+ or less $10y16	Inc from Ashland	Handicapped
Age: 7	$55 25 15	Less 10%w/10+ or less 10%y16	Inc from Ashland	Handicapped; may extend trip if cfs over 20,000

Name– Max. cfs	Starting	Raft type	Put-in– Take-out	Miles Camp Facilities
KROE No max	D May 15—Sep 30	pb, ob op, o/pa op, ik op	Ferry Point-Coon Creek	8
KROE No max	D May 15—Sep 30	pb, ob op, o/pa op, ik op	Happy Camp-Ferry Point	11
O.R.E. Inc. 30,000	D May 1—Sep 30	pb	Happy Camp-Ferry Point	11
River Country 5,000	Tu Apr 15—Sep 30	ob, pb op, ik op ia	Happy Camp-Ferry Point	11
Ti Bar No max	D Jul 1—Sep 30	ob, pb ob, o/pa op, ik op	Oak Bottom-Dolan's Bar	8
Tributary Whitewater No max	D Apr 1—Oct 31	pb	Oak Bottom-Orleans	9

LOWER KLAMATH—2 DAY

Name– Max. cfs	Starting	Raft type	Put-in– Take-out	Miles Camp Facilities
All- Outdoors No max	D May 15—Sep 15	pb, o/pa op, ik op	Happy Camp-Coon Creek	19 On-river Porta
ARR No max	D Apr 1—Oct 31	ik, ob op, pb op	Happy Camp-Coon Creek	19 On-river Porta
Eagle Sun 50,000	Mo, We, Fr May 1—Sep 30	ob, pb op, o/pa op	Horse Creek-Seattle Creek	26 On-river Porta
Electric Rafting Co 15,000	D Jun 1—Oct 31	ob, pb op, o/pa op, ik op	Happy Camp-Coon Creek	19 On-river Porta
Four Seasons Adv No max	Th-Su Jun 15—Sep 30	pb, ik op, ob op	Happy Camp-Coon Creek	19 On-river Chem
Great Out of Doors 50,000	D Mar 1—Sep 30	pb, ob op, o/pa op, ik s/b op	Happy Camp-Independence Crk	13 On-river Porta
Headwaters No max	D Apr 1—Oct 31	pb, ob op, s/b op, o/pa op	Happy Camp-Coon Creek	19 On-river Porta
James Henry 6,000	Jul 8, 15; Aug 26	pb, ob op ia, ik op	Happy Camp-Dillon Creek	24 On-river Porta

Recom. Require. Min. Age	Cost Max. Grp. Min. Grp.	Discounts	Transportation	Comments
Req: Exp for children. Age: 10	$50 25 3	Less 10%w/6-14 or less 15%w/ 15+		
Req: Exp for children. Age: 10	$50 25 3	Less 10%w/6-14 or less 15%w/ 15+		
Req: Group of 12+. Age: 8	$45 25 12	(Less 10%w/12+ and 1Fw/12) or less 10%w/3 immediate family members	Shuttle not inc	
Age: 12	$50 15 5	1 Fw/10		
Age: 6	$50 25 4	1 Fw/6		
Req: Children must swim, like water. Age: 12	$75 25 6	Less $5wd and (less 10%w/10+ or 1 Fw/10 or less 30%y16 or less 30% handicapped or less 30%s65)		Handicapped
Req: Wetsuit until Jun 20. Age: Call	$179 25 25	1 Fw/12 and less $10wd		
Age: 10	$145 25 12	1 Fw/12	Avail from Yreka	Beer, wine inc; van from Yreka for 4+, add $5
Age: 8	$150 24 6	Less 10%w/6+ and 1 Fw/8	Inc from Medford, Ashland	Handicapped; lodge op, add $25
Age: 8	$135 25 8	Less 10%w/12-19 or less 15%w/ 20+ or less 10%s65 or less 10%y14	Inc from Eureka/ Arcata	Handicapped; wine tasting trips Jul 12, Aug 23, add $20; lodge op, add $40
Age: 6	$140 25 6	Less 10%w/10	Inc from Ashland	Handicapped
Age: 8	$135 25 12	Less $10y12 and 1 Fw/12		
Age: 7	$150 25 15	Less 10%w/10+ or less 10%y16	Avail from Ashland, Medford	Bus from Ashland, Medford, add $40; lodge op, add $30
Age: 7	$145 24 12	Less 25%y16 and (1 Fw/12-15 and less 5%w/12-15) or (1 Fw/16 and less 10%w/16-24)		Wine inc

Name– Max. cfs	Starting	Raft type	Put-in– Take-out	Miles Camp Facilities
KROE No max	Mo, We, Fr, Sa May 15— Sep 30	pb, ob op, o/pa op, ik op	Happy Camp-Coon Creek	19 On-river Porta
Noah's No max	Jun 12, 26; Jul 3, 17, 24, 31; Aug 7, 21, 28	pb s/b, ik s/b op, ob s/b op ia	Happy Camp- Cottage Grove	20 On-river Porta
O.R.E. Inc. 30,000	Sa, Tu May 24—Sep 30	ob	Happy Camp-Coon Creek	19 On-river Porta
Ouzel **Outfitters** No max	D Apr 1—Oct 1	pb, ob op, ik op	Happy Camp-Coon Creek	19 On-river Porta
River **Country** 5,000	Tu Apr 15—Sep 30	ob, pb op, ik op ia	Happy Camp-Coon Creek	19 On-river Porta
Smith's River **Adv.** No max	Mo, Th May 15—Sep 15	ob, pb op	Seiad Vly Br-Happy Camp	26 Lodge
Ti Bar No max	D Jul 1—Sep 30	ob, pb op, o/pa op, ik op	Happy Camp-Coon Creek	19 On-river Porta
Tributary **Whitewater** No max	D Apr 1—Oct 31	pb, ob op	Happy Camp-Ti Bar	27 On-river Porta
Trinity River **Raft** 25,000	D May 15—Sep 13	pb, ik op	Happy Camp-Coon Creek	19 On-river Chem
Trinity **Wilderness** No max	D May 10—Oct 11	pb, ik op, ob op	Happy Camp-Coon Creek	19 On-river Porta
Turtle River No max	Jun 28; Jul 14; Aug 9	pb, ik s/b op, ob op, o/ pa op	Happy Camp-Coon Creek	19 On-river Porta
Wild River **Tours** 8,000	D Jun 1—Sep 30	pb, ob op	Happy Camp-Ti Bar	27 On-river Porta
WW Rapid **Transit** No max	D May 1—Sep 30	pb s/b	Happy Camp-Ti Bar	27 On-river Porta

Recom. Require. Min. Age	Cost Max. Grp. Min. Grp.	Discounts	Transportation	Comments
Req: Exp for children. Age: 10	$150 25 3	Less 10%w/6-14 or less 15%w/ 15+		
Age: 6	$138 25 6	(Less 10%w/8+ or less 25%y17) and 1 Fw/12	Inc from Medford, Ashland, Yreka	Lodge op, add $20; gold panning; fishing for trout and steelhead (late Aug, Sep); handicapped; riverside sauna
Age: 8	$170 25 12	(Less 10%w/12+ and 1 Fw/12) or less 10%w/3 immediate family members	Shuttle not inc	You-oar; Asian cooking; wine inc
Age: 5	$160 25 6	Less 10%w/12-17 or 1 Fw/12 or less 20%w/18+ or 2 Fw/18	Shuttle not inc ($15/car)	Handicapped; gourmet; Oregon wines inc
Age: 12	$120 15 5	1 Fw/10		
Age: 10	$180 20 4	1 Fw/8 or less 10%w/6-14 or less 20%w/15+	Inc from Medford, Ashland	Beer, wine inc
Age: 6	$150 25 4	1 Fw/6		Lodge op, add $45
Req: Children must swim, like water. Age: 12	$165 25 6	Less $30wd and (less 10%w/10+ or 1 Fw/10 or less 30%y16 or less 30% handicapped or less 30%s65)		Handicapped; on-river op, chem
Req: Exp if cfs over 15,000. Age: 7	$120 25 12	1 Fw/12 and less 20%w/20+ and (10% less w/ payment 60 days in advance or less 5% w/ payment 30 days in advance)		
Age: 8	$130 25 12	Less 10% for returnees or less 10%w/12+ or less 10%y16		
Age: Call	$130 25 6	(1 Fw/10 or .5 Fw/ 6) and less 25% before May 15 and less 20%y12	Shuttle is coop style	
Rec: Tents. Age: 7	$175 25 12	Less 10%w/12+ and 1 Fw/23		
Age: 6	$150 25 6	1 Fw/12	Avail from Sacramento	Bus from Sacramento, add $10

Name– Max. cfs	Starting	Raft type	Put-in– Take-out	Miles Camp Facilities
LOWER KLAMATH—3 DAYS				
Action **Adventures** No max	D Jun 1—Aug 31	pb, ob op, ik s/b op	Sarah Totten-Happy Camp	35 On-river Porta
Action **Adventures** No max	D Jun 1—Aug 31	pb, ob op, ik s/b op exp	Happy Camp-Ti Bar	27 On-river Porta
All- **Outdoors** No max	D May 15—Sep 15	pb, o/pa op, ik op	Happy Camp- Presidio Bar	26 On-river Porta
ARR No max	D Apr 1—Oct 31	ik, ob op, pb op	Seiad Valley-Happy Camp	24 On-river Porta
ARTA No max	Jul 18, 25; Aug 1, 8, 15, 22	pb, ik s/b op ia, ob op	Happy Camp- Presidio Bar	26 On-river Porta
Charter **River Adv.** No max	Tu, Fr Aug 1—Aug 31	ob, pb op	Happy Camp-Ti Bar	27 On-river Porta
Eagle Sun 50,000	Mo, We, Fr May 1—Sep 30	ob, pb op, o/pa op	Seiad Valley-Coon Creek	43 On-river Porta
Four **Seasons Adv** No max	Th-Su Jun 15—Sep 20	pb, ik op, ob op	Happy Camp- Presidio Bar	26 On-river Chem
Get Wet **River Trips** 10,000	Jun 6, 13; Aug 15, 22, 29	ik s/b	Happy Camp-Coon Creek; Fort Goff- Seattle Creek	25 On-river Porta
Great Out of **Doors** 50,000	D Mar 1—Sep 30	pb, ob op, o/pa op, ik s/ b op	Happy Camp-Dillon Creek	24 On-river Porta
Headwaters No max	D Apr 1—Oct 31	pb, ob op, s/b op, o/pa op	Happy Camp- Presidio Bar	26 On-river Porta
James Henry 6,000	Jun 27, Jul 11	pb, ob op ia, ik op	Happy Camp-Dillon Creek	24 On-river Porta
KROE No max	Mo, We, Fr, Sa May 15— Sep 30	pb, ob op, o/pa op, ik op	Happy Camp- Presidio Bar	26 On-river Porta
Noah's No max	Jun 11, 25; Jul 2, 16, 23, 30; Aug 6, 20, 27	pb s/b, ik s/b op, ob s/b op ia	Grider Creek- Cottage Grove	43 On-river Porta
NOC No max	D May 1—Oct 30	ob, pb op	Happy Camp-Ti Bar	27 On-river Porta

Recom. Require. Min. Age	Cost Max. Grp. Min. Grp.	Discounts	Transportation	Comments
Age: Call	$159 25 10	Less 10%w/11 + or less 20%y13	Avail from Yreka	Van from Yreka for 1-5, add $50
Rec: Exp for children. Age: Call	$159 25 10	Less 10%w/11 + or less 20%y13	Avail from Yreka	Van from Yreka for 1-5, add $50
Req: Wetsuit until Jun 20. Age: Call	$249 25 25	1 Fw/12 and less $20wd		
Age: 10	$210 25 12	1 Fw/12	Avail from Yreka	Beer, wine inc; van from Yreka for 4 +, add $5
Age: 7	$255 25 12	Less $35y17 and less 10%w/10 + and 1Fw/20		Family trips Jul 18, Aug 22, less $80y17
Age: 12	$230 24 20	Less $15w/10 +		Beer, wine, sleeping pads, tents (weather demanding) inc
Age: 8	$225 24 6	Less 10%w/6 + and 1 Fw/8	Inc from Medford, Ashland	Handicapped; lodge op, add $25
Age: 6	$210 25 6	Less 10%w/10	Inc from Ashland	Handicapped
Age: 8	$319 24 6	Less 5%w/8-11 or less 10%w/12 +	Inc from Medford, Ashland	Boutique varietal wines, beer, rain gear inc; lodge op, add $130
Age: 8	$185 25 12	Less $10y12 and 1 Fw/12		
Age: 7	$235 25 15	Less 10%w/10 + or less 10%y16	Avail from Ashland, Medford	Bus from Ashland, Medford, add $40; lodge op, add $50
Age: 7	$260 24 12	Less 25%y16 and (1 Fw/12-15 and less 5%w/12-15) or (1 Fw/16 and less 10%w/16-24)		Wine inc; sports medicine Jul 11, 2 units credit; guided imagery and self-healing Jun 27; massage training Jun 27, Jul 11
Req: Exp for children. Age: 10	$245 25 3	Less 10%w/6-14 or less 15%w/ 15 +		
Age: 6	$195 25 6	(Less 10%w/8 + or less 25%y17) and 1 Fw/12	Inc from Medford, Ashland, Yreka	Lodge op, add $40; gold panning; fishing for trout and steelhead (late Aug, Sep); handicapped; riverside sauna; all-woman trip (age 16 +) Aug 13
Req: Wetsuit if water below 50 deg F. Age: Call	$231 25 6	1 Fw/12 and .5 Fy14		

Name– Max. cfs	Starting	Raft type	Put-in– Take-out	Miles Camp Facilities
Orange Torpedo 15,000	Mo-Fr May 1—Sep 30	ik s/b	Walker Creek-Thompson Creek; Happy Camp-Coon Creek	29 On-river Porta
Orange Torpedo 15,000	Mo-Fr May 1—Sep 30	ik s/b	Walker Creek-Thompson Creek; Happy Camp-Coon Creek; Oak Bottom-Orleans	38 On-river Porta
O.R.E. Inc. 30,000	Sa, Tu May 24—Sep 30	ob, pb op	Happy Camp-Presidio Bar	26 On-river Porta
Outdoor Adv./UCD 20,000	May 24; Jul 4; Aug 30	pb	Happy Camp-Presidio Bar	26 On-river Porta
Outdoors Unlimited No max	Jul 5, 9, 12, 16; Aug 2, 6, 9, 12, 23, 27	ob, pb op, ik op	Thompson Creek-Presidio Bar	43 On-river Porta
Ouzel Outfitters No max	Fr Apr 1—Oct 1	pb, ob op, ik op	Happy Camp-Presidio Bar	30 On-river Porta
River Country 5,000	Fr Apr 18—Sep 26, except Jul 4; Jul 2	ob, pb op, ik op ia	Happy Camp-Coon Creek	19 On-river Porta
River Trips Unlimited No max	Su Jun 15—Aug 31	ik, ob op	Tree of Heaven-Beaver Creek; Seiad Vly Bridge-Seattle Bar; Happy Camp-Ferry Point	33 Lodge
Rivers West No max	Jun 20, 27; Jul 18; Aug 1, 22	ob, pb op, ik s/b op	Happy Camp-Presidio Bar	26 On-river Porta
Rubicon No max	D Jun 1—Sep 30	ik, pb op, ob op	Happy Camp-Ti Bar; Somes Bar-Orleans	35 Com. Com.
Sierra Whitewater No max	Mo, Fr Jun 16—Sep 15	pb, ik op, ob op	Happy Camp-Presidio Bar	26 On-river Porta
Smith's River Adv. No max	D May 15—Sep 15	ob, pb op	Tree of Heaven-Beaver Creek; Seiad Valley-Seattle Creek; Happy Camp-Ferry Point	32 On-river Porta
Ti Bar No max	D Jul 1—Sep 30	ob, pb op, o/pa op, ik op	Happy Camp-Presidio Bar	26 On-river Porta

Recom. Require. Min. Age	Cost Max. Grp. Min. Grp.	Discounts	Transportation	Comments
Age: 10	$270 12 8	Less $25MoTu	Inc from Grants Pass, Medford, Ashland	Beer, wine inc; lodge op, add $55; groups of 24 w/ 2 weeks' advance notice
Age: 15	$300 12 8	Less $25MoTu	Inc from Grants Pass	Beer, wine inc; lodge op, add $55; groups of 24 w/ 2 weeks' advance notice
Age: 8	$248 25 12	Less $13wd and (less 10%w/12 + and 1Fw/12) or less 10%w/3 immediate family members	Shuttle not inc	
Age: 8	$108 24 12		Shuttle not inc	Food op, add $15
Age: 5	$230 20 16	1 Fw/10 and less 10%w/20		
Req: None. Age: 5	$240 25 6	(Less 10%w/12 + or 1 Fw/12 +) and (less 50%y12w/2 full fare adults)	Shuttle not inc ($15/car)	Handicapped; gourmet; Oregon wines inc
Age: 12	$215 15 5	1 Fw/10		Hike to Ukonom Falls inc
Age: 4	$300 12 4		Inc from Medford, Ashland	
Age: 7	$265 26 6	Less 10%w/12 + and .75 Fw/12 or less 10% w/3 same family or less 10%y16		Wine inc; extra day can raft CS w/ 4 wks advance registration
Age: Call	$200 25 12	1 Fw/12 and less 10%w/20		1 night off-river, chem; 1 night on-river, porta
Age: None	$240 25 6	(1 Fw/12 or 2 Fw/ 20) and less $20wd and (less 10%w/10 + or less 20%w/20 or less 20%y16)	Avail from Medford	Van from Medford, add $5
Age: 10	$250 20 4	1 Fw/8 or less 10%w/6-14 or less 20%w/15 +	Inc from Medford, Ashland	Beer, wine inc
Age: 6	$195 25 4	1 Fw/6		Lodge op, add $45

Name— Max. cfs	Starting	Raft type	Put-in— Take-out	Miles Camp Facilities
Tributary Whitewater No max	D Apr 1—Oct 31	pb, ob op	Happy Camp-Ti Bar	27 On-river Porta
Trinity River Raft 25,000	D May 15—Sep 13	pb, ik op	Happy Camp-Ti Bar	27 On-river Chem
Trinity Wilderness No max	D May 10—Oct 11	pb, ik op, ob op	Happy Camp-Presidio Bar	26 On-river Porta
Turtle River No max	Jun 6, 13, 20; Jul 4, 11, 25; Aug 1, 15, 22, 29; Sep 5, 12, 19; Oct 3, 10, 14	pb, ik s/b op, ob op, o/ pa op	Happy Camp-Presidio Bar	26 On-river Porta
W.E.T. 15,000	D Jun 1—Aug 31	ob, pb op, ik op	Happy Camp-Presidio Bar	26 On-river Porta
Whitewater Voyages 50,000	Jul 4, 11; Aug 1, 22, 30	pb, ob op	Happy Camp-Presidio Bar	26 On-river Porta
Wild River Tours 8,000	D Jun 1—Sep 30	pb, ob op	Happy Camp-Ti Bar	27 On-river Porta

LOWER KLAMATH—4 DAYS

Name— Max. cfs	Starting	Raft type	Put-in— Take-out	Miles Camp Facilities
James Henry 6,000	Jun 19; Jul 2, 17; Aug 21	pb, ob op ia, ik op	Seiad Valley-Dillon Creek	48 On-river Porta
O.R.E. Inc. 30,000	Sa, Tu May 24—Sep 30	ob, pb op	Seattle Creek-Presidio Bar	38 On-river Porta
Trinity River Raft 25,000	D May 15—Sep 13	pb, ik op	Happy Camp-Green Riffle	37 On-river Chem
Turtle River No max	Jun 12, 26; Jul 3, 10, 17, 24; Aug 7, 14, 28; Sep 4	pb, ik s/b op, ob op, o/ pa op	Happy Camp-Green Riffle	37 On-river Porta

Recom. Require. Min. Age	Cost Max. Grp. Min. Grp.	Discounts	Transportation	Comments
Req: Children must swim, like water. Age: 12	$240 25 6	Less $40wd and (less 10%w/10 + or 1 Fw/10 or less 30%y16 or less 30% handicapped or less 30%s65)		Handicapped; on-river op, chem
Age: 7	$180 25 12	1 Fw/12 and less 20%w/20 + and (10% less w/ payment 60 days in advance or 5% w/ payment 30 days in advance)		
Age: 8	$185 25 12	Less 10% for returnees or less 10%w/12 + or less 10%y16		
Age: Call	$195 25 6	(1 Fw/10 or .5 Fw/ 6) and less 25% before May 15 and less 20%y12	Shuttle is coop style	All youth July 24; Aug 12; all ik Jul 4
Rec: Camping exp. Age: 6	$200 24 12	Less $40y12 and 1 Fw/12		
Age: 7	$246 24 24	Less 10%w/12 + or less 10%y16	Avail from LA, SF	Cocktails inc; bus from LA, add $80; bus from SF, add $45; bus trip inc breakfast day 1
Rec: Tents. Age: 7	$210 25 12	Less 10%w/12 + and 1 Fw/23		
Age: 7	$350 24 12	Less 25%y16 and (1 Fw/12-15 and less 5%w/12-15) or (1 Fw/16 and less 10%w/16-24)		Wine inc; natural history trips for 3 units biology credit inc for will call dates
Age: 8	$285 25 6	(Less 10%w/12 + and 1Fw/12) or less 10%w/3 immediate family members	Shuttle not inc	You-oar; Asian cooking; wine inc
Req: Exp if cfs over 15,000. Age: 7	$240 25 12	1 Fw/12 and less 20%w/20 + and (less 10% w/ payment 60 days in advance or less 5% w/payment 30 days in advance)		
Age: Call	$234 25 6	(1 Fw/10 or .5 Fw/ 6) and less 25% before May 15 and less 20%y12	Shuttle is coop style	Wine, beer inc; handicapped; culture, myths and issues of local Indians Jul 10,; all-woman Jul 24, Aug 14; timid water-lovers Jun 26; storyteller & harp Jul 3; wildlife photography Jun 19; whitewater leadership workshop Jul 17; mother-daughter Jun 26

Name– Max. cfs	Starting	Raft type	Put-in– Take-out	Miles Camp Facilities
W.E.T. 15,000	D Jun 1—Aug 31	ob, pb op, ik op	China Creek-Presidio Bar	45 On-river Porta

LOWER KLAMATH—5 DAYS ━━━━━━

Name– Max. cfs	Starting	Raft type	Put-in– Take-out	Miles Camp Facilities
KROE No max	Mo, Th, Sa May 15—Sep 30	pb, ob op, o/pa op, ik op	Seiad Valley-Green Riffle	61 On-river Porta
Ti Bar No max	D Jul 1—Sep 30	ob, pb op, o/pa op, ik op	Happy Camp-Coon Creek	19 On-river Porta
Trinity River Raft 25,000	D May 15—Sep 13	pb, ik op	Happy Camp-Coon Creek; Somes Bar- Weitchpec	41 On-river Chem

LOWER KLAMATH—6 DAYS ━━━━━━

Name– Max. cfs	Starting	Raft type	Put-in– Take-out	Miles Camp Facilities
Action Adventures No max	D Jun 1—Aug 31	pb, ob op, ik s/b op	Sarah Totten-Ti Bar	62 On-river Porta
Outdoors Unlimited No max	Jul 5; Aug 2, 23	ob, pb op, ik op	Seiad Valley-Presidio Bar	50 On-river Porta
Trinity River Raft 25,000	D May 15—Sep 13	pb, ik op	Happy Camp-Ti Bar; Somes Bar- Weitchpec	49 On-river Chem
W.E.T. 15,000	D Jun 1—Aug 31	ob, pb op, ik op	Sarah Totten- Presidio Bar	61 On-river Porta

North Fork of the Smith

Introduction. The remote and beautiful North Fork of the Smith attracts the experienced wilderness rafting enthusiast.

Level of difficulty/water level concerns/flow information.
Class IV. The season is unusually difficult to predict. The minimum water for rafting is 400 cfs. Call (916) 322-3327 for flow information; the flow

Recom. Require. Min. Age	Cost Max. Grp. Min. Grp.	Discounts	Transportation	Comments
Rec: Camping exp. Age: 6	$250 24 12	Less $45y12 and 1 Fw/12		
Req: Exp for children. Age: 10	$420 25 3	Less 10%w/6-14 or less 15%w/ 15+		
Age: 6	$250 25 4	1 Fw/6		3-day horse-packing Marble Mountain Wilderness, add $45; only days 4 and 5 on river
Req: Exp if cfs over 15,000. Age: 7	$300 25 12	1 Fw/12 and less 20%w/20+ and (less 10% w/ payment 60 days in advance or less 5% w/ payment 30 days in advance)		
Age: Call	$299 25 10	Less 10%w/11+ or less 20%y13	Avail from Yreka	Will visit (1) Jade Mine up Indian Creek with native host who has bear, deer (non-domesticated) living at his homesite and (2) gemological display showing precious, semi-precious stones found along river; van from Yreka for 1-5, add $50
Age: 5	$405 20 16	1 Fw/10 or (less 10%w/20 and 1 Fw/19)		
Req: Exp if cfs over 15,000. Age: 7	$360 25 12	1 Fw/12 and less 20%w/20+ and (less 10% w/ payment 60 days in advance or less 5% w/ payment 30 days in advance)		
Rec: Camping exp. Age: 6	$395 24 12	Less $125y12 and 1 Fw/12		

Abbreviations

Mo,Tu,We	Monday, Tuesday, Wednesday, etc.	porta	Porta-potty or lime can at camp
D	Daily	exp	(Rafting) experience
will call	Outfitter will call you to arrange dates	Camping exp	Camping experience
ob	Oar boat	F	Free
o/pa	Oar boat with paddle assist	w/	With
pb	Paddle boat	wd	Weekday
ik	Inflatable kayak	we	Weekend
s/b	Self-bailing	y	Youth
op	Optional	y16	Youth, age 16 and under
ia	If available or if appropriate	s	Senior
on-river	Camp is beside the river	s65	Senior, age 65 and over
off-river	Camp is not beside the river	inc	Included
lodge	Overnight at a lodge or motel	avail	Available
flush	Flush toilets at camp	#	pound
chem	Chemical toilets or outhouse at camp		

Name– Max. cfs	Starting	Raft type	Put-in– Take-out	Miles Camp Facilities
NORTH FORK OF THE SMITH—1 DAY ━━━━━━━━				
Noah's 6,000	Apr 12, 26; May 10, 17	o/pa s/b, pb s/b op exp ia	Low Divide Rd-MF Conf + 2	15
Turtle River 4,000	Will call	pb, o/pa op, ik s/b op	Low Divide Rd-MF Confluence	13
NORTH FORK OF THE SMITH—2 DAYS ━━━━━━━				
Headwaters 4,000	D Apr 1—Jun 1	pb, ob op, s/b op, o/pa op	Low Divide Rd-Hwy 199 Bridge	24 On-river Porta
Noah's 6,000	Apr 12, 26; May 10, 17	o/pa s/b, pb s/b op exp ia	Low Divide Rd-Hwy 199 Bridge	24 Lodge

at the put-in is approximately one-third the flow at Jedediah Smith State Park.

Permit system/time to raft. See South Fork of the Smith.

Commercial rafting. See South Fork of the Smith.

Gear/safety/who can come. Rain gear and wetsuit. Because of the absence of road access, this run is recommended only for those in excellent health with Class IV rafting experience.

Distinctive features. Some call the North Fork the most beautiful river in the state. It flows through a rocky valley alive with orchids, daisies, lamb's tongues, pitcher plants, rhododendra, and azaleas.

River access. At put-in and below the Middle Fork of the Smith confluence.

Environment. Many of the wildflowers and other plants that grow along the banks of the Smith are endangered species —don't pick them. Ask your guide to point them out to you. Otter live in the river; deer and bear may visit it.

Summary of river between put-ins. Summary provided by Noah Hague of Noah's World of Water. See *California White Water* for river maps.

Low Divide Rd to Middle Fork Confluence (13 miles)—Eight Class IV rapids, more than twenty Class IIIs.

Middle Fork Confluence to Middle Fork Confluence + 2 miles (2 miles)—Class III rapids.

Middle Fork Confluence + 2 miles to Highway 199 Bridge (9 miles)—One Class V rapid (Oregon Hole), one Class IV, many Class IIIs. Old-growth redwoods along the riverbanks.

Recom. Require. Min. Age	Cost Max. Grp. Min. Grp.	Discounts	Transportation	Comments
Rec: Good health. Req: Wetsuit; excellent health for pb. Age: 14	$75 16 6	(Less 10%w/8 + or less 25%y17) and 1 Fw/12	Inc from Crescent City	Start date confirmation required
Age: 16	$65 20 6	(1 Fw/10 or .5 Fw/ 6) and less 25% before May 15 and less 20%y12		
Rec: Wetsuit. Age: 12	$170 25 15	Less 10%w/10 + and 1 Fw/20 or less 10%y16	Avail from Medford for 8 +	Bus from Medford, add $30
Rec: Good health. Req: Wetsuit; excellent health for pb. Age: 14	$180 16 6	(Less 10%w/8 + or less 25%y17) and 1 Fw/12	Inc from Crescent City	Start date confirmation required

River status. The North Fork of the Smith has wild and scenic status, under the "wild" classification.

See South Fork of the Smith for lodgings and campgrounds.

South Fork of the Smith

Introduction. A pool and drop river with rather more drop than pool, the South Fork of the Smith combines continuous excitement with moderate rapid difficulty.

Level of difficulty/water level concerns/flow information. Class IV. The season is unpredictable. The minimum water to raft is 500 cfs. For flow information, call (916) 322-3327; take one-third to one-half the level at Jedediah Smith State Park.

Permit system/time to raft. Because of the very low level of commercial rafting use of the Forks of the Smith, there are no limits to starts or to group sizes. The river itself limits usage; its season is short, and the timing of runnable periods varies dramatically from year to year. If you want to raft the Smith, call an outfitter and put your name on a will-call list.

Commercial rafting. As of December 1985, no company had a permit to raft the Smith. However, no permit is needed for "incidental use" by commercial outfitters (although proof of insurance is required). No statistics are available on 1985 usage.

Gear/safety/who can come. Bring your rain gear and wetsuit; the weather in April and May will surprise you. The South Fork of the

Smith should not be your first river (unless you can arrange with an outfitter to take out before the last mile, see below). Non-swimmers should note the Class V rapid.

Distinctive features. Clean, clear turquoise water.

River access. Road along but above the river.

Environment. Black-tailed deer, raccoons, and even bear call the river canyon their own. A few bald eagles roam the skies, but should they be elsewhere you could use your binoculars to spot blue heron. Coastal rain feeds a mountain greenery of Douglas fir, Port Orford cedar, and even some redwoods. In the final mile, the canyon narrows to a gorge, and a rain forest appears. The walls of the gorge are covered with moss and ferns; viny maples, alders, ash, and myrtle also enjoy the weather.

Abbreviations

Mo,Tu,We	Monday, Tuesday, Wednesday, etc.	porta	Porta-potty or lime can at camp
D	Daily	exp	(Rafting) experience
will call	Outfitter will call you to arrange dates	Camping exp	Camping experience
ob	Oar boat	F	Free
o/pa	Oar boat with paddle assist	w/	With
pb	Paddle boat	wd	Weekday
ik	Inflatable kayak	we	Weekend
s/b	Self-bailing	y	Youth
op	Optional	y16	Youth, age 16 and under
ia	If available or if appropriate	s	Senior
on-river	Camp is beside the river	s65	Senior, age 65 and over
off-river	Camp is not beside the river	inc	Included
lodge	Overnight at a lodge or motel	avail	Available
flush	Flush toilets at camp	#	pound
chem	Chemical toilets or outhouse at camp		

Name– Max. cfs	Starting	Raft type	Put-in– Take-out	Miles Camp Facilities
SOUTH FORK OF THE SMITH—1 DAY				
Noah's 5,000	Apr 11, 25; May 9, 16/will call	o/pa s/b, pb s/b op exp ia	South Fork Rd Br-MF Confluence	13
SOUTH FORK OF THE SMITH—2 DAYS				
Electric Rafting Co 5,000	D Apr 1—Jun 30	ob, pb op, o/pa op	South Fork Rd Br-MF Confluence	13 On-river Porta
Trinity River Raft 1,000	D May 15—Sep 13	pb, ik op	South Fork Rd Br-MF Confluence	13 On-river Chem
Turtle River 5,000	Will call	pb, o/pa op, ik s/b op	South Fork Rd Br-MF Confluence	13 On-river Porta

Summary of river between put-ins. Summary provided by Noah Hague of Noah's World of Water. See *California White Water* for a river map.

South Fork Rd Bridge to Middle Fork Confluence (13 miles)—One Class V rapid, two Class IVs, many Class IIIs. The more difficult rapids are all in the last mile of the run.

River status. The South Fork of the Smith has wild and scenic status, under the "recreational" classification. However, wild and scenic status protects a river only within one-quarter mile of its banks. At present, the Forest Service plans to clear cut 300 to 600 acres per year of old-growth forest land in the Smith River watershed for at least the next 20 years. Friends of the River and the Save-the-Redwoods League, concerned about both the irreplaceable loss of old-growth forest and the impact clear cutting may have on sedimentation in the river, have proposed the Smith River watershed for national park status. Designation as a national park would require the recommendation of the National Park Service and the approval of Congress.

Motels and lodges. Abbreviations used in the following listings are: L, R = Turn left, Turn right; H = Highway; I = Interstate; N, S, E, W = North, South, East, West; mi = miles; n/p = price or service not provided.

El Patio Motel, 655 H St, Crescent City, CA 95531. (707) 464-5114. Directions: H-101N to Crescent City; L on 6th St. Cost per room for one:

Recom. Require. Min. Age	Cost Max. Grp. Min. Grp.	Discounts	Transportation	Comments
Rec: Good health. Req: Wetsuit; excellent health for pb. Age: 14	$75 16 6	(Less 10%w/8 + or less 25%y17) and 1 Fw/12	Inc from Medford, Ashland, Yreka, Crescent City	
Req: Wetsuit. Age: 14	$135 15 8	Less 10%w/12 + or less 10%s65 or less 10%y14	Inc from Eureka/ Arcata	Lodge op, add $35
Age: 7	$120 40 12	1 Fw/12 and less 20%w/20+ and (less 10% w/ payment 60 days in advance or less 5% w/ payment 30 days in advance)		
Age: 16	$130 20 6	(1 Fw/10 or .5 Fw/ 6) and less 25% before May 15 and less 20%y12		

$22-32; for two: $24-34; for three: $26-36; for four: $28-38.

Pelican Beach Motel, 16855 Highway 101 North, Smith River, CA. (707) 487-7661. Directions: H-101N to just before the Oregon border. Cost per room for one: $29; for two: $29; for three: $34; for four: $39.

Crescent City has many motels.

Private campgrounds. Crescent City Redwoods KOA. 4241 Highway 101 North, Crescent City, CA 95531. (707) 464-5744. Open: All Year. Directions: H-101 to Crescent City; 5 mi N of city. Cost for tenters: $11; for RVs: $13.50; for showers: free.

Village Camper Inn. 1543 Parkway Dr, Crescent City, CA. (707) 464-3544. Open: All Year. Directions: H-101 to Crescent City; exit Parkway Dr. Cost for tenters: $7/2; for RVs: $9; for showers: $2.

Ship Ashore Resort. 12370 Highway 101 North, P.O. Box 75, Smith River, CA 95567. (707) 487-3141. Open: All Year. Directions: H-101 to Crescent City; 17 mi N of city. Cost for tenters: $5 for 2; for RVs: $10 for 2; for showers: $2.

Public campgrounds can be found in Redwood National Park.

New Commercial Rivers for 1986

Some companies have reported that they will offer commercial tours on new rivers in 1986, going where no outfitter has gone before (or where others have gone, but given up on rafting). If you are a pioneer and a purist, then these may be the runs for you. Call the outfitter with questions about them.

All of these runs require full wetsuits.

South Fork of the Eel

Class IV-V; 2 days. This is a rainy season run on a rain-fed river; the trip is offered by Nonesuch Whitewater from January to April on a will-call basis. Run from Branscomb to Big Bend: 16 miles, about 12 major rapids. Suitable for cold-weather tolerant rafters (the outfitter requires age 12+, but age 16 may be more appropriate) with Class IV paddling experience. $150. See *California White Water* for river description and map. See Main Eel for lodgings and campgrounds.

Mad

Class III; 2 days, runnable on a will call basis from January 15 to May 15. 16 rapids. Another rainy season river, one that you won't find described in any book. Run from Maple Creek to Blue Lake, 16 miles. $135. Also a Class II 1 day trip, run from Swasy Dam to Highway 101, 11 miles, $45. Like the South Fork of the Eel, this river requires that rafters be age 12 or older and tolerant of the cold. Call Electric Rafting Company if you are interested. Obtain the Northwestern California AAA map from your local CSAA office (or ask a friend who is an AAA member to get one for you) to locate the river. The Mad runs north of the Main Eel and south of the South Fork of the Trinity, near Eureka. Ask Electric Rafting about places to stay.

Wooley Creek

Class V; 5 days, 3 of which are on the river. Runnable during most of the Cal Salmon season. Raft from Fowler's Cabin to Oak Bottom: 9 miles, six Class V rapids, eight Class IVs. For the hardy and adventurous; you should have Class IV paddle experience. The outfitter requires a minimum age of 21. Phone interview and swimming test required. Offered at $630 by Wilderness Adventures. Not in any river guide: if you need a visual, write away for a Klamath National Forest map. Send $1 in check or money order, made out to USDA Forest Service, to USDA Forest Service, Office of Information, 630 Sansome Street, Room 529A, San Francisco, CA 94111. Wooley Creek is a tributary of the Cal Salmon; see that river for lodgings and campgrounds.

Middle Fork of the Feather

To rafting enthusiasts, the Middle Fork of the Feather may represent the ultimate whitewater wilderness challenge in the United States. Thirty-two miles of Class V+ rapids, strung out over five days. Runnable April to June. Suitable only for those who have rafted the Upper Tuolumne and feel ready for five days of major paddling. Expect a Class V paddle test. Backpacking experience will help, as you will be traveling very light, eating freeze-dried food, etc. For an awe-inspiring description of this river, as well as a river map, see *California White Water*.

At the request of the Forest Service, this book includes no information on specific trips on the Middle Fork of the Feather. Commercial permits have not yet been issued to run the river. However, there appears to be a possibility that permits will be issued in April. If they are, then Aquatic Adventure Publications will be right on it. If you would like to receive up-to-date trip information on the Middle Fork of the Feather (as well as on the Kyburz run of the South Fork of the American), then send a check for $1.50 and a self-addressed, stamped envelope, along with the last page of this book, to the publisher. If permits are not approved, your check will be returned in late April along with an update on the situation.

South Fork of the American (Kyburz run)

Class V; 1 day on a snow-fed free-flowing high-elevation river runnable until mid-June. Raft Kyburz to Riverton: 7 miles; depending on water levels, up to seven Class V rapids and many Class IVs that run together. For strong, confident swimmers with Class IV paddle experience. Expect a fitness and/or swim test. Highway 50 runs right along the river. See the description in *A Guide to the Best Whitewater in the State of California*. Discussed only briefly in *California White Water*. No river maps available. If you require a map, send $1 in check or money order made out to USDA Forest Service, to USDA Forest Service, Office of Information, 630 Sansome

Street, Room 529A, San Francisco, CA 94111. Request an Eldorado National Forest map.

This year may be your last chance to raft the Kyburz section. The S.O.F.A.R. project, a proposed hydroelectric dam, has been fully licensed and has received all necessary permits. Construction could start as early as spring, 1986, so be sure to check with your outfitter about the status of the project. You may also wish to check with your congressional representative (House Office Building, Washington, DC 20515), as this is one of a number of dams approaching construction whose feasibility depends on tax breaks and rate-payer subsidies unjustified by the current energy market. If built as planned, the dam would partially dewater this section and cause severe flow fluctuations both in this run and in the weekday flows of the main South Fork run downstream.

A permit is expected to be issued on this river by March, 1986. Once again, Aquatic Adventure Publications will have that information when it is available. Your check for $1.50 will cover information on the Kyburz run in addition to the Middle Fork of the Feather, discussed above.

River/Days/ Name	Starting	Raft type	Put-in– Take-out	Miles Camp Facilities
FORKS OF THE AMERICAN RIVER				
MF-Am, NF-Am cmb 2 days Adventours Unlimited	D Apr 5—Jun 8	pb	Oxbow Bend-Ruck-a-Chucky; Iowa Hill Rd-Shirttail Canyon	19 Off-river Flush
SF-Am, NF-Am cmb 2 days Adventure Connection	D Apr 1—Jun 30	pb, ob op, o/pa op on SF; pb ia, ob op, o/pa op on NF	Baachi Ranch-Salmon Falls; Iowa Hill Rd-Ponderosa Way	20 On-river Chem
SF-Am, NF-Am cmb 2 days Libra Expeditions	Mo-Th, Sa Apr 1-Jun 30	pb	Marshall Park-Salmon Falls; Iowa Hill Rd-Shirttail Canyon	20 Off-river Flush
SF-Am, NF-Am cmb 2 days Nonesuch Whitewater	D Apr 1—Jul 15	pb, o/pa op	Chili Bar-Salmon Falls; Iowa Hill Rd-Ponderosa Way	30 On-river Chem
SF-Am, MF-Am cmb 2 days Whitewater Excitement	D May 1—Jun 30	pb	Marshall Park-Salmon Falls; Oxbow Bend-Greenwood Br	31 On-river Flush
SF-Am, NF-Am cmb 2 days Whitewater Excitement	D Apr 1—Jun 30	pb	Marshall Park-Salmon Falls; Iowa Hill Rd-Ponderosa Way	24 On-river Flush
SF-Am, NF-Am cmb 2 days Whitewater Voyages	D Apr 1—Jul 31	pb, ob op	Beaver Point-Salmon Falls; Iowa Hill Rd-Ponderosa Way	22 On-river Chem

Combination Trips

As discussed in Chapter 2, combination trips allow you to stack together two or more river visits. In many cases, outfitters have provided limited start dates for these trips, making your trip somewhat easier to book.

For maximum cfs to raft information, see an outfitter's trip description under the appropriate river.

The following abbreviations identify rivers listed in the combination trips.

MF-Am	Middle Fork of the American
NF-Am	North Fork of the American
SF-Am	South Fork of the American
CS	California Salmon
MF-Eel	Middle Fork of the Eel
LK	Lower Klamath
UK	Upper Klamath
NF-Smith	North Fork of the Smith
SF-Smith	South Fork of the Smith

Recom. Require. Min. Age	Cost Max. Grp. Min. Grp.	Discounts	Transportation	Comments
Req: Wetsuit on NF-Am. Age: 13	$185 40 6	1 Fw/7-17 or 2 Fw/18-27 or 3 Fw/ 28-35 or 4 Fw/36	Avail from LA, Orange Cty	Bus from LA, Orange Cty (wine, beer inc), add $35; breakfast on day 1 inc; on-river op, porta
Rec: Exp; good physical condition. Req: Wetsuit. Age: 14	$175 50 12	1 Fw/12 and less $10w/24+ and less $10wd and less $10y15	Avail from LA	Breakfast day 1, 2 nights' camping, beer, wine inc; bus from LA, add $45
Rec: Exp. Req: Good health; wetsuit. Age: 14	$165 50 8	Less $15wd and 1 Fw/14 and less $10w/20+	Avail from Anaheim, Irvine, Torrance, San Fernando Valley	Bus from Anaheim, Irvine, Torrance, San Fernando Valley, add $45
Req: Wetsuit; Class III paddling exp. Age: 12	$160 24 8	Less 10%w/12+		
Age: 12	$155 24 24	1 Fw/12		
Rec: Healthy; active. Req: Wetsuit. Age: 14	$155 24 24	1 Fw/12		
Req: Wetsuit on NF. Age: 14	$170 24 24	Less $18wd and (less 10%w/12+ or less 10%y16)	Avail from LA	Cocktails inc; bus from LA, add $55; bus trip inc breakfast day 1

River/Days/Name	Starting	Raft type	Put-in–Take-out	Miles Camp Facilities
SF-Am, NF-Am cmb 2 days Wild Water West, Ltd.	D Apr 26—Jun 30	pb	Chili Bar-Camp Lotus; Iowa Hill Rd-Ponderosa Way	18 On-river Flush
MF-Am, NF-Am cmb 3 days Adventours Unlimited	D Apr 5—Jun 8	pb	Oxbow Bend-Mammoth Bar; Iowa Hill Rd-Shirttail Canyon	28 Off-river Flush
SF-Am, MF-Am, NF-Am cmb 3 days Whitewater Excitement	D Apr 1—Jun 30	pb	Marshall Park-Salmon Falls; Oxbow Bend-Greenwood Br; Iowa Hill Rd-Ponderosa Way	40 On-river Flush

EEL RIVER

River/Days/Name	Starting	Raft type	Put-in–Take-out	Miles Camp Facilities
MF-Eel, Main Eel cmb 7 days Rubicon	D May 1—May 15	ik, ob op, pb op	Black Butte-Alderpoint	77 On-river Porta

KLAMATH RIVER AND TRIBUTARIES

River/Days/Name	Starting	Raft type	Put-in–Take-out	Miles Camp Facilities
UK, Scott cmb 2 days Noah's	Apr 5, 19; May 16, 29; Jun 7	o/pa s/b	John Boyle-Copco Lake; Canyon Creek Scott Bar	29 Lodge
UK, CS, Scott cmb 3 days Eagle Sun	Sa Apr 1—Jun 30	ob, pb op, o/pa op	John Boyle-BLM Access; Indian Scotty-Sarah Totten; Nordheimer Crk-Wooley Creek	38 Lodge
UK, Scott, CS cmb 3 days Noah's	May 16, 29; Jun 7	o/pa s/b, pb s/b op exp ia	John Boyle-BLM Access; Canyon Creek-McGuffy Creek; Nordheimer Crk-Wooley Creek	30 Lodge
Scott, CS cmb 3 days Wilderness Adventures	May 17, 31; Jun 7	o/pa	Kelsey Creek-Scott Bar; Methodist Creek-Oak Bottom	32 Com. Porta
CS, Scott cmb 4 days All-Outdoors	May 10, 27; Jun 14	o/pa, pb op ia	Nordheimer Crk-Oak Bottom; Kelsey Creek-Sarah Totten	26 On-river Porta
LK, UK cmb 4 days ARTA	Jul 21, 28; Aug 18	pb	Happy Camp-Coon Creek; John Boyle-Copco Lake	36 On-river Porta
LK, UK cmb 4 days Headwaters	D Apr 1—Oct 31	pb, ob op, s/b op, o/pa op	Happy Camp-Coon Creek; John Boyle-Copco Lake	36 On-river Porta
UK, Scott, CS cmb 4 days Noah's	May 16, 29; Jun 7	o/pa s/b	John Boyle-BLM Access; Canyon Creek-McGuffy Creek; Nordheimer Crk-Dolan's Bar	40 Lodge
LK, UK cmb 5 days Noah's	Jun 25; Jul 2, 16, 23, 30; Aug 6, 13, 20, 27	pb, ik op on LK; o/pa, pb op exp ia on UK; all s/b	Grider Creek-Cottage Grove; John Boyle-Copco Lake	60 On-river Porta

Recom. Require. Min. Age	Cost Max. Grp. Min. Grp.	Discounts	Transportation	Comments
Req: Wetsuit on NF. Age: 13	$160 28 10	(1 Fw/12 or 2 Fw/ 20) and less $15wd		Beer, wine inc
Req: Wetsuit on NF. Age: 13	$250 40 6	1 Fw/7-17 or 2 Fw/18-27 or 3 Fw/ 28-35 or 4 Fw/36	Avail from LA, Orange Cty	Bus from LA, Orange Cty (wine, beer inc), add $35; breakfast on day 1 inc; on-river camp op, porta
Rec: Healthy. Req: Wetsuit. Age: 14	$225 24 24	1 Fw/12		
Req: Wetsuit. Age: 12	$450 16	1 Fw/10		Fishing for steelhead on Main Eel
Rec: Exp. Req: Wetsuit; excellent health. Age: 16	$180 16 6	(Less 10%w/8 + or less 25%y17) and 1 Fw/12	Inc from Medford, Ashland, Yreka	
Req: Class III exp. Age: 18	$300 24 6	Less 10%w/6 +	Inc from Medford, Ashland	
Rec: Exp. Req: Wetsuit; excellent health. Age: 16	$250 16 6	(Less 10%w/8 + or less 25%y17) and 1 Fw/12	Inc from Medford, Ashland, Yreka	
Req: Wetsuit. Age: 16	$370 20 8	1 Fw/15		1 night in lodge, 1 night on-river
Req: Wetsuit; exp. Age: 16	$355 20 20	1 Fw/12		
Age: 12	$350 20 12	Less $75y17 and less 10%w/10 +		
Rec: Healthy, active; wetsuit Apr, May, Sep, Oct; exp for paddlers. Age: 14	$350 25 15	Less 10%w/10 + and 1 Fw/20 or less 10%y16	Inc from Ashland, avail from Medford	Bus from Medford, add $15; 1 night lodge op, add $75
Rec: Exp. Req: Wetsuit; excellent health. Age: 16	$325 16 6	(Less 10%w/8 + or less 25%y17) and 1 Fw/12	Inc from Medford, Ashland, Yreka	
Req: Good health. Age: 10	$295 25 6	(Less 10%w/8 + or less 25%y17) and 1 Fw/12	Inc from Medford, Ashland, Yreka	Gold panning; fishing for native wild trout (UK) and steelhead (LK); riverside sauna; all-woman (age 16 +), Aug 13

River/Days/ Name	Starting	Raft type	Put-in– Take-out	Miles Camp Facilities
CS, Scott cmb 5 days Sierra Whitewater	May 22; Jun 4	o/pa	Forks of Salmon-Dolan's Bar; Bridge Flat-Scott Bar	34 On-river Porta
LK, UK cmb 5 days Sierra Whitewater	Aug 11, 18	pb, ik op ia on LK; o/pa on UK	Happy Camp-Presidio Bar; John Boyle-Copco Lake	43 On-river Porta
LK, UK cmb 5 days Whitewater Voyages	Aug 11, 25	pb, ob op	Happy Camp-Presidio Bar; John Boyle-Copco Lake	43 On-river Porta
UK, Scott, CS cmb 5 days Wilderness Adventures	May 2, 9, 22	ob, pb op, o/pa op	John Boyle-Copco Lake; Kelsey Creek-Scott Bar; Nordheimer Crk-Wooley Creek	37 Lodge
CS, Scott, UK cmb 6 days All-Outdoors	May 10, 27; Jun 14	o/pa, pb op ia	Nordheimer Crk-Oak Bottom; Kelsey Creek-Sarah Totten; John Boyle-Copco Lake	43 On-river Porta
UK, LK cmb 11 days Wilderness Adventures	Mar 31	ob	John Boyle-Copco Lake; Iron Gate Dam-Pacific Ocean	178 On-river Porta

FORKS OF THE SMITH RIVER

River/Days/ Name	Starting	Raft type	Put-in– Take-out	Miles Camp Facilities
SF-Smith, NF-Smith cmb 3 days Noah's	Apr 11, 25; May 9, 16	o/pa s/b, pb s/b op exp ia	South Fork Rd Br-MF Confluence; Low Divide Rd-Hwy 199 Bridge	37 Lodge
NF-Smith, SF-Smith cmb 3 days Turtle River	Will call	pb, o/pa op, ik s/b op	Low Divide Rd-MF Confluence; South Fork Rd Br-MF Confluence	26 On-river Porta

Whitewater Schools

Whitewater schools offer you the chance to become your own guide, by teaching you the necessary skills to run a safe and well-planned rafting trip. Many outfitters use these schools as a training ground for their own guides.

These tours have the advantages of relatively low cost and a low passenger (student) to guide ratio. In addition, schools are usually offered in the early spring, before other boaters start to crowd the rivers.

Whitewater schools include food and on-river camping, unless otherwise noted.

Notes on the school descriptions

Rivers. The following abbreviations are used for rivers in the guide school tables.

Recom. Require. Min. Age	Cost Max. Grp. Min. Grp.	Discounts	Transportation	Comments
Req: Wetsuit. Age: 12	$395 12 12	1 Fw/12 and less 10%w/12 and less 20%y16	Avail from Medford	Van from Medford, add $5
Age: 8	$375 20 8	(1 Fw/12 or 2 Fw/ 20) and less $20wd and (less 10%w/10 + or less 20%w/20 or less 20%y16)	Avail from Medford	Van from Medford, add $5
Rec: Wetsuit. Age: 12	$398 20 20	Less 10%w/12 + or less 10%y16		Cocktails inc
Req: Wetsuit. Age: 16	$530 20 10	1 Fw/15		
Req: Wetsuit; exp. Age: 16	$525 20 20	1 Fw/12		
Req: Wetsuit. Age: 16	$915 20 6	1 Fw/15		You-oar on LK; portage Ishi-Pishi
Rec: Good health. Req: Wetsuit; excellent health for pb. Age: 14	$250 16 6	(Less 10%w/8 + or less 25%y17) and 1 Fw/12	Inc from Crescent City	Start date confirmation required; last 1.5 mi on SF o/ pa only
Req: Exp for pb, ik. Age: 16	$195 20 6	(1 Fw/10 or .5 Fw/ 6) and less 25% before May 15 and less 20%y12		

MF-Am	Middle Fork of the American
NF-Am	North Fork of the American
SF-Am	South Fork of the American
CS	California Salmon
EF-Car	East Fork of the Carson
L Kern	Lower Kern
U Kern	Upper Kern
LK	Lower Klamath
UK	Upper Klamath
Mer	Merced
Mok	Mokelumne
U Sac	Upper Sacramento
Stan	Stanislaus
U Tri	Upper Trinity

Also, two outfitters run a portion of their guide school on the Rogue, a Class III river in southern Oregon.

Days. The first number refers to the total number of days of the school; the second number refers to the number of days spent on the river.

Hired 1985. Percentage of those who finished the school who were hired as guides by the outfitter in 1985. n/a = not applicable; n/p = school not provided.

Skills taught. Some companies will teach you both oar and paddle captaining skills, while other companies will teach you only one or the other.

Company Name	River(s)	Days	Start Dates	Student: Guide Ratio	Hired 1985	Cost	Skills Taught	Comments
Action Adventures	NF-Am; MF-Am; SF-Am, LK	26(20)	Feb 28; Mar 21	5:1	90%	$500	Oar, paddle captaining; cooking; bad weather survival; First aid; CPR	Certificates issued by the AGA; first 6 days free classroom training; next 10 days on-river, $500; next ten days advanced training for company guides only, free
Adventours Unlimited	MF-Am; NF-Am	8(6)	Apr 5-- Aug 31	4:1	60%	$350	Oar, paddle captaining; safety; repair; ecology; river etiquette; cooking; First aid	First aid certificates awarded
Adventure Connection	SF-Am; MF-Am; NF-Am ia	7(6)	Mar 24	6:1	50%	$425	Paddle captaining; rigging boats; repair; emergency procedures; customer relations; river etiquette; kitchen skills	Class tailored to meet individual needs of participants
All-Outdoors	SF-Am	6(6)	Apr 5	5:1	50%	$395	Oar, paddle captaining; safety; commercial skills	
ARR	NF-Am; SF-Am	7(7)	Mar 31; Apr 5	6:1	50%	$350	Oar, paddle captaining; wilderness camping; cooking; river rescue; boat rigging; repair; reading whitewater	
ARTA	CS; Rogue; UK	10(9)	Jun 6	4:1	n/a	$600	Advanced oar, paddle skills; advanced safety	Class V workshop, exp required
ARTA	SF-Am; MF-Am or NF-Am	7(7)	Apr 13; May 11; Jun 15	5:1	40%	$400	Oar, paddle captaining; cooking; knot tying; repair; safety	
A WW Connection	MF-Am; SF-Am	7(7)	Mar 26	4:1	75%	$400	Oar, paddle captaining; basic river running; knots; river rescue; equipment repair; P.R. skills; flora; fauna; history	
California River	MF-Am; SF-Am	7(7)	Mar 22; May 18; Aug 17	4:1	20%	$400	Oar, paddle captaining; safety; rescue; food preparation; sanitation; minimum impact camping; trip planning	Scholarships avail

Company Name	River(s)	Days	Start Dates	Student: Guide Ratio	Hired 1985	Cost	Skills Taught	Comments
Chuck Richards' SOC	L Kern; U Kern	2(2)	Sa, Mo Apr 1--Jul 31	5:1	n/a	$140	Basic paddle, basic oar captaining	Food, camping not inc
Chuck Richards' SOC	L Kern; U Kern	6(6)	Su Apr 1- -Jul 31	5:1	n/a	$400	Oar, paddle captaining; emergency, rescue procedures; repair; maintenance; reading whitewater; rigging; equipment selection	
Chuck Richards' WW	L Kern; U Kern	6(6)	Mar 30; Apr 5	5:1	100%	$300	Splashyak, paddle captaining; ropes; knots; rescue; emergency procedures; camp organization; cooking; customer handling and problem solving; personality skills; company policy; Forest Service permit requirements	Meals not inc; students need current CPR and first aid certification; interview required; motel op, student arranges
Earthtrek Expeditions	MF-Am; NF-Am; SF-Am	7(7)	Mar 24; Jun 9; Sep 1	6:1	25%	$425	Paddle captaining; reading whitewater; rigging boats; knots; equipment repairs; emergency rescue procedures; cooking	
Great Valley	Mok; Stan	5(5)	Jun 16; Jul 21	6:1	80%	$300	Paddle or oar captaining; safety; rescue; equipment repair; trip planning skills; river hydraulics	Course outlines inc; weekend courses start Apr 5, 26; May 3, 24; Jun 7, 28; Jul 5, 26; Aug 2, 23; Sep 20; three weekends required to complete course; off-river camp op
Headwaters	CS; UK; Scott	7(7)	Sep-Oct/ will call	3:1	n/p	$550	Class V techniques	Advanced school; work on individual basis to meet needs of students
Headwaters	LK; UK	7(7)	Mar-May/ will call	3:1	n/p	$450	See Beginner school; more details	Intermediate school
Headwaters	LK; Rogue	5(5)	Mar-May/ will call	3:1	n/p	$325	Paddle, oar captaining; group dynamics; knots; rigging; reading whitewater; emergency rescue, procedures, equipment; safety; cooking; First aid; river ecology; food planning; equipment purchasing, maintenance, repair	Beginner school; inc daily classroom, Day 1 instruction on lake
Mariah	SF-Am	7(7)	Apr 12	6:1	80%	$350	Oar, paddle captaining; reading whitewater; safety; equipment maintenance and repair	
NOC	SF-Am; EF-Car	8(5)	Mar 1; Mar 24; May 17; Jun 7	6:1	95%	Com.	Oar, paddle captaining; rescue; repair; equipment maintenance; reading whitewater; cooking; emergency procedures	Food, camping not inc; wetsuit required; instruction is free, charges are for equipment rental (rafts, etc.), put-in, take-out fees, carpooling only; designed to qualify individuals to rent rafts for private raft trips

Company Name	River(s)	Days	Start Dates	Student: Guide Ratio	Hired 1985	Cost	Skills Taught	Comments
OARS	MF-Am; SF-Am; Mer; Mok	9(7)	Mar 22, Jun 7	4:1	50%	$610	Boating theory; knot tying; safety; rescue; repair; leadership skills; river conservation; camp craft; guide/passenger relations; dutch oven cooking; reading whitewater	Off-river camp op
Ouzel Voyages	CS; LK	7(7)	Mar 23	5:1	56%	$350	Oar, oar/paddle assist, paddle captaining; camp skills; Class III, IV navigation	
RAM River	MF-Am; NF-Am	7(7)	Mar 22	3:1	75%	$225	Oar, paddle captaining; safety; rescue	
River Runners, Inc.	NF-Am; SF-Am	9(9)	Mar 22	5:1	100%	$450	Oar, paddle captaining; repair; safety; ecology; rescue	
Sierra Whitewater	LK; UK	5(5)	Aug 4	3:1	100%	$375	Oar, paddle captaining; reading whitewater; repair; First aid; natural history; cooking; packing; rigging	Exp recommended
Trinity Wilderness	LK; U Tri	6(6)	Mar 22; May 24	4:1	20%	$275	Oar, paddle captaining; reading whitewater; emergency procedures; boat maintenance, repair; cooking	
Turtle River	SF-Am; U Sac; Scott	5(5)	Apr 9	6:1	20%	$325	Oar, paddle captaining; reading whitewater; safety; river ecology; repair; equipment maintenance; rescue; leadership	
Whitewater Voyages	MF-Am; NF-Am; SF-Am	7(7)	Mar 23; Jun 22	4:1	80%	$550	Paddle or oar captaining; reading whitewater; signals; unwrapping rafts; emergency procedures; equipment maintenance, repair; knot tying; wilderness cooking; menu planning; safety	Copies of *The Guide's Guide*, and *Class V Briefing* by William McGinnis (chief instructor) inc
Whitewater Voyages	L Kern; U Kern	7(7)	Apr 13	4:1	80%	$575	Paddle or oar captaining; reading whitewater; signals; unwrapping rafts; emergency procedures; equipment maintenance, repair; knot tying; wilderness cooking; menu planning; safety	Copies of *The Guide's Guide*, and *Class V Briefing* by William McGinnis (chief instructor) inc

---

Chapter 4

Outfitters Operating in California

Now for the saddest weakness of the book. All the outfitters listed have their required permits, yet I can't go through the list and say this company is good, or that company is not. There are too many outfitters offering too many trips. To make a judgment based on one trip (and one guide) from each outfitter (assuming I could afford it, which I can't) would be like a restaurant reviewer advising one restaurant over another on the basis of having sampled only the salads. Further, I am unwilling to suffer a lawsuit by repeating industry gossip.

However, I can report that I have rafted with Adventure Connection, All-Outdoors, Earthtrek Expeditions, Noah's World of Water, Sierra Mac, Turtle River Rafting, and Whitewater Voyages and that all of these companies provided fine trips with good food and well-qualified guides. I would raft again with any of them, and I probably will.

But these companies represent only a tenth of those operating in the state. Further, my selection of companies was frequently based on which outfitter was running a river when I wanted to raft (although price was also a factor). Other companies may (a) offer superior trips, or (b) provide a better match with your concept of a desirable tour.

In choosing an outfitter, be sure to spend some time on the phone, talking with the outfitter and judging the company's ability to provide a safe and reliable service. Ask about the training program for guides. Ask about the screening process for passengers. Who will or will not be permitted to raft a certain river? A company should be willing to sacrifice potential revenue for safety. Ask about the maximum number of people that would be put in a paddle boat. Ideally, this number should be six, and under no circumstances should it be more than eight. On some rivers, for example the Middle Fork of the American, you can calculate the maximum number per boat from the number of boats permitted and the maximum group size.

This book provides other information that may be useful to you in your company analysis. Naturally, every outfitter will express that his or her company is quite conservative about safety. However, check the maximum level at which a company is willing to run a river and also the minimum age at which a company will permit a child to raft a river (see

—*Sierra Shutterbug/Paul Ratcliffe*
An oar boat travels through a Class I stretch of the East Fork of the Carson

Chapter 3). These data often reflect a company's attitude towards safety.

Also, be aware that an alarming number of "commercial" trips are run by companies or individuals that do not have the required permits for the river rafted. These are known as "pirate" or "rogue" trips. Companies or persons providing such trips (a) do not have to have insurance (now very expensive and difficult to obtain), (b) do not have to pay fees for river access, river maintenance, etc., (c) do not have to meet guide training standards, (d) do not have to meet group or boat-load limitations, and (e) do not have to meet equipment standards. It should come as no surprise whatsoever that pirate trips are frequently offered at a very, very large discount. I urge you, for safety's sake, to avoid this kind of illegal bargain.

Every trip listed in this book was verified by a river authority as a legal trip in December, 1985. In addition, some legitimate companies could not be reached or chose not to be listed here. For any company's trip that is not listed, you can ascertain whether or not the trip is legal by asking the outfitter for the name and phone number of the officer in the Forest Service, Bureau of Land Management, or State or local agency responsible for permits on the river. Call the officer to verify that the company has an active permit.

The following descriptions were designed to provide you with information that may differentiate outfitters, as well as each company's view of its qualities.

Notes on the company descriptions

Address. You may find arranging transportation easier with a company based near your home. Also, your long distance phone bill will be lower. On the other hand, you may find greater expertise on a particular river, as well as lower prices, offered by companies located near the river you wish to raft.

Phone answered. These are the times the phone number is answered by a person who can make a reservation. This information is provided to avoid the annoyance of placing a long-distance phone call and reaching only an answering machine. Larger, more established companies employ permanent office staff to answer the phone and return phone calls during regular office hours. Also, some of the larger companies have "800" numbers.

Charge cards accepted. AX is American Express; MC is Mastercard; V is Visa.

Year company started. As reported by the outfitter.

Rafting/river associations. These associations work to advance the sport of river running, to improve or provide services to the commercial outfitting industry, and/or to protect rivers. Only California, regional, or national associations are listed. Friends of the River did not verify by deadline that the outfitters correctly reported their membership.

The following abbreviations are used in the listings:

AGA	American Guides Association
ARCC	American Rivers Conservation Council
ARRA	American River Recreation Association
EDPO	El Dorado Professional Outfitters
FOR	Friends of the River
KCRO	Klamath Canyon River Outfitters
NORS	National Organization for River Sports
WRGA	Western River Guides Association

Wetsuit Rental. If you will be rafting at a time of year or on a river requiring a wetsuit, you can save time and effort by renting one through your outfitter. Rafting companies also provide thinner wetsuits specially designed for rafting. However, you can often save money by renting elsewhere. See the appendix *Where to Buy or Rent Equipment.*

Where prices are shown, they refer to just a wetsuit, unless "w" is used for wetsuit and "b" for booties. Prices vary substantially from outfitter to outfitter. This book uses the following abbreviations:

no	Outfitter does not provide or rent wetsuits
inc	wetsuit rental is included in the trip fee
w/b inc	wetsuit and booties are included in the trip fee
/day	per day
/add day	per additional day
/we	per weekend
/trip	per trip
/day 1	for the first day of the rental
/day 2	for the second day of the rental

Rates. Rates are either "guaranteed", in which case an outfitter has stated that rates will remain the same throughout 1986, or "subject to change", in which case the outfitter has indicated that rates may rise during the 1986 season. Note that in the case of at least one outfitter, Chuck Richards' WW/SOC, prices for 1986 were not finalized at deadline (November, 1985) and the prices quoted here are 1985 rates.

Rivers. Some companies specialize in only certain rivers, while others provide a wide variety (Oregon companies may offer many trips in that state not listed here). Just because an outfitter reports a rafting trip does not mean that the outfitter runs that river frequently or even at all. It simply means that the outfitter has a permit and has chosen to have that trip listed.

The river list also allows you to decide on a company first and then select a river that the company rafts.

Some rivers have restrictive permit systems. As a result, outfitters on these rivers either (a) have extensive experience on the river, and/or

(b) were selected in a competitive bid-prospectus system. Companies operating on these rivers (Kern, Kings, Merced, Tuolumne, and Yuba) are almost all well-established, full-time, professional outfitters.

The following abbreviations, organized alphabetically by the main river name, are used in the rivers section.

MF-Am	Middle Fork of the American
NF-Am	North Fork of the American
SF-Am	South Fork of the American
CS	California Salmon
EF-Car	East Fork of the Carson
MF-Eel	Middle Fork of the Eel
EB-NF-Fea	East Branch of the North Fork of the Feather
L Kern	Lower Kern
U Kern	Upper Kern
LK	Lower Klamath
UK	Upper Klamath
Mer	Merced
Mok	Mokelumne
U Sac	Upper Sacramento
NF-Smith	North Fork of the Smith
SF-Smith	South Fork of the Smith
Stan	Stanislaus
U Tri	Upper Trinity
BRG	Burnt Ranch Gorge (on Trinity River)
SF-Tri	South Fork of the Trinity River
Main T	Main Tuolumne
Upper T	Upper Tuolumne
NF-Yuba	North Fork of the Yuba

Statement. Finally, each company received the opportunity to say 50 words about either its philosophy of operation or those qualities that its management felt made the company excellent or unique. As previously mentioned, this statement was edited only for length and for the word "gourmet" (see Gourmet trips, in Chapter 2).

Action Adventures Wet n Wild
Box 13846
Sacramento, CA 95853
(800) 238-3688 in CA
24 hrs
(916) 662-5431
24 hrs
Charge Cards: AX
Company Started in 1958
Rafting/River Associations: AGA, WRGA
Wetsuit rental: No
Rates: Guaranteed

Rivers: MF-Am; NF-Am; SF-Am; CS; Main Eel; LK; Mer; Main T; Guide School
To provide a maximum level of enjoyment in a wilderness setting for persons of all socioeconomic strata without regard to age, prior experience, or handicaps. Our priorities are (1) safety, (2) fun, (3) comfort. We are the oldest operator of California rivers. We have a 100% safety record during our history of operation.

Adventours Unlimited
P.O. Box 218/207 Main St.
Seal Beach, CA 90740
(213) 594-8153
Mo-Fr 9:30 am-5 pm
(213) 493-6824
Mo-Fr 9:30 am-5 pm
Charge Cards: MC, V
Company Started in 1980
Rafting/River Associations: ARCC,
ARRA, EDPO, FOR
Wetsuit rental: No
Rates: Guaranteed
Rivers: MF-Am; NF-Am; Guide
School
Adventours Unlimited is a multi-faceted adventure company with an emphasis on safety and comfort. Whitewater rafting is our specialty.

Adventure Connection
P.O. Box 475
Coloma, CA 95613
(916) 626-7385
Mo-Sa 9 am-5 pm
(800) 556-6060 in CA
Mo-Sa 9 am-5 pm
Charge Cards: MC, V
Company Started in 1978
Rafting/River Associations: ARRA,
EDPO, FOR, WRGA
Wetsuit rental: No
Rates: Guaranteed
Rivers: MF-Am; NF-Am; SF-Am;
Guide School
Adventure Connection strives to share with our guests our belief that rafting is a three-fold adventure—a connection between nature, self, and shared experience. Our goal is to provide safe, comfortable, exciting, and fun adventures for people from varied backgrounds.

All-Outdoors Adventure Trips
2151 San Miguel Drive
Walnut Creek, CA 94596

(415) 932-8993
Mo-Fr 8 am-5 pm
Charge Cards: No
Company Started in 1974
Rafting/River Associations: ARRA,
EDPO, FOR, KCRO, WRGA
Wetsuit rental: No
Rates: Subject to change
Rivers: MF-Am; NF-Am; SF-Am;
CS; Mer; LK; UK; Main T; Scott;
Guide School
All-Outdoors is a professional whitewater company with 17 years' experience conducting adventure trips for clubs, schools, employee groups, and individuals. All-Outdoors has a reputation for commitment to serving our guests prior to, during, and after our trips. We are a company that prides itself in offering a professional and organized service.

American River Recreation (ARR)
11257 S. Bridge St.
Rancho Cordova, CA 95670
(916) 635-4516
Oct 1—Mar 31 Tu-Sa 10 am-6 pm
(916) 635-4516
Apr 1—Sep 30 D 10 am-6 pm
Charge Cards: MC, V
Company Started in 1974
Rafting/River Associations: ARRA,
EDPO, FOR, WRGA
Wetsuit rental: w: $5/day, $4/add day; b: $1/day, $1/add day
Rates: Guaranteed
Rivers: MF-Am; NF-Am; SF-Am;
CS; EF-Car; LK; UK; Guide School
Started in 1974 as a small raft rental on the lower American River in Sacramento, American River Recreation has become the largest raft rental in California. We also have a large retail store, kayak school, inflatable boat repair center, sailboard school, and of course, one of the

fastest growing, full-service whitewater rafting companies in the state.

American River Touring Association (ARTA)
445 High St.
Oakland, CA 94601
(415) 465-9355
Mo-Fr 9 am-5:30 pm
Charge Cards: No
Company Started in 1963
Rafting/River Associations: ARRA, EDPO, FOR, WRGA
Wetsuit rental: No
Rates: Guaranteed
Rivers: MF-Am; NF-Am; SF-Am; CS; EF-Car; LK; UK; Mer; Main T; Guide School
Special places, special people. At ARTA, we believe that you should be just as concerned about who you are going with as you are about where you are going. Our guides are friendly, entertaining, humorous, and safe; people with whom you will enjoy spending your vacation.

A Whitewater Connection
P.O. Box 270
Coloma, CA 95613-0270
(916) 622-6446
Mo-Fr 9 am-5 pm
(800) 336-7238 in CA
Mo-Fr 9 am-7 pm
Charge Cards: No
Company Started in 1980
Rafting/River Associations: ARRA, EDPO, FOR
Wetsuit rental: No
Rates: Guaranteed
Rivers: MF-Am; NF-Am; SF-Am; UK; Guide School
We feel our employees and cuisine are the most important factors in making your river journey a mem-

orable one. Therefore, we hire only the most qualified and personable people available and we provide the finest meals in the industry—steak and lobster dinners, local wine selections, buffet deli lunches, etc.

California Adventures
UC Dept of Recr Sports
2301 Bancroft Way
Berkeley, CA 94720
(415) 642-4000
Mo-Th 10 am-6 pm; Fr 10 am-8 pm; Sa 8 am-1 pm
Charge Cards: MC, V
Company Started in 1980
Rafting/River Associations: FOR
Wetsuit rental: Inc
Rates: Guaranteed
Rivers: SF-Am; EF-Car
As leaders in the field of Outdoor Recreation, we at California Adventures are committed to providing low cost recreational experiences, while acting as an example of safe and environmentally conscientious outdoor recreation. Our programs are unique in that we offer transportation, as well as attractive discounts on already low prices.

California River Trips
P.O. Box 460
Lotus, CA 95651-0460
(916) 626-8006
Feb—Oct Mo-Fr 9 am-5 pm
Charge Cards: No
Company Started in 1978
Rafting/River Associations: ARRA, EDPO, FOR, WRGA
Wetsuit rental: No
Rates: Guaranteed
Rivers: MF-Am; NF-Am; SF-Am; Guide School
California River Trips believes in smaller trips, with quality camps,

and a low passenger-to-guide ratio (6:1). We also believe in sharing the complete canyon, the birds, history, and ecology, through our exceptionally qualified guides. We discourage the use of drugs and alcohol.

Charter River Adventures
P.O. Box 7098
San Jose, CA 95150
(408) 985-7733
Sep 1—Apr 30 Mo-Fr 5 pm-7 pm
(408) 985-7733
May 1—Aug 31 Mo-Fr 9 am-5 pm
Charge Cards: No
Company Started in 1982
Rafting/River Associations: FOR
Wetsuit rental: b inc
Rates: Guaranteed
Rivers: MF-Am; EF-Car; LK
Charter River Adventures is "Rafting with Style". We call it luxurious backpacking; our whitewater rafts carry all the gear. You get wilderness camping on spectacular rivers and amenities found with no other company. Experience the difference. Enjoy a first class river trip with Charter River Adventures. Gift certificates are available.

**Chuck Richards' Whitewater, Inc./
Sequoia Outdoor Center**
Box WW Whitewater
Lake Isabella, CA 93240
(619) 379-4685
Mo-Fr 9 am-5 pm
(800) 624-5950 in So. CA
Mo-Fr 9 am-5 pm
Charge Cards: MC, V
Company Started in 1975
Rafting/River Associations: ARCC, WRGA
Wetsuit rental: w: $10/day; b: $3.50/day
Rates: Subject to change

Rivers: Forks-Kern; U Kern; L Kern; Guide School
Whitewater! It's born on the Kern. Here's Southern California's closest whitewater river with thundering rapids that pale all others we've seen from Alaska to Chile. Plus warm water and perfect sunshine, and great guides grinning and dripping in our paddle rafts and our dynamite 2-person splashyaks. Come on!

Eagle Sun, Inc.
P.O. Box 873
Medford, OR 97501
(503) 772-9910
D 7 am-8 pm
Charge Cards: No
Company Started in 1976
Rafting/River Associations:
Wetsuit rental: No
Rates: Guaranteed
Rivers: CS; LK; UK; Scott
Eagle Sun Expeditions are designed for those who enjoy getting involved in outdoor experiences. We offer both "paddle yourself" and "guide-powered" trips. Our guides thoroughly instruct you on boat-handling techniques and water safety procedures. You become part of a highly personalized team that works together to master river exploration.

Earthtrek Expeditions
1534 E. Edinger, Ste. #6
Santa Ana, CA 92705
(714) 547-5864
Mo-Fr 9 am-5 pm
Charge Cards: MC, V
Company Started in 1977
Rafting/River Associations: FOR
Wetsuit rental: w: $12/we; b: $3/we
Rates: Guaranteed
Rivers: MF-Am; NF-Am; SF-Am; Guide School

Earthtrek prides itself on the personal touches we add to our river journeys. We go the extra mile, insuring that the finest guides, safety equipment, and culinary experiences will be had on every trip. While the river creates the magic, it's our personal touch that brings the magic to heart.

ECHO: The Wilderness Co.
6529 Telegraph Ave.
Oakland, CA 94609
(415) 652-1600
Mo-Fr 9 am-5 pm
Charge Cards: MC, V
Company Started in 1971
Rafting/River Associations: FOR, WRGA
Wetsuit rental: w/b: $20/trip
Rates: Guaranteed
Rivers: NF-Am; SF-Am; Main T
To provide the best river trips possible: safe, well-organized, exciting adventures that promote a great appreciation of wilderness and wild rivers and that offer a special, meaningful experience for everyone involved.

Electric Rafting Co.
P.O. Box 3456
Eureka, CA 95501
(707) 445-3456
Mo-Fr 9 am-5 pm; Sa 10 am-3 pm
Charge Cards: MC, V
Company Started in 1979
Rafting/River Associations: AGA, FOR
Wetsuit rental: $10/day, $3/add day
Rates: Subject to change
Rivers: CS; LK; SF-Smith
The Electric Rafting Company is the only whitewater recreation service native to the golden state's "North Coast". We get a "charge" out of sharing our knowledge of California's North Coast rivers with rafters. We also do custom river trips that are runnable only during the winter.

Four Seasons Adventure
290 Helman
Ashland, OR 97520
(503) 482-8352
Mo-Su 9 am-6 pm
Charge Cards: No
Company Started in 1982
Rafting/River Associations:
Wetsuit rental: w/b inc
Rates: Guaranteed
Rivers: LK
We personalize our programs, activities, and leaders to offer the best possible outdoor recreation opportunity for all persons in as many safe and affordable areas of recreation as we can. All activities can be adapted to meet special needs.

Friends of the River
Fort Mason Ctr. Bldg. C
San Francisco, CA 94123
(415) 771-0400
Mo-Fr 9:30 am-5 pm
(916) 442-3155
Mo-Fr 9:30 am-5 pm
Charge Cards: No
Rafting Started in 1978
Rafting/River Associations:
Wetsuit rental: No
Rates: Guaranteed
Rivers: SF-Am
Friends of the River, a non-profit organization, works to protect rivers. Outfitters donate equipment; professional guides volunteer, spending extra time explaining the river's natural history and ecology. Our passengers report that FOR trips provide a relaxing, communal, and friendly atmosphere. Join us and help FOR preserve our rivers.

(FOR operates under an umbrella permit.)

Get Wet River Trips
P.O. Box 697
Ashland, OR 97520
(503) 482-1254
D 8 am-10 pm
Charge Cards: No
Company Started in 1981
Rafting/River Associations: FOR, WRGA
Wetsuit rental: Inc
Rates: Guaranteed
Rivers: CS; LK
Get Wet is for the outdoor adventurist who can appreciate floating a whitewater river with well-trained, courteous professionals who use only the best equipment and provide the small details. Get Wet is to outfitting as Mercedes is to automobiles.

Gold Rush River Runners
P.O. Box 1013
Diamond Springs, CA 95619
(916) 626-7631
Mo-Fr 9 am-5 pm
(800) 344-1013 in CA
Mo-Fr 9 am-5 pm
Charge Cards: No
Company Started in 1978
Rafting/River Associations: ARRA, EDPO
Wetsuit rental: No
Rates: Guaranteed
Rivers: SF-Am
Gold Rush River Runners is a family-owned company offering quality trips with personal service. By combining 34 years of experience, high standards, and individual attention, Gold Rush provides the ultimate river trip vacation. Gold Rush specializes by offering trips only on the American River.

Great Out of Doors
16475 Julie Lane
Red Bluff, CA 96080
(916) 527-1417
Sep 1—Apr 30 Mo-Fr 7 am-8 am; 6 pm-10 pm
(916) 527-1417
May 1—Aug 31 24 hrs
Charge Cards: No
Company Started in 1979
Rafting/River Associations: AGA, FOR, KCRO
Wetsuit rental: No
Rates: Guaranteed
Rivers: CS; LK; UK; U Sac; SF-Tri; U Tri
Our operation is a family business so owners Julie or Koll are usually trip guides. We prefer smaller trips (6-18 people) as this allows us to be more accommodating to our guests and encourages an environment where passengers begin our trips as strangers, but leave as friends.

Great Valley Canoe and Raft Trips
3213 Sierra St.
Riverbank, CA 95367
(209) 869-1235
D 8 am-9 pm
Charge Cards: No
Company Started in 1978
Rafting/River Associations: FOR
Wetsuit rental: No
Rates: Guaranteed
Rivers: Stan; Guide School
Great Valley Canoe and Raft Trips offers guided and self-guided river trips throughout central California. All of our trips emphasize education and personal skills development in river sports. We encourage beginners to take classes; we offer certified instruction to beginner and intermediate paddlers, and we customize their particular lesson packages.

Headwaters River Adventures
P.O. Box 1086
Ashland, OR 97520
(503) 488-0583
D 9 am-5 pm
Charge Cards: MC, V
Company Started in 1980
Rafting/River Associations: FOR
Wetsuit rental: $8/day
Rates: Subject to change
Rivers: CS; LK; UK; U Sac; Scott;
NF-Smith; BRG; U Tri; Guide
School
No gimmicks or frills—simply the most exciting river trips possible at reasonable, competitive prices. Guaranteed. We specialize in daring whitewater and supply state-of-the-art equipment, and the most skilled and experienced guides and instructors available anywhere. Well-planned, safe, and always operated with our guests' desires and expectations foremost. Try us.

James Henry River Journeys
P.O. Box 807
Bolinas, CA 94924
(415) 868-1836
Mo-Fr 9 am-5 pm
Charge Cards: No
Company Started in 1973
Rafting/River Associations: ARRA, FOR
Wetsuit rental: No
Rates: Guaranteed
Rivers: MF-Am; EF-Car; MF-Eel; LK
Since 1973 our natural history-oriented participatory journeys have provided a nurturing space for enjoying wilderness living. Traveling at a leisurely and informal pace and blending individual discovery with group camraderie has provided memorable vacations. Maturity, professional competence, good hu-mor, creative cookery, and a perfect safety record have fostered our reputation.

Kern River Tours
636 Maryann Street
Ridgecrest, CA 93555
(619) 379-4616
Oct 1—Jan 31 8:30 am-12:00 pm
Feb 1—Sep 30 8:30 am-5:30 pm
Charge Cards: MC, V
Company Started in 1974
Rafting/River Associations: ARRA, FOR, WRGA
Wetsuit rental: No
Rates: Subject to change
Rivers: SF-Am; Forks-Kern; L Kern; U Kern; Mer
KRT tries to make your river experience something that will challenge you and make you grow. We offer trips for both the novice and the expert that emphasize teamwork and self-awareness. We take great pride in the qualifications of our guides and in our 100% safety record.

Kings River Expeditions
211 N. Van Ness
Fresno, CA 93701
(209) 233-4881
Mo-Fr 8 am-5 pm
Charge Cards: MC, V
Company Started in 1972
Rafting/River Associations: WRGA
Wetsuit rental: w: $7; b: $3
Rates: Guaranteed
Rivers: Kings
To provide top quality river trips, including comfortable camp facilities, excellent food service, friendly guides, and an exciting river to run.

Klamath River Outdoor Expeditions (KROE)
P.O. Box 369

Orleans, CA 95556
(916) 469-3391
D 8 am-8 pm
(916) 469-3351
D 8 am-8 pm
Charge Cards: No
Company Started in 1979
Rafting/River Associations: FOR
Wetsuit rental: No
Rates: Guaranteed
Rivers: CS; LK
Being a locally owned and operated company gives us a chance to offer truly deluxe river trips and to tailor your trip to your every need. Personal service and attention to detail make our trips a memorable experience. We specialize in small groups.

Libra Expeditions
P.O. Box 4280
Sunland, CA 91040-4280
(818) 352-3205
Mo-Th 9 am-5 pm; Fr 9 am-3 pm
(800) 228-4121 in CA
Mo-Th 9 am-5 pm; Fr 9 am-3 pm
Charge Cards: AX, MC, V
Company Started in 1980
Rafting/River Associations: ARRA, EDPO, FOR, WRGA
Wetsuit rental: No
Rates: Guaranteed
Rivers: MF-Am; NF-Am; SF-Am
Libra Expeditions offers exceptional paddle rafting trips with the finest in staff, gear, campsites, and food. Our commitment to quality ensures that your river experience will be a superb one that you will remember for years and tell your friends about! Call us now to start your adventure.

Mariah Wilderness Expeditions
P.O. Box 248
Pt. Richmond, CA 94807

(415) 233-2303
Mo-Fr 9 am-5 pm
Charge Cards: AX, MC, V
Company Started in 1982
Rafting/River Associations: ARRA, EDPO, FOR
Wetsuit rental: No
Rates: Guaranteed
Rivers: MF-Am; NF-Am; SF-Am; Mer; Guide School
To provide a safe, growth-producing, and fun environment in which a person can learn that he/she is physically and emotionally strong, and to have fun in a wilderness environment rafting, cross country skiing, and sea kayaking.

National Outdoor College (NOC)
11383A Pyrites Way
Rancho Cordova, CA 95670
(916) 638-7900
Tu-Sa Sep 2—May 15 10 am-6 pm
(916) 638-7900
D May 15—Sep 1 10 am-6 pm
Charge Cards: MC, V
Company Started in 1977
Rafting/River Associations: None
Wetsuit rental: $9.50/day, $15/we
Rates: Subject to change
Rivers: MF-Am; NF-Am; SF-Am; EF-Car; LK; Guide School
NOC was formed as a professional human service organization of recreation, fun, and safety in the outdoors. Recreation reduces stress and facilitates our well-being physically, emotionally, socially, spiritually, and intellectually. We leave little or no trace on the environment. Join us this summer for the time of your life.

Noah's World of Water
P.O. Box 11
Ashland, OR 97520
(503) 488-2811

Apr 1—Sep 30, Mo-Sa 8 am-9 pm
Oct 1—Mar 31, Mo-Fr 9 am-5 pm;
7 pm-9 pm
Charge Cards: MC, V
Company Started in 1974
Rafting/River Associations: FOR
Wetsuit rental: w/b inc
Rates: Guaranteed
Rivers: CS; LK; UK; Scott; NF-Smith; SF-Smith
We are dedicated to adventure and to sharing with you the thrill of whitewater, our love and knowledge of the great out-of-doors, and our appreciation and respect of the magnificent and precious forces of the world. We never compromise safety for momentary excitement.

Nonesuch Whitewater
4004 Bones Rd.
Sebastopol, CA 95472
(707) 823-6603
Mo-Su 8 am-8 pm
Charge Cards: No
Company Started in 1971
Rafting/River Associations: EDPO, FOR, NORS, WRGA
Wetsuit rental: No
Rates: Guaranteed
Rivers: MF-Am; NF-Am; SF-Am; CS; EF-Car; MF-Eel; Scott
We encourage trip members to be active participants in the planning and operation of their trips. We prefer to work in small and charter groups and focus on enjoying the wilderness or outdoor aspects of the river trip. We believe participation makes a better, safer trip.

OARS, Inc.
P.O. Box 67
Angels Camp, CA 95222
(209) 736-4677
Mo-Fr 8 am-5 pm
(800) 344-3284 out of CA

Mo-Fr 8 am-5 pm
Charge Cards: AX, MC, V
Company Started in 1969
Rafting/River Associations: FOR, WRGA
Wetsuit rental: $15/day 1, $10/day 2, $5/add days
Rates: Guaranteed
Rivers: MF-Am; NF-Am; SF-Am; CS; EF-Car; Mer; Main T; Guide School
OARS uses only oar-powered or paddle-powered rafts. We keep our group sizes small and strive for the personal interaction between guides and passengers that makes a trip special. This allows our guides to share their love of and commitment to the outdoors with the passengers.

Orange Torpedo Trips, Inc.
Box 1111
Grants Pass, OR 97526
(503) 479-5061
D 8 am-8 pm
(503) 476-3383
D 8 am-8 pm
Charge Cards: MC, V
Company Started in 1968
Rafting/River Associations: WRGA
Wetsuit rental: $10/trip
Rates: Guaranteed
Rivers: Main Eel; LK
Participation in the challenge is the essence of a true wilderness experience. Specializing in inflatable kayaking for 18 years, we feature lodge trips and expert instruction from guides who average over 7 years of experience. Most of our lodge trips are highlighted by free videotaping which is previewed in the evenings.

O.R.E. Inc.
30493 Lone Pine Dr.
Junction City, OR 97448

(503) 689-6198
Mo-Fr 9 am-12 pm; 1 pm-5 pm
Charge Cards: No
Company Started in 1978
Rafting/River Associations: WRGA
Wetsuit rental: No
Rates: Guaranteed
Rivers: LK; U Tri

O.R.E. Inc. is the Northwest's second largest river trip outfitter. We offer participatory "row it yourself" trips (using specially designed 12' rafts) and "paddle raft" trips. Most trips have a naturalist, geologist, or musician along. O.R.E. is the choice of the National Audubon Society, the Nature Conservancy, and the Sierra Club.

Outdoor Adventures
MU Recreation
UC Davis
Davis, CA 95616
(916) 752-1995
Mo-Fr 10 am-6 pm
Charge Cards: MC, V
Company Started in 1971
Rafting/River Associations:
Wetsuit rental: $4/day, $3/add day
Rates: Guaranteed
Rivers: NF-Am; SF-Am; CS; LK

Outdoor Adventures is an outdoor recreation program at the University of California at Davis that offers a wide variety of outdoor experiences. Our cooperative trips are run by highly qualified guides and are educational in emphasis. Join us for an inexpensive, friendly, and enjoyable river experience.

Outdoors Unlimited
P.O. Box 22513
Sacramento, CA 95822
(916) 452-1081
Mo-Fr 9 am-5 pm
(408) 624-2193

Mo-Fr 9 am-5 pm
Charge Cards: MC, V
Company Started in 1969
Rafting/River Associations: ARRA, FOR, WRGA
Wetsuit rental: Inc on Mer, Main T
Rates: Guaranteed
Rivers: NF-Am; LK; Mer; Main T

For 17 years Outdoors Unlimited has outfitted on the finest rivers that the West has to offer, establishing a reputation for excellence, consistency, and safety. If you are looking for a different vacation, one that offers adventure and a taste of personnal challenge, then join OU on the river.

Ouzel Outfitters
P.O. Box 11217
Eugene, OR 97440
(503) 747-2236
Mo-Sa 9 am-6 pm; Su 8 am-12 pm
Charge Cards: MC, V
Company Started in 1979
Rafting/River Associations: KCRO, WRGA
Wetsuit rental: $10/we
Rates: Guaranteed
Rivers: CS; LK; UK

Ouzel Outfitters strives to provide extremely high quality participatory river trips on rivers of all levels throughout the Northwest. Our primary goal is to attain a high level of guest involvement and satisfaction by skillfully blending formal and informal instruction in an atmosphere of support, encouragement, and comraderie.

Ouzel Voyages
314 W. 14th St.
Chico, CA 95926
(916) 893-5029
Sep 1—Feb 28 7 pm-9 pm
(916) 891-0520

Mar 1—Aug 30 Mo-Fr 9 am-5 pm
Charge Cards: No
Company Started in 1978
Rafting/River Associations: AGA, ARRA, EDPO, FOR, KCRO
Wetsuit rental: No
Rates: Guaranteed
Rivers: CS; UK; Scott; Guide School
Ouzel Voyages provides friendly, informal, personal catering and emphasizes "taking in" the energies of the wilderness to increase your perceptions. Our patrons engage in activities such as swimming, hiking, fishing, meeting new friends, or rest and good food, tanning, solitude, camping under the stars, and learning the wisdom of the wilderness.

Pacific Adventures
P.O. Box 502
Coloma, CA 95613
(916) 622-6919
D 10 am-9 pm
Charge Cards: No
Company Started in 1976
Rafting/River Associations:
Wetsuit rental: No
Rates: Guaranteed
Rivers: MF-Am; NF-Am
Pacific Adventures takes small groups of 20 people or less on wilderness rivers. We provide quality camp cookery, top-of-the-field guides, and safety-conscious tours.

RAM River Expeditions
P.O. Box 70892
Reno, NV 89570-0892
(702) 826-2307
Mo-Fr 6 am-9 pm, Sa-Su 7 am-8 pm
Charge Cards: No
Company Started in 1980
Rafting/River Associations: AGA, FOR, WRGA
Wetsuit rental: $10/day, $5/add day

Rates: Guaranteed
Rivers: MF-Am; NF-Am; EF-Car; Guide School
RAM River Expeditions is both oriented to easy-going family trips as well as wild Class V exploratory adventures. We pride ourselves in having the best guides in the business: all are congenial, mature individuals and all have their E.M.T.'s. Safety is our main concern; our 12-year record in rafting is untarnished.

River Country Rafting
P.O. Box 57
Chico, CA 95927
(916) 891-1002
Mo-Fr 8 am-5 pm
Charge Cards: No
Company Started in 1985
Rafting/River Associations:
Wetsuit rental: No
Rates: Guaranteed
Rivers: Main Eel; LK
We are a new outfit with all the old experience. We enjoy the calm and serene along with the breath-taking. Some of our floats are designed for canoes and inflatable kayaks. We are set up to provide high quality service for the private party. The owners go on every float.

River Mountain Action Tours
22409 Baltar St.
Canoga Park, CA 91304
(800) RMA-RAFT in So CA
Mo-Fr 8 am-6 pm
(818) 348-3727
Mo-Fr 8 am-6 pm
Charge Cards: AX, MC, V
Company Started in 1979
Rafting/River Associations: AGA
Wetsuit rental: No
Rates: Guaranteed
Rivers: SF-Am

Safety, comfort, and courtesy are our creed. Clean-cut, drug-free professional guides, outstanding meals, complimentary beer and wine, hot showers, flushing toilets and 3" thick foam mattresses provided. Our discerning guests appreciate our standard of excellence, whether they book direct with our friendly, helpful office or through travel agents.

River Riders Whitewater Tours
10512 Abbottford Way
Rancho Cordova, CA 95670
(916) 363-7874
D 9 am-7 pm
(916) 366-RAFT
D 9 am-7 pm
Charge Cards: No
Company Started in 1979
Rafting/River Associations: AGA
Wetsuit rental: No
Rates: Guaranteed
Rivers: MF-Am; NF-Am; SF-Am
River Riders specializes in giving small trips. We want to give each customer a pleasurable experience. Time has shown that this goal can be achieved only when the groups are small (6-24 passengers). Small groups allow everyone a chance to ask questions, have closer contact, and share more of the rafting experience.

River Runners, Inc.
23801 Killion St.
Woodland Hills, CA 91367
(916) 622-5110
D 7 am-10 pm
(818) 340-1151
D 7 am-10 pm
Charge Cards: No
Company Started in 1973
Rafting/River Associations: ARRA, FOR, WRGA

Wetsuit rental: No
Rates: Guaranteed
Rivers: NF-Am; SF-Am; Guide School
River Runners wants you to have a fun-packed, adventurous vacation where you will meet new friends, enjoy great food and entertainment, work as a team in the spirit of cooperation while riding wild rapids, and have the time of your life using the safest rafting equipment and excellent guides.

River Trips Unlimited
4140 Dry Creek Road
Medford, OR 97504
(503) 779-3798
24 hrs
Charge Cards: No
Company Started in 1966
Rafting/River Associations: WRGA
Wetsuit rental: No
Rates: Guaranteed
Rivers: LK
A philosophy? People go to be on the water, to try something they probably have never done before, and to have a good time.

Rivers West Whitewater Specialists
1565 West 7th St.
Eugene, OR 97402
(503) 686-0798
Mo-Fr 9 am-6 pm; Sa 9 am-5 pm; Su 8am-12 pm
Charge Cards: MC, V
Company Started in 1975
Rafting/River Associations:
Wetsuit rental: w/b inc
Rates: Guaranteed
Rivers: CS; LK
Rivers West invites you to share truly memorable experiences. We provide the highest quality equipment from rafts and inflatables to wetsuits and tents. Our guides are

highly-trained professionals in rafting and kayaking. We seek to provide enjoyment and promote learning from each river experience.

Rollinson River Rafting Ltd.
332 Palmer Ave.
Aptos, CA 95003
(408) 688-8551
Mo-Fr 9 am-5 pm
Charge Cards: No
Company Started in 1979
Rafting/River Associations: ARRA
Wetsuit rental: No
Rates: Guaranteed
Rivers: MF-Am; NF-Am; SF-Am
We run small, personal raft trips, limiting the group size to about 24. All of our trips are by paddle boat with each person actively participating in maneuvering the raft. Above all, we strive to be professional yet friendly, and safe yet fun.

Rubicon Whitewater Adventures
9336 Champs Elysees
Forestville, CA 95436
(707) 887-2452
24 hrs
Charge Cards: No
Company Started in 1971
Rafting/River Associations:
Wetsuit rental: No
Rates: Guaranteed
Rivers: NF-Am; SF-Am; CS; Main Eel; MF-Eel; Pillsbury-Eel; LK; UK; Scott; U Tri
Rubicon runs river trips with the proven notion that the best way to enjoy the experience is to participate. We encourage you to help plan and operate your trip. Informative talks on safety, camp procedures, and river ecology will help develop your confidence and sensitivity to the environment.

Sierra Mac River Trips
P.O. Box 366
Sonora, CA 95370
(209) 532-1327
D 8:30 am-5:30 pm
(209) 532-6113
D 8:30 am-5:30 pm
Charge Cards: No
Company Started in 1965
Rafting/River Associations: FOR
Wetsuit rental: Inc
Rates: Guaranteed
Rivers: Main T; Upper T
Sierra Mac River Trips specializes in Tuolumne whitewater. We pioneered the first trips on the Class V Cherry Creek/Upper Tuolumne, which has become our hallmark. Sierra Mac strives to provide exciting, fun, educational, and safe rafting tours by utilizing all self-bailing whitewater rafts, veteran guides, and outstanding foods.

Sierra Whitewater Expeditions
P.O. Box 1330
Springfield, OR 97477
(503) 741-2780
D 8 am-6 pm
Charge Cards: MC, V
Company Started in 1975
Rafting/River Associations: FOR, KCRO, WRGA
Wetsuit rental: $5/day
Rates: Guaranteed
Rivers: CS; LK; UK; Scott; Guide School
Sierra Whitewater strives to offer the highest quality trips at a reasonable cost. Our guides enjoy sharing their knowledge of river lore and natural history. S.W.E. enjoys its pioneering spirit, having offered the first commercial rafting trips on the California Salmon, Scott, Middle Fork American, and numerous Oregon rivers.

Smith's River Adventures
2036 Crestbrook Road
Medford, OR 97501
(503) 779-3706
Mo-Fr 6 pm-12 am
Charge Cards: MC, V
Company Started in 1978
Rafting/River Associations: AGA
Wetsuit rental: No
Rates: Guaranteed
Rivers: LK; UK
We strive to provide each person with individual service. We have excellent guides who cater to our customers. We furnish good food, good wine, safety, adventure, and fun.

South Bay River Rafters
Box 243
Hermosa Beach, CA 90254
(213) 545-8572
Mo-Th 10 am-6 pm, Fr 10 am-12 pm
(213) 376-2226
Mo-Th 10 am-6 pm, Fr 10 am-12 pm
Charge Cards: MC, V
Company Started in 1977
Rafting/River Associations: FOR
Wetsuit rental: No
Rates: Subject to change
Rivers: SF-Am
South Bay River Rafters is committed to providing its guests with the very finest experience in whitewater rafting. From our new luxury buses to our first class riverfront camping facility, unequalled among rafting companies, to our highly trained culinary staff and river guides, South Bay River Rafters fulfills that commitment.

Spirit Whitewater
1001 Rose Ave.
Penngrove, CA 94951
(707) 795-7305
Mo-Fr 8 am-5 pm

Charge Cards: No
Company Started in 1979
Rafting/River Associations: FOR, WRGA
Wetsuit rental: No
Rates: Guaranteed
Rivers: Kings
With an emphasis on quality and safety, all trips are owner-supervised to insure our guests enjoy a professional, well-run river experience. We have built our reputation on the excellent food we serve, the skill and friendliness of our guides and, most of all, on the incomparable Kings River.

Sunshine River Adventures
P.O. Box 1445
Oakdale, CA 95361
(209) 847-8908
Mo-Fr 8 am-10 pm; Sa-Su 8 am-6 pm
Charge Cards: AX, MC, V
Company Started in 1984
Rafting/River Associations: FOR
Wetsuit rental: $5/day
Rates: Guaranteed
Rivers: Mok, Stan
We believe in offering a high quality outdoor recreational experience at a reasonable rate that the majority of the population can afford. We believe that active outdoor recreation (canoeing, rafting, etc.) is good for all aspects of the human being including the mental, physical, and spiritual well-being.

Ti Bar Guide Service
2033 Ti Bar Road
Somes Bar, CA 95568
(916) 469-3349
Mo-Fr 9 am-9 pm
Charge Cards: No
Company Started in 1980
Rafting/River Associations: FOR

Wetsuit rental: No
Rates: Guaranteed
Rivers: CS; LK
Ti Bar Guide Service can help make your vacation a truly memorable experience. We are all local guides and guide the Klamath and Salmon rivers all year long. We are "local, full-time guides". We can make it happen for you.

Tributary Whitewater Tours
55 Sutter St., Suite 65
San Francisco, CA 94104
(415) 428-2035
Oct 1—Feb 28 Mo-Fr 5 pm-8 pm
(415) 428-2035
Mar 1—Sep 30 Mo-Fr 8 am-12 pm
Charge Cards: No
Company Started in 1978
Rafting/River Associations: FOR
Wetsuit rental: No
Rates: Guaranteed
Rivers: MF-Am; NF-Am; SF-Am; CS; EF-Car; LK; UK; Scott; BRG; U Tri; NF-Yuba
Tributary is a company dedicated to providing inexpensive, friendly, unforgettable, and, most important of all, safe river trips down California and lower Oregon's most beautiful rivers. Tributary believes that rivers bring out the best in people.

Trinity River Rafting Centre
Box 151255
San Diego, CA 92115
(619) 483-4687
Sep 15—May 15 Mo-Fr 8 am-1 pm
(916) 629-3646
May 16—Sep 14 D 8 am-8 pm
Charge Cards: No
Company Started in 1979
Rafting/River Associations: WRGA
Wetsuit rental: No
Rates: Guaranteed
Rivers: CS; LK; SF-Smith; U Tri
Trinity River Rafting Centre offers safe and high-quality paddle rafting trips at discount prices. Our guides are trained in river safety, interpretive techniques, and outdoor cooking. They enjoy sharing these skills to make your rafting adventure an experience you'll never forget. We cater to groups.

Trinity Wilderness Travel
P.O. Box 4321
Chico, CA 95927
(916) 891-8734
Mo-Sa 9 am-8 pm
Charge Cards: No
Company Started in 1983
Rafting/River Associations: FOR
Wetsuit rental: No
Rates: Guaranteed
Rivers: Main Eel; EB-NF-Fea, LK; SF-Tri; U Tri; Guide School
Trinity Wilderness Travel is dedicated to providing small personalized trips which allow participants to experience the beauty and tranquility of California's wild rivers and mountains, enjoy the solitude of quiet, forested canyons, and pulse with excitement while negotiating whitewater rapids. Allow us to treat you to a safe and enjoyable trip.

Turtle River Rafting Co.
507 McCloud Ave.
Mt. Shasta, CA 96067
(916) 926-3223
Su-Fr 7:30 am-8 pm
Charge Cards: No
Company Started in 1976
Rafting/River Associations: AGA, ARCC, ARRA, EDPO, FOR, KCRO, NORS, WRGA
Wetsuit rental: $4/day, $16 max
Rates: Guaranteed
Rivers: SF-Am; CS; MF-Eel; LK;

UK; U Sac; Scott; NF-Smith; SF-Smith; U Tri; Guide School
Our unique capabilities, and trip options such as Audubon Float Trips, Women's Trips, Hot Spring Resorts, challenging Class IV and V rivers, and Family Adventures do not, in themselves, make us special. We are well-known for our commitment to full-on, people-oriented, participatory river adventures. Join us!

W.E.T. - Whitewater Expeditions & Tours
P.O. Box 160024
Sacramento, CA 95816
(916) 451-3241
24 hrs
Charge Cards: MC, V
Company Started in 1979
Rafting/River Associations: ARRA, EDPO, FOR, KCRO, NORS, WRGA
Wetsuit rental: No
Rates: Subject to change
Rivers: MF-Am; NF-Am; SF-Am; CS; EF-Car; LK; Scott
WET retains a small company atmosphere while providing the finest river trips, state of the art equipment, veteran guides (up to 16 years experience), incredible on-river food (our meals are opulent without additional cost), and secluded, private camps. No drive-in camps.

Whitewater Excitement
6552 Craighurst St.
North Highlands, CA 95660
(916) 338-3532
D 8 am-6 pm
(916) 722-2229
D 6 pm-9 pm
Charge Cards: No
Company Started in 1978
Rafting/River Associations:
Wetsuit rental: No

Rates: Guaranteed
Rivers: MF-Am; NF-Am; SF-Am; CS; UK
To provide our guests with a safe, enjoyable outdoor experience at an affordable price.

Whitewater Rapid Transit
3705 Gratia Ave.
Sacramento, CA 95821
(916) 484-7153
Mo-Fr 6:00 pm-11:30 pm
Charge Cards: No
Company Started in 1982
Rafting/River Associations:
Wetsuit rental: No
Rates: Guaranteed
Rivers: MF-Am: NF-Am; EF-Car; MF-Eel; LK; UK; Scott
Whitewater Rapid Transit is a small Sacramento-based outfitter specializing in small groups and personal service. Excellent food and drinks are provided. Safety and quality are assured by the owner's presence on each trip.

Whitewater Voyages
P.O. Box 906
El Sobrante, CA 94803
(415) 222-5994
Mo-Fr 9 am-5 pm
Charge Cards: MC, V
Company Started in 1975
Rafting/River Associations: ARRA, EDPO, FOR, KCRO, WRGA
Wetsuit rental: $12/day 1, $8/day 2, $6/add day
Rates: Guaranteed
Rivers: MF-Am; NF-Am; SF-Am; CS; EF-Car; Forks-Kern; L Kern; U Kern; LK; UK; Mer; Scott; BRG; NF-Yuba; Guide School
Whitewater Voyages is a pioneer in the world of whitewater, opening up new rivers, advancing the state of the art, and fostering a warm,

supportive style of guiding that places the enjoyment and safety of our clients uppermost. We devote ourselves wholeheartedly to making each trip the finest possible.

Wild River Tours
P.O. Box 500
Lotus, CA 95651
(916) 626-5042
Mo-Fr 9 am-6 pm; Sa 10 am-12 pm
(800) 821-0183 in CA
Mo-Fr 9 am-6 pm; Sa 10 am-12 pm
Charge Cards: No
Company Started in 1972
Rafting/River Associations: EDPO, FOR
Wetsuit rental: No
Rates: Guaranteed
Rivers: MF-Am; NF-Am; SF-Am; EF-Car; LK; UK; Mer
Our purpose is to help people experience and appreciate their heritage of wild rivers. Our goal is to conduct the type of trips that we enjoy: safe, high-quality, environmentally-sound trips, conducted in a friendly, personal manner. Our 13 years of experience are reflected in every trip.

Wild Water West, Ltd.
2 Virginia Gardens
Berkeley, CA 94702
(415) 548-0782
Mo-Fr 9 am-5 pm
Charge Cards: MC, V
Company Started in 1979
Rafting/River Associations: ARRA, EDPO, FOR, KCRO, WRGA
Wetsuit rental: $8/day, $4/add day
Rates: Guaranteed
Rivers: MF-Am; NF-Am; SF-Am; CS; UK; BRG; Scott; NF-Yuba
Although we offer excellent introductory and intermediate trips, our specialty and first love is advanced

whitewater expeditions. Using high-tech, self-bailing rafts, we challenge many Class IV and V rivers. We've made an impressive record of first descents on California's wildest rivers. You will find extraordinary guiding skill at Wild Water West.

Wilderness Adventures
P.O. Box 938
Redding, CA 96099
(916) 243-3091
D 7 am-7 pm
Charge Cards: MC, V
Company Started in 1979
Rafting/River Associations: KCRO
Wetsuit rental: No
Rates: Guaranteed
Rivers: CS; LK; UK; U Sac; Scott; U Tri
Owner/operator Dean Munroe is recognized for the first documented runs of the Upper Klamath and Wooley Creek. He gave the Upper Klamath its designation "The Hell's Corner Gorge" and named all of its major rapids. Join Munroe for the most exciting and complete whitewater services in the North State.

Zephyr River Expeditions, Inc.
P.O. Box 3607
Sonora, CA 95370
(800) 431-3636 in CA
Mo-Fr 8:30 am-5 pm
(209) 532-6249
Mo-Fr 8:30 am-5 pm
Charge Cards: MC, V
Company Started in 1973
Rafting/River Associations: ARRA, EDPO, FOR, WRGA
Wetsuit rental: w: $10/day, $3/add day; b: $3/day, $1/add day
Rates: Guaranteed
Rivers: MF-Am; SF-Am; EF-Car; Kings; Mer; Main T
To offer the best river trips possible

for individual, family, group enjoy- to explore the known, yet unfamiliar,
ment and resurrection of the spirit; and to make it familiar.

—*O.R.E., Inc.*

A you-oar oar boat rides through a Class III rapid on the Lower Klamath

Chapter 5

Booking a River Trip

The first four chapters of this book have assisted you in selecting a trip and choosing some outfitters. This chapter provides advice on booking a trip that will not be canceled, as well as some useful hints on organizing a large group.

How you book your trip should depend on the number of people with whom you plan to raft: fewer than six (you would have to join another group) and six or more (usually large enough to custom charter a tour). Note that sometimes the minimum for a custom tour is four people, sometimes twelve or more. Be sure to check the trip descriptions. Check also the special instructions for booking a trip on the South Fork of the American, if that river is your destination.

Important: When booking a trip, tell the outfitter you received information about the trip from this book. This gives the outfitter the opportunity to tell you if any aspect of the trip has changed since deadline. If the price has changed, and the outfitter listed his or her rates here as guaranteed, then he or she should have a good story to tell. Let me know about it.

Groups of five or less

If your group is small (five or less) then you should avoid selecting a trip that may be canceled later due to insufficient reservations. This is a special problem on (a) weekday trips, (b) rivers with low commercial demand, or (c) rivers with an oversupply of outfitters.

I recommend that you phone to make a reservation. If on the day you want to raft a trip is full, or worse, empty, you do not have to waste time writing and waiting for a response. Some companies are not speedy with their correspondence.

With the phone, you can go beyond finding out whether there is room on a particular date for you. You can also ask three important questions.

(1) What kind of group am I joining?
(2) How many people are in the group?
(3) How many people have sent in a deposit?

The people in the group may also affect how comfortable you feel on your tour. I was once informed as I set up camp the night before a trip that I would be joining a group of fathers and their sons. Somehow this particular grouping was not desirable. Also, church groups frequently go together on river trips. I regret to say that when I start sliding down into a wildly churning eight-foot hole, some of my language is suitable for neither church nor children. If you too suffer from barely controllable verbal responses to immediate hazards, then you may wish to consider who will be accompanying you in your raft.

Also, if you join one large group you may find it difficult to learn the names of 20 people. Further, you may feel like an outsider on your own tour. However, the more people there are in the group you plan to join, the less likely it is the trip will be canceled.

You are better off with a number of small groups making up the trip. Then, in the event that one group cancels at the last minute, the trip will still run.

Finally, you should ask how many people have sent in a deposit. An outfitter will book you on a trip if in his or her expectation, the trip will collect enough people (deposit received or not). But make plans around a trip only if at least the minimum group has sent in a deposit.

Trips may also cancel in the springtime due to high water. I recommend that you call the company you are booked with both two weeks before the trip, to see how reservations and the water are running, and also two days before the trip, for the same information. This is especially appropriate if you are away from home and the company would have no way to reach you if the trip were in fact canceled. Be sure to take this book with you on your vacation; if it is necessary to reschedule your trip, you will have the phone numbers of companies to call as well as their schedules.

Some companies recommend travel insurance so that if your trip cancels, you can recover expenses such as plane fare, motel charges, etc. To me, however, this is asking you to take responsibility for the company's failure to provide a dependable service. Certainly in the event of a rapid and unexpected rise in the water level, a trip may have to be canceled at the last minute for safety's sake. However, if you are booked on a trip that you have been assured will run, and it is later canceled due to reasons other than high water, or it is canceled at the put-in when the water level has been the same all week, I would like to hear about it. Write to me care of the publisher. Note that travel insurance may be appropriate if you are concerned about coverage in the event of a rafting injury.

All companies state in their brochures that in the event of a cancellation they will refund only the amount you paid the company for the trip. However, a good company will in addition offer you a discount on a future trip, which should somewhat recompense you for the loss of your planned trip. Also, the outfitter should recommend trips offered by other companies.

Many companies accept credit cards; those that do are identified in the Chapter 4. For the remainder, a check will reserve your place.

Request that the company send you a brochure, a list of items to bring, and instructions for getting to the put-in point or the meeting place. If the trip is a week or less away, then get instructions to the put-in or meet point over the phone.

Groups of six or more

All the rules described above also apply to medium-sized groups, except that such groups will no longer be limited to dates when trips are already scheduled or look likely. If you have enough people in your group to make up a custom trip minimum, then I strongly recommend that you do so. Try to schedule the trip for a weekday. With a larger group, you may have problems trying to join a weekend trip at the last moment. You must still call the outfitter to make sure your trip date is available. Weekend trips on some rivers, especially the rivers south of the Tuolumne, can fill up months in advance. Also, unless your group size equals the maximum group size, the outfitter will probably add other rafters to your tour.

When calling the outfitter, be sure to request enough brochures and flyers for the people in your group.

Organizing and booking a large group, or how to get a free trip

Outfitters prefer to deal with large groups; they therefore offer substantial discounts for group parties and often free trips to group organizers. The outfitter obtains two advantages: better use of the reservations and river staffs, and a guaranteed minimum party to which individual rafters can be added. You, of course, get the free trip.

However, several hole-like hazards lie in the path of organizing a large trip. The first and most important is the selection of a date. First-time organizers will try calling everyone they know who has ever expressed an interest in rafting, spend literally hours on the phone and, in all likelihood, be totally unable to find a date that pleases everyone. The irony of this effort is that within a week of your scheduled date, perhaps 20 percent of your group will cancel due to unavoidable last minute responsibilities. More on how to alleviate that problem later.

Therefore, in selecting a date for your trip, ask at most three others what dates would be acceptable to them. The earlier you anticipate your trip, the more dates will be acceptable. Several months in advance is not unreasonable. Be sensitive to the type of people you plan to invite. Certain professions require people to be on the job Monday through Friday except vacations; other professions may permit the rearranging of schedules to get time off during the week. Remember, you will find weekday trips cheaper, easier to book, and a more pleasant experience.

When you find a company with your preferred date open, reserve the date and explain that you are organizing a large group. Request flyers, posters, and other information. You may be required to send a deposit within a week to hold the date for your group, especially if it is a weekend date.

Many outfitters offer special, very low rates for scout groups. Ask about them.

Next, calculate the cost you will charge the other people who want to take part in the trip. Note that this is **not** the discounted price listed in the company's brochure. The price differential comes from your not only being the trip organizer, but also the beverage purchaser, long distance connection to the company, mailer of all information, and provider of tips. You may even have to arrange transportation.

A special caveat for overnight trips with regard to beer: be sure to calculate how much your group could possibly consume, and then double it. In the very unlikely event any is left over, it can be distributed to the trip participants. However, if your supply runs dry, the finger of blame will point directly at you. If your group plans to be together at a campsite the night before the trip, the campfire carousing will add yet another night of beer drinking to your river nights.

Glass containers are almost always forbidden on the river, but nevertheless, I have seen rafts carry wine in glass bottles on rare occasions. Also, on non-wilderness tours, camping gear is not taken on the raft, so glass bottles make no difference. Before you buy wine for your group, be sure to ask the outfitter.

OK. Now you have taken the discounted trip price and added $6 per adult per night for beer; $2 for postage, xerox, and phone; $5 for tip, and an appropriate amount for wine and other expenses. Be careful: it will be a royal pain to go back for more contributions.

Once you have determined the price of the river trip, start letting your friends and associates know about it. Post information about the trip in your office, work place, or school. You may be able to list the trip in a newsletter of an organization of which you are a member. Indicate that space on the trip is limited and held only with full payment.

But, you say, full payment is not required until a month before the trip. Well, a month before a trip, a person's schedule looks a little different than it did three months before a trip, with the likely result of a cancellation. No one said you had to cash the person's check until payment is due.

Should the number of persons making reservations exceed the space available, return the checks of the overflow rafters, and tell them you will put their names on a waiting list. Then, should someone cancel at the last minute, it would be the canceling rafter's responsibility to contact people on the waiting list to find a replacement.

One final piece of advice: try to disseminate information and make your contacts with your group by mail. With a group of any size, repeated phone conversations and the efforts of trying to reach people by phone can take up much of your time and patience.

You will still deserve that free trip.

━━

What to Bring (and what not to bring)

Hamlet at one time said: "the readiness is all" (Act V, Scene II), and nowhere is this more true than in river rafting. Proper preparation avoids headaches, both literally and figuratively.

On a one-day trip always bring:

Sunscreen. Choose a high sun protection factor (15+) water-insoluble type, even if you never burn. Bring plenty as you will no doubt have to share with those who come unprepared.

Extra clothing. Bring an entire extra set, including footwear. Absolutely everything you wear on the river will get soaked.

River clothing. Keep it comfortable and quick drying. Nylon is a good river fabric. Avoid cotton unless you expect to be too hot (40 degree river water can cool you off quickly). In the summer, rafters wear bathing suits and/or shorts and short-sleeved sport shirts. A bikini can be quite uncomfortable under a life jacket. Raft tubes can become hot in the sunshine, so women should wear shorts over a bathing suit. If you sunburn easily, long-sleeved white shirts and white pants are good choices. In the late spring and early fall, bring polypropylene long underwear, a wool sweater, wool or synthetic pants, wool socks, and rain gear (a rain jacket or nylon windbreaker and rain pants are preferable to a poncho). In spring or fall, bring a wetsuit (see below).

Footwear. Sneakers and/or divers' booties (not just divers' socks) must be worn at all times while rafting, both to facilitate your keeping your footing while you are in the boat, and to protect your feet when you are not. Sneakers cost less than booties, keep your feet cooler on hot days, and cause less wear and tear on the feet during hikes and portages. Try to get sneakers with all-cloth uppers, like tennis, basketball, or deck shoes. On the other foot, booties keep your feet warm when the water is cold, which on Sierra rivers is most of the time. Booties can keep your entire body comfortable if you are rafting in late spring without a wetsuit, because they reduce heat loss from your feet. Unless your craft is self-bailing, your feet will be in water for most of the trip. If the water temperature dictates booties, and the day's schedule calls for hiking, bring along a pair of sneakers in the day bag. One final word of caution about booties: you may find that wearing them causes dehydration of the feet and ankles. One rafter I know has solved this problem by wearing polypropylene socks (wool socks also help) under his booties. I have found that applying Neutrogena Norwegian Formula hand cream to my feet twice daily for about a week after wearing booties is the only way to stop the skin from peeling.

Sunglasses. Reflections from the river will intensify sunlight about three times, which is why river sunburn is so serious. Protect your eyes by wearing dark sunglasses that have tint extended over the entire lens. Avoid mirrored sunglasses, as the curvature and mirror will cause light to reflect onto your nose. Not only will this result in probable sunburn today, but practices like wearing mirrored sunglasses may eventually result in Ronald Reagan nose. Bring some kind of strap to hold your glasses or else they will almost certainly be washed away. In addition, bring a safety pin and pin the strap to your shirt. And after all that, be sure they are cheap sunglasses. One guide tells the story of diving to the bottom of a rapid and pulling up a pair of expensive French sunglasses. That treasure in turn lasted almost the entire day, until the guide, too, lost the sunglasses going through a rapid.

Towel. Don't forget your towel. It should hitchhike with your dry clothing. [Don't bring large towels on overnight trips, when space is limited].

Comb or brush. Often forgotten, which causes that river rat look you see on people on the road.

Optional things to bring on a one-day trip:

Hat. Required for men who are balding, because of the sunburn hazard. Recommended for all others as a protection against sunstroke. You may wish to look into the equivalent of a French Foreign Legion hat, which has several advantages: (a) the white reflects sunlight and keeps your head cool; (b) the visor protects your forehead and eyes; (c) the tails protect your neck; (d) the hat can be used as a bucket to dump water on your head; (e) it's great for starting conversations; and (f) the effect is rather dashing on men with dark complexions. Available by phone order from Adventure 16, (619) 283-2362, for $12.95 postage paid (ask for the Desert Hawg Hat and be prepared to provide your hat size).

Bandana. You can obtain a more western appearance and protect your neck at the same time by wearing a bandana. A Riverguide map bandana will also show where you are going: two-color river maps are printed on them. Available from Cascade Outfitters, (800) 223-RAFT or (503) 747-2272 in Oregon, for $5.95 plus $2.65 shipping. Specify a bandana for the South Fork of the American, the North and Middle Forks of the American, the Upper Kern, the Lower Kern, or the Main Tuolumne.

Camera and film. Be sure to read what not to bring, below. Over and over again I have seen people risk their cameras on river trips and take few if any pictures. It is extremely difficult to take good photos while in a raft, and it usually requires the cooperation of the guide and the rest of the crew to get you in the proper position.

For photographing rafts going through rapids, James Henry River Journeys recommends a long lens (200-300 mm), and 400 ASA slide film. It's better to take pictures on land, but your opportunities are few, and you will have to be concerned about trespassing.

If you want photographs to be a product of your tour, then try an oar boat on a relatively calm river. The East Fork of the Carson has stunning scenery. Remember your UV filter at that altitude. Also, Turtle River Rafting will offer in 1986 a wildlife photography trip on the Lower Klamath.

The outfitter will usually provide, free of charge, a waterproof container for your camera equipment; be sure to ask when making your reservations. Remember that every time you want to take a picture, the camera will have to be removed from the container. That container or any container you purchase may not be 100% reliable. If you insist on bringing your camera with you, get insurance.

A better option than your regular camera, which will suffer an expensive death when drenched, is a small waterproof camera. Tie it to your life jacket and keep it tucked inside when not in use.

On certain rivers, professional photographers will take photographs of your tour. When you see a photographer on the shore, ask your guide which company the photographer is from. Water Colors, (619) 379-4976, takes photographs of rafters on all three sections of the Kern. Sierra Shutterbug, (916) 622-FILM, takes photographs of the rafts of certain companies running the South Fork of the American. Rapid Shooters, (800) 4 RAPIDS, takes photographs of boaters on the three Forks of the American. All of these companies will take orders over the phone: simply tell the company (a) the date of your trip, (b) the name of your outfitter, (c) the name of your guide, and (d) your position in the boat.

If you want a good photograph, grin when you go through that rapid.

Cigarettes and Matches. If you cannot live without a cigarette in your hand, then you may prefer an oar boat, where you won't be called upon on a moment's notice to dispose of your cigarette in an ecologically sound manner (put the butt in your pocket) and place two hands on your paddle. I recall a smoker who, upon reboarding the raft after a rather stressful Class V swim, reached into his life jacket and withdrew a pack of soggy cigarettes. Your cigarettes belong in a Ziploc® storage bag or in a waterproof container. Also, bring extra, as someone will no doubt forget and/or suffer soggy cigs.

Plastic water bottle. I carry a one-pint plastic bottle with a blue loop at the top; similar bottles are available at outdoor equipment stores. The loop can attach the water bottle to the lines on the raft, to your belt, to your life jacket, or to the oar frame, if your craft is an oar boat. Often, but not always, a communal water bottle is carried with each raft. Be sure to request that a water bottle be provided, if you do not plan to bring your own water. See the section on dehydration, in the appendix *Safety*. [On an overnight trip, your own plastic water bottle is particularly convenient for brushing your teeth, washing up, etc.]

Wetsuit. On most spring and fall trips, and on most Class V rivers, a wetsuit is required. A wetsuit will protect you against the considerable danger of hypothermia from repeated splashing by (or perhaps swimming in) snow-melt water. Also, wetsuits bounce rather better off sharp rocks than people do. Wetsuits also prevent bailing bucket shins (see *Safety*). They come in a variety of types and thicknesses. Full wetsuits encase you from ankle to wrist, in one or two pieces. Shorty wetsuits start at mid-thigh. Farmer John wetsuits resemble tight overalls, leaving your shoulders and arms unencumbered for paddling. Temperature will dictate the type of wetsuit necessary; ask your outfitter when you book your trip. Be aware that the thicker the wetsuit, the more stiff and uncomfortable you will find it. Try to rent or obtain a ⅛ inch thick wetsuit, preferably from a shop that serves river runners and/or wind surfers. Dive shops may stock only the thicker suit required for diving. An advantage of renting your wetsuit through your outfitter (in addition to saving time trying to find one) is that an outfitter will usually have the right kind of suit. If you do try one on in a dive shop or other store, try to get one that is a little loose, to facilitate getting in and out of it. Cecil Kuhne, in his fine book *Advanced River Rafting*, recommends sprinkling a little talcum powder inside to smooth your way into that tight wetsuit.

Gloves. On cold days, in cold water, divers' gloves can keep your hands warm and your grip powerful. They also give you that NFL wide receiver look. Available at any diving shop or outdoor supply store that serves the river market.

On a camping trip always bring:

Everything listed as required for a one-day, and also the following:

Sleeping bag. Yes, I have known these to be forgotten. Be sure that your sleeping bag is rated to keep you warm below 40 degrees in summer and 0 degrees in spring and fall. It's cold in them thar hills, and you would rather not have to swaddle yourself like a mummy in your mummy bag.

Pad or air mattress. Optional only if you don't really care about sleeping. If it's been awhile since you camped on the cold hard ground, you will find it colder and harder than you remember. So, since you don't have to carry the pad like a backpacker, find a thick one. An air mattress also works, but doesn't insulate as effectively.

Tarp, blanket, or space blanket. Any one of these serves as a ground cloth under your pad or air mattress, which keeps you from waking up with sand on your sleeping bag and in your hair. A space blanket has the advantage of insulating against the ground. A tarp can be strung up as a tent in the event of inclement weather.

Sleep wear. Choose something warm that you don't mind being seen in by strangers. Polypropylene long underwear is warm, comfortable, and attractive. A sweatsuit is warm, comfortable, and socially acceptable even if it's not sexy.

Flashlight. Add fresh batteries. There are no city lights in the mountains, although a full moon over the river canyon can be an acceptable substitute.

Toothbrush, toothpaste, and dental floss. Store these in a Ziploc® storage bag to keep your toothbrush clean and the rest of your gear dry.

Biodegradable soap. Available at outdoor supply stores. Also keep in a Ziploc® storage bag, because even though biodegradable soap comes in a plastic bottle, it may leak (mine does). When you use it, be sure you are above the water line. Fish do not care for soap.

Dry clothes for camp. The second thing you will do after getting to camp is change out of your wet clothing. Be sure to bring along footwear for camp, as you do not want to be walking around in your wet sneakers.

Mosquito repellent. Mosquitoes follow Rena's Rule of Adverse Element Repellence. If you bring along repellent, then mosquitoes will not choose to visit your camp. Leave your repellent off-river, and you will go home bitten. As space is frequently at a premium when packing for a river trip, get a small plastic bottle of 100% N,N-diethyl-meta-toluamide, available at any outdoor supply store. One bottle will be enough for your whole group in the unlikely event that mosquitoes show up in violation of the rule. N.B. The same rule applies to rain gear.

Toilet paper. Veteran backpackers know the trick of finding a roll that has only one-quarter (or less) of the sheets remaining and pulling out the cardboard from the inside of the roll. Pack the toilet paper in a Ziploc® storage bag to protect it.

Pack all your gear, with the exception of the sleeping bag and pad, in a stuff bag, small duffel bag or soft backpack. Don't bring a suitcase. On rivers without road access, you will have to repack your non-food items into a waterproof bag.

Optional things to bring for a camping trip:

Pillow case. Can be stuffed with clothes to create a pillow. If you have a stuff bag for your sleeping bag, use that.

Aloe vera gel. After following to the letter the instructions in this book, you may expect that you will not get sunburned. This is false. You will miss a spot somewhere. Aloe vera gel will relieve the sunburn some-what and will also make you very popular among the seriously sunburned persons on your trip. Note that if you are organizing a group, one jar of aloe vera gel will generally be sufficient for 25 people who used sunscreen and for five people who did not. Also, if you are organizing a group, you may wish to bring along one of the many medicated products for sunburn relief.

Tent. It's rare to see a tent on a river trip, outside of the spring or fall rainy seasons, when one is recommended. A free-standing dome tent is best. Space may be limited, so use a backpacking type tent.

Nylon rope, 10 to 20 feet. Part of the rope can be used as a belt during the day, and pieces can be cut off to use for tying down hats, sunglasses, plastic bottles, etc. In camp, the rope can be tied between trees as a clothes line for drying your wet river clothes. Finally, in the event of unexpected rain, the rope can be used to secure your tarp as a tent.

Beer. See extensive discussion under etiquette. No glass bottles.

Utensils. Some outfitters require you to bring your own utensils. Be sure to ask. Plastic knives, forks, and spoons are convenient, but the knives in particular are insufficient to handle steak, if that's on the menu. Again, ask.

Cup. Likewise, you may be required to bring your own cup. Metal or plastic only. A Sierra Club cup, available at any outdoor supplier, is a good choice. Better a large cup than a small one, as you will be using the cup to carry water, especially if you fail to bring a plastic water bottle.

Gloves. On a multi-day trip, hands unused to heavy work can develop blisters from paddling. To prevent blisters, wear biking gloves (leather palms, macrame backs) in the summer, and divers' gloves in the spring and fall.

Binoculars. In this, the rafting season of Halley's comet, river runners in the sparsely populated and naturally lit mountain areas will have an excellent opportunity for viewing the comet. *Astronomy* magazine reports that from April 2 to April 13, the comet will be at its brightest, traveling low in the southern sky, between the tail of Scorpius and the northern part of Centaurus. From April 26 to May 10 and from May 25 to June 10, the comet will be located south of Leo and west of Corvus. The best viewing, as you no doubt know by now, will be in the south, so try the Kern for your combination rafting/comet trip. The comet will be low in the sky, so look for it before you descend into the river canyon.

Star guide. It may be that you don't know how to find Scorpius, or indeed any other constellations. It may even be that the star you wish upon is a planet. To resolve these and other stellar concerns, obtain the Star and Planet Locator from the Edmund Scientific Company ($2.50). This and other publications of use to river runners are distributed by Westwater Books, (702) 293-1406.

Flora, fauna, bird, tree, geology or river history guides. Any of these can deepen your immersion in a wilderness and natural history experience. Audubon paperback guides are complete, contain photographs, and are available in most bookstores. Nature Study Guild Books (P.O. Box 972, Berkeley, CA 94701) publishes compact, inexpensive, and easy-to-use guides to birds, flowers, trees, etc. Specific river history guides are recommended for many rivers in Chapter 3.

Gold pan. Miners have scoured many California rivers for gold for over a century. Your river trip offers you the same opportunity. Any heavy metal pie pan can substitute for the real thing.

Musical Instrument. Be sure to inquire as to whether there will be road access to your camp, as you may not be able to bring a guitar along on a raft. Most outfitters on the Tuolumne allow guitars—ask, and don't bring along an expensive one.

Personal articles. Occasionally you will find on rafting trips women so compulsive as to bring makeup and men so compulsive as to bring shaving kits. Freud had names for these people. Their intentions are almost invariably brought to naught because they forget to bring mirrors.

Sanitary napkins or tampons, if needed.

Swiss army knife or equivalent. I always seem to find a use for this, be it for the toothpick, the knife, the scissors, and, yes, sometimes, the corkscrew.

Medicine. Bring along anything you shouldn't leave home without. The outfitter will always provide a good first aid kit.

Muscle ointment. Some of you may not keep your bodies in exemplary condition. You may not exercise at all. Your body may not be ready for paddling, and if you do, your body may just tell you so. To make it to the next day of paddling, bring some muscle ointment. Even if you don't need it, someone on your trip probably will.

Hydrocortisone cream. If you are allergic to poison oak, then the better part of itch prevention may involve accepting your fate and bringing along hydrocortisone cream, which is available both generically and under various brand names.

Ear Plugs. Especially indicated if there are old frat brothers on the trip.

Sleep mask. When a full moon flies like a flashlight in your eyes, a sleep mask can protect your sleep. Also, those early morning dawns that you may miss at home in bed can be hard to ignore if you are sleeping out in the open.

Fishing gear. On rivers with road access, bring what you have. For wilderness trips, collapsible poles are preferred. Whitewater Voyages recommends light fly or spinning gear that fits into a compact protective case. Be sure you have a current California fishing license, available at most sporting goods stores.

Extra sunglasses or optical glasses, with a head strap.

What not to bring

Never bring anything on the river you are not willing to lose. I repeat, **never bring anything on the river you are not willing to lose.**

Keys. After the unusual injury, the most tragic thing that can happen on river is for a rafter to lose his or her car keys. You have several options for the protection of your keys. First, hide the key on the car. Second, bury the key near the car. Third, give the key to the shuttle driver. Fourth, ask the motel where you are staying to hold it for you. If none of these options is acceptable to you, then loop your key ring through your belt and hope that your belt does not break. This may be uncomfortable, but it beats losing your keys.

Wallet/Purse. Same as above, except a wallet or purse may be locked in your car. However, cars can be broken into and personal items stolen. When packing for your trip, try to bring along a minimum of cash and just the credit cards you expect to need.

Non-waterproof watches and jewelry.

Personal stereo or record player. Even at river access camps where these can be brought in, they represent a serious intrusion into the peace of others.

Firearms of any kind.

Pets.

Appendix B
Safety

This section is not included to fill you with fear, but rather to help you develop a healthy awareness for the various ways the river can reach out and touch the disrespectful. Always listen to your guide; he or she knows the river better than you do.

Any activity on or near water has the potential for drowning. Whitewater rafting is no exception. People who fall into the water without life jackets on can drown. People who are tied to a boat that flips can drown. Non-swimmers who fall out in Class V rapids, or in rivers at flood stage, can drown. While commercial rafting companies on the whole have an excellent safety record, safety remains an outfitter's first concern, and it should be yours also.

There is no substitute for personal training in learning rafting safety, and this section is not intended to replace that training. Before you raft, listen carefully to your guide's safety instructions and discuss your safety questions with him or her.

The key to safety is avoiding any situation where you may be held underwater. Everything else in this appendix is commentary. There are two important ways to reduce the likelihood of being held underwater.

First, when in the boat, keep free of lines or ropes. If you feel the need to hold on, then hold on (discreetly, of course), but do not wrap lines around your hands or feet in an effort to keep yourself from leaving the boat. In the unlikely event the boat were to turn over, you would want to be able to swim away. Loose lines present a similar hazard; keep all lines coiled or tucked in pouches.

Second, if you fall out of the raft in the middle of a rapid, don't panic. If at all possible, hang on to your paddle. I have yet to meet a really experienced rafter whose has never fallen out of a boat; it's rather like a skier who has never fallen down in the snow. Consider it a baptism. Consider it a challenge. As a guide once told me after he navigated a particularly long and difficult rapid on his back: "Anybody could do it in a raft". Consider it value for money: Disney never could, never would, give you a ride like this one.

And, you had better plan to keep your feet up, point them downstream, and stay away from submerged trees and bushes, or your ass will be grass. By keeping your feet up, you prevent them (and the rest of you) from being trapped by the rocks on the river bottom. By pointing your feet downstream, you make your feet the first point of impact with any rocks you may meet along the way. This is usually preferred to hitting a rock with the other end of your body. Finally, while you can bounce off rocks and continue downstream, water can travel through the branches of submerged trees and bushes, and you can't. Branches that let water through, but not boats or people, are called "strainers". Swim away from them and make landfall later.

As you float through a rapid, the waves and turbulence may make it impossible for you to breathe whenever you feel like it. The best place to catch a breath is in the troughs of the waves. The water is calmest there. In general, it is best to hold your breath in between good breathing opportunities.

Listen to your guide. Sticking close to the raft when you fall out is not always the best position. Most notably, avoid a location where rocks are just downstream and the boat is just upstream. In such circumstances the guide will instruct you to swim away from the boat, as he would rather not use your body as a buffer between a rock and 1500 pounds of boat, passengers, guide, and gear.

Now it's time to consider how you are going to get back to the boat. This could be accomplished three ways:

(1) Float until you reach a relatively calm area and then swim for the boat. This is my favorite.

(2) If the current remains swift, and you perceive some hazards downstream, then swim into an eddy. An eddy is a pool of calm water that sits downstream of a boulder or riverside promontory. Ask your guide to point one out to you early in the trip. I found (in a controlled, reproducible experiment) that the fastest way into an eddy is with a powerful overarm backstroke. Jim Cassady also recommends a backstroke, so you can see obstacles downstream. However, Mark Helmus of Wild Water West recommends freestyle on Class V rivers, for greater speed and power.

(3) Receive a toss line from a boat or shore and be pulled towards your rescuer. Grab the toss line by the rope, not the bag, as there are several score feet of rope in the bag that would have to be pulled in before you. Again, never tie or wrap the line around your wrists or any other part of your body, as the line may drag you underwater. Should you be held for an extended time underwater, you will probably want to let go of the line. Otherwise, hold the line over your shoulder and close to your chest while facing up and away from the thrower. Take a deep breath and hold it; breathe between waves.

That's it for the key safety factors. What follows are miscellaneous safety hints.

Alcohol. Never drink before or while rafting. Alcohol slows your response time and reduces your resistance to cold. If you show up at the put-in under the influence, you won't be rafting. When companies report that they provide beer or wine or spirits, they mean at camp or at the take-out. Also, if you come off the river cold, wet, and shivering, and you are thinking how nice some brandy would be, then don't hit the bottle. Alcohol compounds the effects of hypothermia. Alcohol is also a diuretic; it can cause dehydration (see below).

Attention. Keep your eyes downstream; remain attentive to the river. Invariably, the rock you didn't see and prepare for will be the one to knock you out of the boat. This doesn't mean you should stare downstream and miss the beautiful wilderness around you. But before you start daydreaming about some timeworn natural monument, do check the river.

Bailing. In conventional (not self-bailing) boats, water collects at the bottom of the boat. If too much water remains in the boat after going through rapids, the weight of the water may impede the paddlers or guide from maneuvering the boat. This can be less than optimal on difficult rivers.

In calm water, if water in the boat has reached the level of your ankles, you should reach or ask for a bailing bucket and start bailing. In rapids, ask the guide before you start to bail.

Bailing buckets. Bailing buckets are made of hard plastic. Persons sitting in the bow of the raft will frequently end the day with an amazing assortment of shin bruises caused by bouncing bailing buckets. To avoid bailing-bucket shins, keep the buckets tightly attached to the bow rope or the bow carabiner when they are not in use.

Bee stings. If you are allergic to bee stings, be sure to notify your outfitter in advance.

Campfires. Upon rare occasions a guide may forget to completely douse a fire before leaving a campsite. The coals should be absolutely cold to the touch. If you have any concerns at all about the campsite you are leaving, then discreetly mention something to a guide.

Class V rapids. Class V rapids are hazardous. Before you run a Class V rapid, join the guides in scouting it. Consider how you would deal with falling out of the raft. If you have any doubts at all, walk around. If you decide you want to run it, ask where you should swim in the event you do fall out (river left, river right, etc). Non-swimmers should walk around the rapid.

Dehydration. The sun can dry you out in spite of all that water. Alcohol- and caffeine-containing drinks are diuretics: they contribute to this problem. Drink plenty of water while on the river (or at camp, if you will be consuming alcohol). The first sign of dehydration is a slight headache; subsequent symptoms include an intense headache, nausea, and fainting. At the first twinge in the brain, drink a pint of water.

Discretionary swimming and diving. Because of the danger of unseen underwater rocks, never dive into the river. Also, do not just jump in the water, even calm water, merely because it seems like the place to be. Ask the guide first; he or she knows what is coming around the bend. Stay near the boat. Never jump into the river in an attempt to rescue someone else. This gives the guide two people to save. Controlling your direction and/or swimming against rapids is much, much harder than you might think.

Experience. Perhaps the worst safety violation occurs before ever reaching the river. This is deceiving a friend or relative about the difficulty of a Class IV+ or Class V river, when he or she has never rafted before. Don't say "it's not that bad." It's that bad. In the same manner, you are doing yourself and your brother or sister rafters a disservice if you deceive an outfitter as to the extent of your experience. Outfitters set experience requirements because on some rivers you will need that experience to respond quickly and appropriately to difficult situations. An inappropriate response might put you or others at risk.

Feet. One way to stabilize yourself in the raft is to wedge your feet under the side tubes or thwarts. Your feet should be flat on the floor of the raft at all times. If you twist your feet sideways at the ankles, in an effort to better hold your feet under the tubes, they become vulnerable to rocks near the surface of the water. If the raft rides over a rock, you will receive a rock bruise to end all rock bruises. This effect can occur to a lesser extent with other parts of your body. If you are on your knees (or tail bone) in the bottom of the boat, your knees (or tail bone) could also be seriously bruised should the boat move over a rock. So, if you fall to the bottom of the boat, get to your feet, even in a squatting position, as soon as possible.

Flips. The smaller the boat, and the wilder the water, the more likely it is that the boat will turn over. Certainly inflatable kayaks in Class III and IV whitewater flip often. So, if the boat turns over, which it very well may, just treat it with the aplomb you normally reserve for falling out of a boat. However, you could have an additional concern. You may just end up underneath the boat. In this case, swim out from underneath, preferably upstream (so you won't end up between the raft and a hard place, like a rock). Otherwise, you will cause considerable concern to your guides, who hate to see a passenger apparently disappear. See Underneath the raft, below.

High side. It may be a natural reaction for a person to edge away from a swiftly approaching rock. This reaction is exactly the one you want to avoid. Your shifting will weight the boat on the side away from the rock, making the side that will impact the rock a "high side". And, the higher that side is, the farther up the boat will slide on the rock. So, when there is a danger of a raft sliding up a rock (and perhaps getting stuck, called "wrapping", perhaps even flipping), the guide will call out "high side", and that means you should get off your tube and over to the side of the boat approaching the rock.

Hold on. When you position yourself in your raft for the first time, look around for a line or strap inboard that you could grab in an emergency. Test it out by quickly reaching and tugging as though you actually believed you might otherwise lose your balance. In a paddle boat, practice tucking your paddle shaft under your outside armpit before you reach for your security strap with your inside hand. Securing your paddle will prevent it from hitting one of your fellow rafters in the head, the kidneys, or other more painful locations.

Holes. A hole is a place in a river where the river level drops sharply. The main portion of the current follows the river bottom, while the surface current curls back upstream. Holes can provide some good times, such as rafting upstream, surfing in an inflatable kayak, and other tricks with which your guide will surprise you. However, swimmers can be trapped in holes and circulate around and around. The strategy for escaping a hole is to swim to the side of the hole to catch the downstream current. If the hole extends the entire width of the river, then swim down to the bottom, where the main current can carry you downstream.

Hypothermia. Hypothermia is generally defined as a potentially dangerous loss of body heat. On a river trip, hypothermia can be defined as the failure to wear a wetsuit on a spring, fall, or winter run. Because outfitters are well aware that some people are reluctant to wear wetsuits, they sometimes reported that wetsuits are "recommended" in situations where they should be required. I urge you to be very conservative in the matter of wetsuits. As a rule of thumb, you should definitely be in a wetsuit if the sum of the river temperature and the air temperature is 100 degrees or less. I use 115 degrees and replace booties with sneakers if it gets too warm. You may also wish to try a two-piece wetsuit if the weather is borderline. Apart from safety concerns, being warm and slightly uncomfortable in a wetsuit is infinitely superior to being cold and miserable without one.

The first symptom of hypothermia is uncontrollable shivering. This is your body doing its best to keep you warm. Should you start shivering, or should you observe someone in your boat obviously suffering from the cold, inform your guide immediately.

Also, if you do not wear a wetsuit in cold weather, and you fall into the water, make every effort to get out of the water as soon as possible. As you get colder, your body will shut off blood flow to your extremities, making it impossible for you to swim.

Illegal drugs. Drugs will have the same impact on rafting performance as alcohol, and again, if a guide even thinks you are under the influence, you won't be rafting.

Inflatable kayaks. Before you head downstream in your kayak, get some instruction from your guides. Practice your back paddling and turns before you need them. Don't crowd other kayakers, especially when traveling through whitewater, or you may become a part of a kayak sandwich, and the rapids will eat you.

Life jackets. Always wear a life jacket when on the river. You may be a strong swimmer, but the calm ripples of a pool bear no resemblance to the power of a strong current in rapids. To check for proper fit, grasp both shoulders of the life jacket and pull up sharply. The life jacket should not rise more than about an inch. If it does, tighten it. If you can pull the shoulders of a life jacket to the level of someone's ears, immersion in water would also lift the life jacket that high. The jacket then would not keep the swimmer's head out of water.

"Macho" rafters. Over and over again, guides report that "macho" rafters create one of rafting's most serious safety hazards. These persons paddle successfully through two or three rapids and then start whining that the river is too easy. They do not consider the potentially serious results of improper river running. In their overconfidence, "macho" rafters fail to respond to a guide's commands or otherwise act without regard to their safety or the safety of others.

People who exhibit "macho" rafter behavior on shore are on occasion not even permitted to raft, because their obvious immaturity presents an unacceptable hazard to the raft's other passengers.

A person who becomes "macho" once on the river should not be surprised if his or her guide (a) heads to shore and makes the passenger walk the remainder of the river, or (b) "accidentally" flips the boat and thus teaches the passenger some humility.

Non-swimmer. If you don't swim, tell your guide!

Off-river. One of the hazards of writing a book like this is having to listen politely to everyone's hard-luck river story. An amazing percentage occur off-river. Be aware that river access and campsites only sometimes are available at flat, sandy beaches. At other times, it may be necessary for you to clamber over large granite boulders in order to exit or enter the river, walk around in campsites, or portage. Persons who suffer from brittle bones and therefore may be more susceptible to broken ankles, etc. should definitely consult with the outfitter before booking a trip. This also applies to seriously overweight people.

Anytime you are close enough to the river to fall in, you should be in your life jacket.

Paddle commands. You will no doubt get complete paddle command instructions on the river. I include this section here, however, because I have been in a boat with someone who does not understand English, and when it comes to paddling through rapids, this can be a safety hazard. Therefore, if you are taking along in a paddle boat, or oar boat with paddle assist, someone who does not understand English (perhaps only Russian), you should tutor that person on the basic paddle commands. Paddle commands may vary slightly from outfitter to outfitter.

(1) Forward Paddle. Reach out with your paddle, and dip it in the water about midway up the blade. Push with your inside (upper) hand, and pull with your outside (lower) hand, until the blade is next to your body. Try using your shoulders, instead of your back. A vision of the Hawaii Five-0 credits should play in your head. Recall how all the paddlers stroked together? In paddling, togetherness is power. If you paddle at

exactly the same time as the person at the right hand bow position of the raft (called the stroke position), your boat will move rapidly and with authority. Well, most of the time. Also, your strokes will have more power if you paddle parallel to the boat; that is, do not paddle along the curvature of the boat, either at the bow or at the stern.

(2) Back paddle. Drive the blade of the paddle into the water behind you, again, with the water about midway up the blade. Rest the shaft of the paddle against your hip. Pull with your inside (upper) hand and push with your outside (lower) hand, until the blade is just forward of your body. You will find that levering the paddle against your hip provides substantially more power.

(3) Stop. Take your paddle out of the water now.

(4) Left turn. Turns are where the problems usually arise. You must avoid looking at what the person on the other side of the raft is doing, or you will become seriously confused. On a left turn the paddlers on the left side back paddle, and paddlers on the right side forward paddle. Try to anticipate this call in your mind; play it through in your mind's eye until you know you would give the proper response if called upon to make a left turn.

(5) Right turn. The paddlers on the right side back paddle and the paddlers on the left side forward paddle.

Poison oak. Widespread throughout California, poison oak is the river souvenir that leaves you scratching when you go. Leaves of poison oak come in sets of three; they resemble wild strawberry plants, but the leaves have no teeth (in early spring, however, the leaves may not have opened yet). If you don't know what poison oak looks like, ask your guide to point it out to you. If you have a strong allergy to poison oak, then inform your outfitter when making a reservation. This may be a factor in your river choice. In addition, you may wish to wear long pants and long-sleeved shirts. Finally, if poison oak touches your skin or your clothes, go immediately to the river and wash.

Pulling someone out of the water. After a member of your raft's party has finished "swimming" in the water, you may be called upon to assist him in reentering the raft. He may reach up his hand for you to help him, and as a well-mannered person, you may feel obliged to take it. Not a good idea. People have a lot of elasticity in their wrists, elbows and shoulders, so if you try to pull someone out by the hand, his arm will simply stretch, or more exciting still, his shoulder may become dislocated. I have seen a two-hundred pound man unable to lift a one-hundred pound woman by this method, and gentlemen, this can be embarrassing for those of us who have to watch. So, ignore that hand reaching out for help. Reach instead for the shoulders of the person's life jacket. Grasp both shoulders firmly. If the person's life jacket is loose, then grasp him or her by the armpits. Say "On three: one, two, three", and on three pull straight up (using your legs, not your back for strength), and fall back into the raft. The count gives the person in the water the opportunity to kick when you pull. Be aware of the location of the metal D-rings on the outside of the raft, as a person's life jacket can clip onto one of these D-rings, making the process of pulling him or her into the boat substantially more difficult. Time is often of the essence in this situation.

Responsibility. You have responsibility for your own safety. In deciding to take a whitewater rafting trip, you are acting to put yourself at risk. All outfitters will require you to sign a statement releasing them from liability for any injury you may suffer while rafting.

River water. Giardia, a nasty little microbe if there ever was one, now has the potential to create intestinal chaos from practically any stream in California. I recommend you never drink river water.

Stance. Little has more effect on whether you will stay in the raft than how you position yourself when going into a rapid. You should keep both feet inboard at all times. To paddle effectively, you have to be able to reach the water, so you should sit on the outside tubes, not on the cross tubes.

If you paddle with your weight centered on your butt, which sits on the side of the raft, then when a rock provides a substantial jolt to both the boat and your person, your butt may be relocated either in or out of the raft. However, if you shift your weight over your feet, then if you are knocked off-balance by an abrupt movement of the raft, you are almost certain to fall inside the raft. You may wonder how much more often you should be willing to fall inside the raft in order to avoid falling outside the raft. Well, falling outside counts for one fall, and falling inside counts for no falls. You can do the math yourself. Always attempt to lean into a rapid; move up and down with the waves as though you were riding a horse. These actions permit you to absorb some of the power of the boat's movement without losing your balance. Finally, never try to fend off an obstacle with your foot, hands, or paddle; the raft is designed to absorb that kind of force, and you are not.

Sunburn/sunscreen. On all but the most hazardous rivers (and perhaps even there), the sun is a much greater source of injury than the stream. Invariably, someone will fail to bring or apply sunscreen and will suffer mightily as a result. Be sure to bring on the raft plenty of high-factor, water-insoluble sunscreen. I recommend Bullfrog, which was in turn recommended to me by a guide who runs rafting trips in Africa. Bullfrog is available at REI, NorthFace, and Holubar Mountaineering stores.

Apply sunscreen at least twice each rafting day. Pay particular attention to those parts of your upper body left bare by the life jacket—around the waist, the shoulders, and the back of the neck. Also, many people wear slacks all summer, only to wear shorts on the water. This is a prescription for the most miserable of all possible sunburns. Be sure to use a high factor sunscreen on your legs.

Do not put sunscreen on your forehead, as when you get water in your face (note that there is no question of if), the water will pick up some of the sunscreen and drip it into your eyes. This is painful. Options to protect your forehead include a hat or a strip of cloth tied in Rambo fashion. Alternatively, purchase a brand of sunscreen that does not say "avoid contact with eyes" on the label.

Finally, never put sunscreen on the backs of your legs, between the hips and the knees. This tends to cause one to go slip-sliding away, out of the raft, at inopportune times.

Underneath the raft. Suppose you fall out of a raft and end up underneath it. Some people might become upset by such a situation. Not you, the well-prepared rafter. You will bring your hands up to the bottom of the raft and come out from under the raft by moving hand over hand, in one direction. Note that if you keep changing directions you'll never get anywhere. Pick a direction, preferably upstream, and stick to it. You can practice this maneuver in a pool, by putting your teenager on an air mattress, swimming under it, and trying to get out from underneath in a hand over hand manner.

Water fights. Water fights can be the most hazardous activity on the river. Several safety precautions are necessary.

(1) Never use your paddle in a water fight. A paddle directed with some force towards another person can come out of your hands and hit that person. Your guide will be glad to recount gruesome examples of what happens next.

(2) Always use river water in the fight, and not the water you have bailed from the boat, which may contain grit from the shoes, socks and legs of the occupants.

(3) If either raft's guide or anyone else in a boat calls a cease fire, then cease firing. There may be danger ahead.

(4) If you see your raft or the raft of the opposition heading for a tree, brush, rock, or other hazard, then you should call a cease fire.

(5) Do not fight in any rapid more difficult than Class I, and only if there are not more difficult rapids ahead.

(6) Never attempt to board another boat during a water fight.

(7) Consult with your guide before starting a water fight.

Appendix C
River Etiquette

Beer. The evening experience of an overnight river tour can seem like a return to Sigma Omicron Beta, especially if the trip's participants are not of the abstemious variety. Due to the exertion of rafting, the heat of the sun and consequent water loss, or perhaps to sheer love of partying, a typical beer-drinking rafter will consume a minimum of one six pack per day. Even if an outfitter does supply beer, it is not usually in this quantity. Also, invariably some group in the tour will have no boy scouts in the bunch and will arrive insufficiently supplied. As beer is relatively inexpensive and a congenial atmosphere on a long trip is much to be desired, estimate how much you and your friends could possibly conceive of consuming, and bring double that amount. Avoid at all costs the fatal error of buying beer in bottles; most tours will not carry bottles on the river for safety reasons.

This discussion is not meant to condone the excessive or abusive use of alcohol, but rather to reflect what I have often seen occur. If you have teenagers or younger children for whom you feel that the fraternity experience is best left until college, then try choosing "family" or one day tours. Also, California River Trips strives to keep the alcohol level down on its tours. The only thing more disconcerting than listening to a mature teenager express disgust at the excesses of immature adults is watching an obviously underage person get blotto, too.

Finally, do not ask your guide if you can have a beer before or while rafting. It's not safe to drink and drift.

Family. River trips are an excellent opportunity to enjoy a challenging outdoors activity with your children. Family members should note, however, that a river trip is a public event. They should agree in advance not to treat each other in a manner that would embarrass strangers. Therefore, teenagers should avoid making remarks such as "Dad, don't be such a wimp!", or shouting "See Mom, I told you you would have to use the bushes!" In return, parents should avoid treating their children as though they are incorrigible, invisible, or mentally deficient. It is not appropriate to tell a 14-year old when to use a fork. You may receive that fork in your small intestine, and a lot of us don't like blood.

Helping out. You can learn much more about outdoor cooking, raft repair and maintenance, rigging, etc., if you assist the guides in preparing meals, setting up camp, and readying the rafts. You will also get fed sooner and hit the water earlier. Note that rafts represent a large investment on the part of outfitters; you can protect that investment by always carrying a raft, rather than dragging it on the ground.

Illegal drugs. Apart from being illegal, bringing drugs on a river trip shows very poor etiquette. Guides are almost always explicitly forbidden to indulge. Bringing drugs on the trip will divide a team that has effectively been forged during a day of rafting, and of course, also make the guides damned uncomfortable.

Sunburn. Someone on your trip will be really smug about not spending the twelve bucks for this book. He will be the fool with the rare roast beef complexion. Squelch, if at all possible, an apparently innocuous but actually infuriating remark such as "Boy, you sure are red". The object of your attention will no doubt be aware that he looks less like a rafter and more like choice prime rib. Instead, whip out your Number 18 sunscreen and spread some on your person. Then offer it to the red object, saying, "would you like some sunscreen, for your [sunburned part]?" This, at least, offers some remedy for his embarrassing and probably painful situation. If he declines, you may follow up with "Are you sure?", after which if he still declines, you should shut up.

Tipping. Tipping is still the exception on the river. If you feel that your guide has done an exceptional job, i.e. provided extensive safety instructions, steered you into exciting whitewater and away from sharp rocks, educated you on the natural history and politics of the river, improved your paddling skills, led your raft to victory in water fights, cooked gourmet food, and increased your repertoire of off-color jokes, then he or she definitely deserves a tip. This is especially appropriate on multi-day trips, when guides working 10-12 hours per day receive pay of $40 to $60 per day. Tip according to the services received; usually $5 to $10 a day is adequate.

Water fights. Something about a whitewater river trip seems to require that people get and stay wet and excited. You knew there was something familiar about this sport. Thus, during flat stretches in the river, water fights seem to spontaneously erupt.

To master any skill, you must first study and then practice. This also applies to water fighting.

Technique. Fill the bailing bucket only one-quarter to one-third full. Any more will substantially reduce the distance you can achieve with your assault. Hurl the water with a side-arm motion. Important: Keep hold of the bucket. Loss of the bucket will not only make you a target for unspeakable ribbing from your crew, but it will leave your boat seriously underdefended in return attacks. I strongly recommend you practice on your garden before you need to act quickly and accurately (in a moving vessel, no less) to defend your ship and your honor. This is also a good way to convince your teenagers to get away from the TV set and start watering the lawn.

Strategy. The wind is the best ally of the water fighter, and it usually comes from downstream. Commercial rafting trips almost always keep the rafts in the same order (that is, the first boat always goes first, etc.). Therefore, your interests lie in attacking the upstream boat. If a raft temporarily moves upstream of your boat, show restraint, as when the rafts resume their regular order, that raft will be able to massacre yours. Also, it is sometimes possible to disarm another boat during lunch. However, never do so without the concurrence of your guide (who knows what lies ahead) and never take a boat's last bailing bucket. Finally, etiquette requires that anyone who wants to should have a chance to take part in the fight. But should the tide of battle, as it were, turn against you, then arm your guide, for he or she is the true gunner amid a crew of swabbies.

Of course, you may just not be interested in having a cold bucket of water thrown into your face. In this case, you should attempt to convince your fellow passengers to declare your raft a "dry boat". Do not bother if there are any teenagers in your raft. When you see a boat full of teenagers and their overage equivalents paddling your way, and some of the rafters have their hands in the boat and an evil look in their eyes, it is because they are holding a bucket one-third full of water and are anticipating Rambo Part III. Immediately bring both hands up where they can be seen, and call out "dry boat". Failure to heed this cry demonstrates unacceptable river etiquette and is grounds for merciless revenge once in camp.

Appendix D
Boat Types

Many manufacturers sell high quality commercial rafts: Avon, Riken, Maravia, etc. On a trip offered by any of the outfitters listed in this book you will travel in either (a) a sturdy, six-chambered 12-16 foot raft or (b) a sturdy, two-chambered approximately 10-foot inflatable kayak. Because of the multiple chambers, even if one chamber were to develop a leak, the raft would keep afloat. Also, the synthetic materials used to make modern rafts are remarkably strong and difficult to puncture.

Some readers may have seen a November 1985 episode of a prime time television show wherein the hero escapes by popping with barbed wire and thereby flipping a commercial-quality raft full of bad guys. The show shall remain nameless because of at least eight technical errors observed in this sequence. Most important, barbed wire would neither pop nor flip a raft. The bullets fired by the bad guys might have made a hole in the hero's raft, but given that the bad guys got hung up in a Class II rapid, it might be too much to expect them to shoot straight.

Then, in late December 1985, on still another television show, the good guys were again pursued by bad guys in a raft (through Class IV rapids, no less). The good guys again got shot at, but this time one bullet did hit their boat. The next sight viewers saw was a totally deflated raft. Wrong again. The other five chambers of the commercial-quality raft would have remained inflated, so the stunt doubles could have continued their merry way downstream.

Media misrepresentation of rafts aside, there is, within common raft types, one feature of which you should be aware: the self-bailing style now available for rafts and inflatable kayaks (abbreviated as s/b in the trip descriptions). Self-bailing rafts come in two forms. A SOTAR (State Of The Art Raft, produced by White Water Manufacturing) looks like a conventional raft from the side, but the floor resembles an air mattress, which keeps it above the water. The floor is laced to the tubes; the lacings provide room for water entering the raft to escape. Other manufacturers have recently produced similar self-bailers; for an extensive discussion of self-bailing rafts, see the Jan/Feb 1986 issue of *River Runner* magazine (available for $3.00 from P.O. Box 2047, Vista, CA 92083).

A second type of self-bailer is the Huck Finn. Imagine, if you will, four torpedoes (sans propellers) lying next to each other and tied together. Change the torpedoes to rubber tubes, and you've got a Huck Finn. This structure offers no place for water to be held, and hence the raft is "self-bailing."

Veteran rafters find the idea of self-bailing rafts very appealing. On rivers with nearly continuous difficult whitewater, like the Upper Tuolumne, bailing between rapids is impossible. Conventional boats rapidly fill with water and become unmaneuverable. Also, you will find some commercial guides who will avoid large, exciting holes for fear of filling a conventional boat with water. Finally, you can obtain far superior footing in a firm-bottomed self-bailer. I strongly recommend rafting in a self-bailer on Class V rivers or on rivers with continuous Class IV rapids. If an outfitter has not specified a self-bailing raft for a particular trip, be sure to ask in advance if one will be provided.

However, a little (or a lot of) water in the bottom of a boat makes it heavier and more stable. Self-bailing boats may therefore flip easier than conventional boats do. Also, some outfitters who have substantial inventories of conventional boats contend that self-bailers are stiff and don't bend well. Finally, you won't be water fighting in a self-bailer, so it isn't a good choice for children.

Another raft innovation of which you should be aware is the development of foot cuffs and foot loops. Either of these helps hold your feet in place while you lean way over the side to paddle. For your first time with cuffs or loops, spend some time practicing getting out of them in a hurry, so you can move quickly for a "high side" command.

Persons concerned with rafting safety should note that Sierra Mac (on the Upper Tuolumne run) ties 18-inch braided "hold on" straps on the cross tubes just to the inside of each rafting position. The braided straps provide excellent grips, are easy to reach, keep rafters in position, and don't entangle rafters.

Inflatable kayaks also come both conventional and self-bailing. One type of self-bailer uses an air-mattress floor similar to that of a SOTAR; another uses a solid foam floor.

If you plan on an inflatable kayaking trip, you should definitely request a self-bailer. Inflatable kayaks sit low on the river and take in gallons of water going through even a Class II rapid. Emptying a conventional inflatable kayak, over and over again, by yourself, has to rival in frustration and annoyance your worst correspondence with the IRS.

Also, if you choose to kayak, you had better be in rather good shape. Refer to the appendix on how to prepare for your trip. On a trip where people rotate in and out of a limited number of inflatable kayaks, a canny rafter will kayak in the morning, before the upstream winds arrive.

Appendix E
How to Prepare for Your River Trip

This appendix identifies several steps to be completed in preparation for your river trip (after you have selected a trip and an outfitter).

First, be sure that you have given all necessary information to your outfitter. Tell the outfitter you read about the tour in this book, as that gives the outfitter the opportunity to indicate if any changes have been made in the tour since the publication of this guide. Also, tell your outfitter the number of people who will be on your trip and if any of them (a) do not swim, (b) are under 18 or over 55, (c) have had recent surgery, (d) have allergies, especially to bee stings or poison oak, (e) have handicaps, or (f) have special dietary requirements or requests. If you want to travel in a type of raft that the outfitter has described as optional, be sure to request it when you make your reservation.

Second, within a week of making your reservation, you should receive a brochure, list of things to bring, and instructions to the put-in. If these do not arrive, call your outfitter again.

Third, check an earlier appendix for a list of things to bring and purchase any needed items. A pilgrimage to your local large outdoor supply store is an efficient way to complete this task.

Fourth, if you will be rafting in the spring, keep track of water levels by calling the flow phone. See the river descriptions.

Fifth, the compulsively prepared person will start to do some exercises every day (check with your doctor first, if you aren't exercising now). Stretching exercises and exercises to strengthen the upper back and shoulders are particularly valuable. If you are a member of a health club, ask about designing a program for yourself. If not, recall some of the stretching exercises you used as a teenager (or get your teenager to show you some). I do push-ups and sit-ups every day. You will find, to your amazement, that each day you can do more, provided you don't push yourself too far. The improvement in your fitness will be evident after a day of paddling.

Sixth, find a pool and swim a few laps. Practice your backstroke, floating on your back, and swimming underwater. If you have to take a swimming test for a Class V river, then practice multiple 100-yard sprints (freestyle). If you can swim 100 yards without stopping in under two and a half minutes, then you should be able to pass the test. The Olympic record for 100 yards is about 50 seconds, and even I clock in at well under two minutes.

Seventh, in the two days before the trip, start to increase your consumption of complex carbohydrates, such as unadorned potatoes, spaghetti, whole wheat breads and cereals, etc. Yes, friends, you will perform better on a river trip if you carbo-load like any other athlete. On the night before a major river trip in 1985, I failed to eat dinner; I nearly wimped out by lunch time the next day. You can avoid such a debacle by eating correctly the night before your trip; I now travel with whole wheat cereal, which I eat straight out of the box as I'm heading for the river. Keep your water bottle handy if you plan to imitate this practice.

Eighth, get plenty of sleep before your trip. If you don't sleep well when camping, you may wish to invest in a motel. For weekend trips within 150 miles of your home, you may want to simply get up early Saturday morning to travel to the meet point, rather than fight Friday evening traffic.

Ninth and most important, bring to the river an upbeat attitude and a determination to have an exciting and enjoyable time. Then you will.

Appendix F
River Fitness Tests

Several companies require physical tests to ensure that river trip participants have the strength, stamina, and swimming ability that may be necessary either in the course of a trip or in an emergency. Descriptions of these tests follow.

Class V paddle test. Required of many rafters who will be in paddle boats on Class V rivers. The description below is reprinted with permission from the Whitewater Voyages brochure.

"—Swim at least 100 yards maintaining a strong, continuous stroke.

—Run a mile without walking or stopping.

—Hang, using both hands, from a round chin up bar for one minute. (You don't need to do chin ups, just hang with arms straight. By the way, we don't recommend doing this on bars with square corners—the corners will murder your hands.)

Use this test—and a frank appraisal of your previous paddling experience—to determine your own readiness to paddle Class V. These trips are strenuous and dangerous, so be sensible. If you cannot pass this test and want to paddle, please select . . . less difficult rivers. We reserve the right to turn away at the put-in those who we feel are not well-suited to these dangerous, strenuous expeditions.

At the river, expect to actually take this test. Also, understand that, at the trip leader's discretion, we may shorten or dispense with the test's land portions in order to concentrate on: Swimming in and out of swift currents catching eddies. Swimming through holes. Flipped raft drills, which include swimming *underwater* from one side of the raft to the other. And toss bag practice. Where a trip begins with a hike to the put-in, the hike substitutes for the run."

In addition, an outfitter may require you to swim the 100 yards using a backstroke, or balance on the ball of one foot for one minute. Check with the outfitter when you make reservations if you have any qualms at all about these tests. See the appendix *How to Prepare for Your Trip.*

Sierra Mac test. Required of rafters on the Upper Tuolumne. The following guide to the fitness required is reprinted with permission from the Sierra Mac brochure.

"**HEART**—The step test requires stepping up and down on a 12-inch box 30 times per minute for 3 minutes. Sit down and take your pulse for 1 minute immediately following the test. Your heart rate should be under 140 beats per minute.

GRIP—Suspend your weight hanging with both hands from a one-inch horizontal bar for 60 to 90 seconds and with one hand for 5 seconds.

LUNGS—Jog 70 to 90 yards on one breath of air.

SWIM—Swim 500 to 600 yards without stopping."

The land portion of this test is administered at the discretion of the guides; all passengers must pass a river swim test to raft. The river test includes swimming across a strong current twice and swimming underneath a raft, both while in full rafting gear.

Libra test. Libra Expeditions uses this test to determine your fitness for inflatable kayaking on the South Fork of the American. The test includes:

— 25 push-ups
— 25 sit-ups
— Balancing for one minute on the ball of one foot
— Entering an inflatable kayak from the middle of the river.

—Turtle River Rafting

A paddle boat in a Class III rapid on the Lower Klamath

Appendix G
Annotated Bibliography

The following books will contribute to your river-running experience. Many are available from Westwater Books: write P.O. Box 365, Boulder City, NV 89005, or call (702) 293-1406, for a free catalog.

Cassady, Jim and Fryar Calhoun, *California White Water*, Richmond, CA: Cassady/Calhoun, 1984, 283pp., $17.95.

> This excellent book provides detailed mile-by-mile river and rapid descriptions, as well as clean and professionally drawn river maps for 45 California rivers (including 28 commercial runs). In addition, the book briefly describes 10 more rivers. The authors offer the perspective of literate and broadly trained former rafting guides on the qualities, difficulty, and boating history of the rivers. Color and black and white photographs.
>
> [Because *California White Water* can contribute so much to a commercial rafting passenger's river choice decision and also to his or her appreciation and enjoyment of a river trip, the publishers of this volume have provided you with a special opportunity to purchase this book. See the last page of this book.]

Cassidy, John, *A Guide to Three Rivers*, San Francisco, CA: Friends of the River, 1981, 295pp., $7.95 + $0.75 shipping.

> This volume provides an extensive and beautifully written mile-by-mile historical guide to the Main Tuolumne, the South Fork of the American, and the lost Camp 9 section of the Stanislaus. The book also includes topographical river maps, descriptions and drawings of plant life and birds, and an introduction to Sierra geology. Black and white photographs.

El Dorado Planning Department, *Information Guide to Whitewater Boating: South Fork of the American River*, 360 Fair Lane, Placerville, CA: El Dorado County, 10pp., free.

> This pamphlet includes a large and detailed map of the South Fork of the American, as well as rules, regulations, safety advice, and miscellaneous river information.

Holbek, Lars and Chuck Stanley, *A Guide to the Best Whitewater in the State of California*, P.O. Box 2685, Stanford, CA: Friends of the River, 1984, 217pp., $14.95 + $0.75 shipping.

> A river guide written for kayakers by kayakers with some references for rafters, this book offers blunt assessments of the strengths, weaknesses, and hazards of 124 river sections (including 26 commercial runs). Multiple "true" river stories. Non-kayakers may find an excessive use of kayaking jargon, but that effect is overcome by the authors' affection for the sport. Black and white photographs.

Kuhne, Cecil, *Advanced River Rafting*, Mountain View, CA: Anderson World, Inc., 1980, 210pp., $5.95.

This guide for the modern private boater contains useful guidance on purchasing equipment, river safety, cooking, photography, and other concerns of rafters. The author also provides a thoughtful analysis of river management issues.

McGinnis, William, *The Guide's Guide*, P.O. Box 906, El Sobrante, CA 94803: Whitewater Voyages/River Explorations Ltd., 1981, 129pp., $7.50 + $1.25 shipping + $0.49 sales tax, (CA residents).

This text is the staff manual for Whitewater Voyages; it provides detailed instructions for guides. Potential pitfalls in commercial trips are fully covered. Some drawings.

McGinnis, William, *Whitewater Rafting*, New York, NY: Times Books, 1975, 361pp., $8.95.

A classic guide for the rafting enthusiast, this book gives complete instructions on preparing for and conducting a private river trip. McGinnis' evocative prose captures the spirit and glory of river running. Black and white photographs and drawings. Available from Whitewater Voyages (+ $1.25 shipping + $0.58 sales tax, CA residents), if you can't find it at a bookstore.

Murphy, Shane, *The Lore and Legend of the East Fork*, P.O. Box 1221, Zephyr Cove, NV 89448: The Carson River Conservation Fund, 1982, 74pp., $5.95.

This mile-by-mile guide to the East Fork of the Carson brings history to life and beguiles through the use of voices from interviews, old letters, and amusing yet factual gazettes. Topographical river maps. Black and white photographs.

Orr, Elizabeth and William Orr, *Rivers of the West*, P.O. Box 5286, Eugene, OR 97405: Eagle Web Press, 1985, 334pp., $14.95.

This volume is a guide to the geology and history of major rafting rivers in Idaho, Oregon, and California. California rivers include the three forks of the American, the East Fork of the Carson, the Main Eel, the Upper and Lower Klamath, the Cal Salmon, the Merced, the Mokelumne, the Stanislaus, and the Main Tuolumne. The book is a good anthropological primer, particularly concerning Indians who lived on or near the rivers, and it is written in a clear style. The geological sections are written at an advanced level and contain numerous maps. Black and white photographs.

Perry, John and Jane Greverus Perry, *The Sierra Club Guide to the Natural Areas of California*, 530 Bush Street, San Francisco, CA 94108: Sierra Club Books, 1983, 320 pp., $9.95.

For 200 natural areas in California, this book provides data on geography, weather, plants, birds, animals, special features, activities, and available publications and maps. Natural areas are listed near every commercially rafted river in California.

Quinn, James M. and James W. Quinn, *Handbook to the Klamath River Canyon*, Redmond, OR: Educational Adventures, Inc., 1983, 180 pp., $14.95.

An extremely readable and useful mile-by-mile guide to the history and rapids of the Upper and Lower Klamath. Supplemental sections identify plant and animal life on the rivers. Especially valuable to fishermen and educational groups. Color and black and white photographs.

Sheafer, Silvia Anne, *Gold Country*, P.O. Box 912, Mariposa, CA 95338: Journal Publications, 1977, 66 pp., $3.50.

This history of the California gold rush locates and describes sites that can be visited today, by car, in the Mother Lode region (from the Tuolumne river area north to the Yuba). Numerous historical black and white photographs and drawings.

Watters, Ron, *The White-Water River Book: A Guide to Techniques, Equipment, Camping and Safety*, 222 Dexter Avenue North, Seattle, WA 98109: Pacific Search Press, 1982, 298 pp., $12.95.

This book is a soup-to-nuts guide to becoming a river runner. The concise and clearly illustrated chapter on reading whitewater is particularly valuable for inflatable kayakers or you-oar boat captains. Many excellent black and white photographs and illustrations.

Wright, Terry, *Rocks and Rapids of the Tuolumne*, Box 279-P, Forestville, CA 95436: Wilderness Interpretation Publications, 1983, 88 pp., $5.95 + $1.25 shipping + $0.30 sales tax (CA residents).

This book is a Tuolumne river trip companion. It provides a mile-by-mile guide to Tuolumne rapids, human history, and natural history. Clear, excellent introduction to and explanation of river geology. Discussions of biology and fishing. Some black and white photographs, some drawings.

Appendix H
Where to Buy or Rent Equipment

The following companies reported that they sell or rent outdoor equipment or wetsuits to river runners. Rates were quoted in December, 1985: call the stores to (a) check wetsuit availability, (b) find out how early you will need to rent in order to be guaranteed a wetsuit for the weekend, and (c) obtain current prices. Recall that thinner wetsuits ($\frac{1}{8}$") are more comfortable and usually more suitable for rafting, while thicker wetsuits ($\frac{1}{4}$") are more readily available.

Of the stores listed below, California Canoe and Kayak and Cal School of Diving reported that they rent drysuits. Drysuits will keep you warm, as will wetsuits; drysuits have the added advantage of keeping you dry.

New England Divers will sell you equipment at a 15-25% discount if you mention this book (tell them the publication discount applies).

Full wetsuit: Covers from ankle to wrist.

Shorty wetsuit: Covers from mid-thigh to shoulders.

Farmer John wetsuit: Covers from ankles to shoulders; resembles overalls.

Please note the following abbreviations:

n/p   information not provided
day 1   first day of rental
add day   additional days of rental

Sport Chalet
Vineyard Center
1511-6 East Valley Pky
Escondido, CA 92027
(619) 746-5958
Outdoor equipment sold, rented
Wetsuits sold, rented
Thicknesses available: $\frac{1}{4}$"
Rental charges for wetsuits:
Two-piece full: $7/day 1, $2/add day

Sport Chalet
Grossmont Center
5500 Grossmont Center Dr.
La Mesa, CA 92041
(619) 463-9381
Outdoor equipment sold, rented
Wetsuits sold, rented
Thicknesses available: $\frac{1}{4}$"
Rental charges for wetsuits:
Two-piece full: $7/day 1, $2/add day

Sport Chalet
University Town Center
4545 La Jolla Village Dr.
La Jolla, CA 92122
(619) 453-5656
Outdoor equipment sold

Sport Chalet
840 B St.
San Diego, CA 92102
(619) 236-9191
Outdoor equipment sold, rented

The Outrigger Dive Shop
2110 Winchester Blvd.
Campbell, CA 95008
(408) 374-8411
Outdoor equipment sold, rented
Wetsuits sold, rented
Thicknesses available: $\frac{1}{4}$"
Rental charges for wetsuits:
Farmer John: $10/we, $5/add day
Two-piece full: $10/we, $5/add day

Bamboo Reef
584 4th St.
San Francisco, CA 94107
(415) 362-6694
Outdoor equipment sold, rented
Wetsuits sold, rented
Thicknesses available: ¼″
Rental charges for wetsuits:
Two-piece full: $6/day 1, $3/add day

Sport Chalet
920 Foothill Blvd.
La Canada, CA 91011
(818) 790-9800
Outdoor equipment sold, rented
Wetsuits sold, rented
Thicknesses available: ¼″
Rental charges for wetsuits:
Two-piece full: $7/day 1, $2/add day

Sierra Diving Center
104 E. Grove
Reno, NV 89502
(702) 825-2147
Wetsuits sold, rented
Thicknesses available: ⅛″, ¼″
Rental charges for wetsuits:
Farmer John: $7/day 1, $3.50/add day
Shorty:$7.50/day 1, $3.75/add day
Two-piece full: $12.50/day 1, $6.25/add day

Western Mountaineering
931 Pacific Ave.
Santa Cruz, CA 95060
(408) 429-6300
Outdoor equipment sold, rented
Wetsuits sold

Pacific River Supply South
955 E. Second St.
Long Beach, CA 90802
(213) 432-0187
Outdoor equipment sold, rented

Wetsuits sold, rented
Thicknesses available: ⅛″
Rental charges for wetsuits:
One-piece full: $8/day 1, $5/add day
Farmer John: $7/day 1, $4/add day
Shorty: $5/day 1, $4/add day
Two-piece full: $12/day 1, $8/add day

Pacific River Supply
6044 Bernhard
Richmond, CA 94805
(415) 232-0822
Outdoor equipment sold, rented
Wetsuits sold, rented
Thicknesses available: ⅛″
Rental charges for wetsuits:
One-piece full: $8/day 1, $5/add day
Farmer John: $7/day 1, $4/add day
Shorty: $5/day 1, $4/add day
Two-piece full: $12/day 1, $8/add day

National Outdoor College Store
11383 A Pyrites Way
Rancho Cordova, CA 95670
(916) 638-7900
Outdoor equipment sold, rented
Wetsuits sold, rented
Thicknesses available: ⅛″
Rental charges for wetsuits:
Farmer John: $9.50/day 1, $5.50/add day

Outdoor Adventure
UC Davis
California & Hutchison
Davis, CA 95616
(916) 752-1995
Outdoor equipment rented
Wetsuits rented
Thicknesses available: ⅛″
Rental charges for wetsuits:
Farmer John: $8/day 1, $12/we

The River Store
P.O. Box 472
1006 Lotus Center
Lotus, CA 95651
(916) 626-3435
Outdoor equipment sold, rented
Wetsuits sold, rented
Thicknesses available: ⅛"
Rental charges for wetsuits:
Farmer John: n/p

American River Recreation
11257 Bridge St.
Rancho Cordova, CA 95670
(916) 635-4479
Outdoor equipment sold, rented
Wetsuits sold, rented
Thicknesses available: ⅛"
Rental charges for wetsuits:
Farmer John: $10/day 1, $6/add
day

California Canoe and Kayak
2170 Redwood Hwy.
Greenbrae, CA 94904
(415) 461-1750
Outdoor equipment sold, rented
Drysuits rented
Thicknesses available: ⅛"
Rental charges for drysuits:
One-piece full: $15/day 1, $10/day
2

Outdoors Unlimited Coop
Parnassus Ave. between 3rd and
4th Ave.
San Francisco, CA 94143
(415) 666-2078
Outdoor equipment rented
Wetsuits rented
Thicknesses available: ⅛"
Rental charges for wetsuits:
Farmer John: $4/day 1, $8/we

Western Mountaineering
550 S. First St.
San Jose, CA 95113

(408) 298-6300
Outdoor equipment sold, rented
Wetsuits sold

New England Divers Inc.
398 5th St.
San Francisco, CA 94107
(415) 434-3614/(415) 974-6440
Outdoor equipment sold, rented
Wetsuits sold, rented
Thicknesses available: ¼"
Rental charges for wetsuits:
Farmer John: $6/day 1, $3/add day
Two-piece full: $6/day 1, $3/add
day

Auburn Ski Hut
585 High St.
Auburn, CA 95603
(916) 885-2232
Outdoor equipment sold, rented
Wetsuits sold, rented
Thicknesses available: ¼"
Rental charges for wetsuits:
Two-piece full: $9/day 1, $6/add
day

Cal School of Diving
1595 University Ave.
Berkeley, CA 94703
(415) 644-2373
Outdoor equipment sold, rented
Wetsuits sold, rented
Thicknesses available: ¼"
Rental charges for wetsuits:
Farmer John: $6/day 1, $3/add day
Two-piece full: $6/day 1, $3/add
day

Ukiah Skin and Scuba
1178 N. State St.
Ukiah, CA 95482
(707) 462-5396
Outdoor equipment sold
Wetsuits sold, rented
Thicknesses available: ¼"
Rental charges for wetsuits:

Farmer John: $10/day 1, $5/add day
Two-piece full: $10/day 1, $5/add day

Marin Skin Diving
3765 Redwood Hwy.
San Rafael, CA 94903
(415) 479-4332
Outdoor equipment sold, rented
Wetsuits sold, rented
Thicknesses available: ⅛″, ¼″
Rental charges for wetsuits:
Two-piece full: $6/day 1, $3/add day

The Pinnacles Dive Center
875 Grant Ave.
Novato, CA 94947
(415) 897-9962
Outdoor equipment sold, rented
Wetsuits sold, rented
Thicknesses available: ⅛″, ¼″
Rental charges for wetsuits:
Farmer John: $7/day 1, $3.50/add day
Two-piece full: $7/day 1, $3.50/add day

The Pinnacles Dive Center
2100 Armory Dr.
Santa Rosa, CA 95401
(707) 542-3100
Outdoor equipment sold, rented
Wetsuits sold, rented
Thicknesses available: ⅛″, ¼″
Rental charges for wetsuits:
Farmer John: $7/day 1, $3.50/add day

Valley Skin Diving Schools
7831 Thornton Rd.
Stockton, CA 95207
(209) 957-0625
Outdoor equipment sold, rented
Wetsuits sold, rented
Thicknesses available: ¼″

Rental charges for wetsuits:
Two-piece full: $8/day 1, $4/add day

Valley Skin Diving Schools
430 W. Lockeford
Lodi, CA 95207
(209) 333-2343
Outdoor equipment sold, rented
Wetsuits sold, rented
Thicknesses available: ¼″
Rental charges for wetsuits:
Two-piece full: $8/day 1, $4/add day

Valley Skin Diving Schools
1209 McHenry Ave. #C
Modesto, CA 95350
(209) 527-2822
Outdoor equipment sold, rented
Wetsuits sold, rented
Thicknesses available: ¼″
Rental charges for wetsuits:
Farmer John: $6/day 1, $3/add day
Two-piece full: $8/day 1, $4/add day

The Stalker
1735 Howe Ave.
Sacramento, CA 95825
(916) 922-8858
Wetsuits sold, rented
Thicknesses available: ⅛″, ¼″
Rental charges for wetsuits:
Farmer John: $6/day 1, $3/add day
Two-piece full: $10/day 1, $4/add day

The Original Steele's
1390 N. McCowell Blvd.
Petaluma, CA 94952
(707) 664-8426/(707) 584-7991
Outdoor equipment sold, rented
Wetsuits sold, rented
Thicknesses available: ⅛″, ¼″
Rental charges for wetsuits:
Farmer John: $7.50/Th-Tu, $11.25/wk

Two-piece full: $15/Th-Tu, $22.50/wk

Keene's Aqua Shop
1517 28th St.
Sacramento, CA 95816
(916) 451-3640
Outdoor equipment sold, rented
Wetsuits sold, rented
Thicknesses available: ¼″
Rental charges for wetsuits:
Farmer John: $7/day 1, $10/we
Two-piece full: $7/day 1, $10/we

Mother Lode Skin Diving Shops
2020 H St.
Sacramento, CA 95814
(916) 446-4041
Outdoor equipment sold
Wetsuits sold, rented
Thicknesses available: ⅛″, ¼″
Rental charges for wetsuits:
One-piece full: $10/day 1, $15/we
Farmer John: $7.50/day 1, $12/we
Shorty: $7.50/day 1, $12/we
Two-piece full: $15/day 1, $20/we

New England Divers Inc.
4148 Viking Way
Long Beach, CA 90808
(213) 421-8939/(714) 827-5110
Outdoor equipment sold, rented
Wetsuits sold, rented
Thicknesses available: ¼″
Rental charges for wetsuits:
Farmer John: $4.50/day 1, $2.25/add day
Two-piece full: $9/day 1, $4.50/add day

New England Divers Inc.
11830 W. Pico Blvd.
Los Angeles, CA 90064
(213) 477-5021
Outdoor equipment sold, rented
Wetsuits sold, rented
Thicknesses available: ¼″

Rental charges for wetsuits:
Farmer John: n/p
Two-piece full: n/p

Original Steele's Water World
147 S. Main St.
Milpitas, CA 94035
(408) 298-4224/(415) 581-1500
Outdoor equipment sold, rented
Wetsuits sold, rented
Thicknesses available: ⅛″, ¼″
Rental charges for wetsuits:
Farmer John: $15/Th-Tu, $22.50/wk
Two-piece full: $15/Th-Tu, $22.50/wk

Original Steele's Water World
5987 Telegraph Ave.
Oakland, CA 94609
(415) 655-4344
Outdoor equipment sold, rented
Wetsuits sold, rented
Thicknesses available: ⅛″, ¼″
Rental charges for wetsuits:
Farmer John: $15/Th-Tu, $22.50/wk
Two-piece full: $15/Th-Tu, $22.50/wk

Nor-Cal Diving
7375 Spring Branch Rd.
Redding, CA 96003
(916) 275-1028
Outdoor equipment sold, rented
Wetsuits sold, rented
Thicknesses available: ¼″
Rental charges for wetsuits:
Two-piece full:$10/day 1, $50/wk

North Coast Sports
418 3rd St.
Eureka, CA 95501
(707) 442-6044
Outdoor equipment sold
Wetsuits sold

Neptune's Realm
2940 Broadway
Eureka, CA 95501
(707) 445-3701
Outdoor equipment sold, rented
Wetsuits sold, rented
Thicknesses available: ⅛", ¼"
Rental charges for wetsuits:
One-piece full: $14/day 1, $4/add day
Farmer John: $8/day 1, $3/add day
Shorty: $6/day 1, $2/add day
Two-piece full: $14/day 1, $4/add day

Wallin Dive Store
517 E. Bayshore
Redwood City, CA 94063
(415) 369-2131
Outdoor equipment sold, rented
Wetsuits sold, rented
Thicknesses available: ¼"
Rental charges for wetsuits:
Farmer John: $5/day 1, $2.50/add day
Two-piece full: $7/day 1, $3.50/add day

Any Water Sports
1080 Saratoga Ave. #11
San Jose, CA 95129

(408) 244-4433
Outdoor equipment sold, rented
Wetsuits sold, rented
Thicknesses available: ⅛", ¼"
Rental charges for wetsuits:
One-piece full: $10/4 days
Farmer John: $10/4 days
Shorty: $10/4 days
Two-piece full: $10/4 days

Diving Equipment Headquarters
584 4th St.
San Francisco, CA 94107
(415) 362-6694
Outdoor equipment sold, rented
Wetsuits sold, rented
Thicknesses available: ¼"
Rental charges for wetsuits:
Two-piece full: $6/day 1, $3/add day

Sport Chalet
16242 Beach Blvd.
Huntington Beach, CA 92647
(714) 848-0988
Outdoor equipment sold, rented
Wetsuits sold, rented
Thicknesses available: ¼"
Rental charges for wetsuits:
Two-piece full: $7/day 1, $2/add day

Appendix I
Friends of the River

Friends of the River is California's leading conservation organization dedicated to protecting free-flowing rivers and conserving water and energy. Its focus is preserving the rivers of California and the Colorado Basin, although it is involved in a number of national issues. It is best known for its efforts involving the Stanislaus, Tuolumne, and Kern.

F.O.R.'s river protection efforts are supported by the education and research-oriented Friends of the River Foundation and their Political Action Committee (RiverPAC).

F.O.R. also runs a free booking and referral service for people interested in running rivers. Call F.O.R.'s Sacramento office for more information at (916) 442-3155 or write F.O.R., 909 12th St., Suite 207, Sacramento, CA 95814.

To join F.O.R., (a) call F.O.R.'s San Francisco office at (415) 771-0400, (b) write to F.O.R., Ft. Mason Ctr., Bldg. C, San Francisco, CA 94123, or (c) complete the form on the last page of this book. Annual membership dues are $20 and include a subscription to the bimonthly newsletter *Headwaters*.

Summary chart of what to bring

On a one-day trip always bring:
Sunscreen
Extra clothing
River clothing
Footwear (sneakers or divers' booties)
Sunglasses
Towel
Comb or brush

Optional things to bring on a one-day trip:
Hat
Bandana
Camera and film
Cigarettes and matches
Plastic water bottle
Wetsuit
Gloves

On a camping trip always bring:
Everything required on a one-day trip
Sleeping bag
Pad or air mattress
Ground cloth
Sleep wear
Flashlight
Toilet paper
Toothbrush, toothpaste
Biodegradable soap
Extra shoes and clothes
Mosquito repellant

Optional things to bring on a camping trip
Pillow case
Tent
Beer
Muscle ointment
Eating utensils
Cup
Binoculars
Flora, fauna, bird, tree, star, geology or river guides
Gold pan
Personal articles
Ear plugs
Sleep mask
Fishing gear and license
Nylon rope
Swiss army knife
Sanitary napkins/tampons
Extra sunglasses
Medicine
Hydrocortisone cream
Musical instrument

Glossary

Above. Upstream of (a place).

Below. Downstream of (a place).

Bow. Front portion of the boat, usually higher than the stern.

Carabiner. A steel clip, about three inches long and two inches wide, used to attach objects together (much like a big, strong safety pin).

Cfs (Cubic feet per second). A measure of water level: the number of cubic feet of water passing through a vertical plane in the river in one second.

Chute. A portion of a rapid characterized by its narrow width and its steep drop.

Class. Level of difficulty of a river or rapid. Reported here on the International Whitewater Scale of I to VI. See Chapter 1.

Class V paddle test. A fitness test used as a qualification requirement on many Class V rivers. See *River Fitness Tests*.

Confluence. A place where two rivers meet.

Continuous (drop rapids). Said of rivers or sections of rivers where the rapids flow into one another, without pools of flat water in between them. Compare Pool and drop.

D-ring. A steel, D-shaped ring about three inches by one and one-half inches, attached to the outside of a raft. D-rings are used to attach straps, lines, and carabiners to the boat.

Dewater. To substantially reduce water levels in a stretch of river. One aftereffect of a dam.

Eddy. A calm section of water just downstream of a large boulder or river promontory. Water may flow upstream in an eddy.

Eddy out. A verb, referring to either a boat or a swimmer: to maneuver out of the main current and into an eddy; frequently also to go to the bank of the river.

Flip. An event where a raft or inflatable kayak turns completely over.

Gradient. The steepness of a river section, usually measured in feet (of elevation lost) per mile (of river).

Guide. An employee of an outfitting company; the person who steers a paddle boat, rows an oar boat, prepares meals on the river, and guards your butt. Always trained in First Aid and CPR.

High side. A command that instructs passengers to move to the rock side of a raft.

Hole. A place in the river where the bottom drops sharply. The main current moves downstream along the bottom of the river, while a portion of the current curls back upstream.

Hydraulics. A term used to describe the large waves, holes, and powerful currents typical of high water or difficult rapids.

Inflatable kayak. Not a kayak at all: an open, inflated raft with a canoe-like shape and no decks. Can be paddled by one or two people. Called a splashyak or funyak by outfitters who do not want to worry that you might confuse one with a hard-shelled kayak.

Lead (boat). The first boat in a group.

Libra test. See *River Fitness Tests*.

Lime can. A porta-potty to which lime is added to reduce methane production.

Line. Used as a verb, to move a raft through an unrunnable rapid using ropes attached to the raft, as opposed to carrying a raft around an unrunnable rapid. See portage.

Lines. Ropes, usually made of nylon and about one-half inch in diameter.

Meet point (also Rendezvous point). The place defined by an outfitter where rafters meet before going on a trip. On rare trips the meet point is at the put-in.

MF. Middle fork.

NF. North fork.

Oar boat (ob). A raft powered by oars, almost always with the guide rowing. See Chapter 1.

Oar boat with paddle assist (o/pa). A raft powered both by oars and by paddlers.

Outfitter. A company that offers commercial rafting trips; also the owner of such a company.

Paddle boat. A raft powered by four to eight (usually six) paddlers and steered by a guide.

Peak. The time or level at which the water is highest (measured in cfs).

Permit. Official permission from a river authority for a company or private group to run a river. Requirements for obtaining permits on different rivers vary.

Permittee. A company that has a permit.

Personal flotation device (PFD). A life jacket.

Pile. Thick nylon clothing that is reasonably effective in keeping you warm. Available at outdoor supply stores.

Pirate (a.k.a. rogue). A person or company that offers trips on a river (a) without a permit, when a permit is required, or (b) in violation of the rules of a permit. No pirate trips are listed in this book.

Pool and drop. Said of rivers or sections of rivers characterized by a rapid followed by a stretch of flat water, followed by another rapid, followed by another stretch of flat water, etc. Compare with Continuous.

Portage. To walk around a rapid or obstruction in the river, carrying all gear.

Porta-potty. A make-shift toilet for solid waste only, consisting of a large ammunition can lined with plastic garbage bags. Well, you were the one who wanted a wilderness river trip.

Put-in. The location on the river where the rafts are "put in" the water.

Rapid. Heaven for river runners. Also, an area in the river where the water (a) falls, (b) passes around or just above rocks and boulders, and/ or (c) rushes through a narrow passage. See Chapter 1 for extensive definitions of the different classes of rapids.

Raft. In this book, a 12 to 16 foot oval-shaped boat with six inflatable air chambers. See appendix on *Boat Type*.

Riffle. Disturbance in the surface of the water too small to count as even a Class I rapid. Affectionately known as a Class 0 rapid.

River hour. One hour spent rafting on the river. Does not include time spent scouting, waiting for boats, eating lunch, etc.

River left. The left side or bank of the river, if you are looking downstream.

River right. The right side or bank of the river, if you are looking downstream.

Runnable. A river, section, or rapid that can be rafted.

Scout. To scout a rapid is to look at it and plan a raft route before you run it, most commonly by going ashore and walking downstream to or past the rapid.

SF. South fork.

Shuttle. The arrangement of transportation from the meet point to the put-in and from the take-out back to the meet point. Almost always provided by the outfitter. In this book, if a company does not provide the shuttle it is noted in the river trip description.

Sierra Mac test. See *River Fitness Tests*.

Stern. Rear portion of the boat.

Strainer. A safety hazard formed by branches of trees or bushes, submerged in the water, that let water through but not boats or people.

Sweep (boat). Last boat in a group.

Take-out. The location on the river where the trip ends and where you and the guides "take out" a raft from the water.

Technical. A river or section of a river that requires a lot of steering and/or turns to maneuver around rocks or through rapids.

Unrunnable. A river, section of a river, or rapid that is too dangerous to run, or cannot be rafted due to too much or too little water.

User day. A measure of the amount of use a river receives. One user day is one person on the river one day.

Water fight. An undignified but often enjoyable activity wherein persons armed with bailing buckets throw water on the passengers of other boats. See discussions under *Etiquette* and *Satety*.

Wetsuit. A body covering made of synthetic material; an important protection against hypothermia. See discussion of wetsuits under optional things to bring on your one-day trip, in *What to Bring*.

Wrap. A situation where the current holds a raft against a rock or boulder. Can result in a flip. Frequently used in the past tense, as in "the passengers didn't 'high side' when I said to and the boat wrapped".

AQUATIC ADVENTURE PUBLICATIONS

_____ I would like to order additional copy(ies) of *The Complete Guide to Whitewater Rafting Tours: 1986 California Edition*. I enclose a check for $11.95 plus $1.55 shipping and handling for the first book and $0.50 for each additional book (California residents add $0.78 sales tax per book, for a total of $14.28 for the first book, $13.23 for each additional book).

_____ I would like information on Middle Fork of the Feather and South Fork of the American (Kyburz run) trips as soon as it is available. I enclose a check for $1.50 and a self-addressed stamped envelope. I understand that if no permits are issued on these rivers, my check will be returned.

_____ I would like free, no-obligation information on *The Complete Guide to Whitewater Rafting Tours: 1987 Western States Edition*.

_____ I would like to purchase *California White Water*. I enclose a check for $17.95, plus $0.95 shipping and handling for each book (California residents add $1.17 sales tax per book, for a total of $20.07). Money back if not satisfied.

_____ I would like to join Friends of the River. I enclose a separate check for $20, payable to Friends of the River.

_____ I want you to know about my (our) experience on (a) a recent river trip or (b) in dealing with an outfitter.

Comments:

_____

_____

_____

_____

_____

Please do/do not quote me. (If you are willing to be quoted, please provide your evening phone number.)(   ) _____ - _____ .

Mail this page to:
Aquatic Adventure Publications
P.O. Box 60494
Palo Alto, CA 94306

Name_____

Street Address_____

City, State, Zip_____

Make checks payable to Aquatic Adventure Publications